D1740765

Design Art of
VILLA
IV

ARTPOWER

Design Art of Villa IV
Copyright © Artpower International Publishing Co., Ltd.

ARTPOWER™

Designer: Chen Ting
Chief Editor: Li Aihong

Address: Room C, 9/F., Sun House, 181 Des Voeux Road Central,
Hong Kong, China
Tel: 852-31840676
Fax: 852-25432396

Editorial Department
Address: G009, Floor 7th, Yimao Centre, Meiyuan Road, Luohu District,
Shenzhen, China
Tel: 86-755-82913355
Fax: 86-755-82020029

Web: www.artpower.com.cn
E-mail: artpower@artpower.com.cn

ISBN 978-988-13542-5-9

No part of this publication may be reproduced or utilised in any form by
any means, electronic or mechanical, including photocopying, recording
or by any information storage and retrieval system, without prior written
permission of the publisher.

All images in this book have been reproduced with the knowledge and
prior consent of the designers and the clients concerned, and every effort
has been made to ensure that credits accurately comply with information
applied. No responsibility is accepted by producer, publisher, or printer for
any infringement of copyright or otherwise arising from the contents of this
publication.

Printed in China

PREFACE

The origin of the Villa dates back to Roman times when "Villa" referred to an upper class country house. From antiquity through the modern era, Villa implies not just living in the country, but being implicitly removed from the city, on the outskirts, becoming one with nature and the land. Certainly, Villas throughout history have maintained this quality, they spread out and they embrace the land.

Spreading out as they do enables the resident great latitude to accomplish much in the way of features, which one cannot obtain in an urban residence, "Domus". Villas commonly contain areas that accommodate many sleeping quarters, varied living spaces both indoor and outdoor, and promote leisure activities with amenities such as tennis courts and swimming pools.

In the recent past, Le Corbusier and Mies Van der Rohe, two of the 20th century's architectural masters, clearly understood these ideals when they titled their early breakthrough modern homes "Villa Savoye" and "Villa Tugenhut". And though, not specifically titled as such, the compositions of Frank Lloyd Wright's "Falling Water" and Walter Gropius's home in Lincoln, Massachusetts, clearly embody the characteristics of the Villa.

It is in this context that the modern homes, or Villas, represented in this book, carry on the traditions. Removed from the city embracing the landscape, spreading their wings, creating vistas to the sea, and openings beyond the common scale of doors and windows. Some Villas anchor to the ground as if to say: "I am here to stay," "I am one with you". Others express a sense of soaring and hovering, they float above the landscape respecting its independence. From the interiors to the exteriors, the modern Villas in this book are truly a work of art.

Stuart Narofsky, AIA, LEED AP

CONTENTS

ACS
Artpower Creative Space

Artpower Creative Space

Artpower, with 10 years' experience in architecture, interior, landscape and graphic design, also the business in the fields such as books' publishing and distribution, cultural / media industry, brand management and artworks market etc., has published more than 600 books, collected about 40,000 outstanding and original works from top design companies and designers all over the world (keep updating).

By launching the magazine Artpower Creative Space (ACS) and the website ACS.CN, Artpower integrates the online resources, and recommends the cutting-edge creative ideas and conceptual design thinking. Besides, Artpower also organizes events and activities on creative design, interviews the world-renowned designers, presents the works of young and aggressive designers, promotes new works, and offers custom publishing and public publishing services etc. With the connection of International design teams, Artpower has provided a global platform of showcase and exchange for professional designers.

What We Do

Sign in to be our member, you will have the chance to have your own homepage, enjoy the rights only for members, upload your works, show your ideas, communicate, exchange and share cooperation opportunities.

Log in to browse more than 40,000 design masterpieces from the renowned designers at home and abroad (well organized, covering the fields of architecture, interior, landscape, graphic, product, environmental design etc.).

DESIGN FOR DESIGN

Searching for New Star

· ACS Online Exhibition Hall

You call the shots here, on your own ACS page. Designers can release their works freely, with the designers all over the world witnessing the growth of you.

· Designers' Press Conference

If you still feel troubled with the label of "freshman", join ACS. We welcome "fresh" but aggressive designers. Release the projects denied by whatever reasons. You may be the new star we are looking for.

· ACS presents the projects to the whole world. No national boundary. Just communicate and exchange ideas on the project with the whole world.

Custom Publishing

ACS, the joint platform, offering the custom publishing service, will edit and publish magazine / portfolio for private clients, enterprises or design studios according to your needs.

Offline Club

Artpower Creative Space Club will invite top designers both at home and abroad, to hold various lectures and salons on creative design, sharing fantastic and interesting creative ideas and inspirations. The club will be a social platform for friends with same interest and taste. Also, it is for corporate brand showcase. Everyone has the opportunity to be next leader of the lectures and salons!

Design · Magazine · Bilingual

ACS is a professional magazine specializing in high-end space design. It is color printing, with 168 pages and the size of 245*325mm. Featured in both Chinese and English, ACS is distributed nationwide and overseas, with even a Lebanese version. As the most cutting-edge counseling magazine, ACS provides readers with the latest works of the very best architects and interior designers and leads the new fashion in space design.

Shenzhen Artpower Culture Development Co., Ltd.
Artpower International Publishing Co., Ltd. (Hong Kong)
Artpower Culture Development Co., Ltd. Beijing Branch
Artpower Culture Development Co., Ltd. Xiamen Branch

For publishing or advertisement cooperation,
please contact Ms. Wang: rainly@artpower.com.cn.
For press or media enquiry, please contact Ms. Mo: artpower@artpower.com.cn.

Scan and follow
the Official Wechat
Account of ACS!

Global excellent design works are all
accessible in ACS Creative Space

WWW.ACS.CN

THE NEWEST CREATING INSPIRATION,
THE LATEST DESIGN CONCEPT.

ACS Creative Space — Official Media Partner of International Youth Designers Association

Scan for surprise!

Scan the QR code to get the unprecedented e-reading
experience! A vast number of outstanding works at your hand.

1232 Sunset Plaza

Architects
Belzberg Architects

Contributor
The Agency

Location
Sunset Strip, Los Angeles

Photography
Jim Bartsch

Only on a rare occasion, we find a drive-on estate in the Sunset Strip of this scale and capacity, located just seconds from the famed boulevard's array of world-class restaurants, shopping and nightlife.

To journey beyond the grand gates and soaring pepper tree hedge of this Hagy Belzberg-designed compound estate is to enter a secluded, resort-like sanctuary where three distinct structures — a Main Residence, Wellness Center and Guest House — summon you forward, beckoning you to journey through their space so they can unveil one surprise after another.

Architecturally inspiring, in both appearance and function, 1232 Sunset Plaza radiates a warm, California modern allure draped in sophistication and delight, while

conveying an unmistakable sense of strength, volume and boldness. Exterior and interior transitional spaces are rich in fluidity so that the capacity to enjoy and entertain is always sensible and effortless.

Sweeping panoramic views of the city, afforded by an endless number of vantage points throughout the estate, are nothing short of breathtaking. Equally stunning are the views of the property itself from within, as architectural and landscape elements serve as artistic expressions and repeatedly delight as one explores the property.

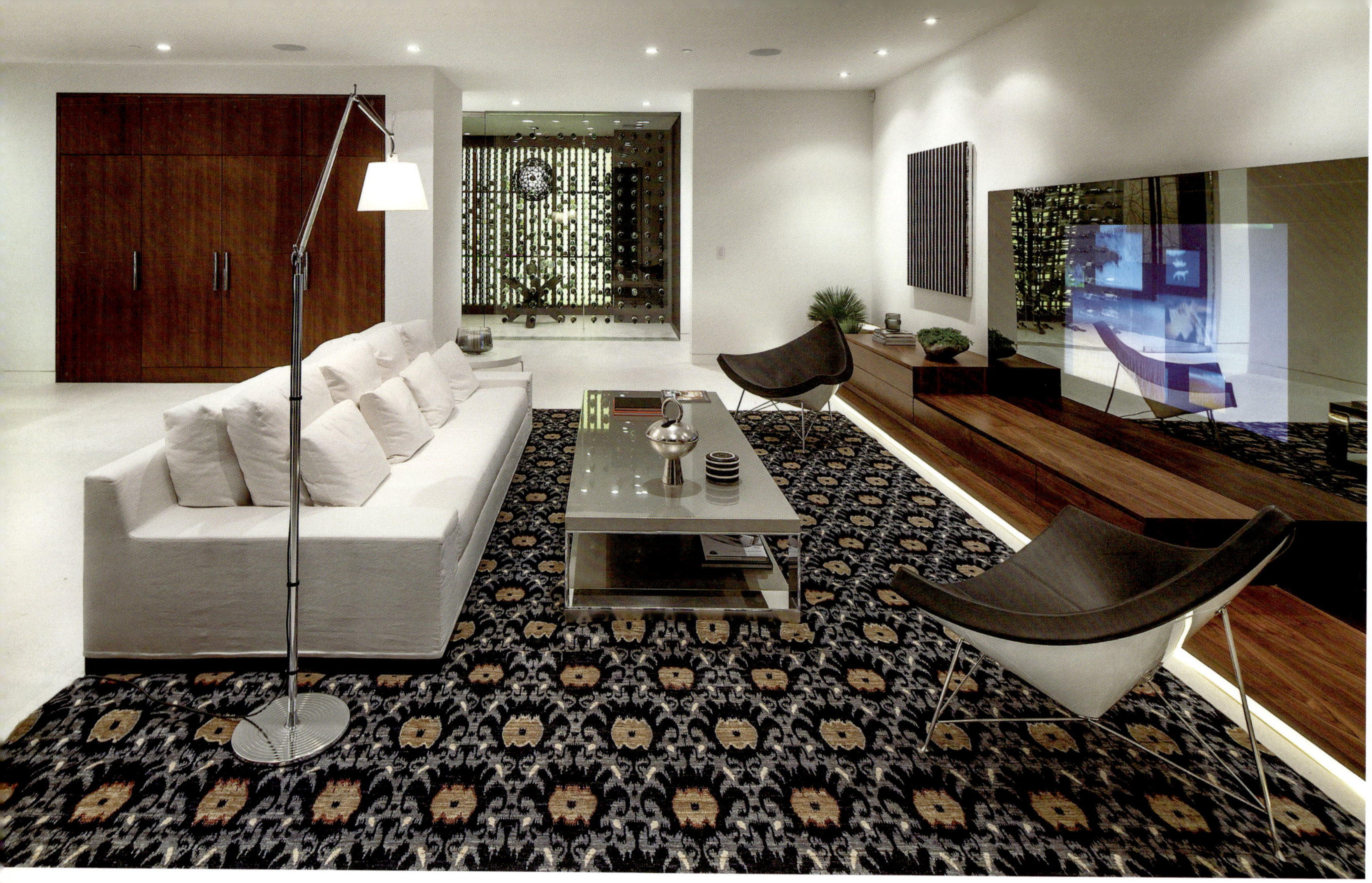

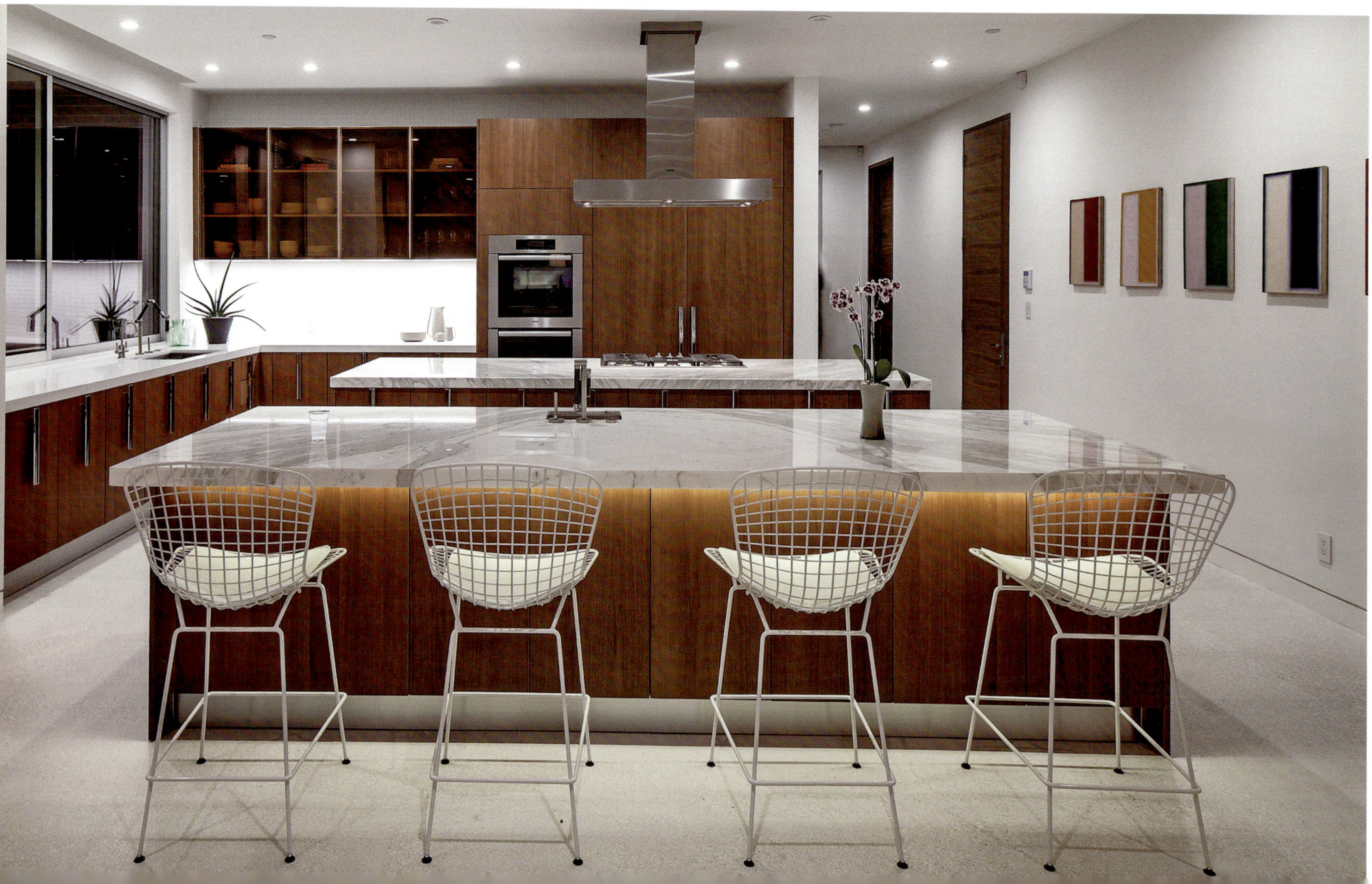

9133 Oriole Way

Contributor
The Agency

Location
Sunset Strip, Los Angeles

Site Area
1,849 m^2

Photography
Simon Berlyn

With sweeping, panoramic views of the entire Los Angeles basin, this stunning contemporary architecture is perched on celebrity-studded Oriole Way, in the highly desirable "Bird Streets" above the Sunset Strip.

The brand new estate was meticulously designed to deliver clean lines with wide open spaces, walls of glass and Fleetwood pocket doors throughout that

seamlessly fuse the interior and exterior, offering the ultimate California lifestyle. The materials, details and natural light are exquisite.

Owner Sean Sassounian, in close collaboration with top design firm In-Ex, focused intently on the well-curated interior, sparing no expense. The impressive list of European manufacturers includes furniture by Acerbis, Arco, Classicon,

Glas Italia, Matteo Grassi and Walter Knoll; custom lighting by Foscarni; closets by Molteni; outdoor furniture by Paola Lenti, Kettal and Roda; and laundry room, kitchen and pantry by DADA. In addition, the art in the house is specially curated by the Michael Kohn Gallery — with notable and emerging artists, many from California.

This is truly a designer home. As such, all furniture is included in the sale price. Main level offers a spacious grey and white lacquer DADA kitchen that flows to attached sitting/media room, facing out to the pool and lush hills. A massive marble island in the kitchen complements the integrated Miele appliances, and a hidden door leads to an entire catering kitchen behind the main kitchen. Formal living room with high-ceilings and spectacular views boasts a full bar and flows to a gorgeous master office with floor-to-ceiling windows. A sophisticated

library/media room provides views over West Hollywood and the Sunset Strip. Tasteful built-in cabinetry throughout. Extremely private, even with the glass and indoor/outdoor flow.

Resort-style backyard offers an infinity edge pool & spa, outside patios with 270° birds-eye views, complete outdoor kitchen, full bath and a spectacular dining and entertaining area. Outdoor kitchen has all Viking appliances and stainless steel Viking cabinets.

Upper level, enjoy 4 bedrooms with wrap-around windows and automated blackout blinds — you feel like you're on an island in the hills floating above the city. Hidden TVs drop from the ceiling. Views everywhere, even the master walk-in closet has a large window and amazing view. All bedrooms are en-suite and feature walk-in closets.

Master suite boasts a huge custom master bath with views overlooking the back pool and canyon, dual rain-heads, deep soaking tub & spa, a mesmerizing hall of mirrors effect. Master bedroom faces west for incredible sunsets and afternoon light. Enjoy a private balcony overlooking pool and an attached office and wet bar.

Lower level, find a full gym with shower, separate massage room, powder room and full bath; wine cellar with its own bar; screening room with custom-installed marble bar-counter; en-suite guest room; and a spacious garage with room for 8 vehicles, plus a carport for 2.

The grand entrance of the home features lush grounds, a fountain, custom blended grey terrazzo floors, and a massive American oak door behind double gates. This is a truly chic, one-of-a-kind home on one of the best streets in Los Angeles.

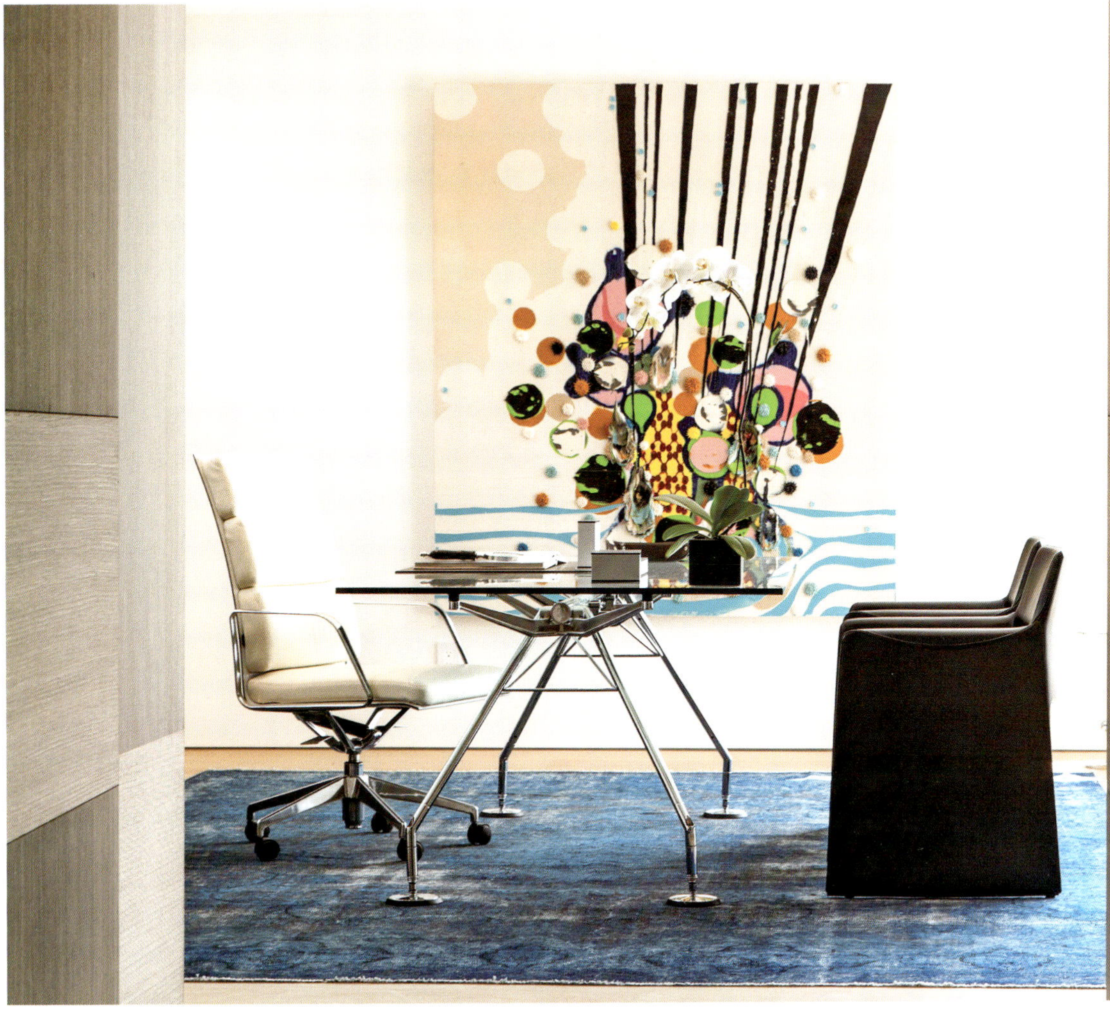

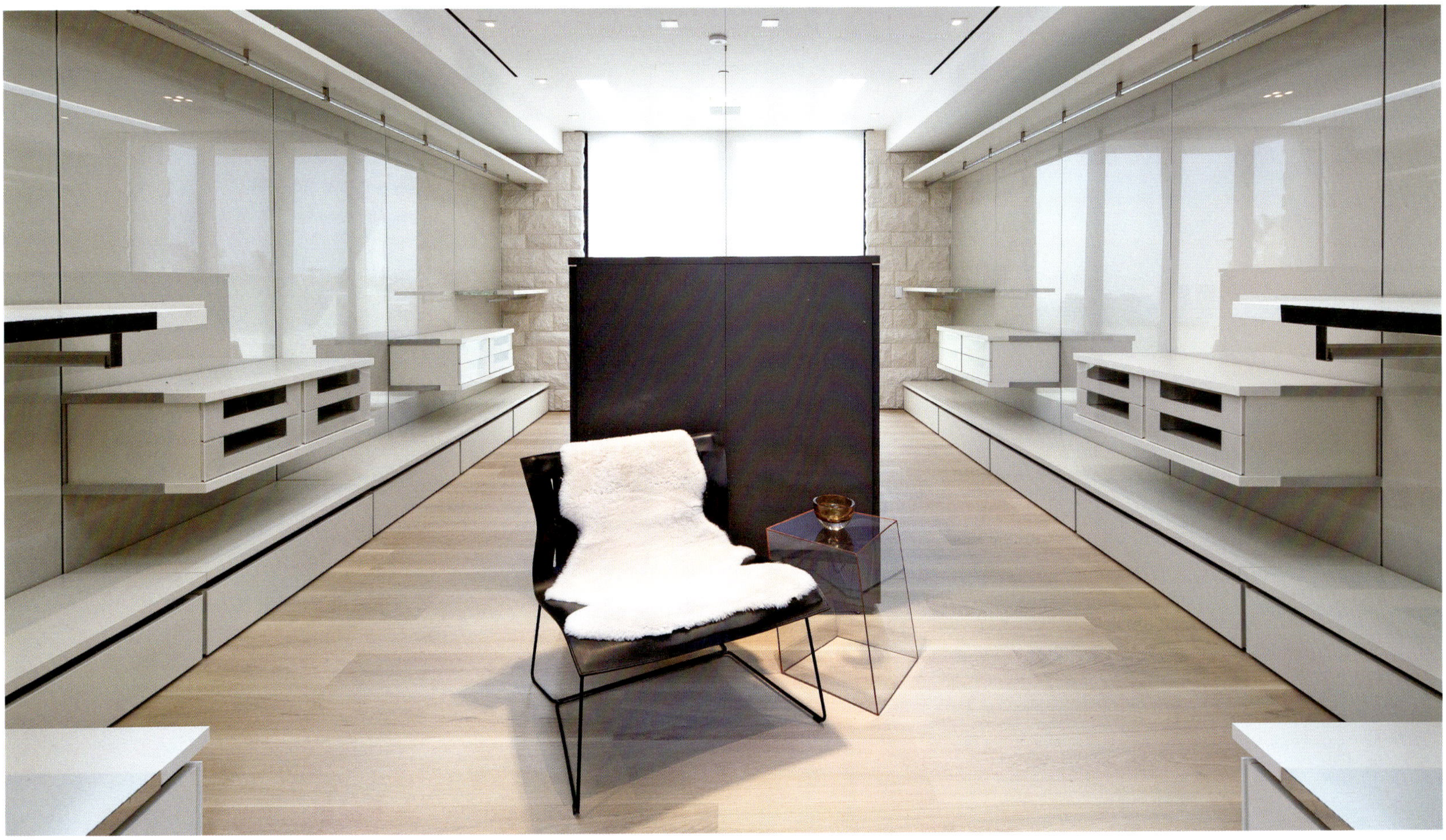

Sands Point Residence

Architects
Narofsky Architecture

Location
Long Island, New York

Photography
Costas Picadas, Michael Grimm Photography

The residence started out as an idea to accommodate 3 generations of the same family. So it took its form, that the private spaces surrounded a great public space, which is the 2-storey central living, dining, entry and lounge space, a sort of indoor court yard. With its larges glazed areas this space as others in this home feel very attached to the outdoors. There is great continuity from indoor to outdoor also reinforced by using the same materials inside and out.

The house is mostly clad in a unique material, which is a 3 mm Slimtech porcelain panel manufactured by Lea Ceramiche from Italy. These panels some as large as 1m x 3m are mounted rain screen fashion (ventilated facade), on vertical insulated furring strips. The entry and the surfaces surrounding the main courtyard are clad in Zinc. All the roofs are green and are all accessible as usable as outdoor terraces.

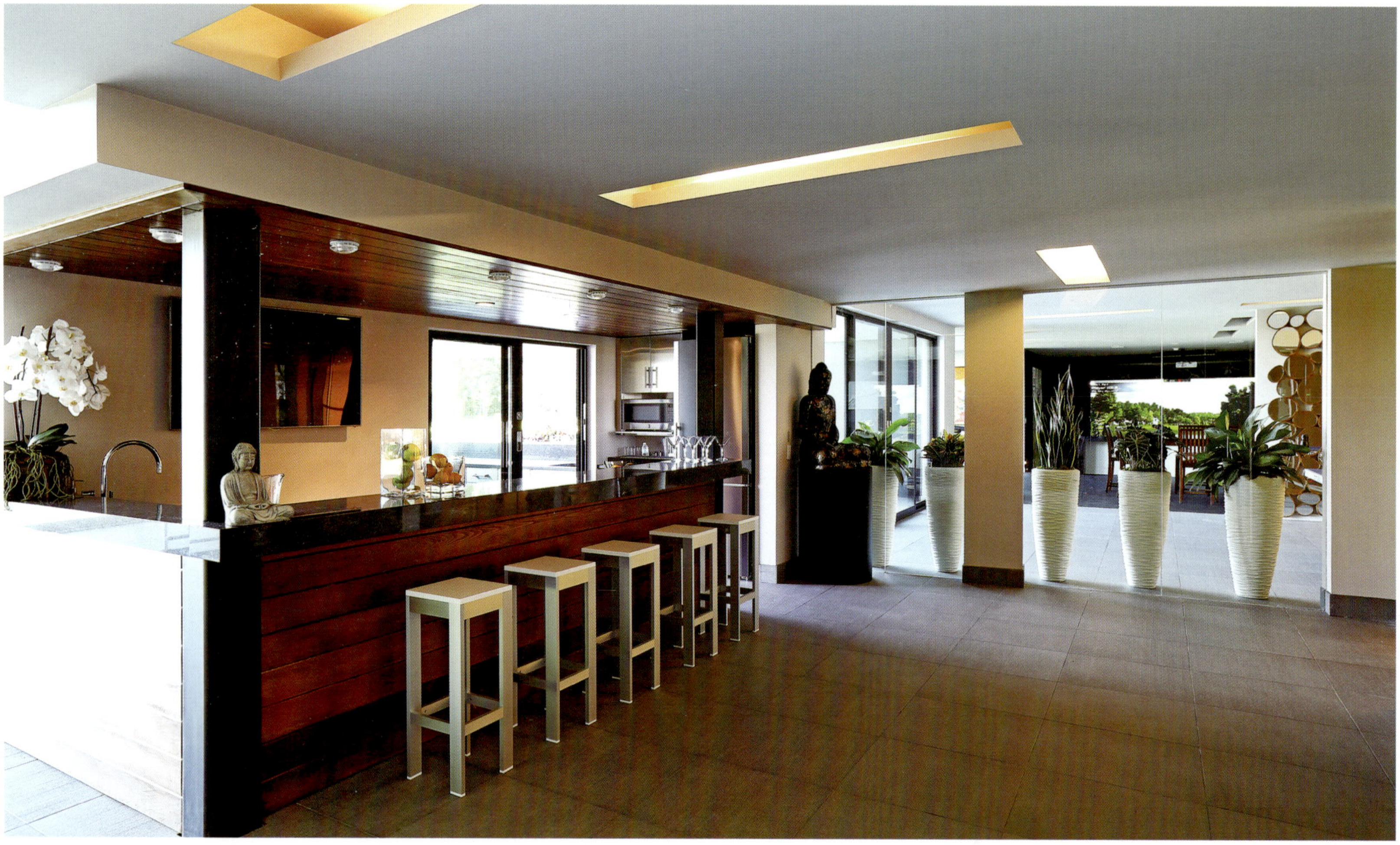

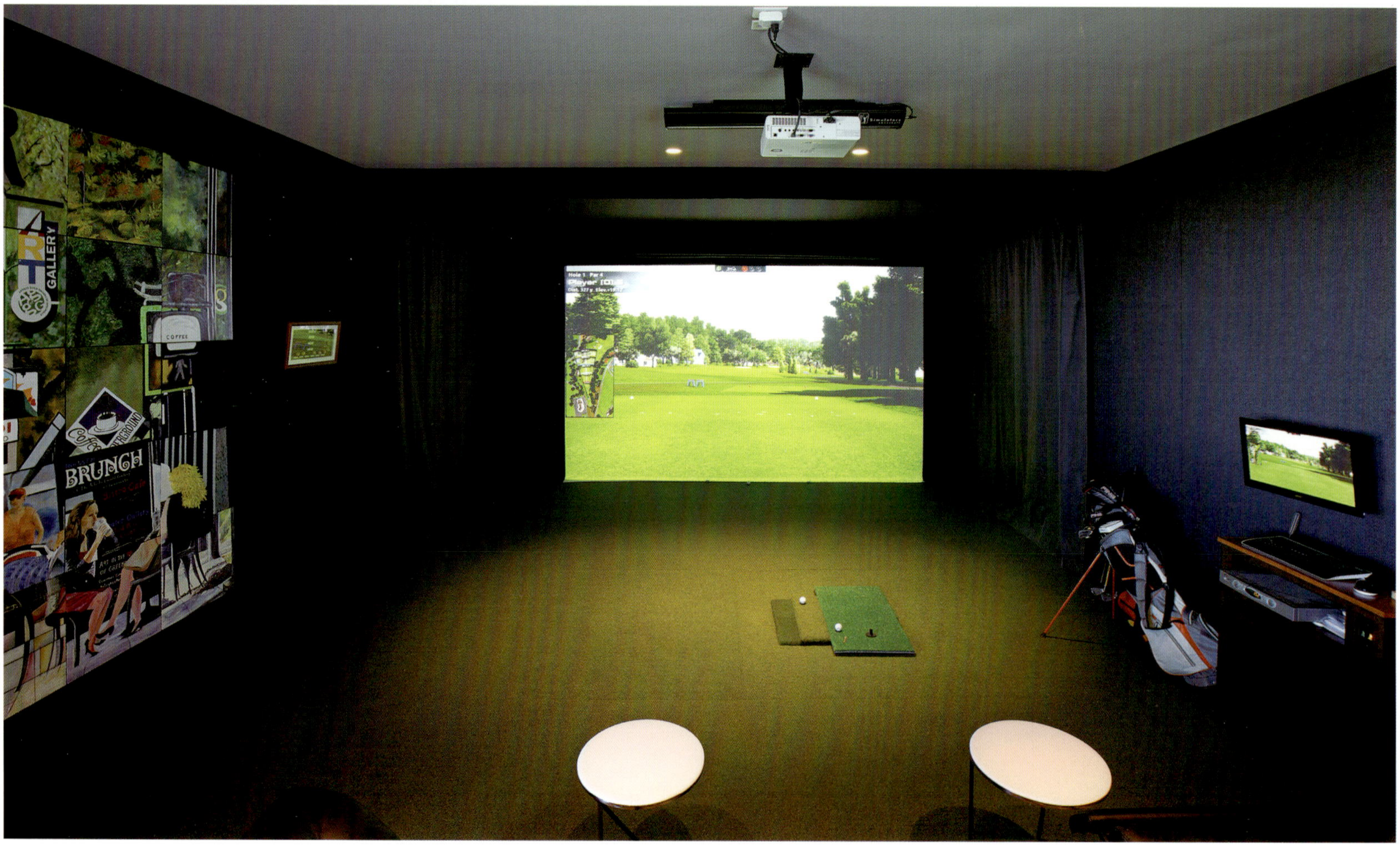
GALLERY
BRUNCH

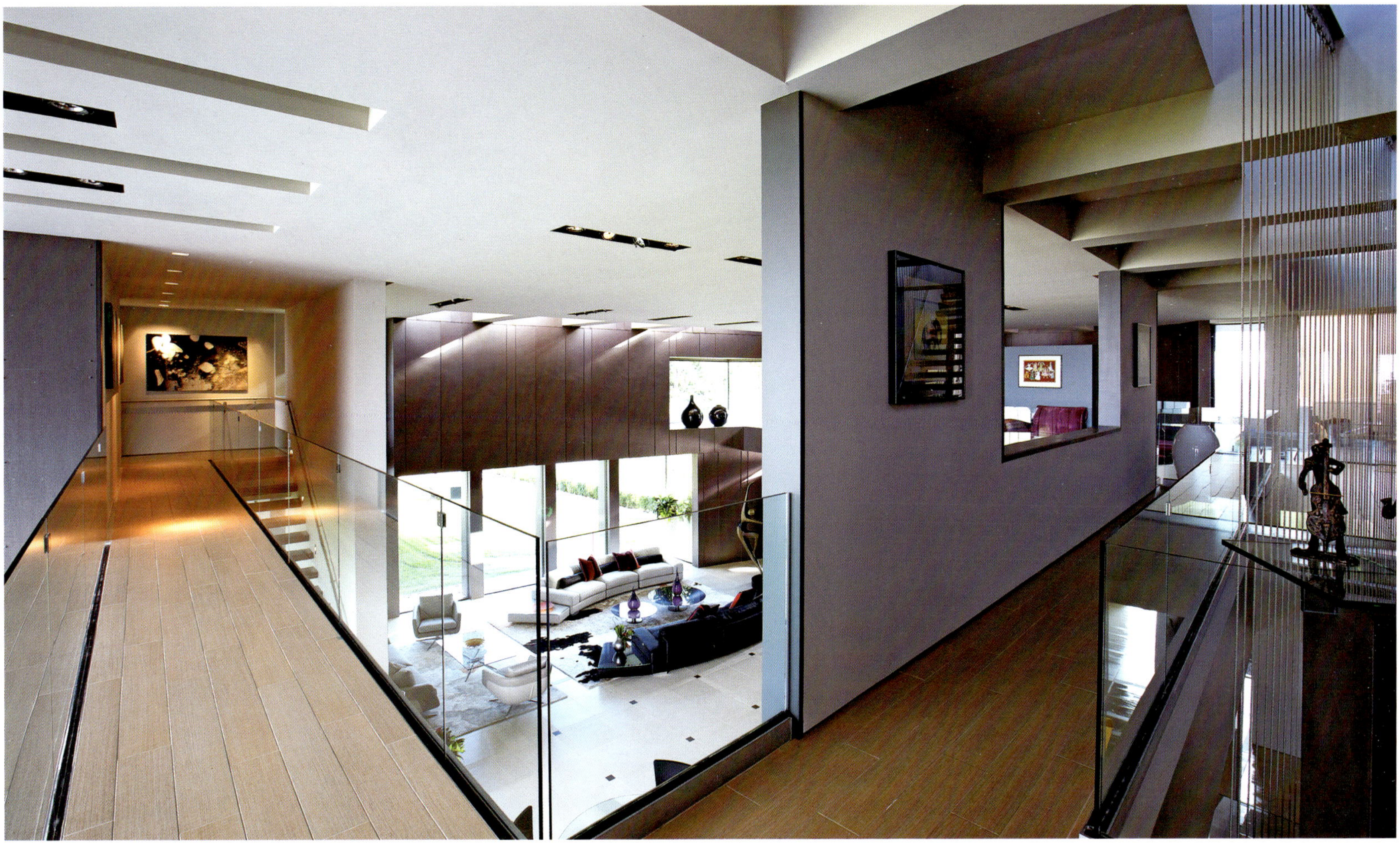

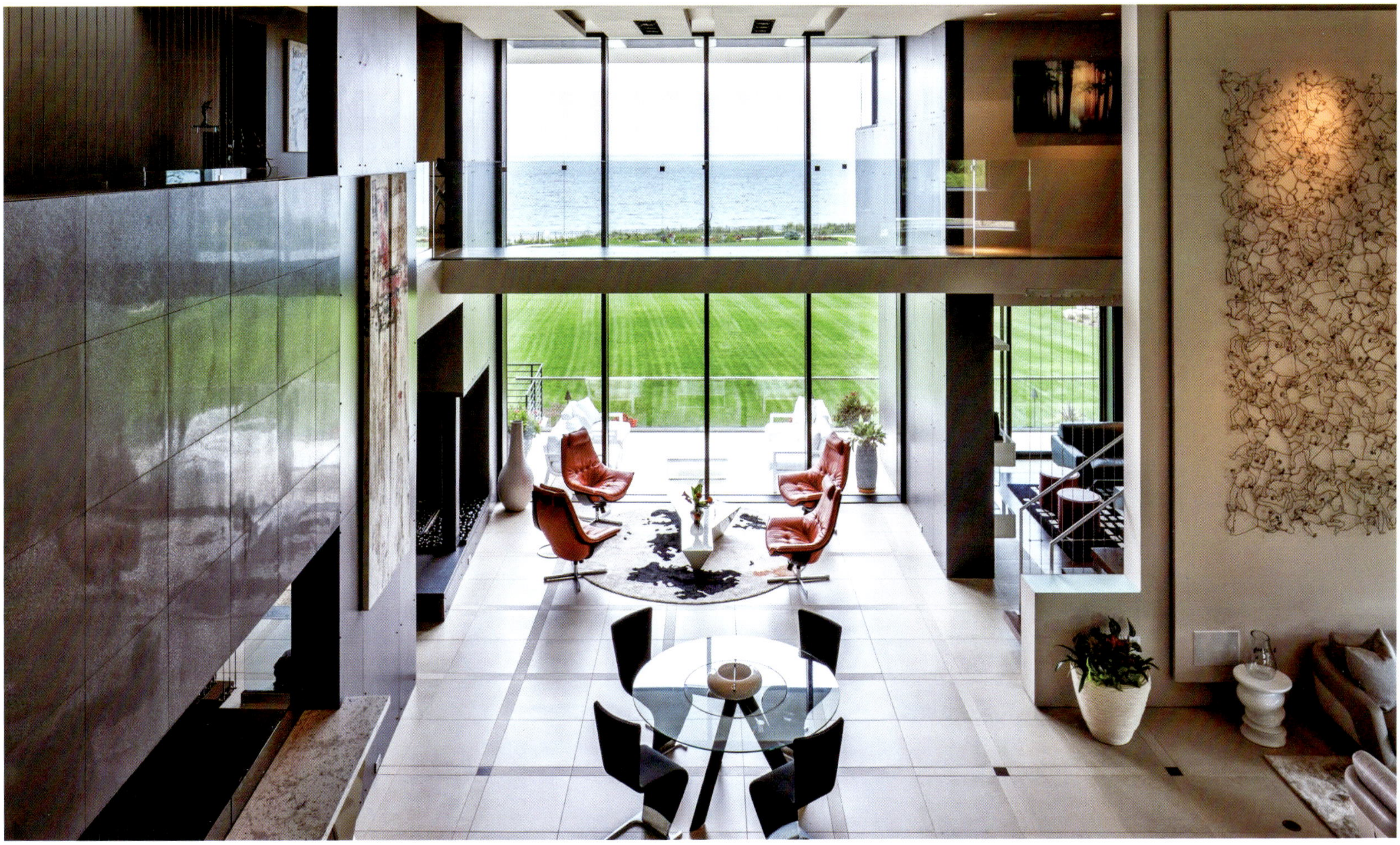

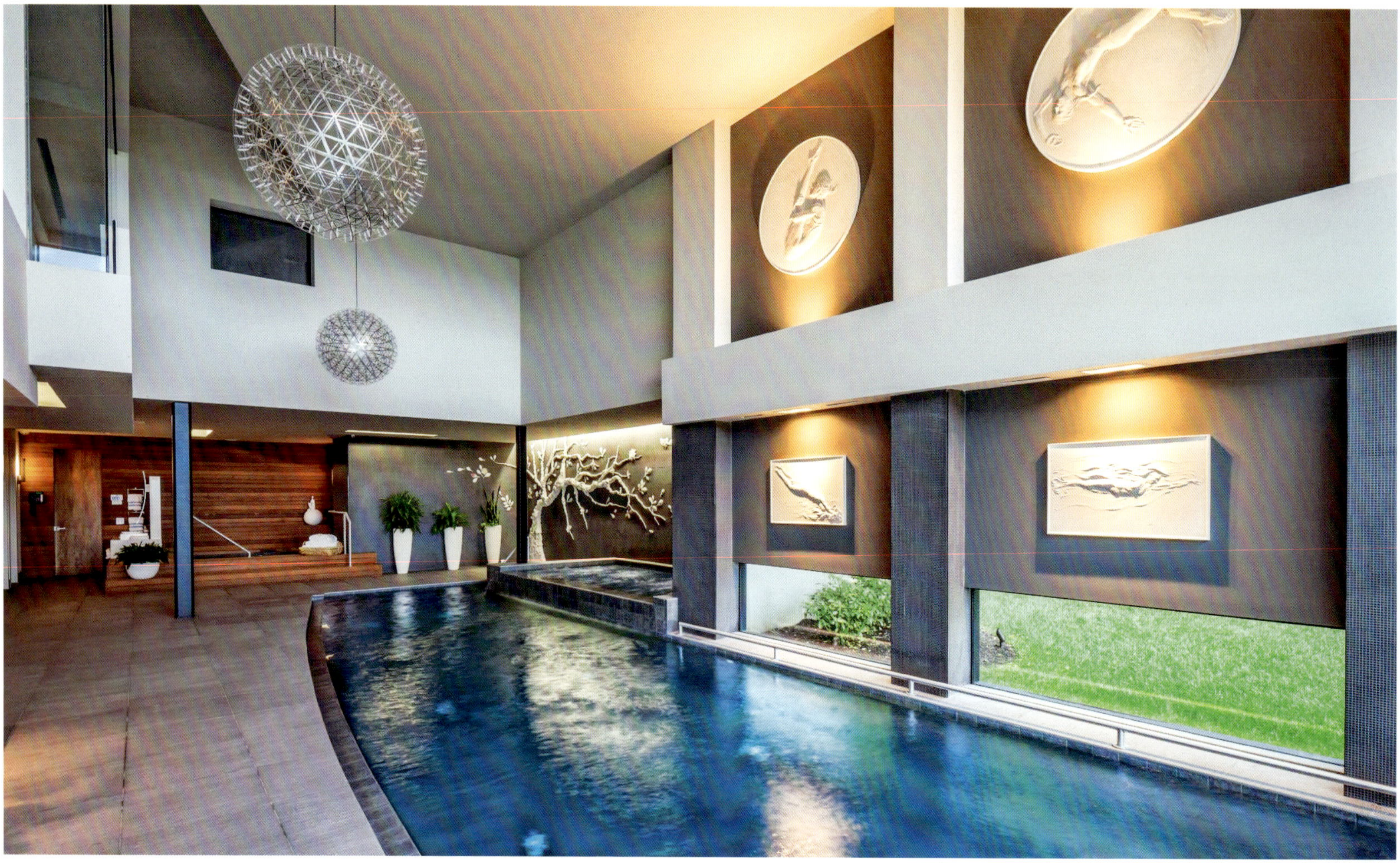

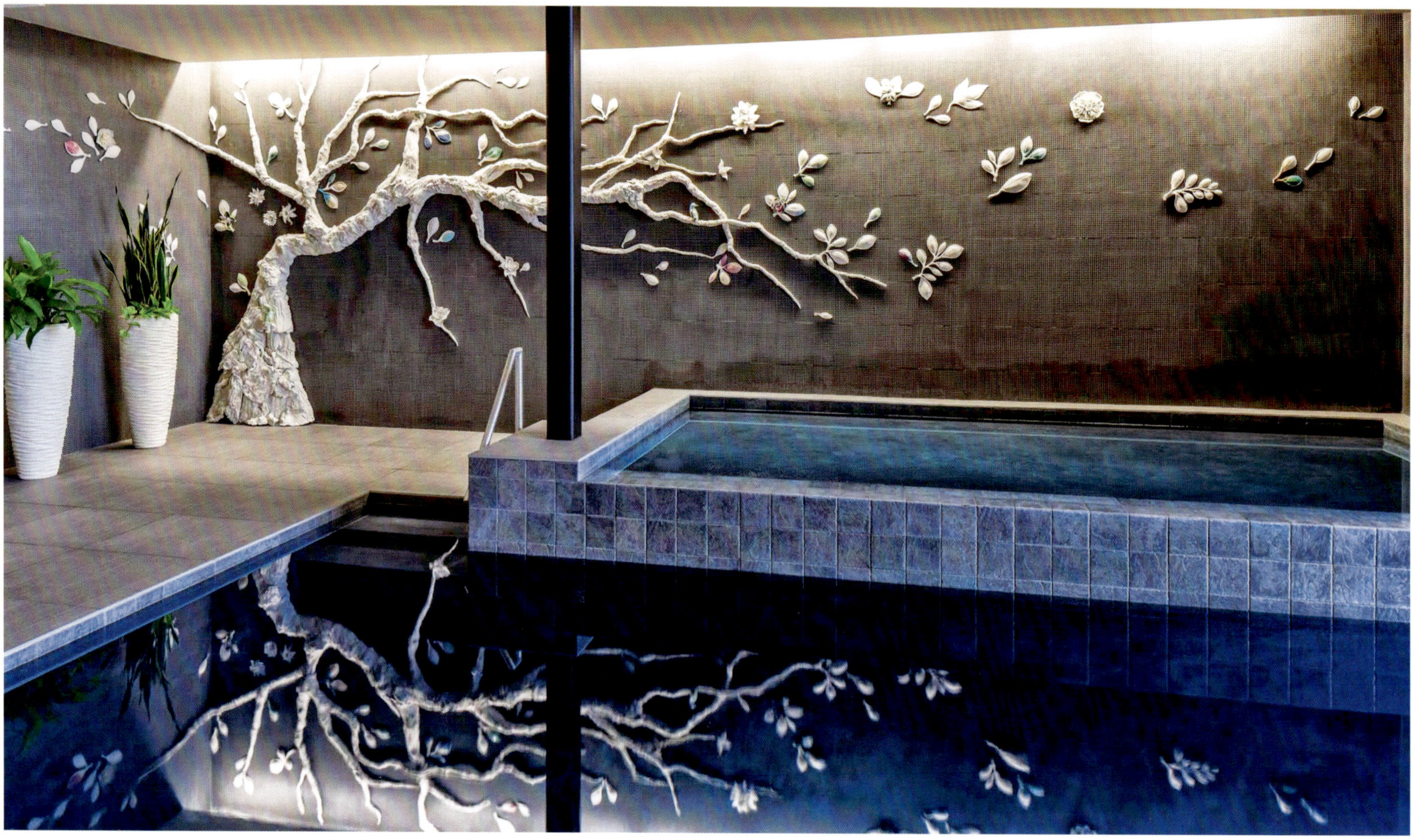

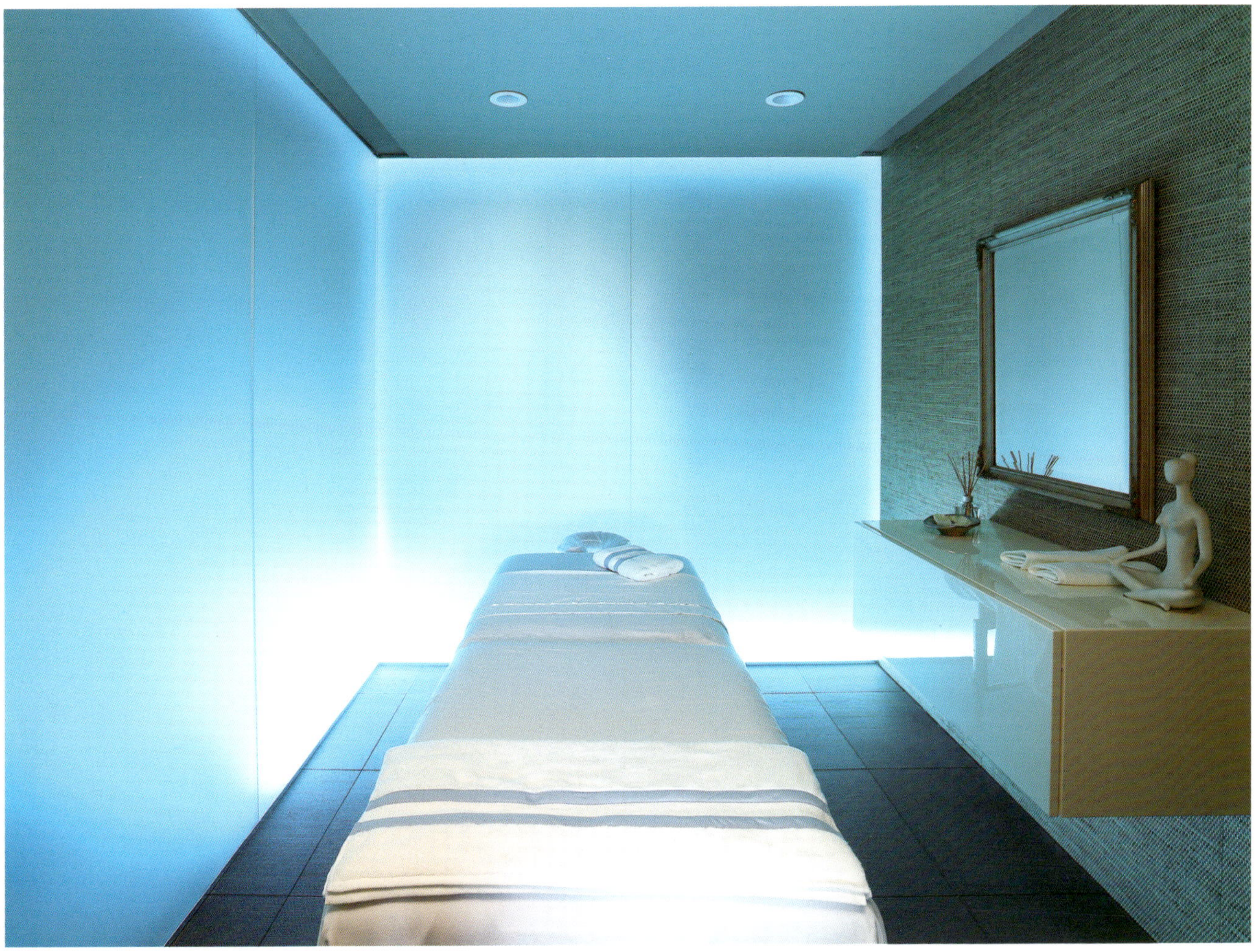

The house is slated to receive a LEED (Leadership in Energy and Environmental Design) for homes Silver as we incorporated many sustainable systems, such as: geothermal heating and cooling (fossil fuel is only used for cooking); LED lighting; water reclaim; super insulation (the entire house is foamed); steel frame (no wood was used); no maintenance materials like the Slimtech and zinc; as well as radiant heat throughout.

Other elements in the house are an indoor /outdoor pool area, with retractable doors for use in the warm weather seasons; an indoor squash/multi court; golf simulator/ theater room; two kitchens (one for cooking Indian food and isolate the spice odors); 7 full bedroom suites; billiard room, family room and a 5 car garage.

It all sits on 1.2 hectare on Long Island's North Shore, right on the Long Island Sound with beach access.

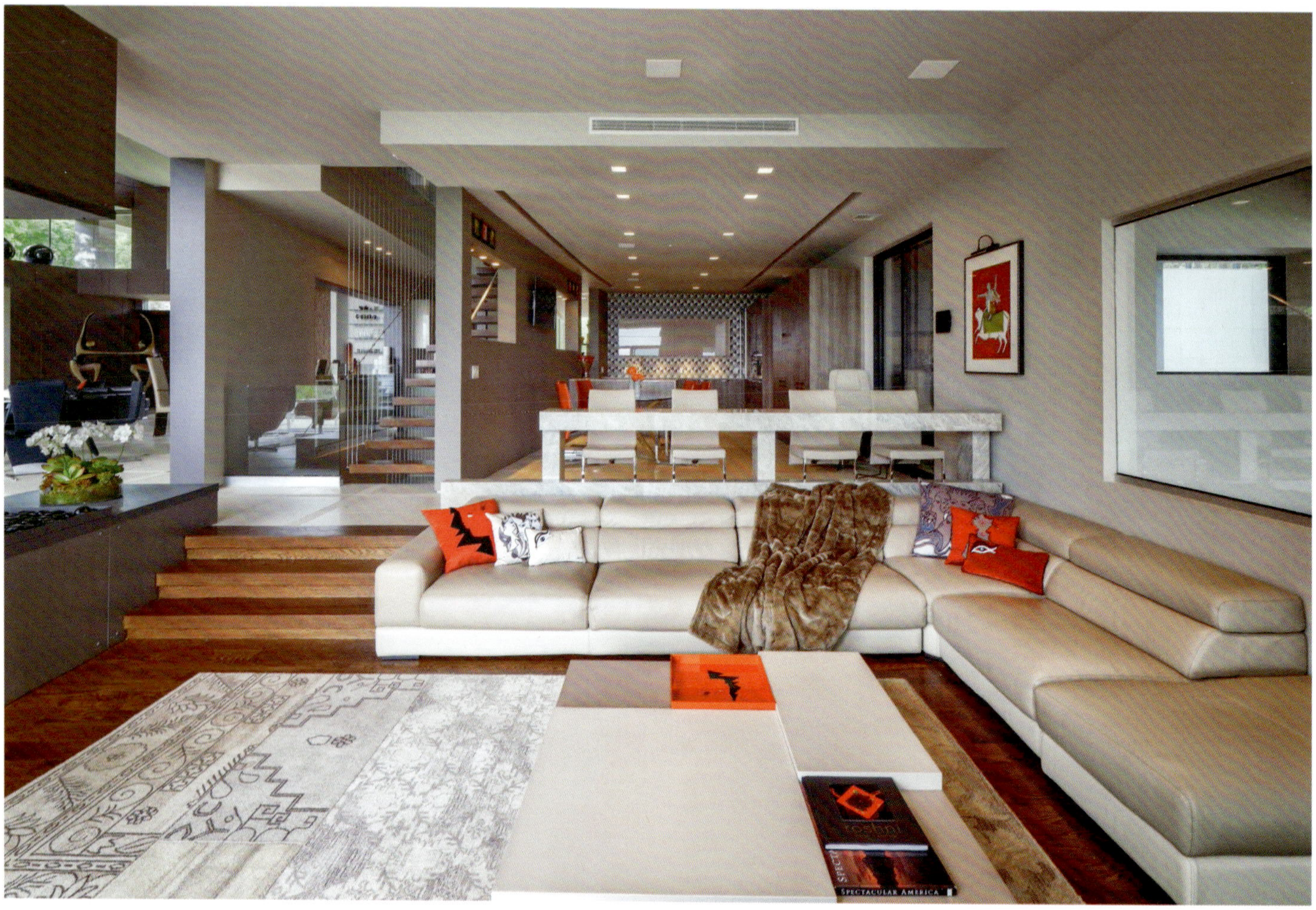
SPECTACULAR AMERICA

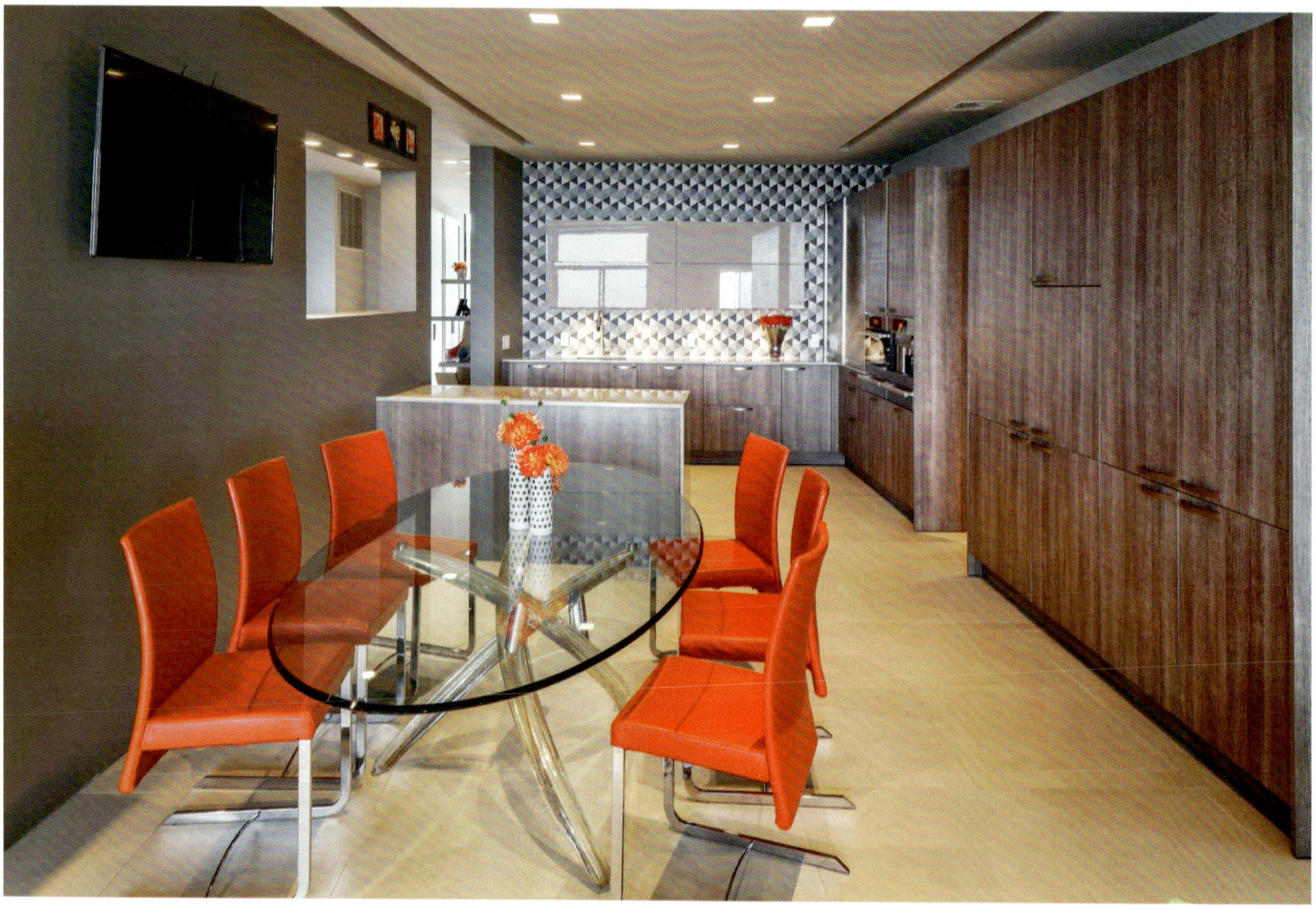

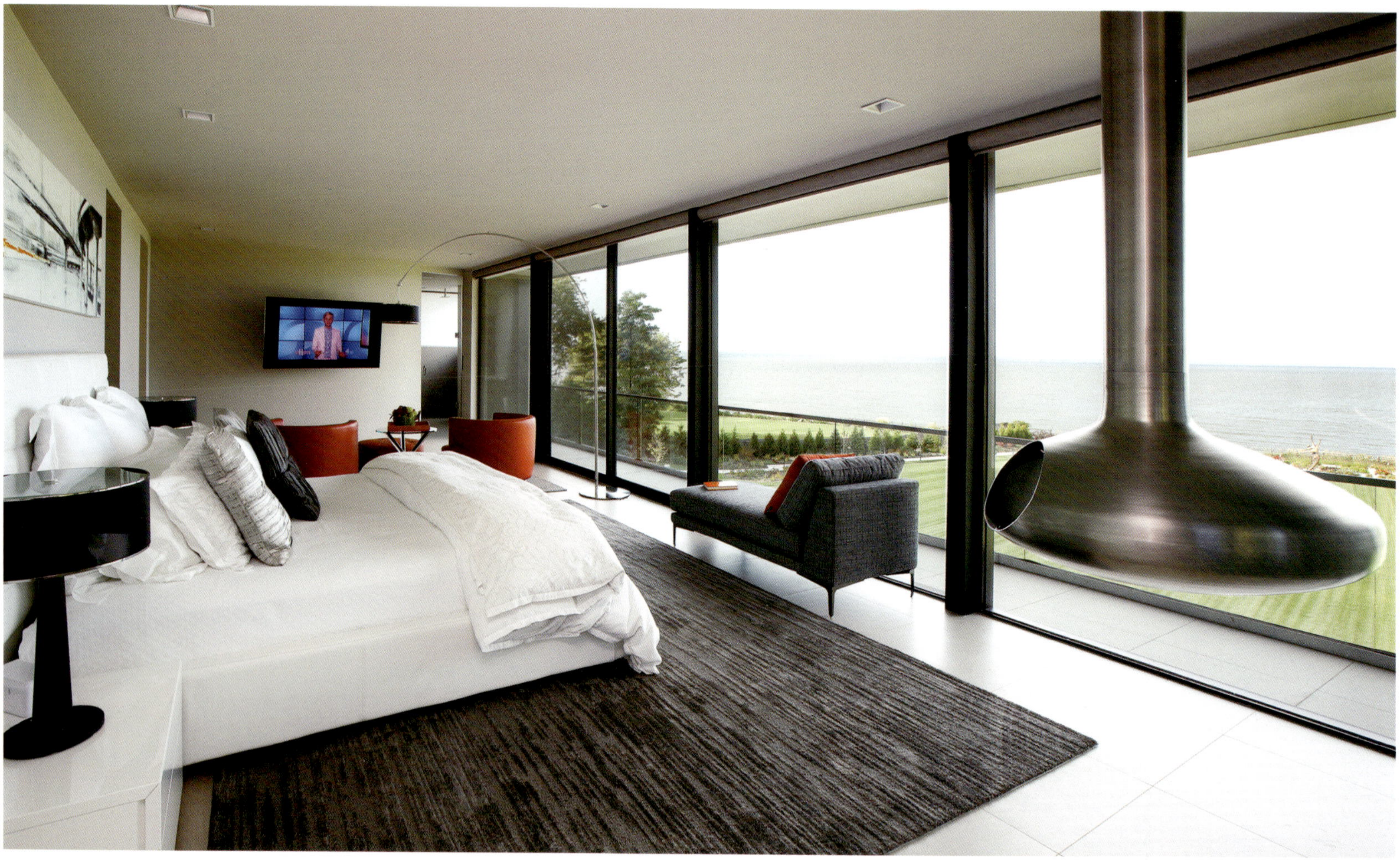

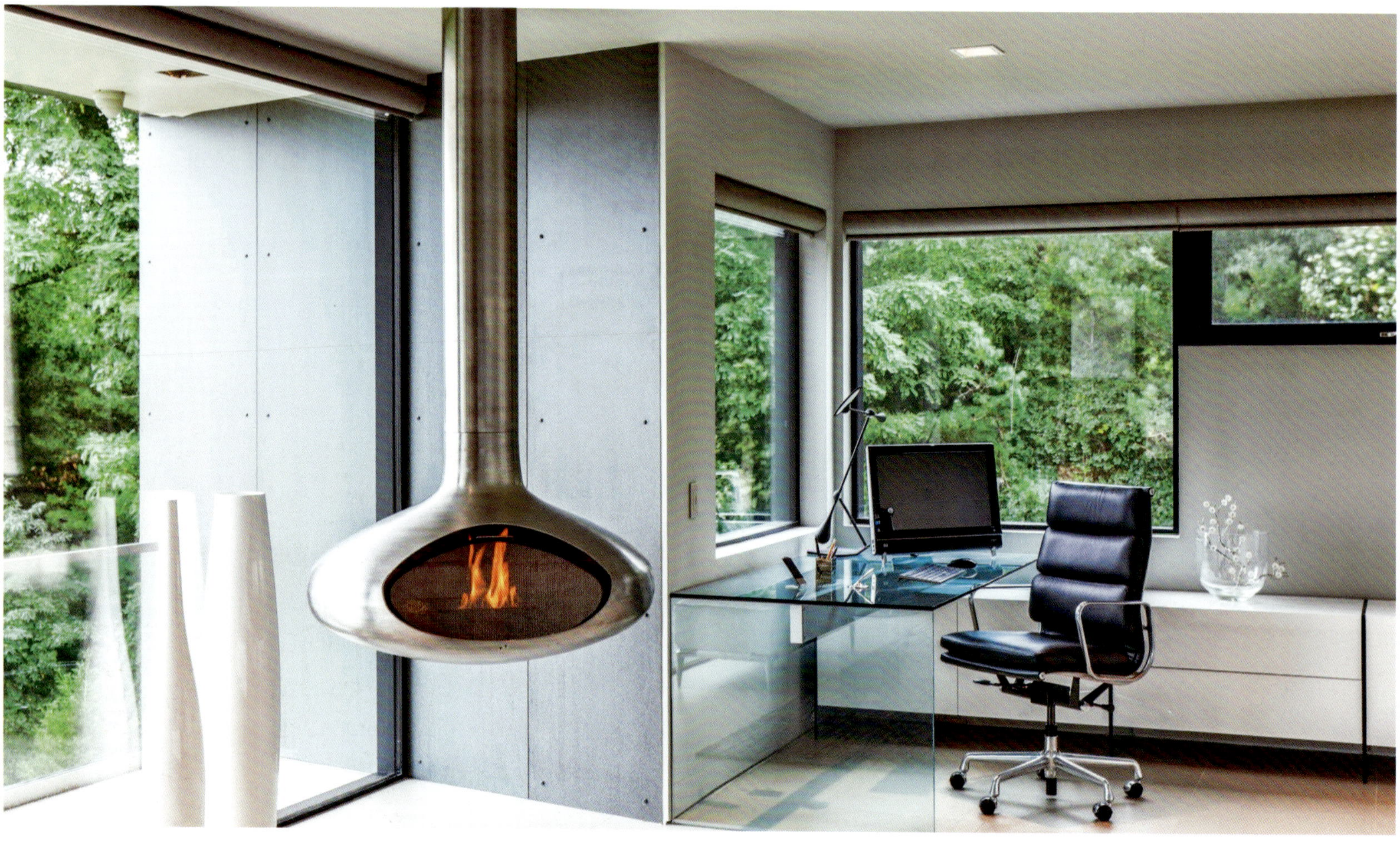

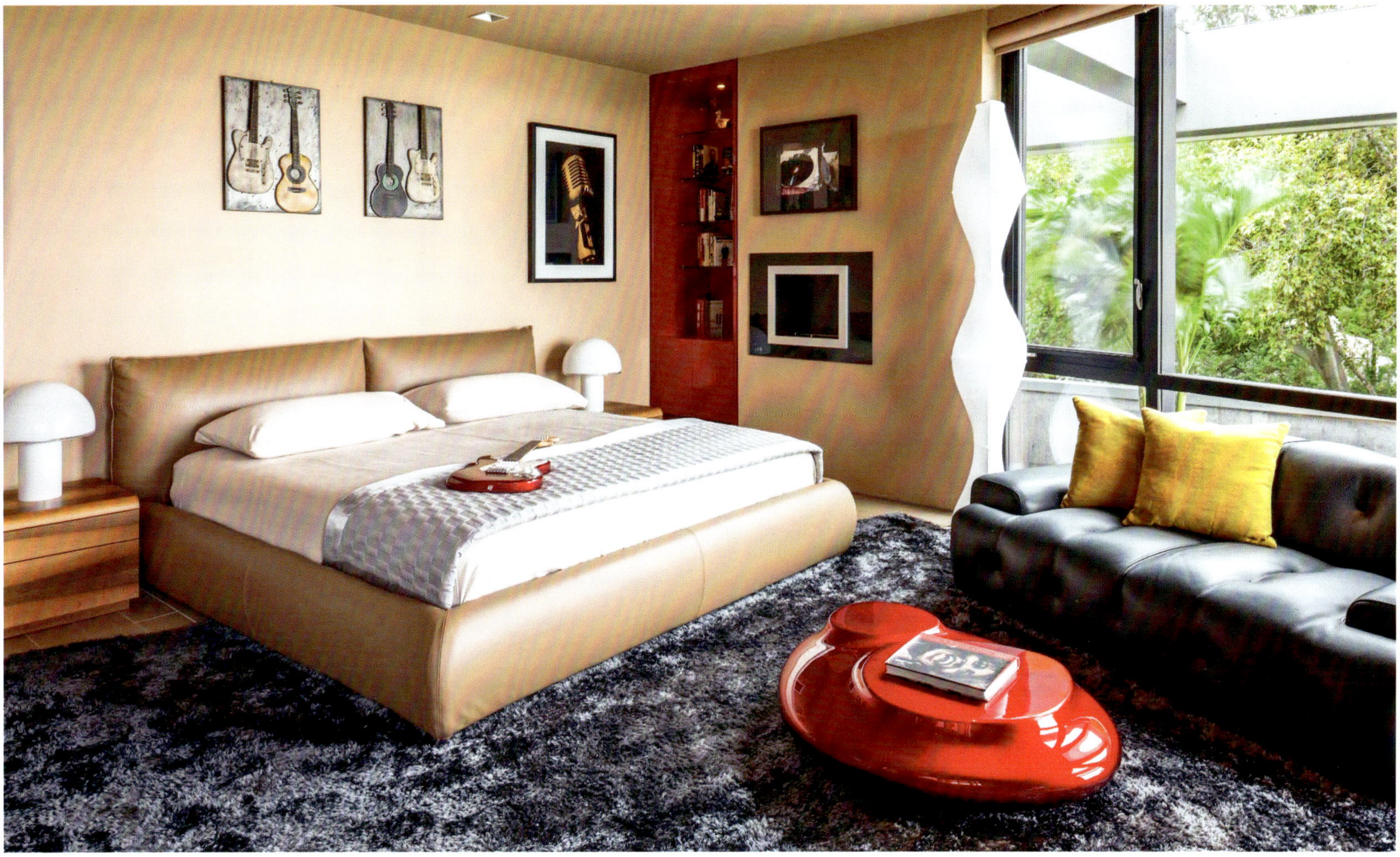

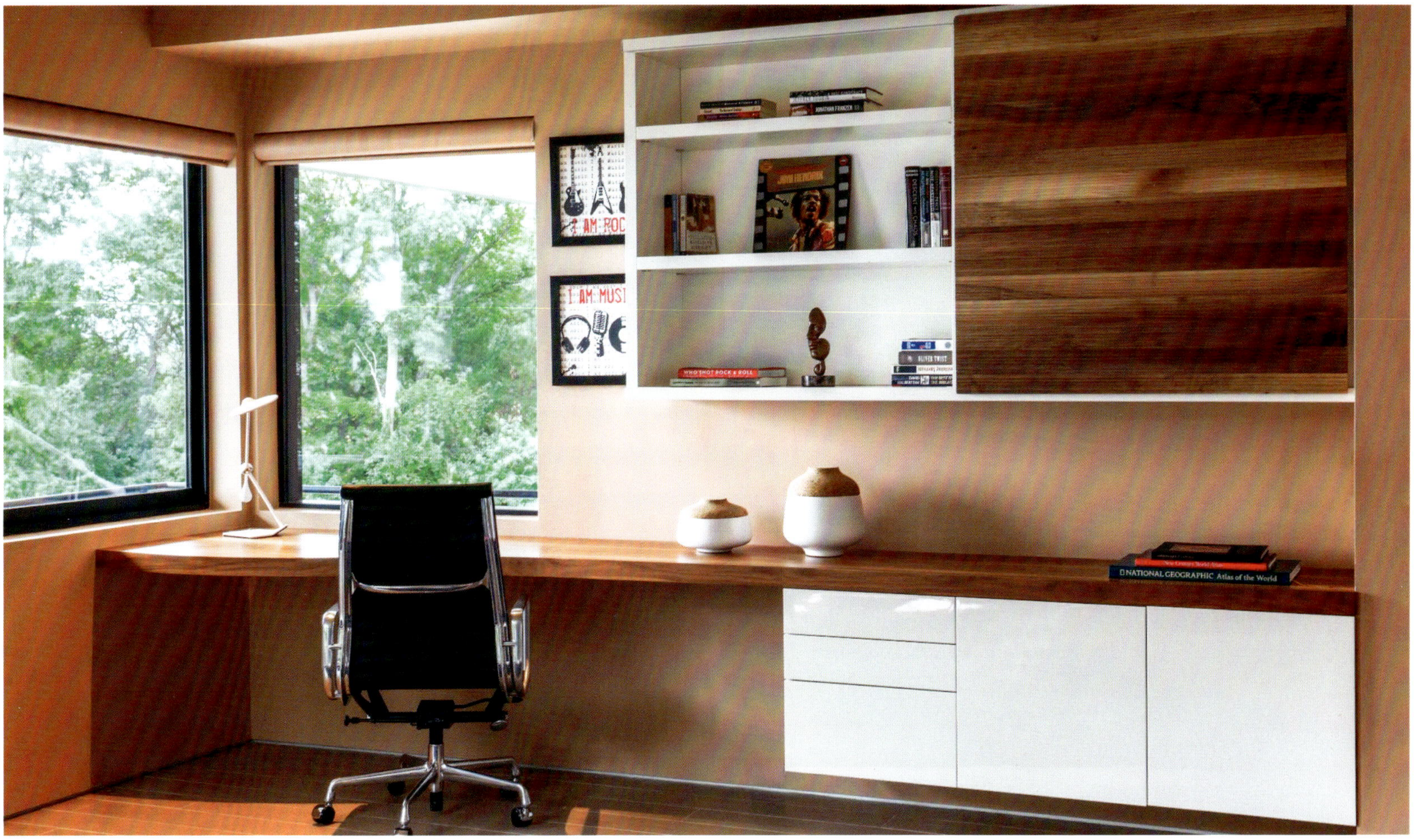
NATIONAL GEOGRAPHIC Atlas of the World

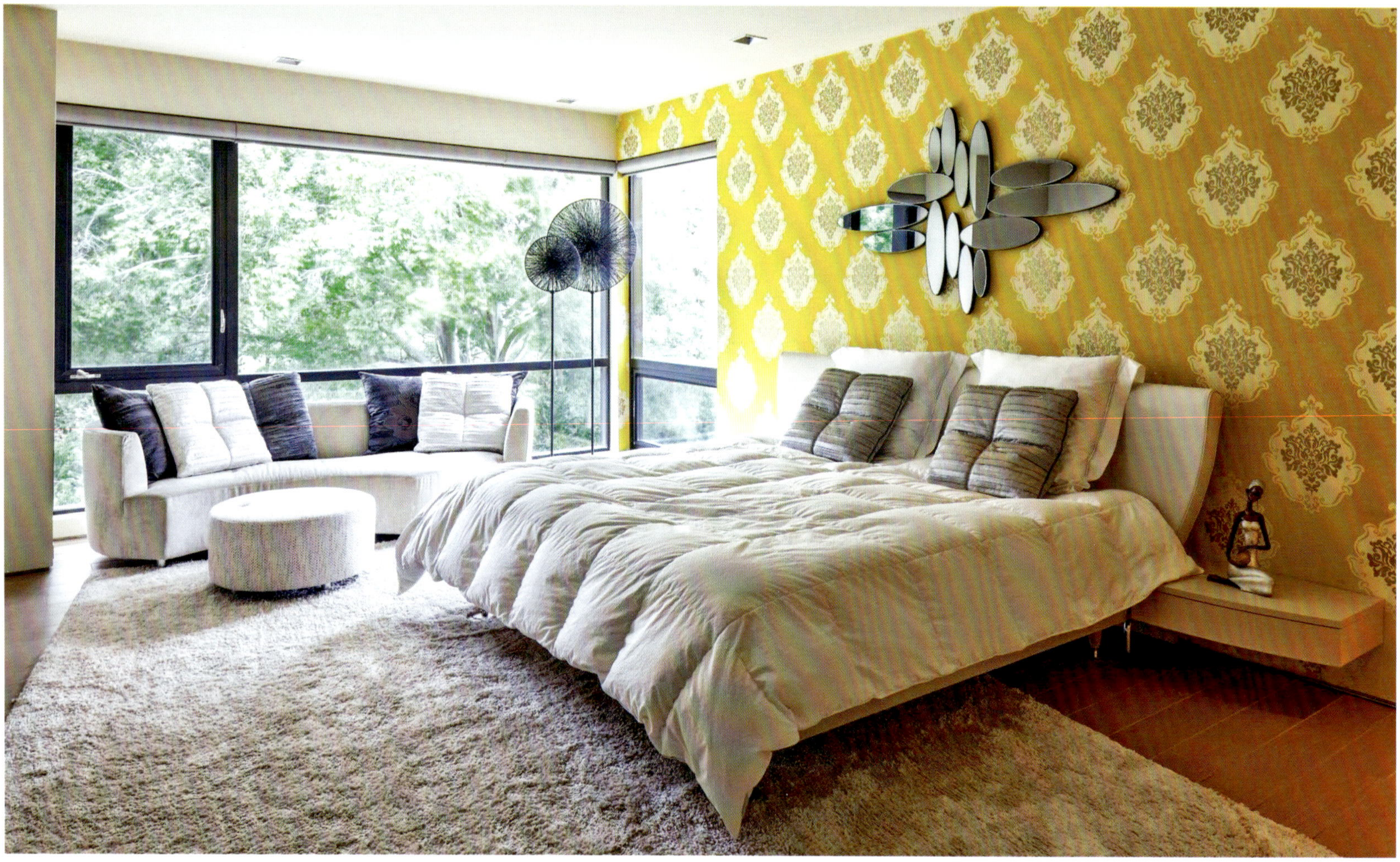

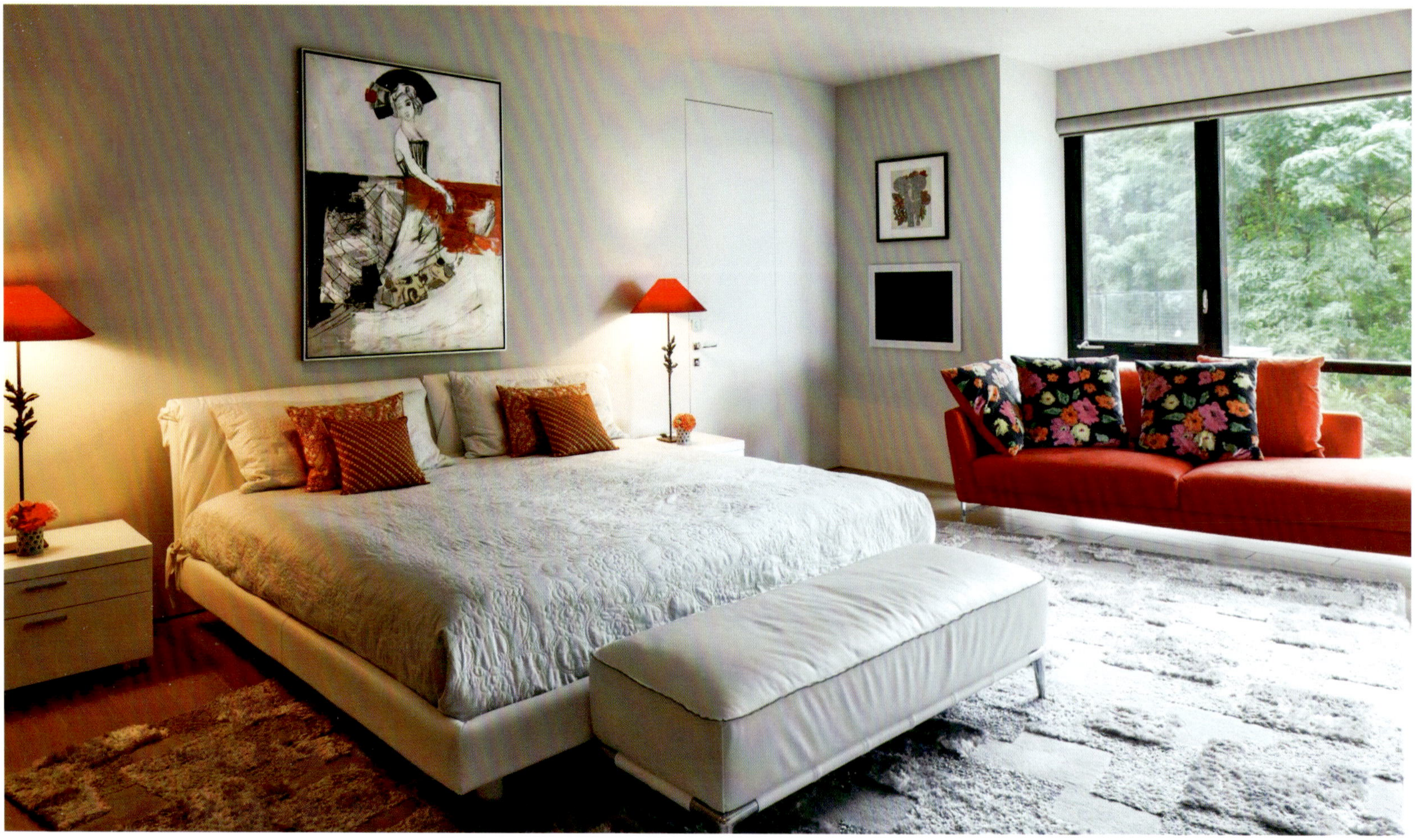

Harker Street, Plettenberg Bay

Architects
Greg Wright Architects

Principal Architect
Greg Scott

Project Team
Liana Abate, Mark Bardon

Location
Harker Street, Plettenberg Bay

Site Area
669 m²

Building Footprint
300 m²

Gross Floor Area
500 m²

Photography
Kate Del Fante Scott

Sited on an exceptionally steep piece of land on the bluff above BI Beach in Plettenberg Bay, the challenge with this project was always going to be how to make a beach house "live" across a vertically driven program. As a wonderful counterpoint to the challenges faced by the extreme topography, it was the steepness the site that offered the extensive, uninterrupted, panoramic views that extend beyond 180° vistas from Robberg Reserve in the south right around to Keurbooms lagoon in the north, the trick was how we balanced the two.

The program was unpacked in such a way that the living area filled the widest of the vertical platforms that was created so that kitchen, dining and living rooms as well as a guest bedroom could open onto a generous, partially covered terrace that made the most of the panorama described above. Pergolas, braai area, canopies level changes and the swimming pool offer a variety of "zones" that can be occupied in various manners depending on whether the terrace is used for a quiet spot of lounging or entertaining friends and family.

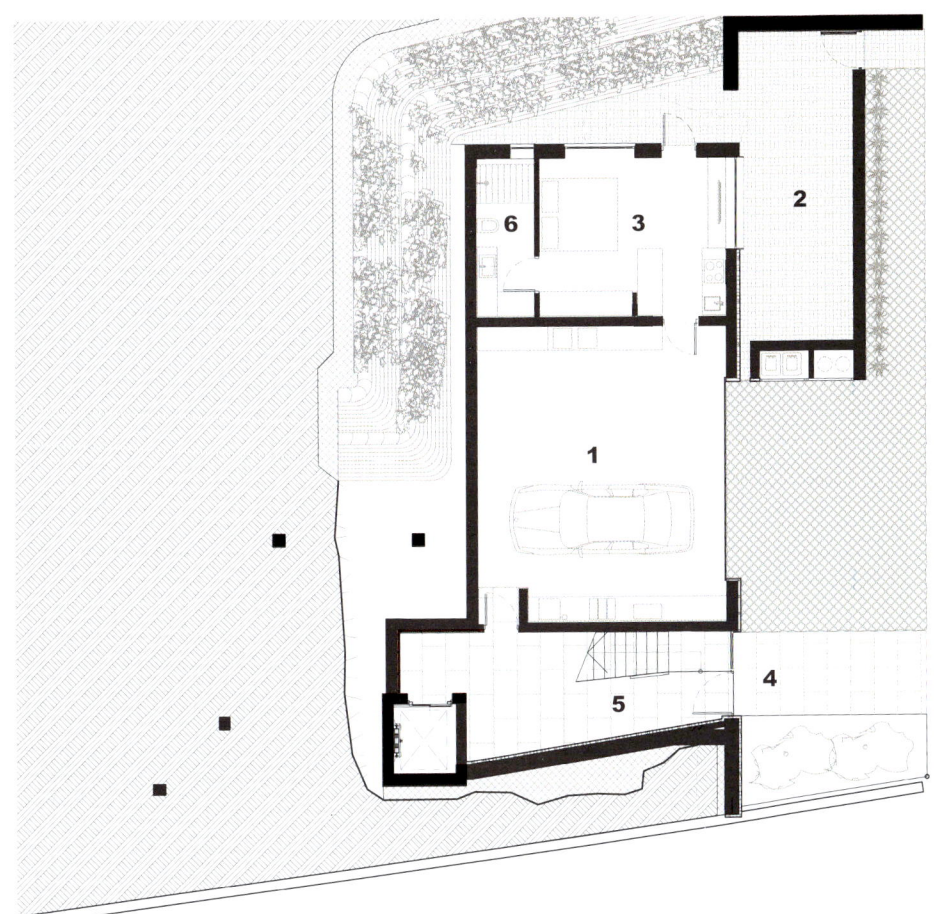

LEGEND

1)	Double Garage	7)	Family Room	13)	Terrace	19)	Scullery
2)	Courtyard	8)	Bedroom 1	14)	Pool	20)	Guest WC
3)	Domestic Quarters	9)	Bedroom 2	15)	Lounge	21)	Main Bedroom
4)	Entrance	10)	Plant Room	16)	Dining	22)	Dressing Room
5)	Foyer	11)	Passage	17)	Bedroom 3	23)	Main Bathroom
6)	En-suite	12)	Double Volume	18)	Kitchen		

The ground floor plays home to garages, staff quarters and a timber and stone clad entrance volume and stairwell; an intermediate level houses 2 other bedrooms and a small TV lounge whilst the top floor plays host to the master bedroom suite that completes the program.

Whilst unashamedly contemporary in the architectural language and interior detailing, a palette of timber and natural stone temper the building both inside and out. The materials are intended to weather into a series of greys and driftwood tones intended to ground the house in its coastal context.

Not only grey though, the house plays host to "green" components as well; the systems of the house are complemented by a series of sustainable features such as rainwater harvesting, PV panels with batteries amongst others.

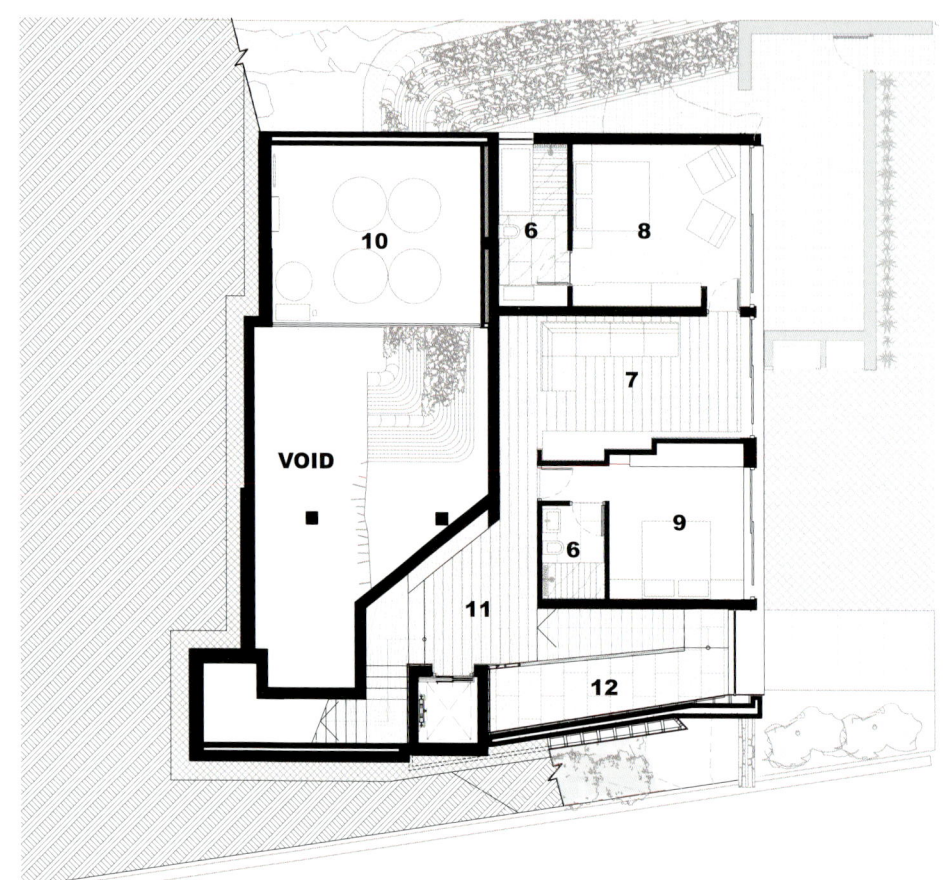

LEGEND

1) Double Garage	7) Family Room	13) Terrace	19) Scullery
2) Courtyard	8) Bedroom 1	14) Pool	20) Guest WC
3) Domestic Quarters	9) Bedroom 2	15) Lounge	21) Main Bedroom
4) Entrance	10) Plant Room	16) Dining	22) Dressing Room
5) Foyer	11) Passage	17) Bedroom 3	23) Main Bathroom
6) En-suite	12) Double Volume	18) Kitchen	

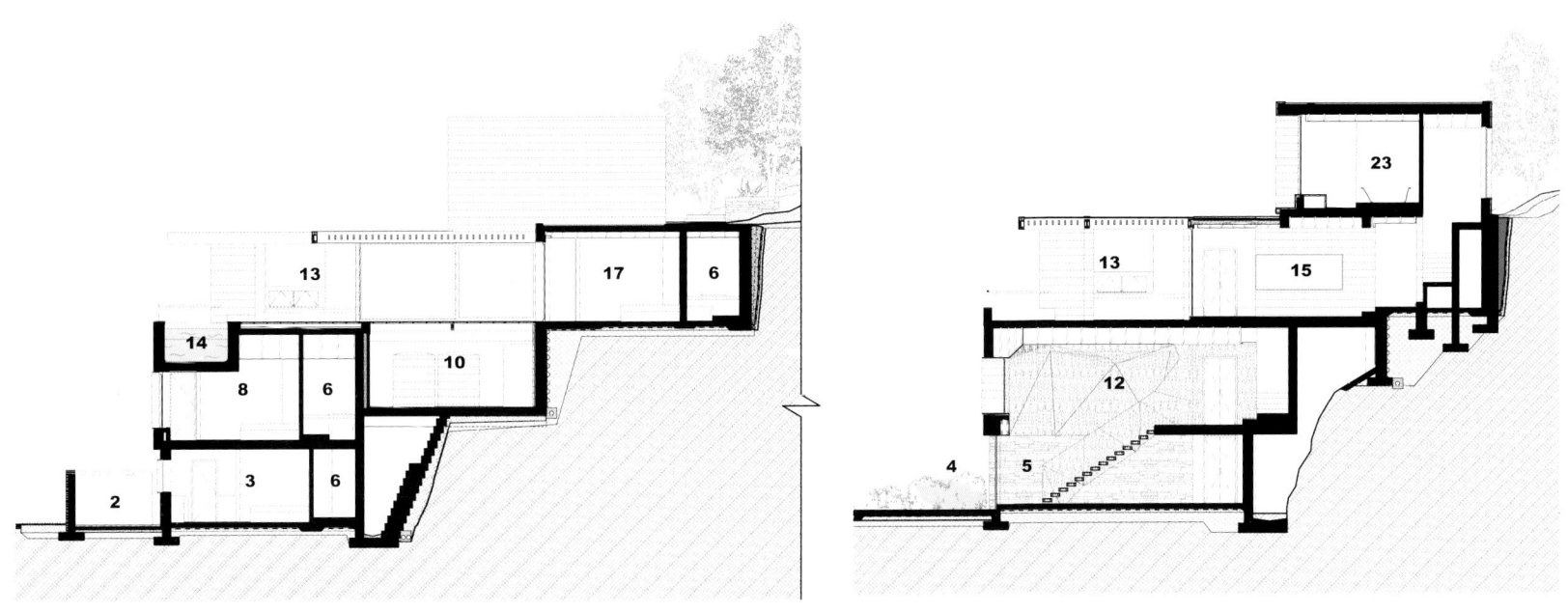

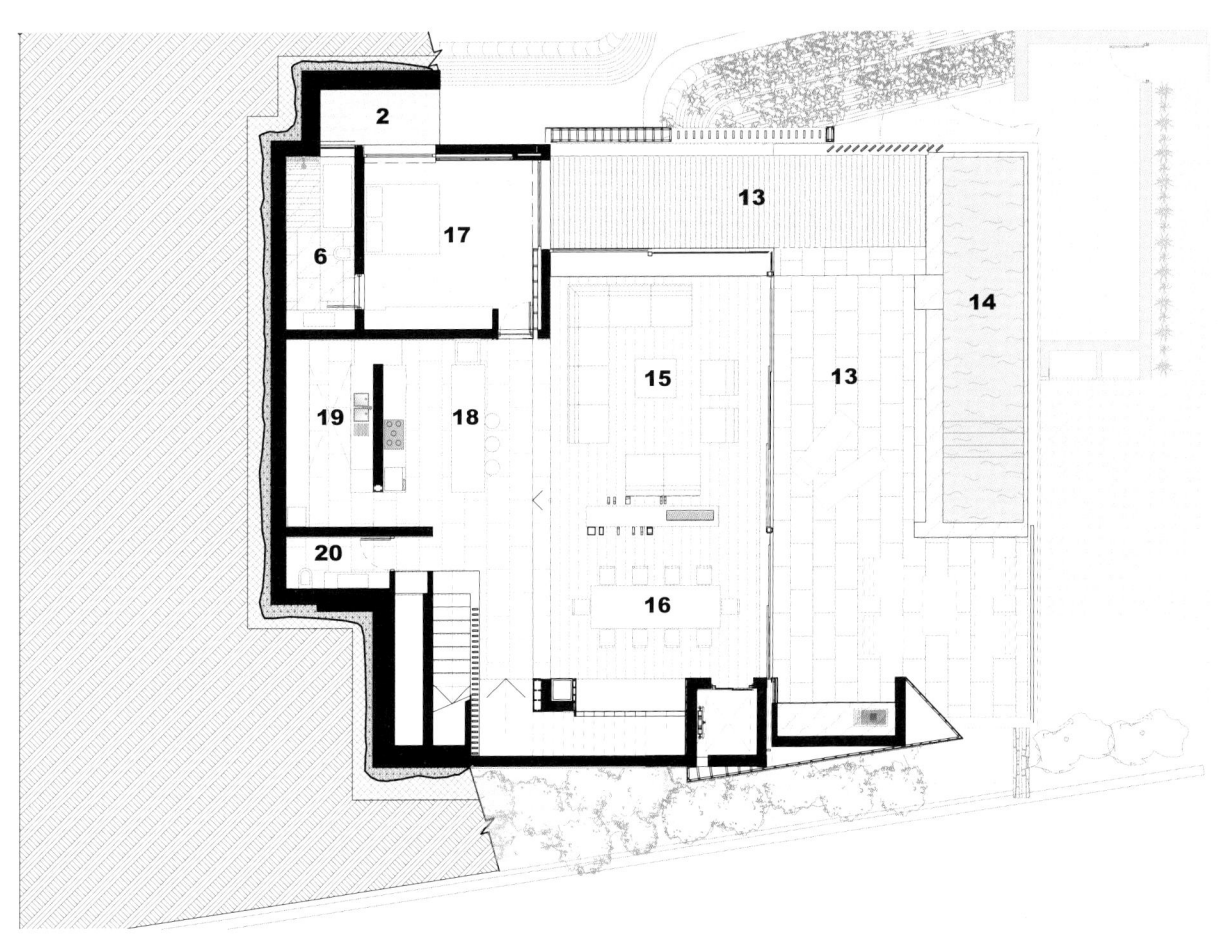

LEGEND

1) Double Garage	7) Family Room	13) Terrace	19) Scullery
2) Courtyard	8) Bedroom 1	14) Pool	20) Guest WC
3) Domestic Quarters	9) Bedroom 2	15) Lounge	21) Main Bedroom
4) Entrance	10) Plant Room	16) Dining	22) Dressing Room
5) Foyer	11) Passage	17) Bedroom 3	23) Main Bathroom
6) En-suite	12) Double Volume	18) Kitchen	

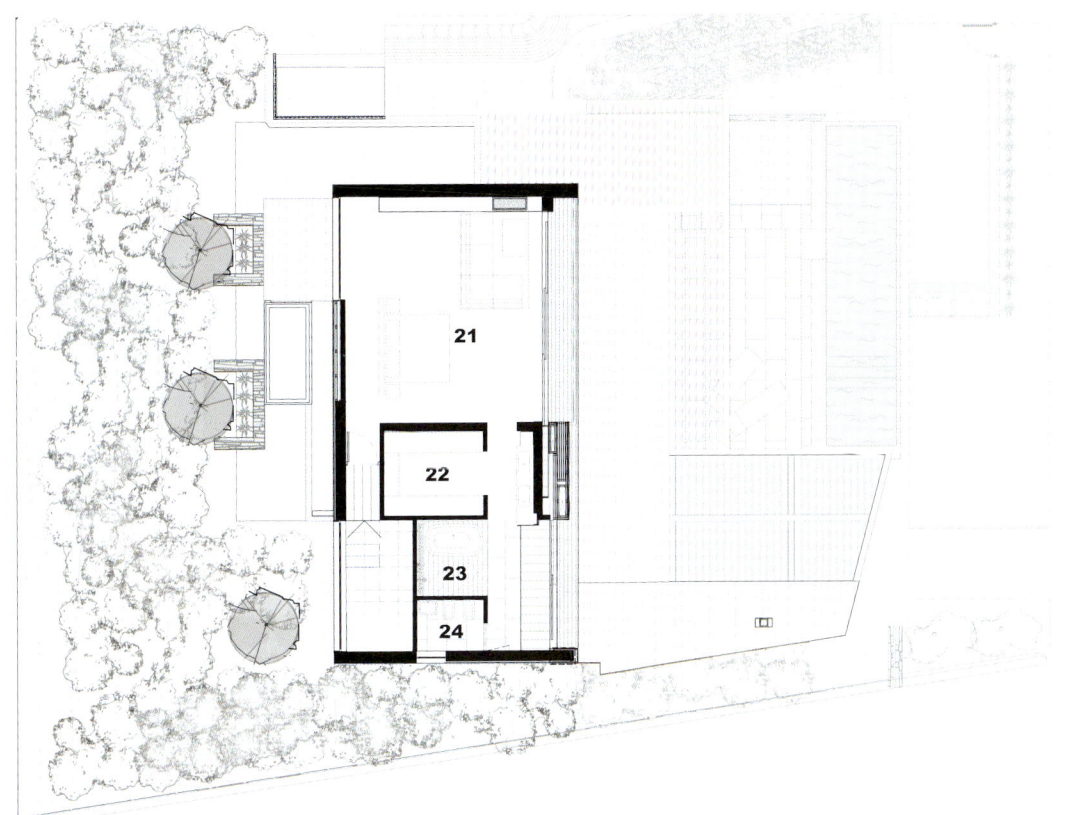

LEGEND

1) Double Garage	7) Family Room	13) Terrace	19) Scullery
2) Courtyard	8) Bedroom 1	14) Pool	20) Guest WC
3) Domestic Quarters	9) Bedroom 2	15) Lounge	21) Main Bedroom
4) Entrance	10) Plant Room	16) Dining	22) Dressing Room
5) Foyer	11) Passage	17) Bedroom 3	23) Main Bathroom
6) En-suite	12) Double Volume	18) Kitchen	

LV House

Architects
A-cero, Joaquín Torres &
Rafael Llamazares architects

Location
Spain

Photography
Plasmalia

A-cero presents a new single-family house located in the north of Spain. This house with an approximate built up area of 1,000 m² is divided in three floors. The project is characterized by its simplicity and its blend of classic style with modern flair. The property is located on a large landscaped garden and a swimming pool with organic shapes.

With a different aesthetic criteria that characterize the studio managed by architects Joaquín Torres and Rafael Llamazares. This house designed by A-cero is provided outdoors and indoors with high standard quality materials and furniture.

When people get into the house through the distributor hall they get surprised by the amazing staircase that connects the three floors. Downstairs, in the ground floor they find the public areas like dining and living rooms as well as the kitchen and the service area. All the rooms have been designed with wide windows. All the rooms are in connection with the garden through the porches.

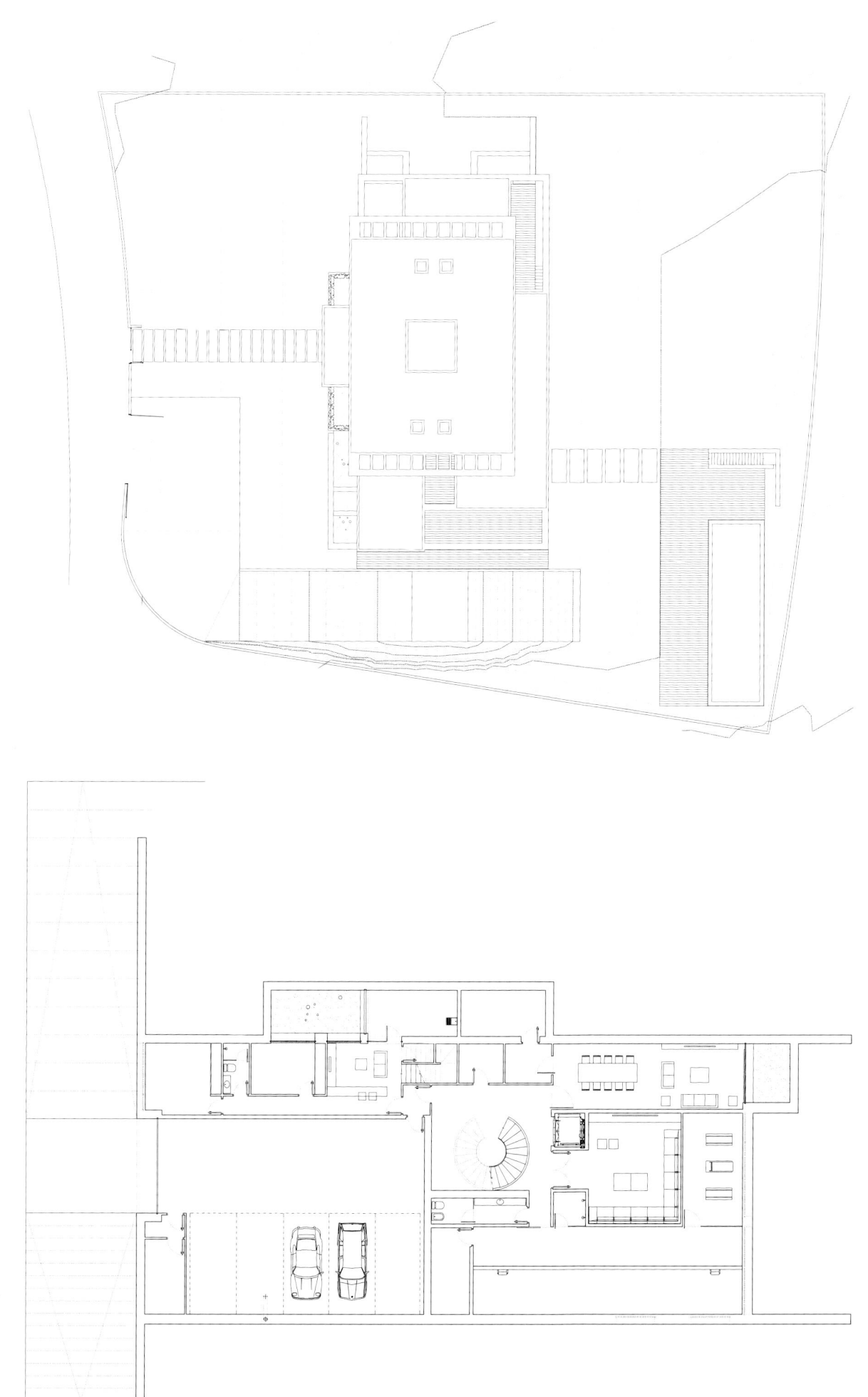

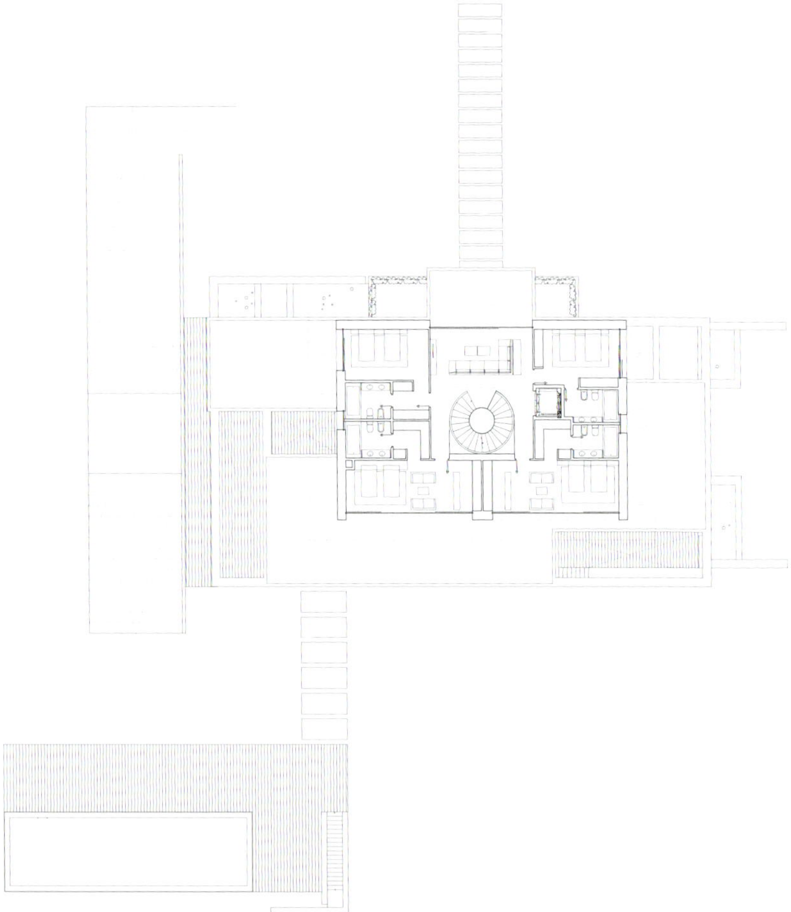

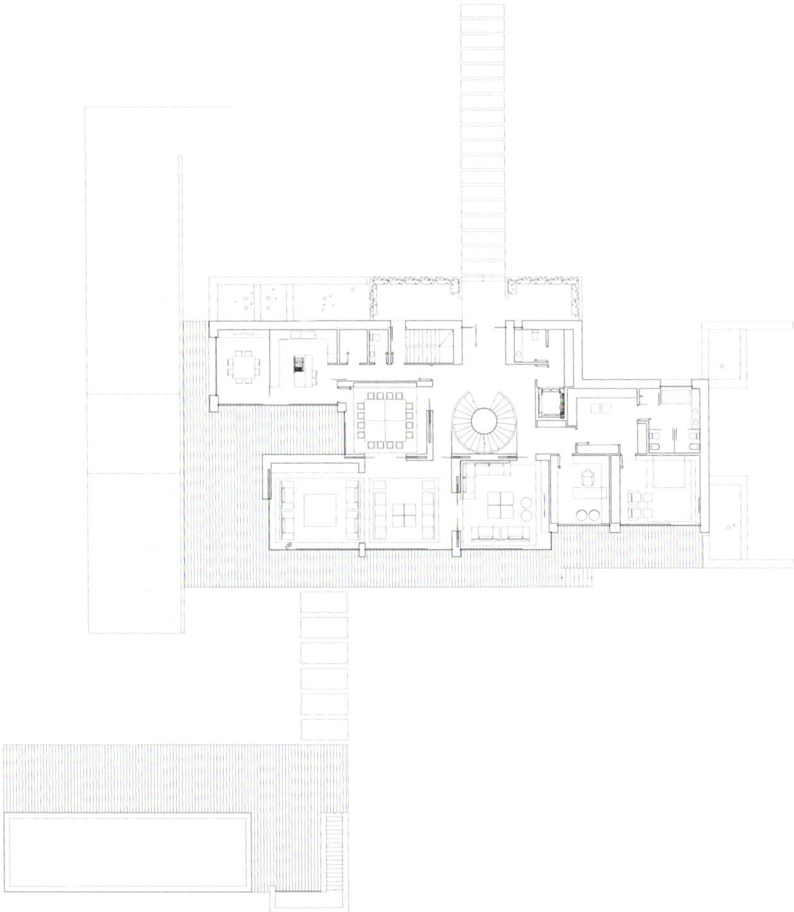

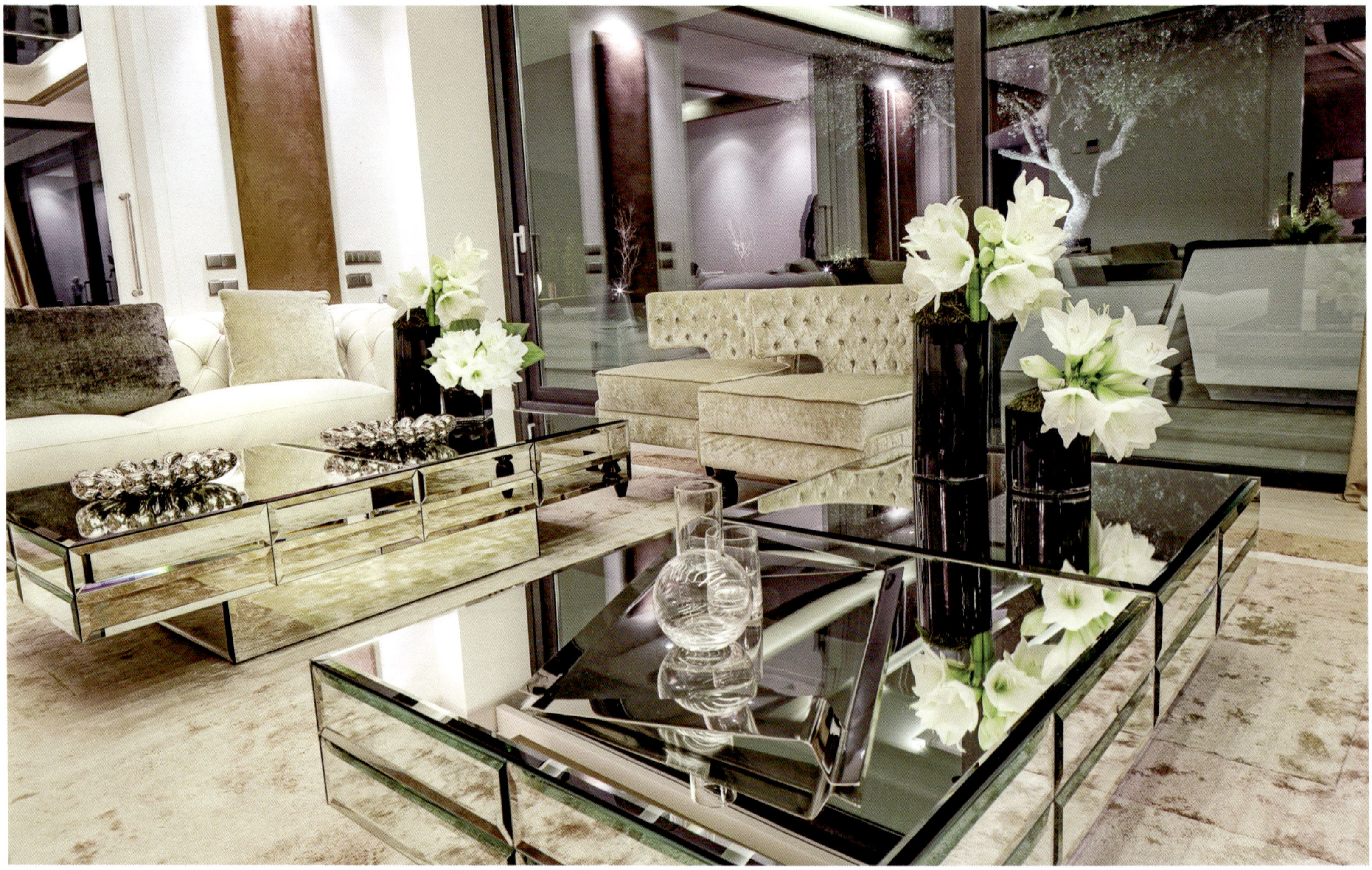

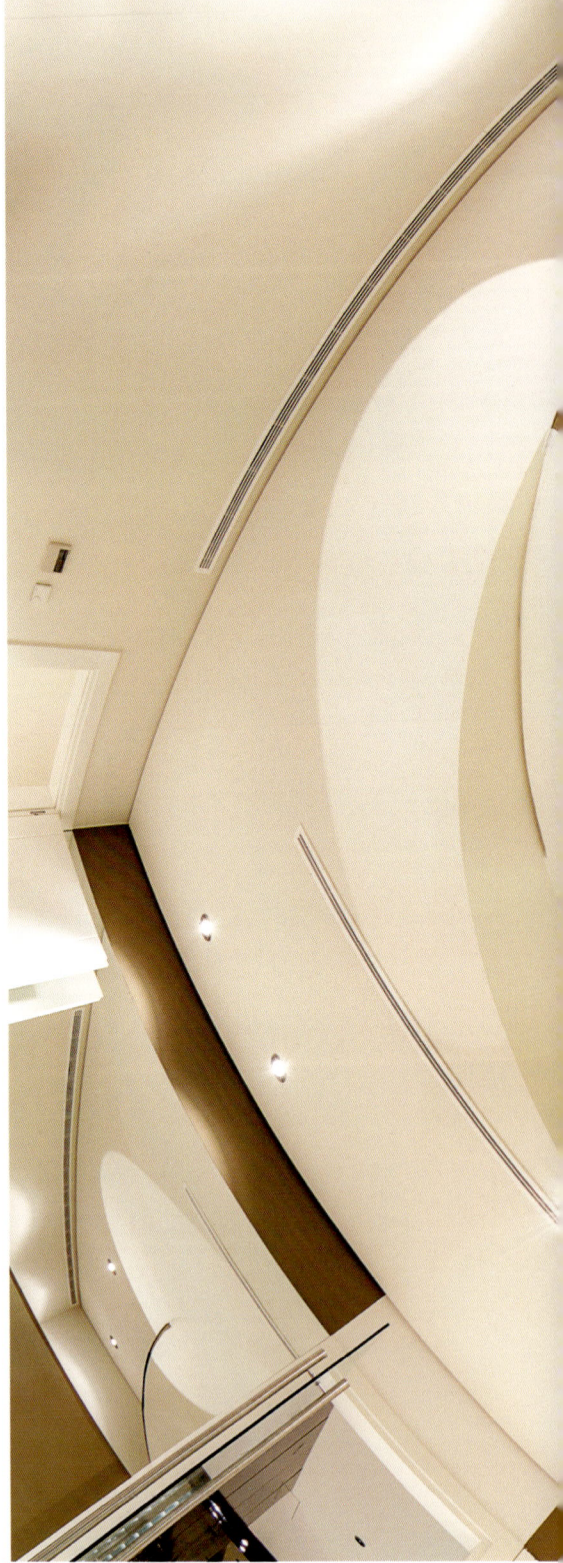

The top floor is reserved for the bedrooms. There is a master bedroom with bathroom and dressing room and 4 other bedrooms also with its own bathroom.

In the basement they find the garage, an entertainment area, which is perfect to meet people and also the indoor pool with gym. The property also has an elevator to connect the different floors.

The interior design and the furniture chosen by the client have different origins. There are several Ipe Cavalli furniture designs as well as A-cero IN designs. Vondom firms the outdoor furniture. The decoration is completed with different objects from the client and also furniture from A-cero IN like sculptures designed by the architectural studio and objects from antique shops or stores like Anmoder and Lou & Hernandez.

San Vicente Residence

Designer
Paul McClean

Location
Los Angeles, CA

Photography
Jim Bartsch

The new residence is located on a large flat lot adjacent to a busy street. The designers' goal was to design a beautiful family home while minimizing street noise. It is essential that the outside world be left behind and their idea focused on creating a zone of decompression as you enter the property. The street is heavily screened with landscaping and high walls. The drive court is separated from the entry courtyard by a glass screen wall. The landscaped courtyard contains a water element to further screen noise and provide an attractive focal point. The house is laid out over 2 levels in an "L" shape configuration around the garden. The kitchen family room opens onto a large covered porch which is lit through a glass floor in the deck above. The pool house provides an attractive focal point from the living spaces across the garden. There are 6 bedrooms in the house as well as formal and family living spaces, media and office. The palette of materials is soft contemporary with extensive use of limestone, wood as well as Italian cabinetry and bronze accents. The garden is the focus of the design incorporating the lawn and pool, various outdoor entertaining spaces, ornamental trees and sculpture.

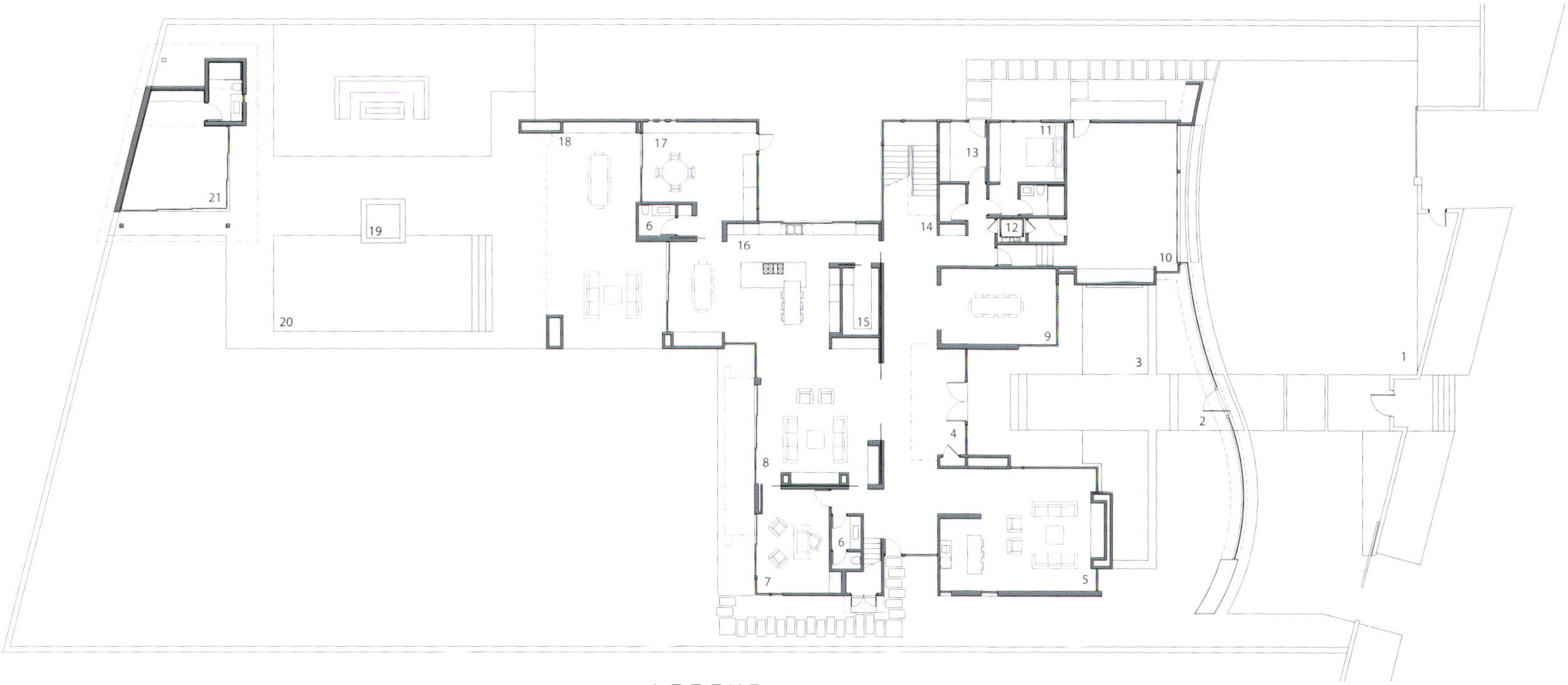

LEGEND

DRIVECOURT	1	DINING ROOM	9	WORK ROOM	17
ENTRY COURTYARD	2	GARAGE	10	PATIO	18
WATER FEATURE	3	MAID'S ROOM	11	SPA	19
ENTRY	4	ELEVATOR	12	POOL	20
FAMILY ROOM	5	MUD ROOM	13	POOL HOUSE	21
POWDER	6	STAIRWELL	14		
OFFICE 1	7	PANTRY	15		
LIVING ROOM	8	KITCHEN	16		

0   10   20

SCALE IN METERS

NORTH

MAIN LEVEL PLAN

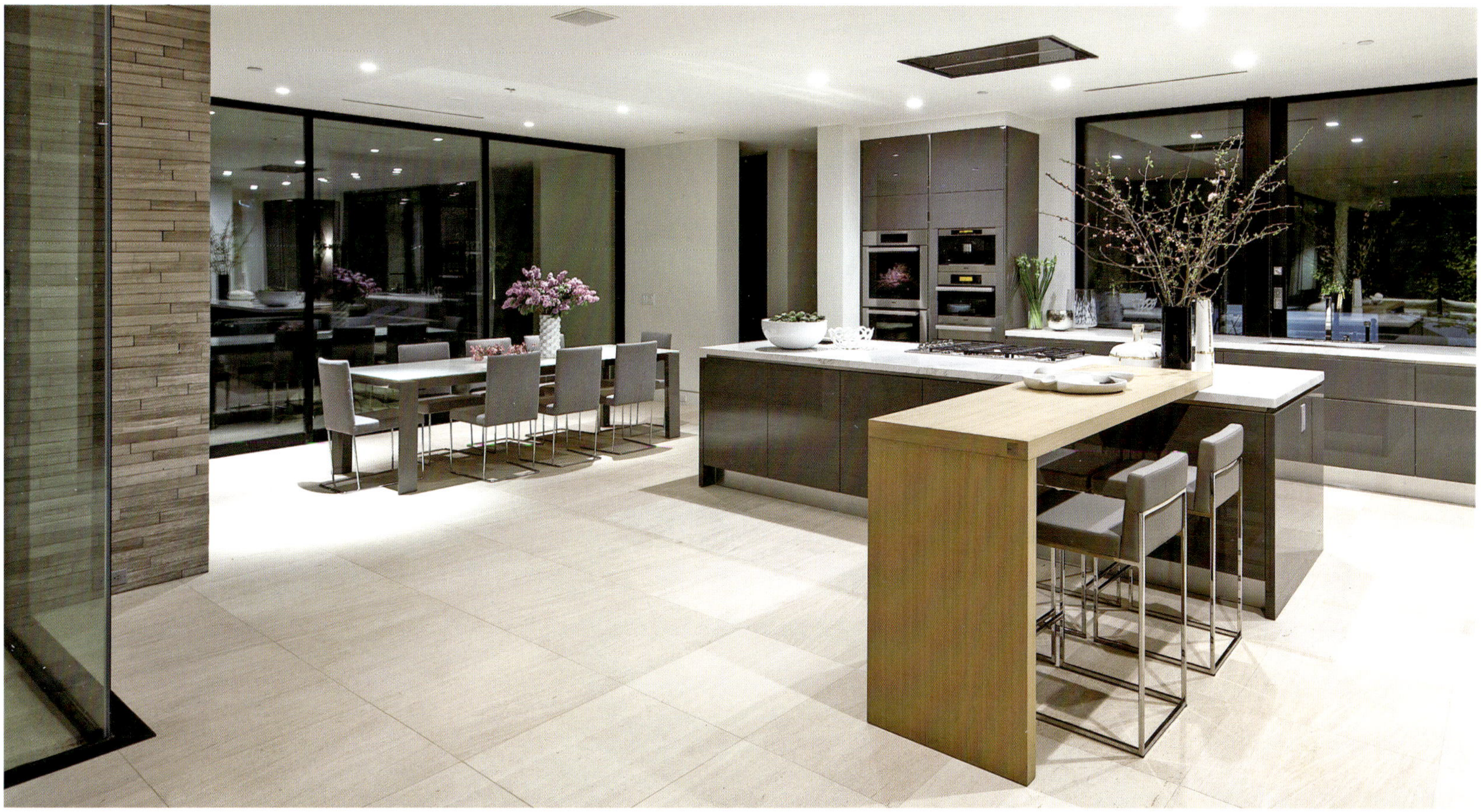
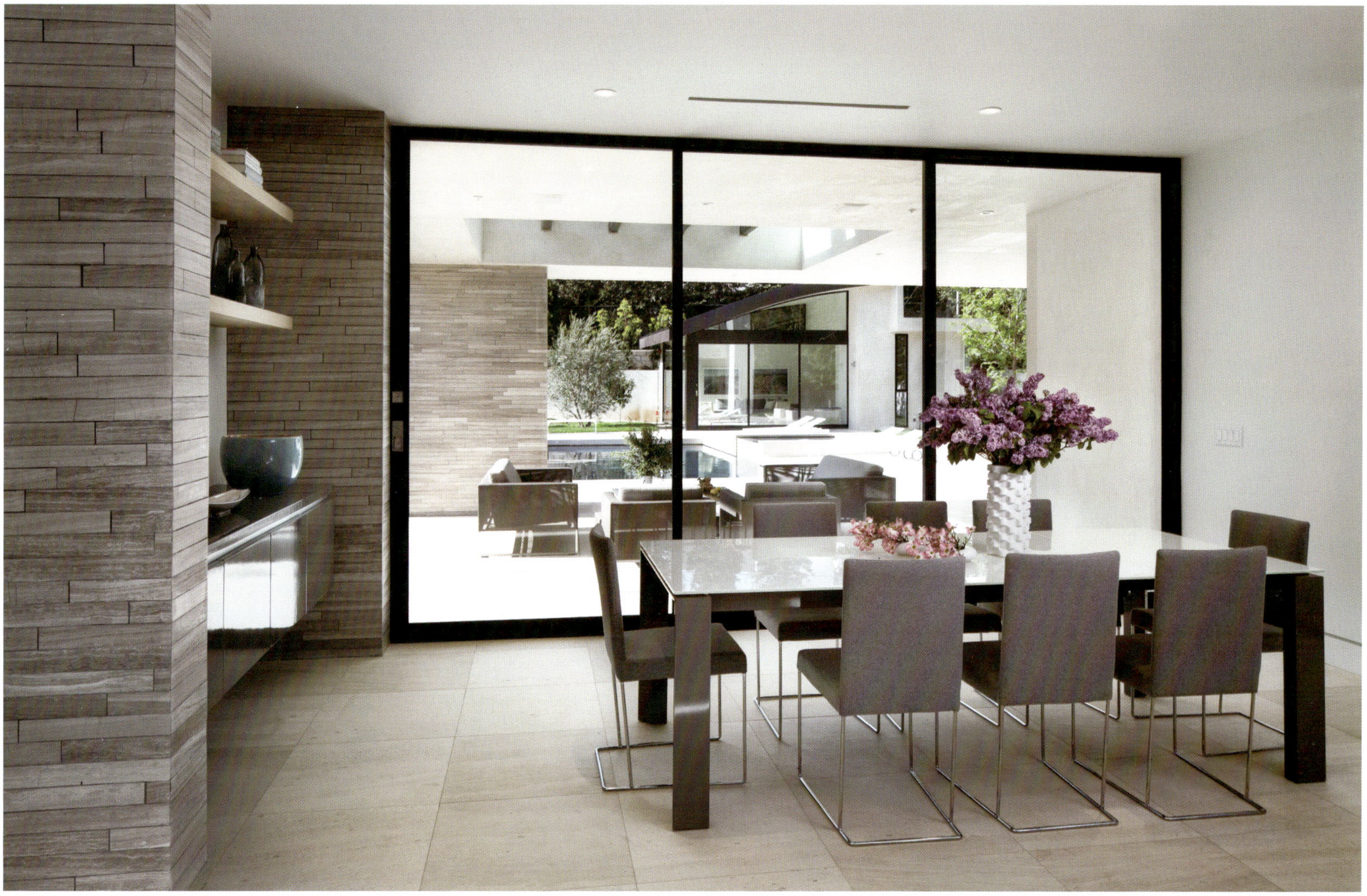

LEGEND

GYM	1	BEDROOM 2	9	M. CLOSET	17
STUDY	2	CLOSET 2	10	M. BATHROOM	18
LAUNDRY	3	BATHROOM 2	11	DECK	19
GUEST BEDRROM	4	BEDROOM 3	12		
FAMILY ROOM	5	BATHROOM 3	13		
BEDROOM 1	6	CLOSET 3	14		
CLOSET 1	7	LOUNGE	15		
BATHROOM 1	8	MASTER BEDRROM	16		

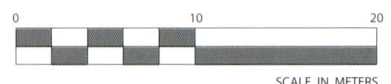

SCALE IN METERS

NORTH

UPPER LEVEL PLAN

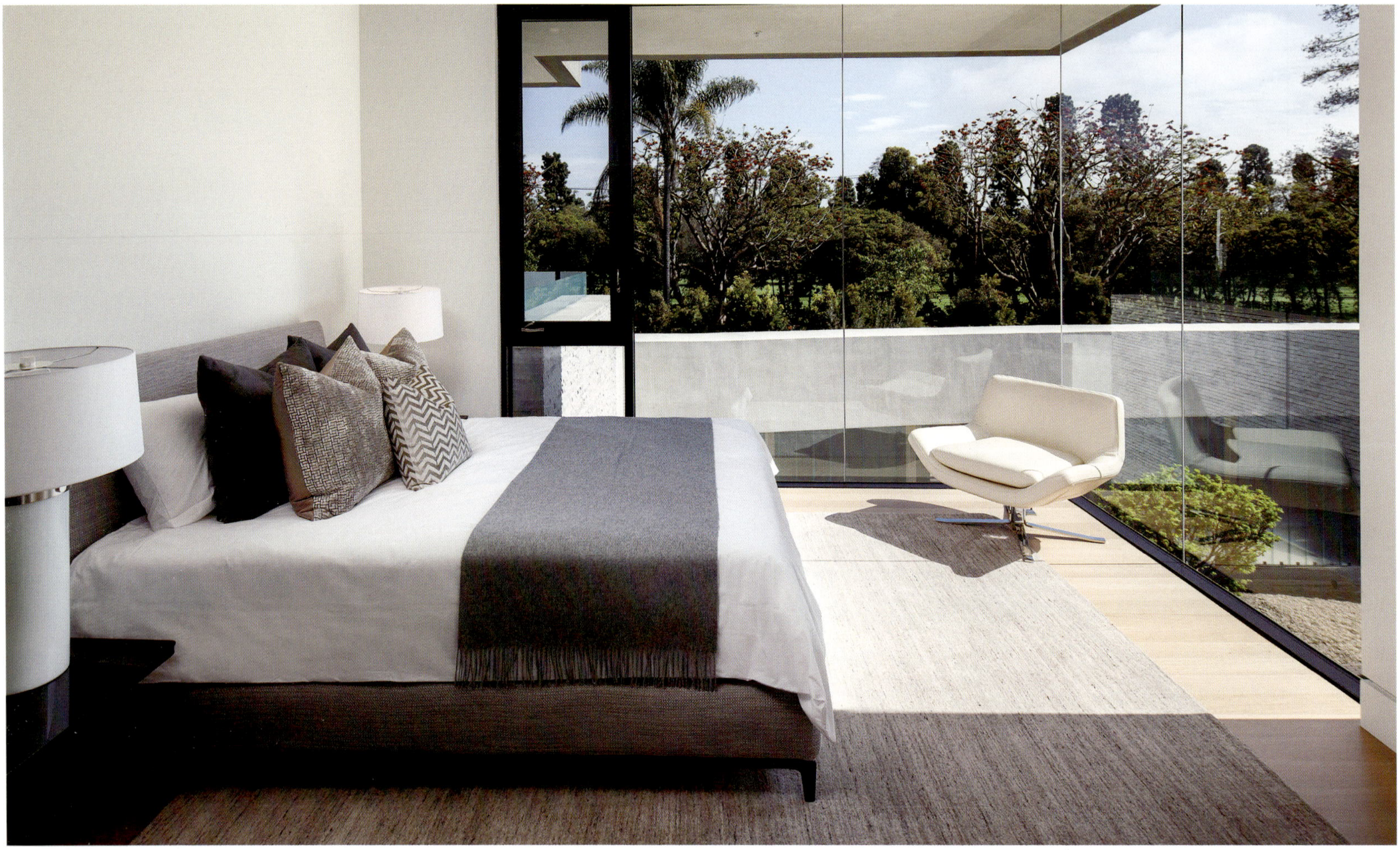

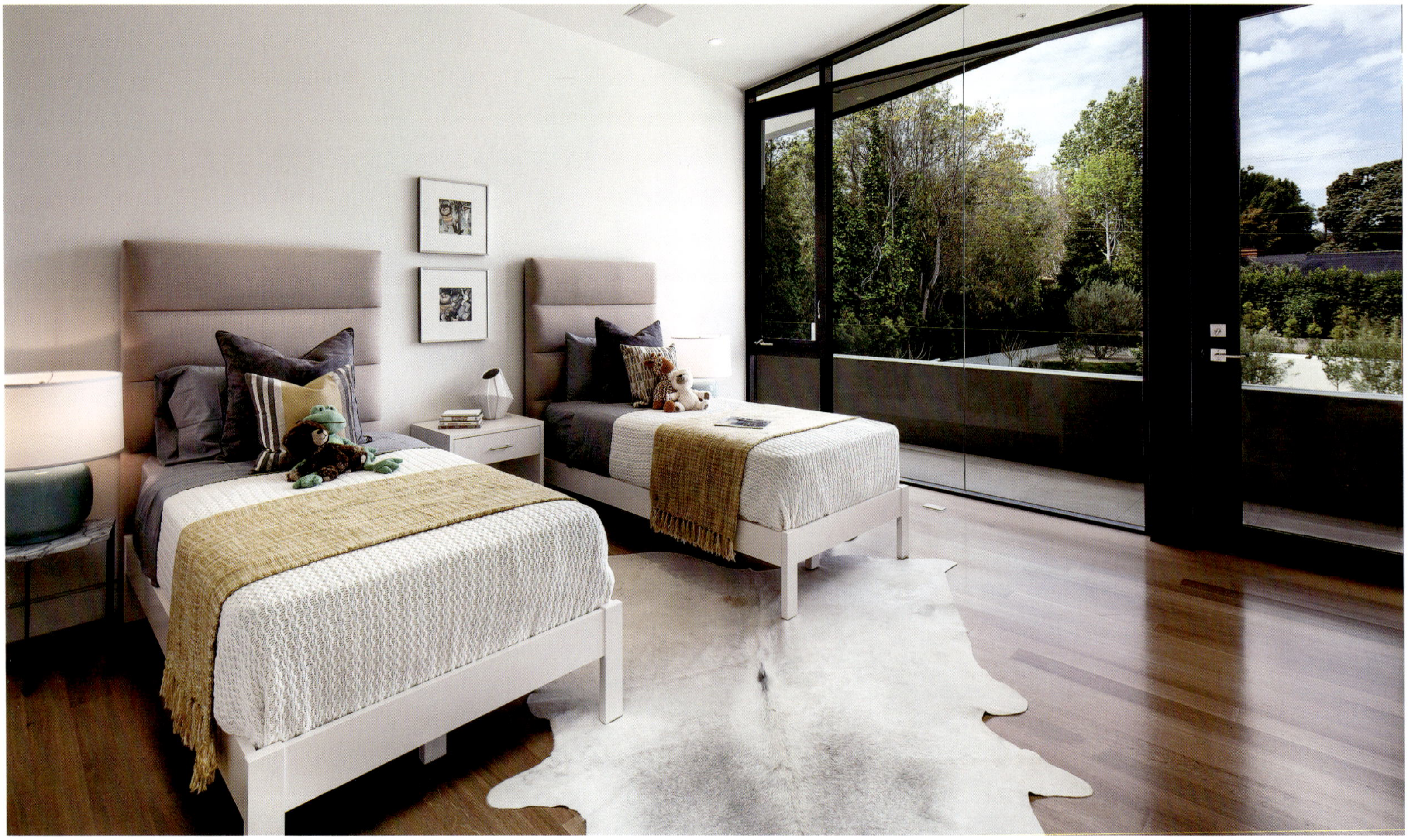

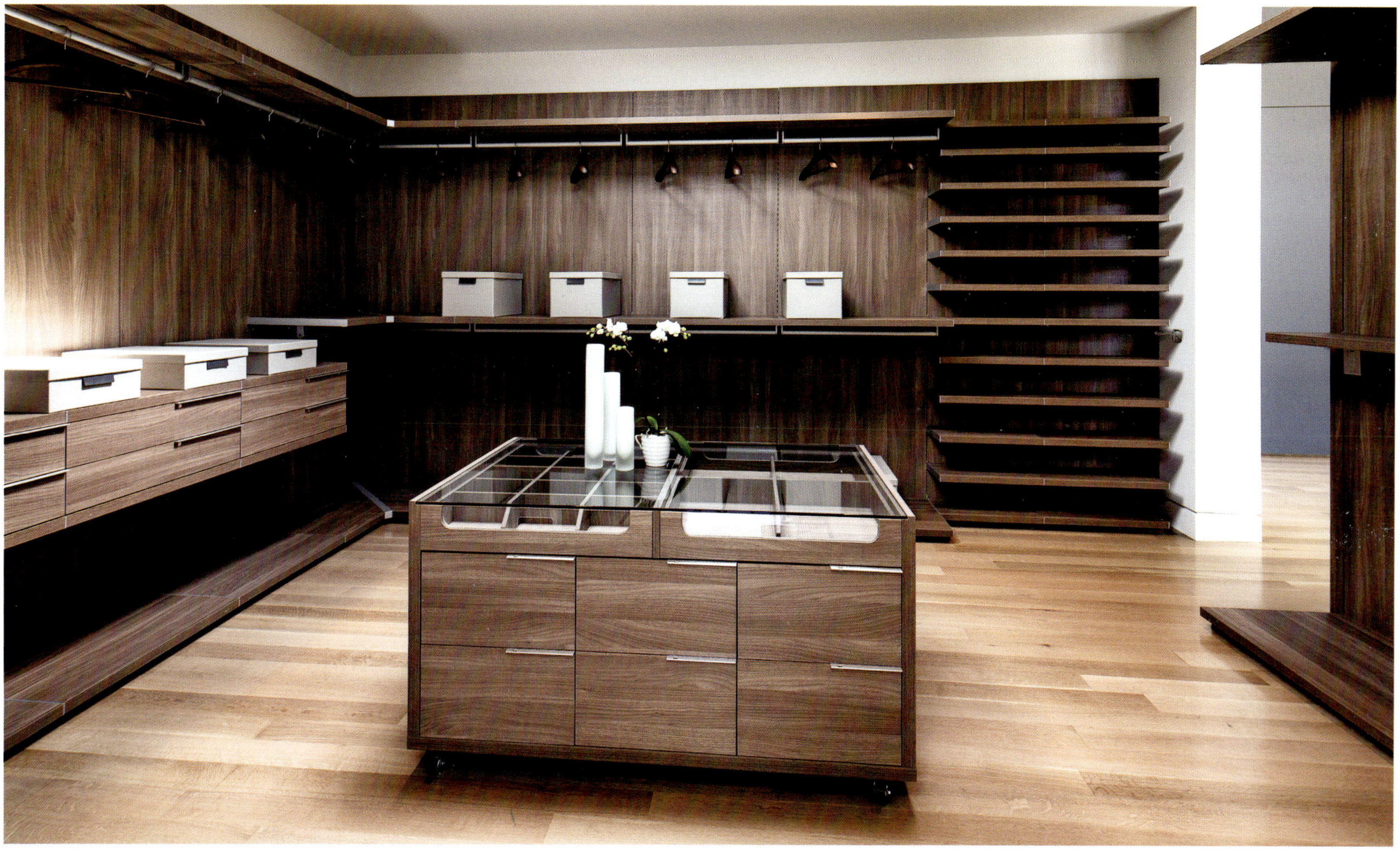

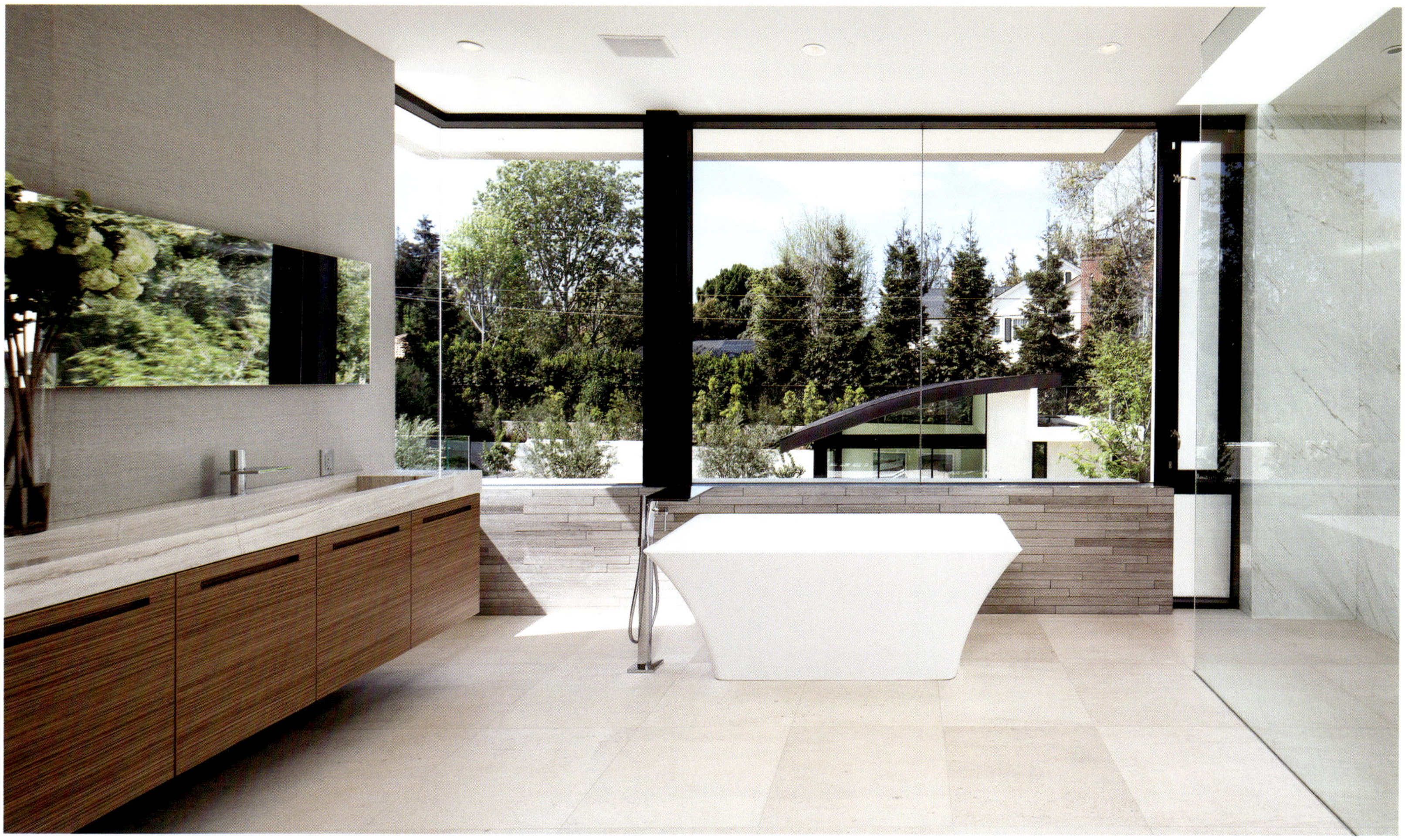

Sunset Strip Residence

Designer
Paul McClean

Location
Sunset Strip, Los Angeles

Photography
Jim Bartsch

The house occupies a hilltop lot in one of the most desirable locations in Los Angeles. It is long and narrow and the primary view was only available from one end of the lot. The designers' solution was to create a compound of three buildings; the main house, garage and wellness as well as a guest house. Passing through the gate, a landscapes hedge leads to the drive court which is centrally located between the three buildings. The garage sits in a spot that enjoys spectacular views of the surrounding canyons so they designed it to be glazed on both sides. All three buildings are connected by a water feature that leads the eye towards the views and entry. The main house is approached along the water feature. The front hallway, glazed and open on three sides, leads to a stairwell where a beautiful chrome and stone stair ascends to the upper level bedrooms.

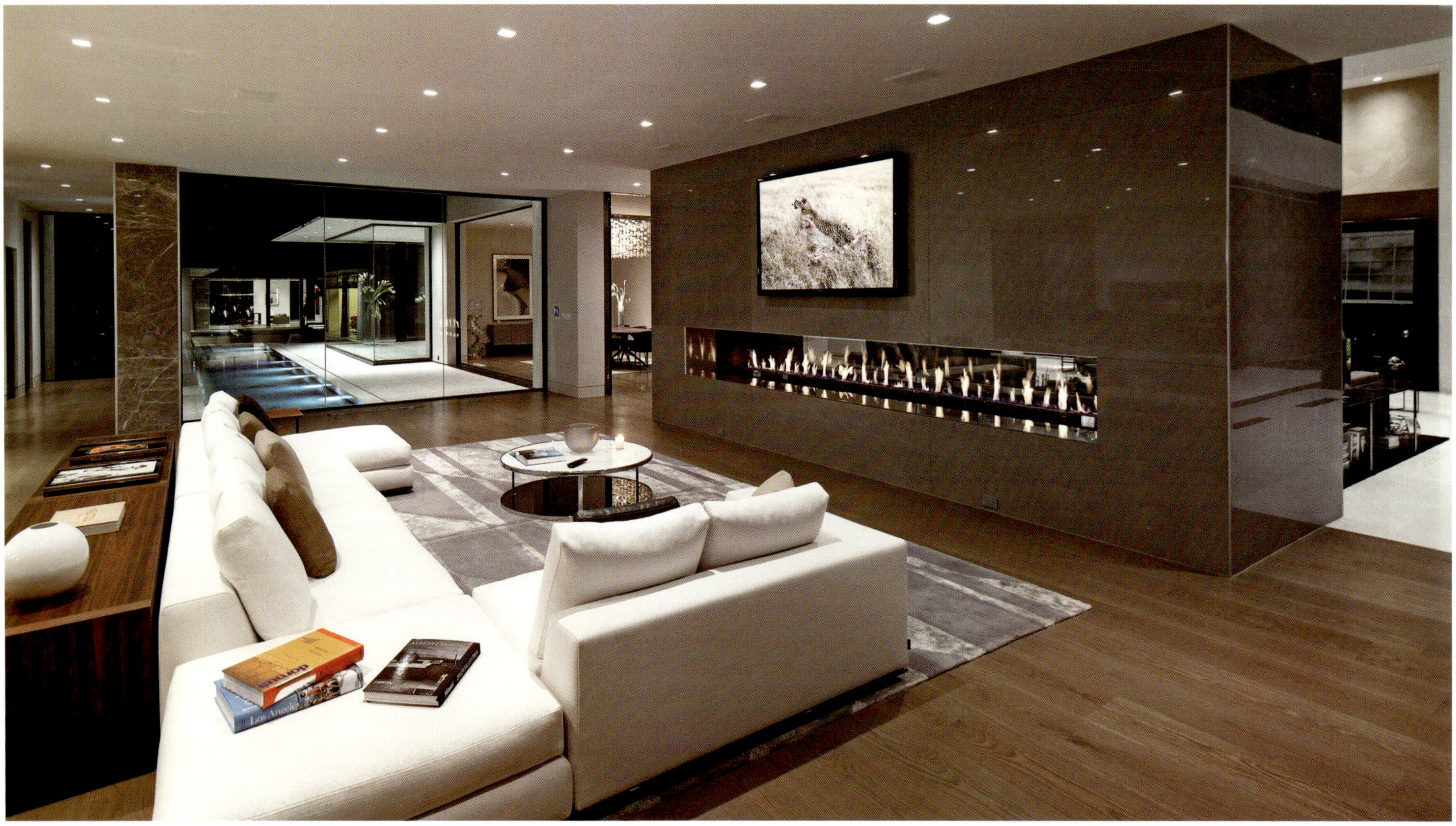

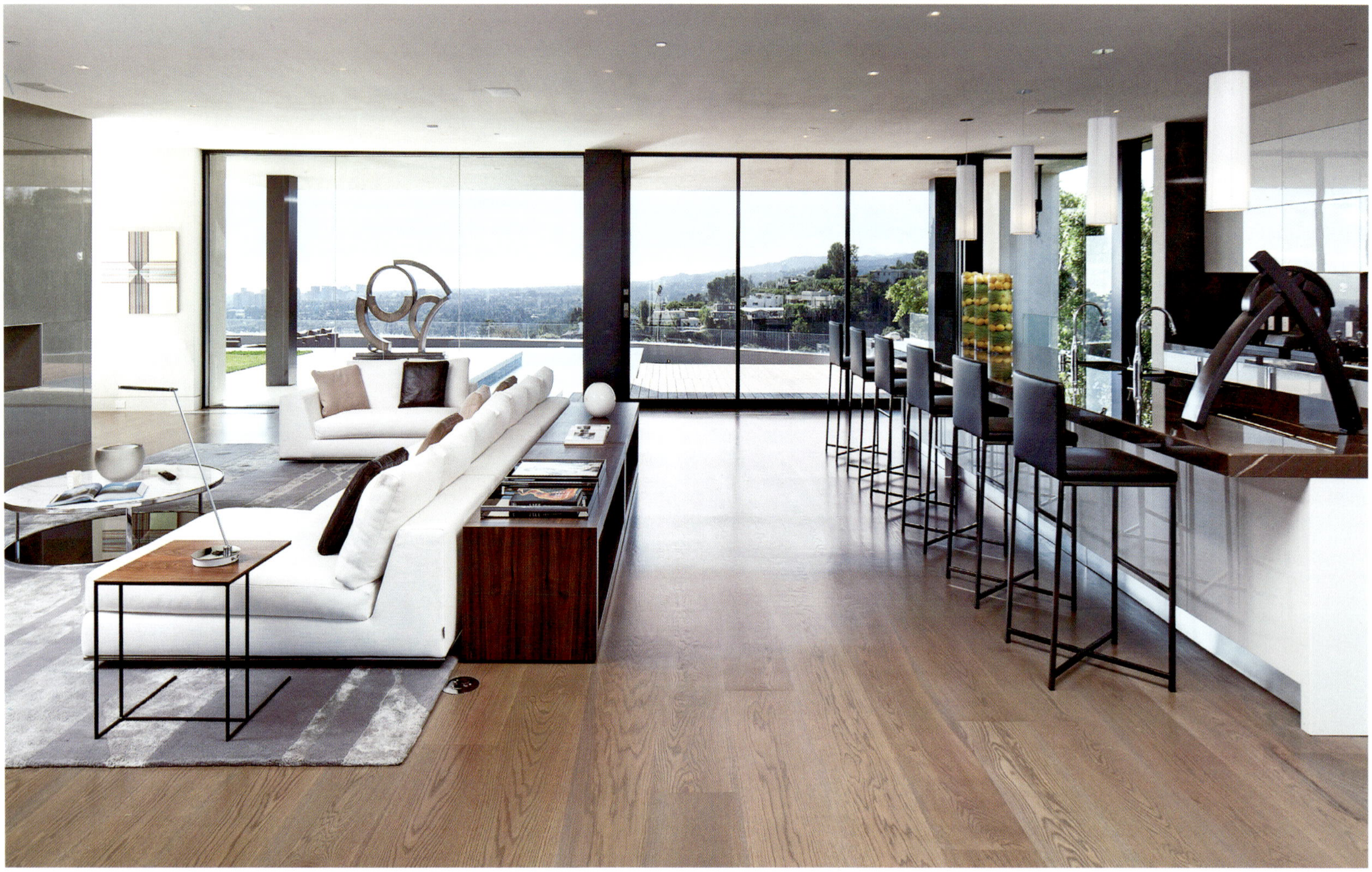

LEGEND

GARAGE 1   DINING ROOM 9   OFFICE 17
DRIVEWAY 2   WINE ROOM 10   POOL 18
WATER FEATURE 3   BAR 11   SPA 19
ENTRY 4   LIVING ROOM 12   DECK 20
MEDIA ROOM 5   FAMILY ROOM 13
LAUNDRY 6   KITCHEN 14
MAID'S ROOM 7   PANTRY 15
POWDER ROOM 8   ELEVATOR 16

0   10   20
SCALE IN METERS   NORTH

MAIN LEVEL PLAN

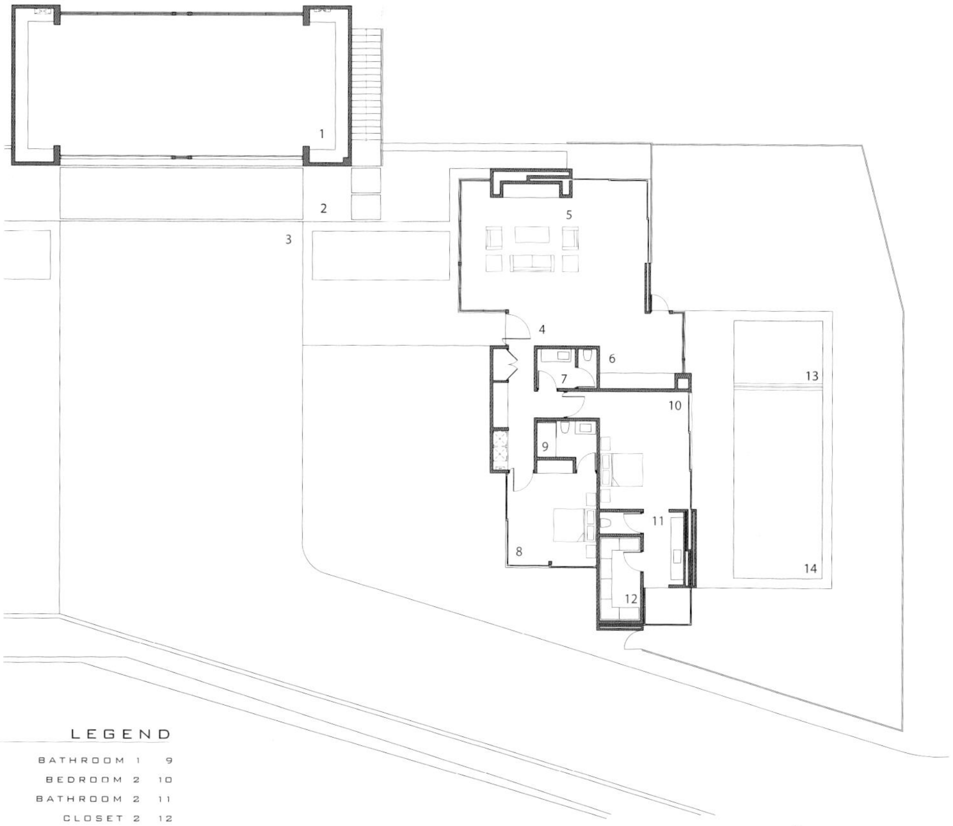

LEGEND

GARAGE 1   BATHROOM 1 9
WATER FEATURE 2   BEDROOM 2 10
DRIVEWAY 3   BATHROOM 2 11
ENTRY 4   CLOSET 2 12
LIVING ROOM 5   SPA 13
KITCHENETTE 6   POOL 14
POWDER 7
BEDROOM 1 8

0   10   20
SCALE IN METERS   NORTH

GUEST HOUSE PLAN

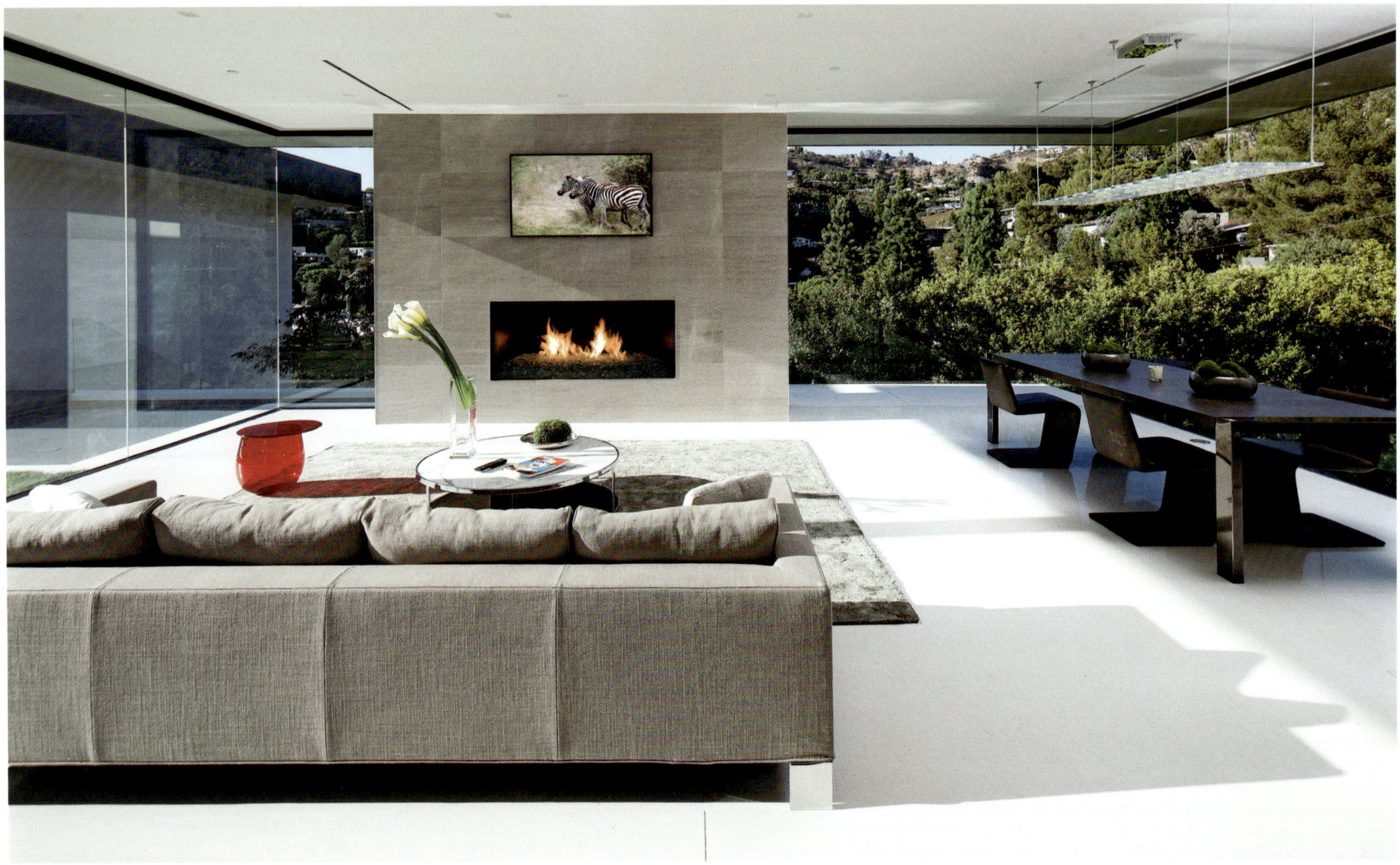

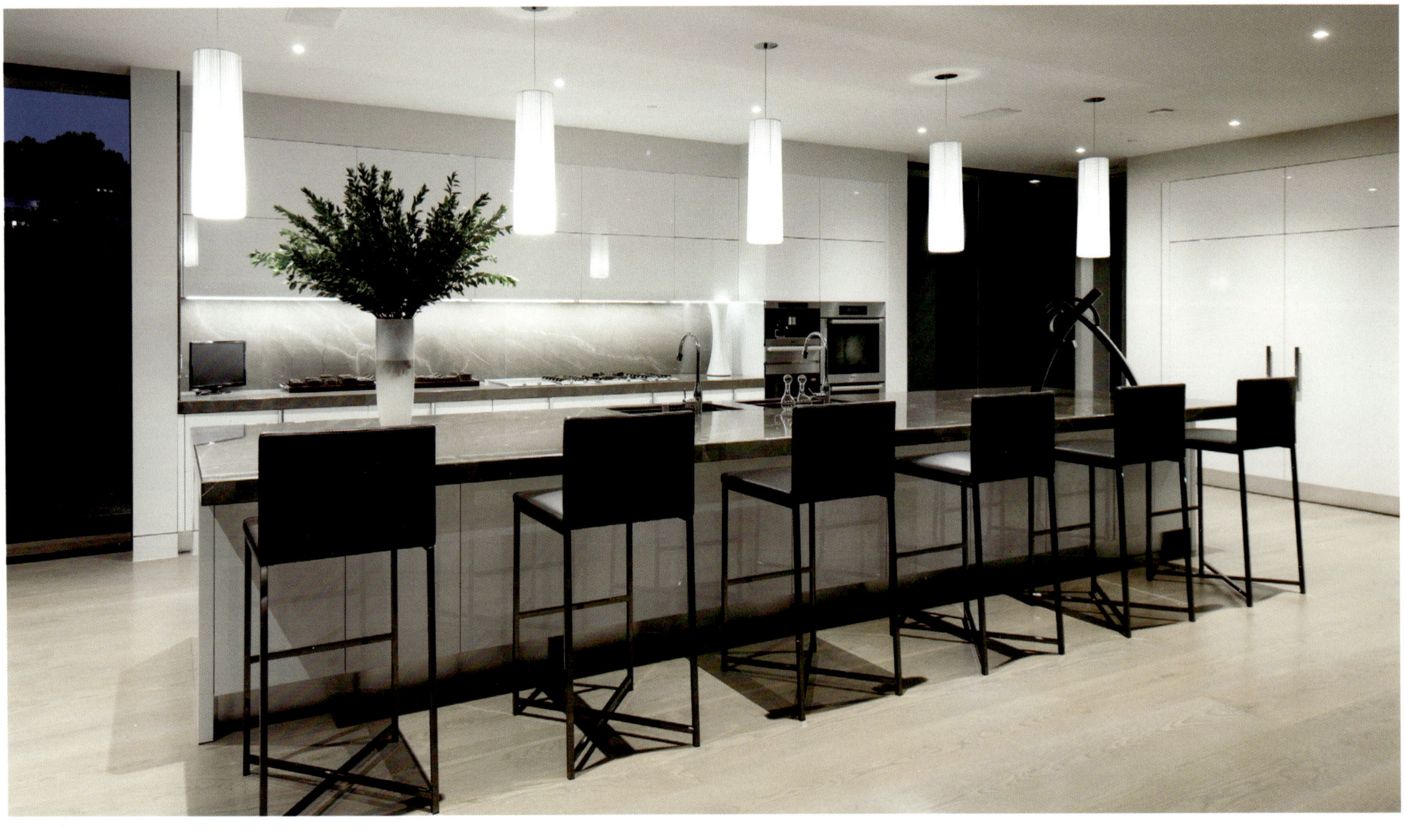

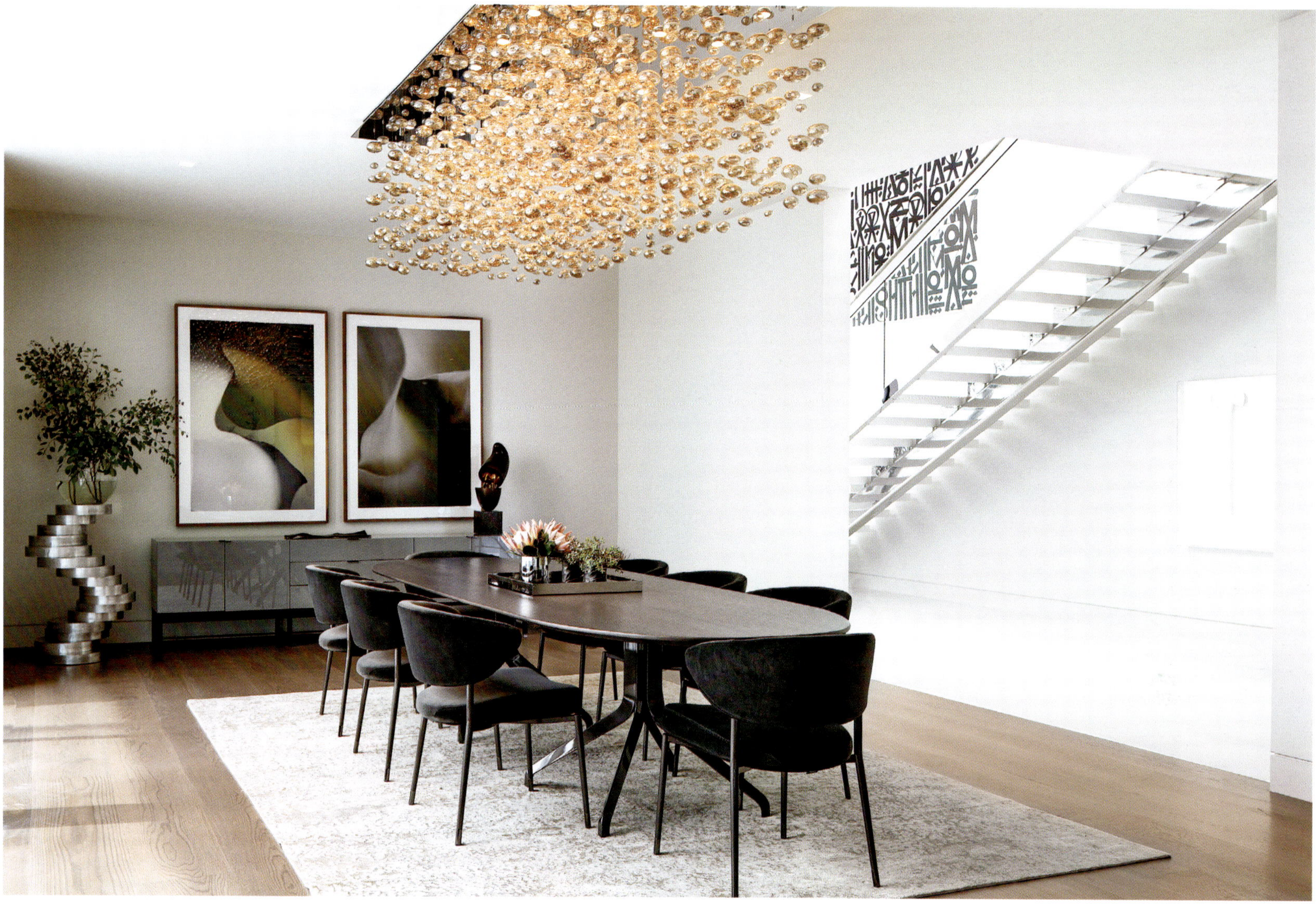

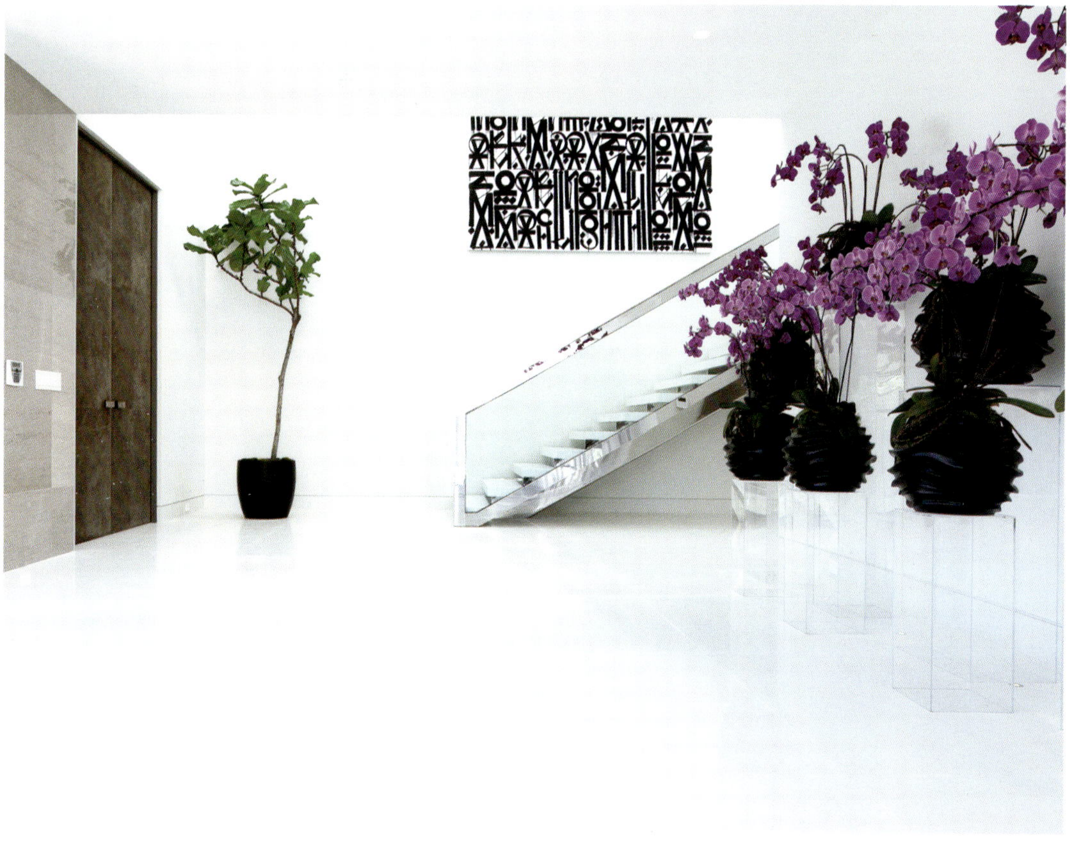

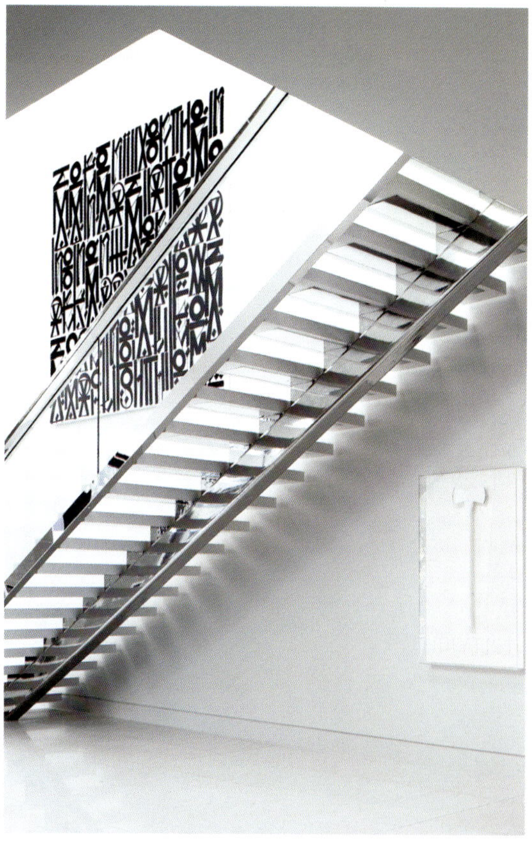

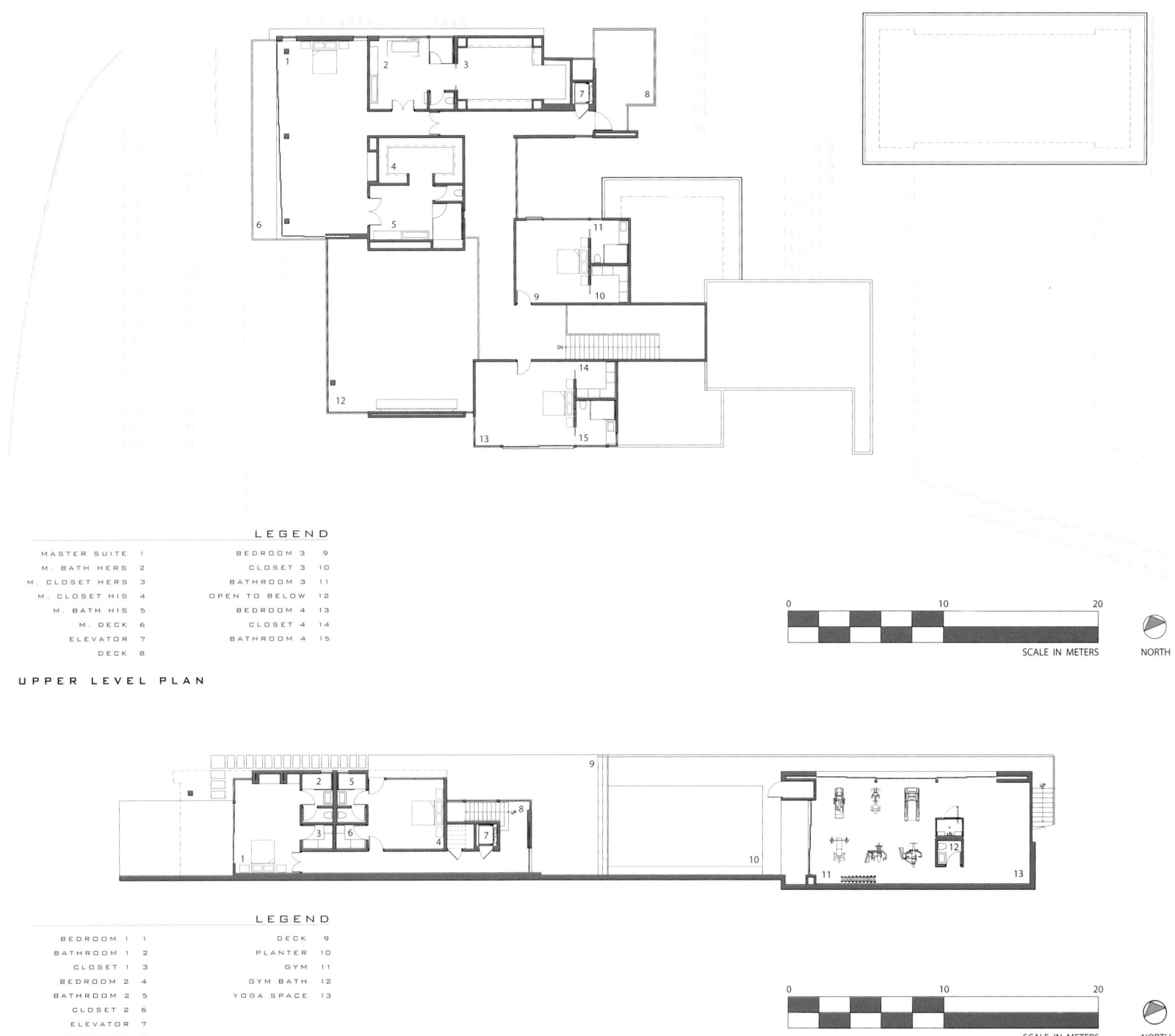

LEGEND

MASTER SUITE	1	BEDROOM 3	9	
M. BATH HERS	2	CLOSET 3	10	
M. CLOSET HERS	3	BATHROOM 3	11	
M. CLOSET HIS	4	OPEN TO BELOW	12	
M. BATH HIS	5	BEDROOM 4	13	
M. DECK	6	CLOSET 4	14	
ELEVATOR	7	BATHROOM 4	15	
DECK	8			

0   10   20

SCALE IN METERS   NORTH

UPPER LEVEL PLAN

LEGEND

BEDROOM 1	1	DECK	9	
BATHROOM 1	2	PLANTER	10	
CLOSET 1	3	GYM	11	
BEDROOM 2	4	GYM BATH	12	
BATHROOM 2	5	YOGA SPACE	13	
CLOSET 2	6			
ELEVATOR	7			
STAIRWELL	8			

0   10   20

SCALE IN METERS   NORTH

LOWER LEVEL PLAN

The main living room is 2-storey tall and enjoys spectacular views of the Los Angeles Basin and the ocean beyond. The room incorporates a bar and glazed wine cellar as well as an elongated see through fire place that is visible from the family room on the other side. The combined kitchen and family room has a more intimate feeling than the living room and appears to float over the water feature. From here it is possible to look back along the water past the garage all the way to the guest house and beyond. This level of the house is completed by service spaces and an office for the owner. The upper level contains the master with his and her baths and closets as well as 2 secondary bedrooms. 2 further bedrooms are located in the basement as well as the guest house across the drive court. The palette of materials is soft contemporary with extensive use of limestone, wood as well as Italian cabinetry and bronze accents.

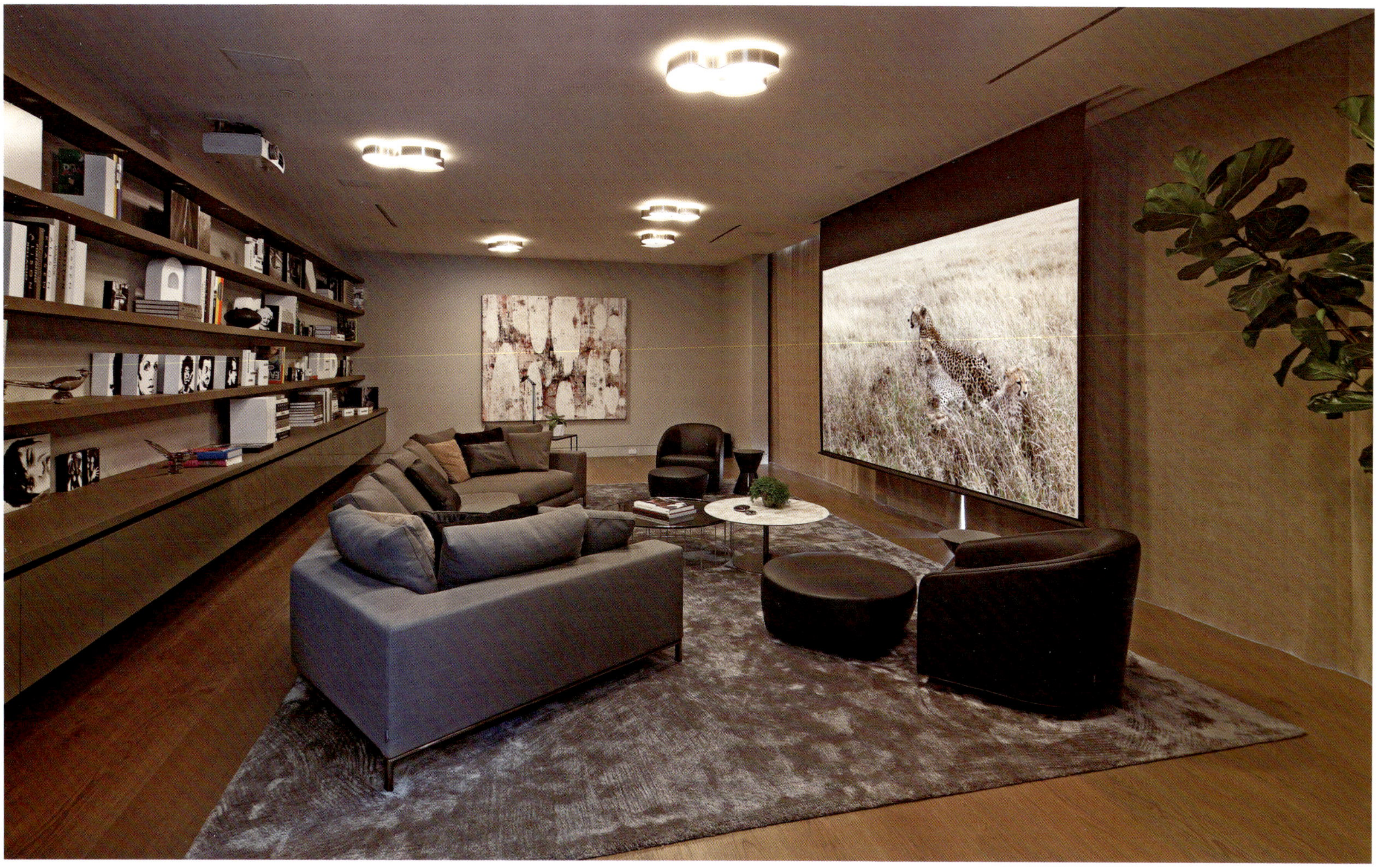

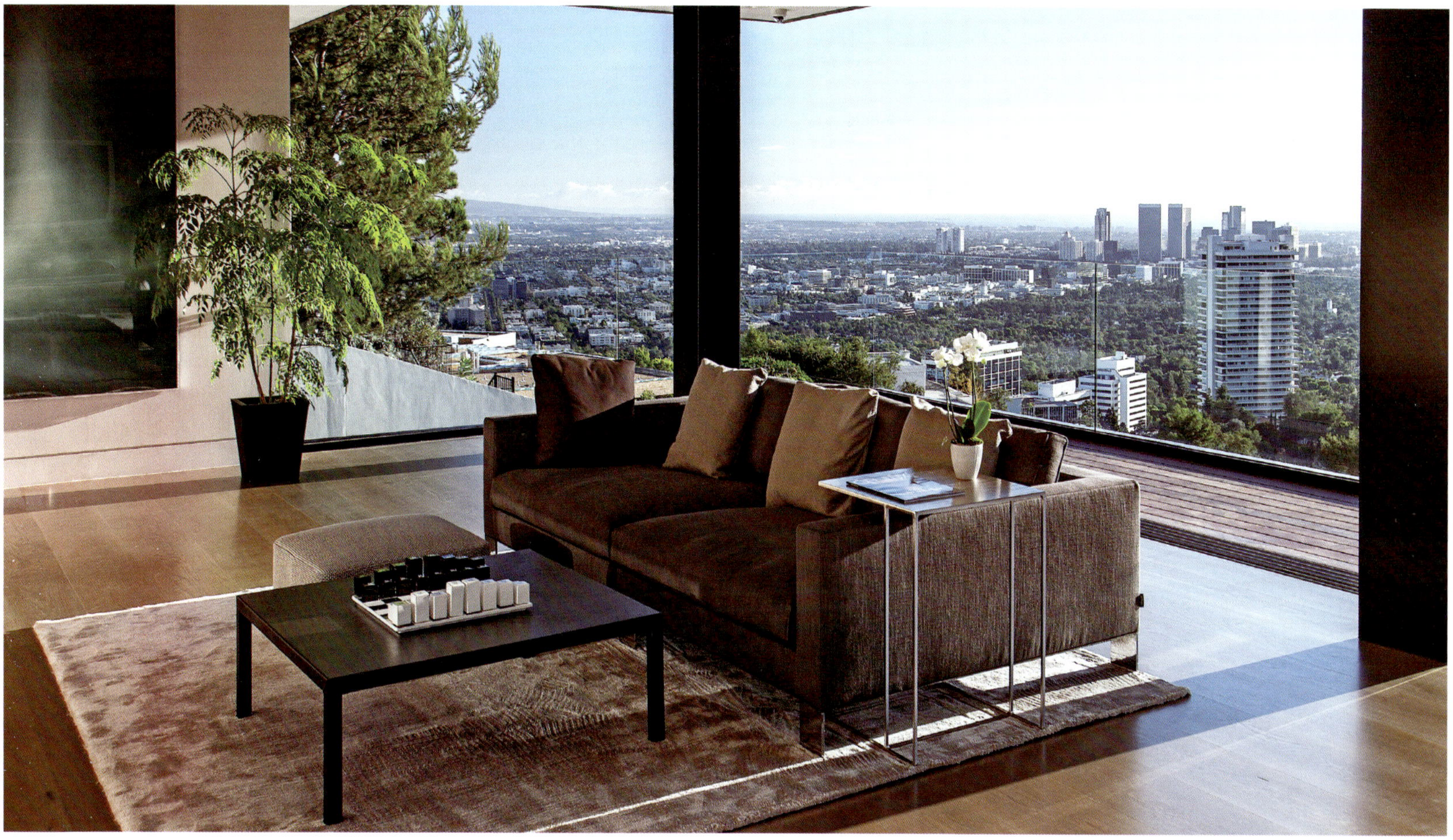

Butterfly House

Architects
jmA

Principal Architect
John Maniscalco

Project Architect
Kelton Dissel

Project Team
John Maniscalco, Kelton Dissel, Marit Gamberg

Interior Furnishings
Shawback Design

Location
San Francisco, CA

Area
462 m²

Photography
Joe Fletcher

In this complete rebuild of a mid-century modern home, the design flows from an analysis of the varied site conditions already present and reinforces key relationships to the site while establishing new ones. From a relocated street level entry, a careful sequence follows the slope and curates the vertical movement through the home from earthbound experience to the open sky and panoramic views. Each level takes on a different purpose first, establishing new ties to the street, then anchoring family spaces to the south-facing garden, turning inwardly focused at the sleeping level, and ultimately dissolving at the top level living spaces and roof deck to reveal panoramic connections to the city and bay.

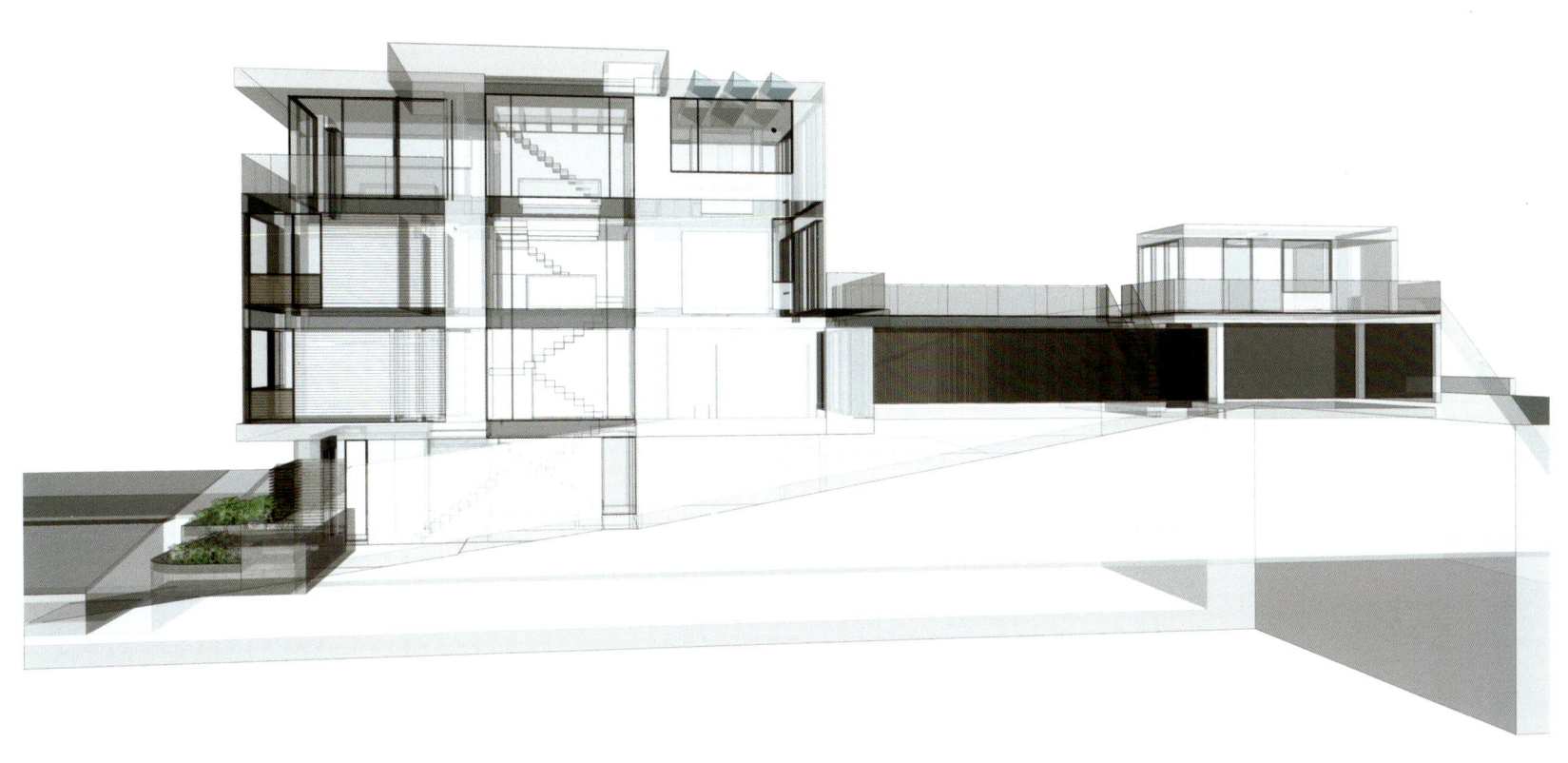

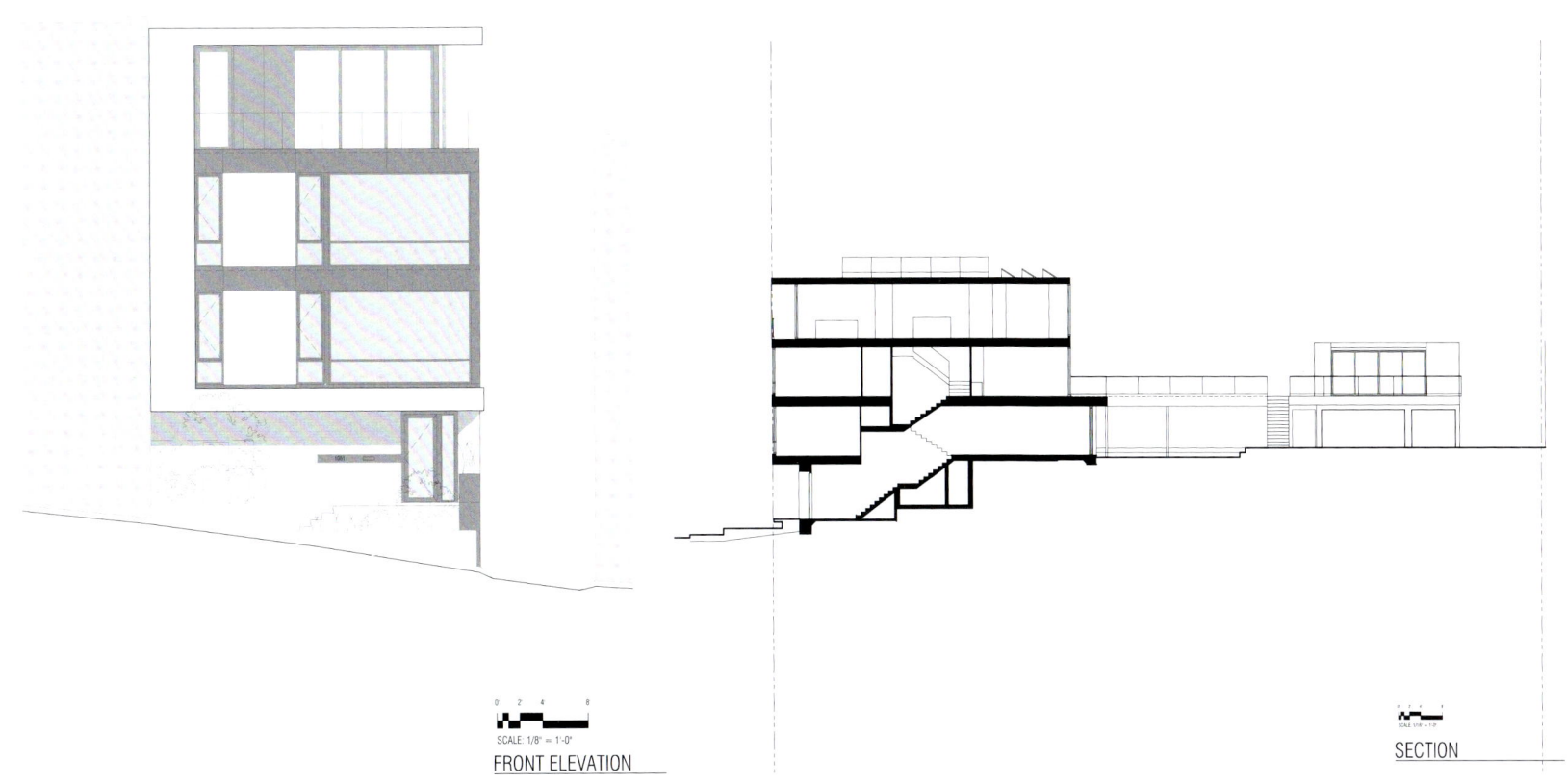

SCALE: 1/8" = 1'-0"

FRONT ELEVATION

SECTION

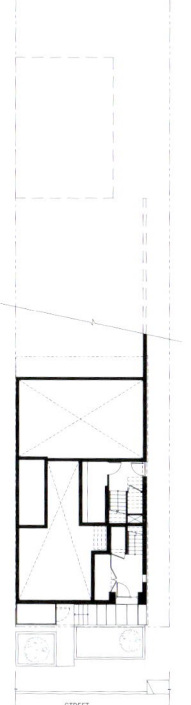

GROUND FLOOR PLAN

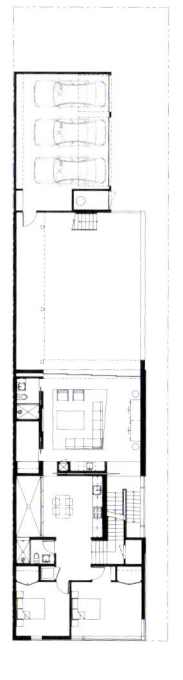

FIRST FLOOR PLAN

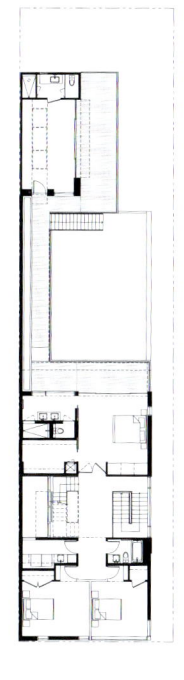

SECOND FLOOR PLAN

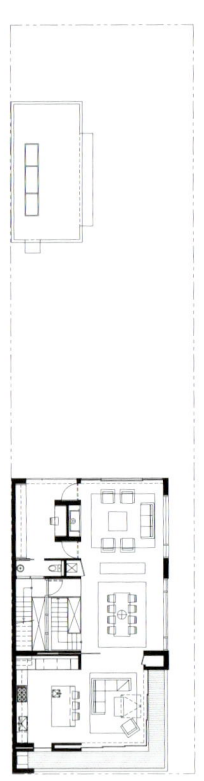

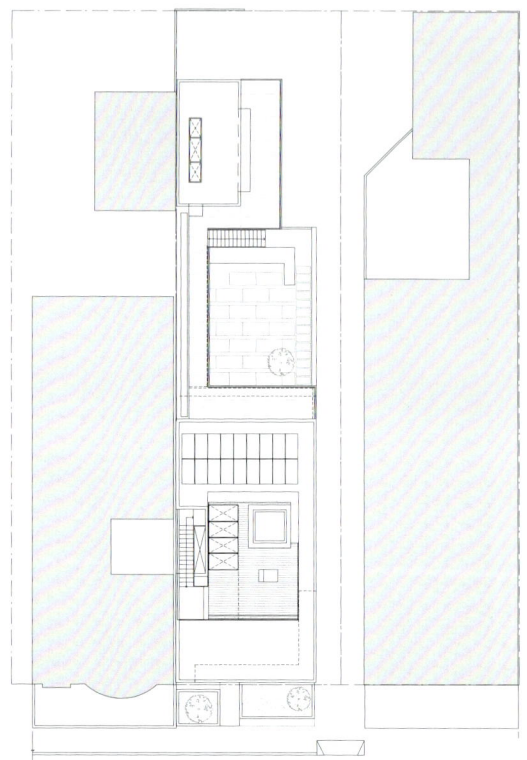

THIRD FLOOR PLAN

ROOF PLAN

SITE PLAN

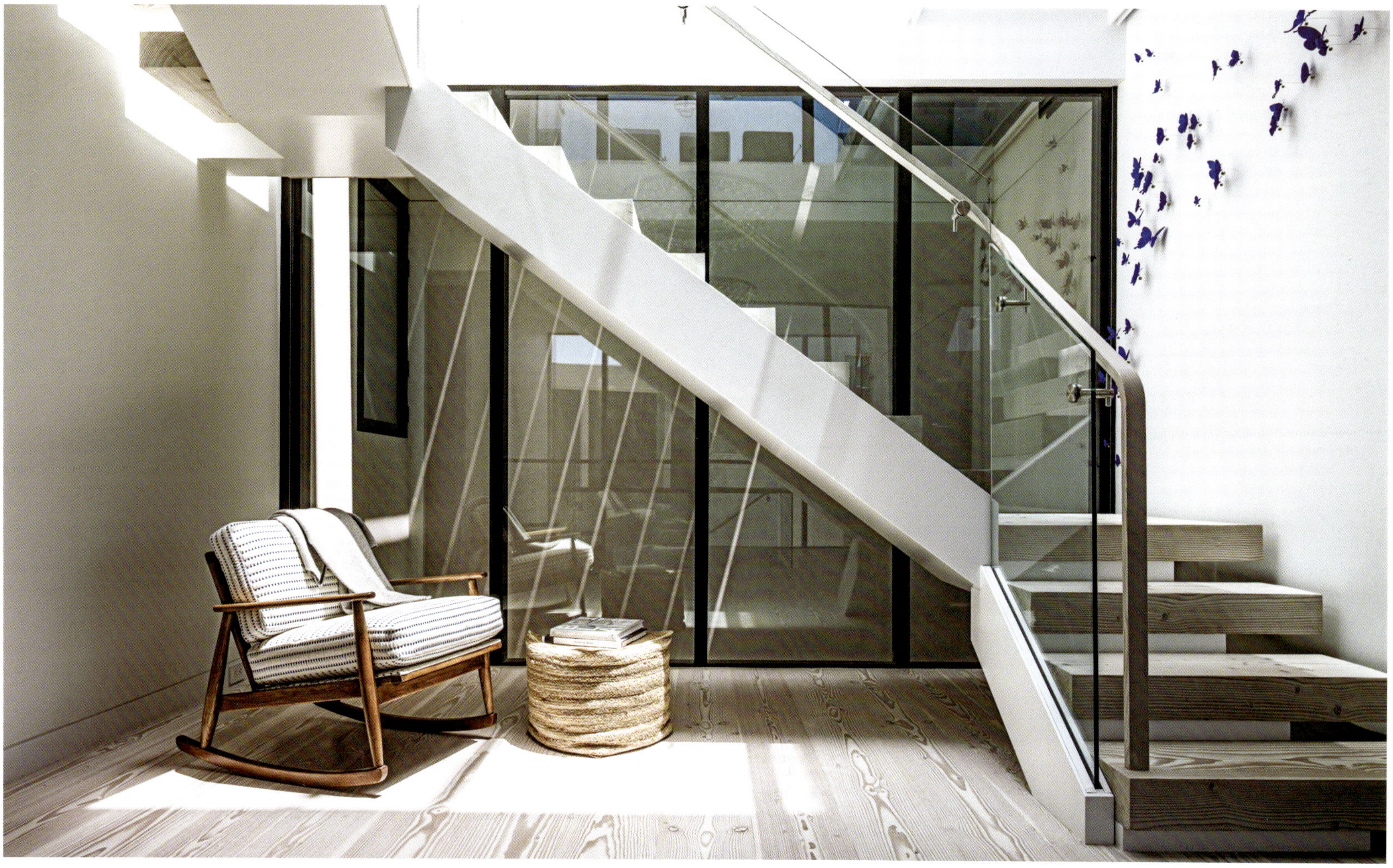

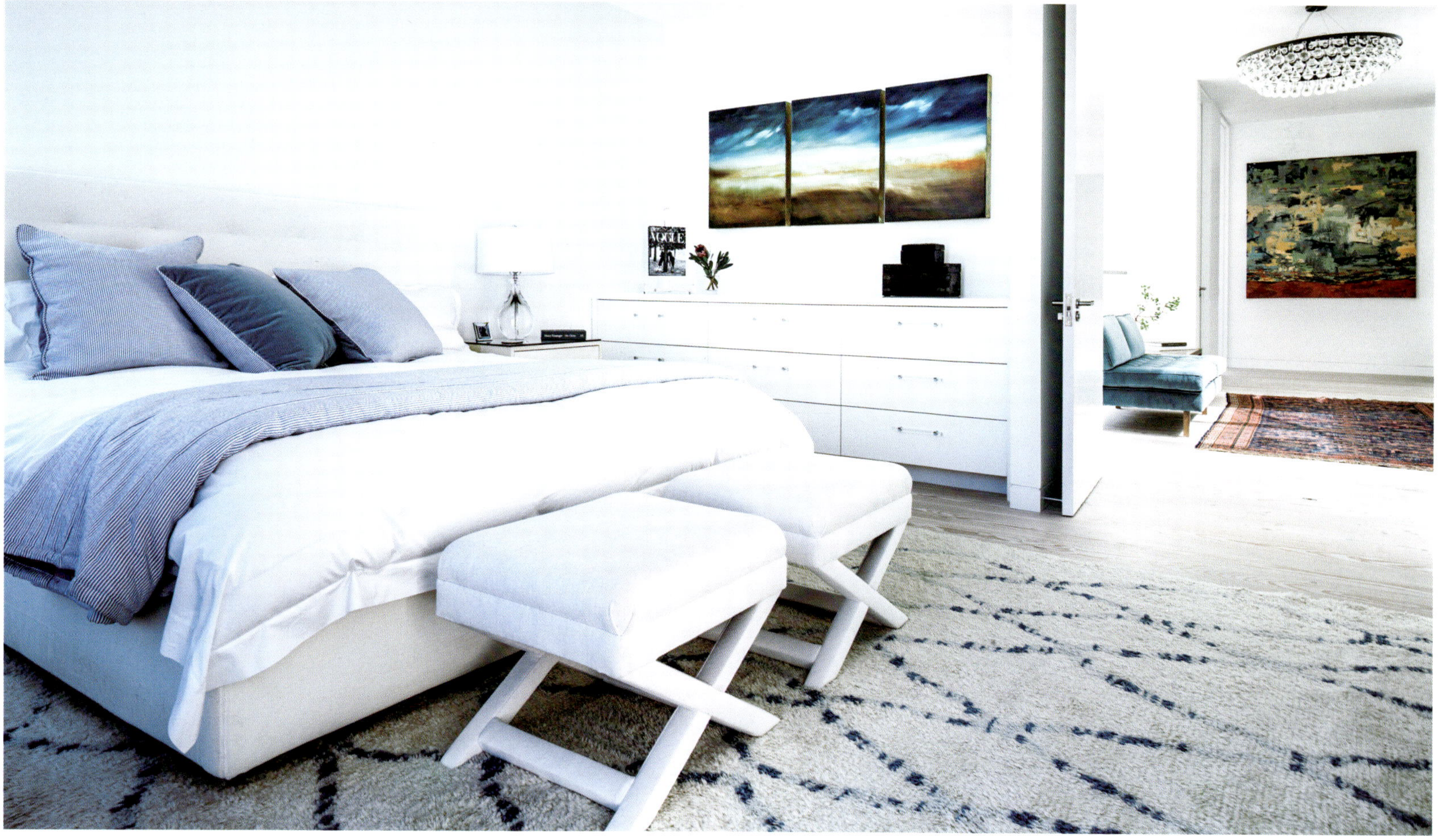

Cliff House

Architects
SAOTA

Architects Project Team
Stefan Antoni, Greg Truen
& Juliet Kavishe

Interior Design
Antoni Associates

Interior Design Team
Mark Rielly & Sarika Jacobs

Main Furniture Supplier
OKHA Interiors

Building Area
1,954m²

Location
Dakar, Senegal

Photography
SAOTA

The ground floor of the house, designed to facilitate seamless indoor and outdoor living and entertainment, is arranged in an "L" shape around the pool, the pool terrace and the garden. The formal living and dining spaces cantilever over the cliff and hang over the Atlantic Ocean enjoying panoramic sea views as well as views back to the house. The kitchen made up of a so called "American" or open kitchen and a separate traditional kitchen as well as the garage and staff facilities run along the east west axis and along the northern side of the boundary. From the entrance one moves past the sculptural circular stair to the entertainment room and the double volume family lounge which connects up with a floating stair to the upper level pyjama lounge. The main and the two children's bedrooms are placed on this upper level.

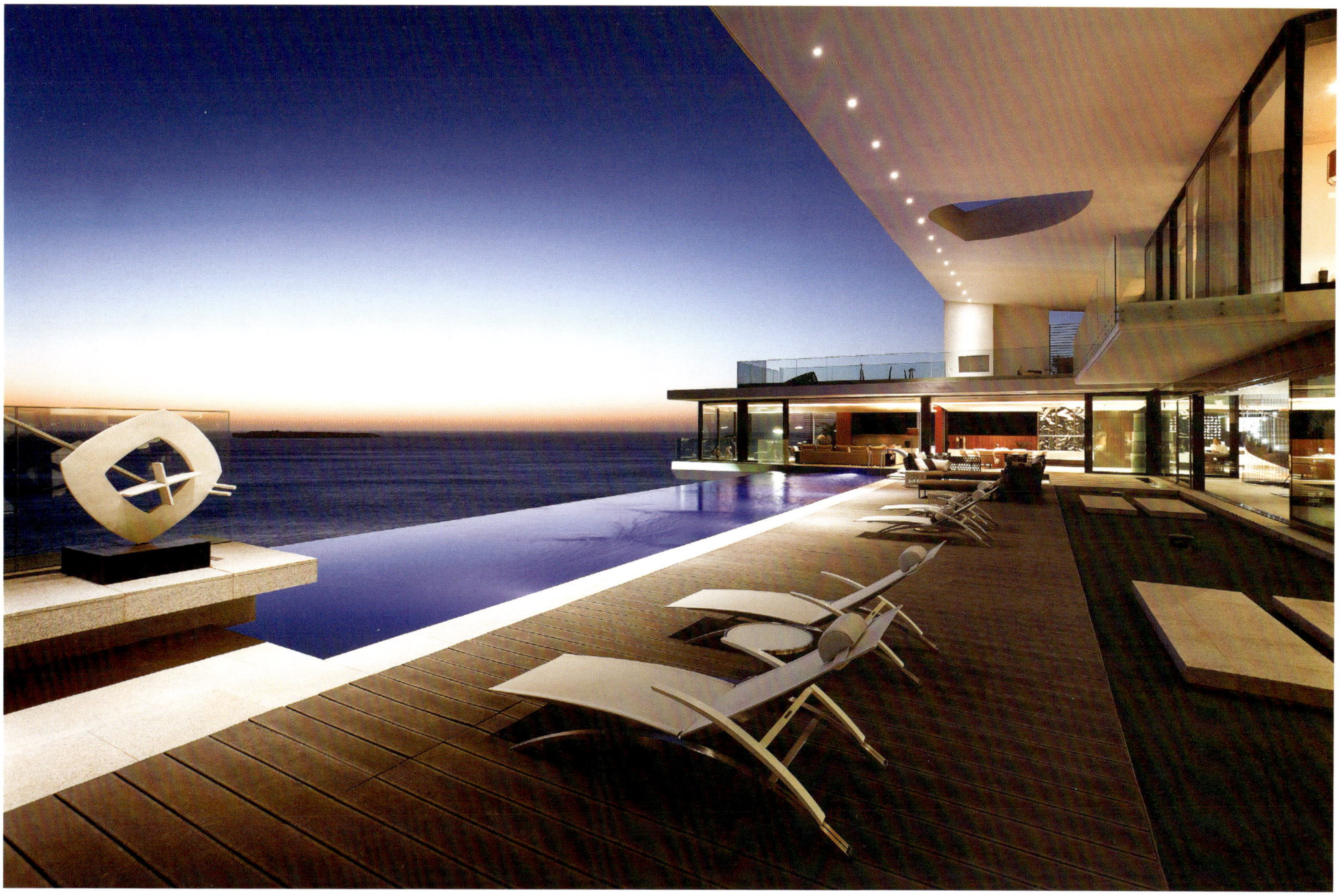

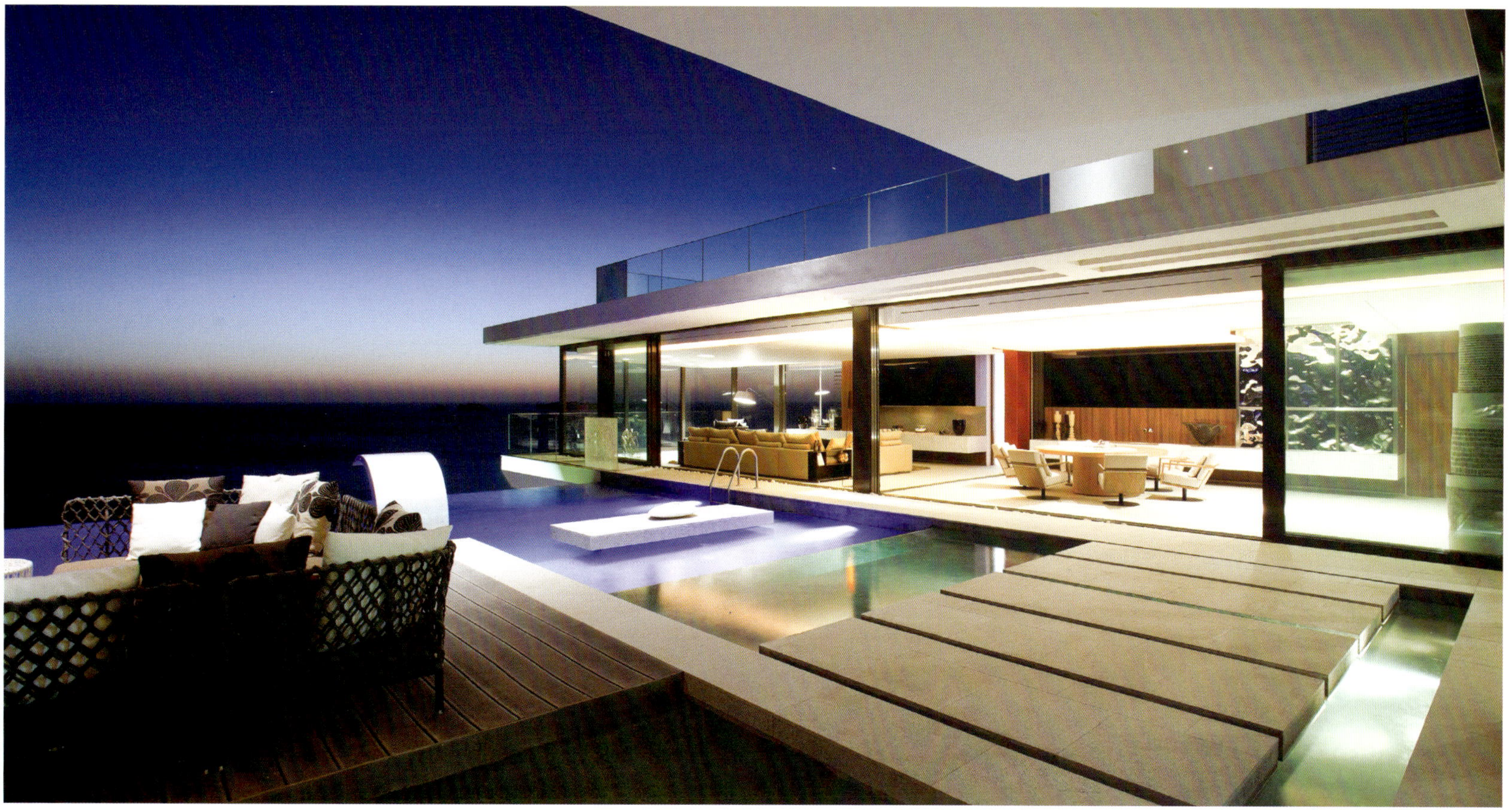

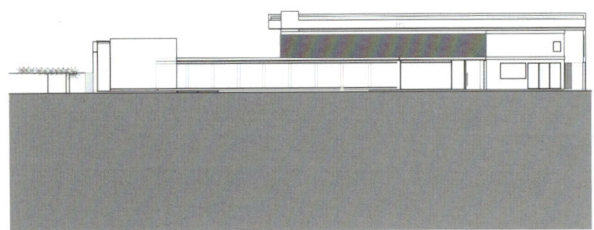

NORTH EAST ELEVATION

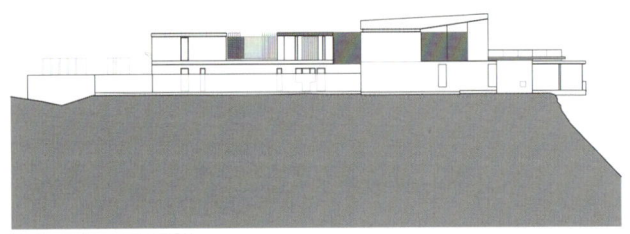

NORTH WEST ELEVATION

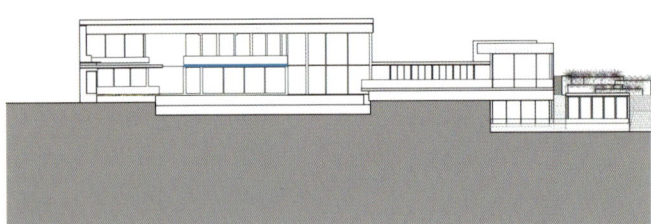

SOUTH EAST ELEVATION

SOUTH WEST ELEVATION

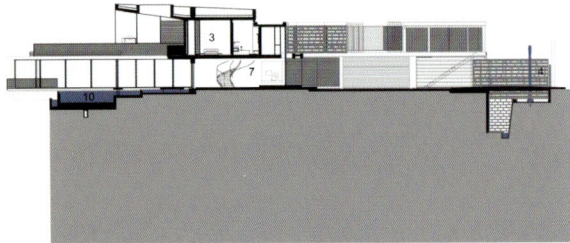

SECTION A-A

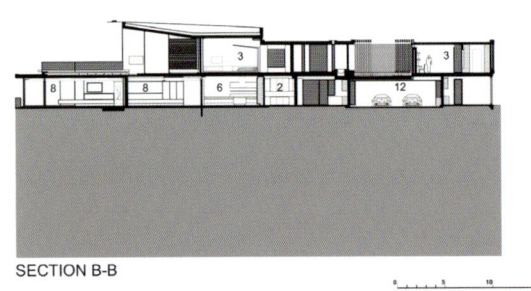

SECTION B-B

LEGEND

1. CINEMA
2. SERVICE AREA
3. BEDROOMS
4. POND
5. GYM
6. KITCHEN
7. ENTRANCE
8. LOUNGE
9. STUDY
10. POOL
11. TERRACE
12. GARAGE
13. ENTRANCE GATE
14. GATE HOUSE

"The huge overhanging roof which projects over the upper level and the outdoor living level creates a dramatic double volume outdoor space and gives the entire home a sense of unity." says partner Stefan Antoni.

One of the features of the house is the spiral staircase, clad in stainless steel, while the treads are clad in white granite. To add to the sense of continuity between the levels the 20 mm in diameter stainless steel rods run from the first floor handrail to the lower ground floor, thus making the stairwell look like a sculptural steel cylinder. A skylight above the stairwell as well as floor to ceiling glazing in the lounges adds to the sense of transparency.

The main bedroom suite opens up onto a large terrace which is the roof of the more formal living wing of the house and the element which projects over to the ocean. The main bathroom opens into a private garden and outdoor shower situated over the garages.

The study / office sits in a separate block and is joined to the main house by a hallway running along the spine of the building. Under the study/office is a separate fully contained guest room, alongside which is a private gym and reflecting pond.

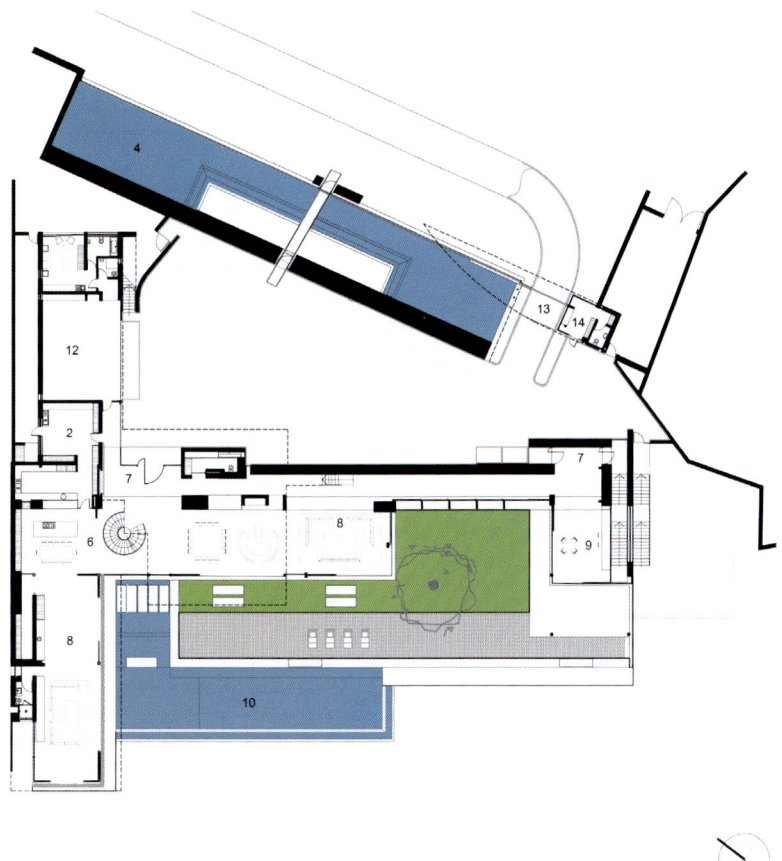

GROUND FLOOR

LEGEND

1. CINEMA
2. SERVICE AREA
3. BEDROOMS
4. POND
5. GYM
6. KITCHEN
7. ENTRANCE
8. LOUNGE
9. STUDY
10. POOL
11. TERRACE
12. GARAGE
13. ENTRANCE GATE
14. GATE HOUSE

0   5   10   15 m

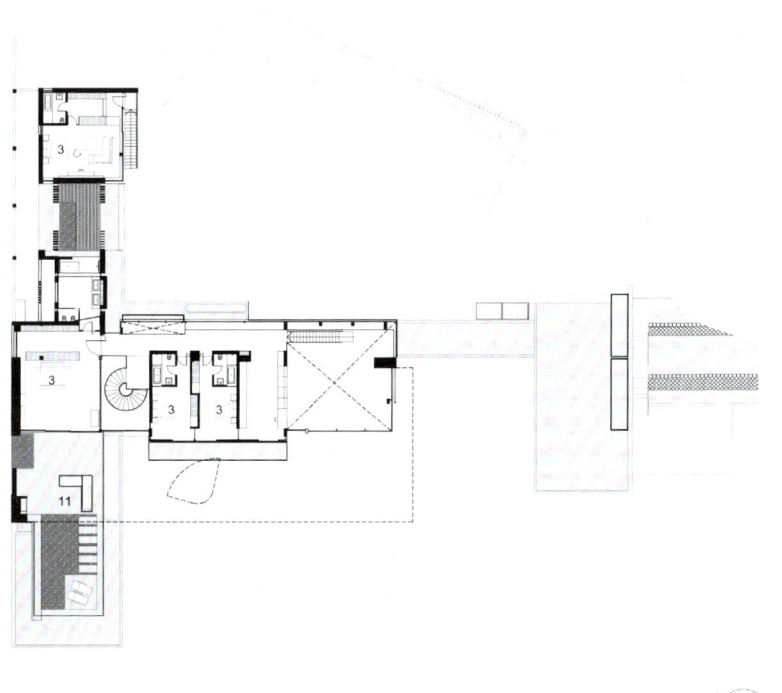

FIRST FLOOR

LEGEND

1. CINEMA
2. SERVICE AREA
3. BEDROOMS
4. POND
5. GYM
6. KITCHEN
7. ENTRANCE
8. LOUNGE
9. STUDY
10. POOL
11. TERRACE
12. GARAGE
13. ENTRANCE GATE
14. GATE HOUSE

0   5   10   15 m

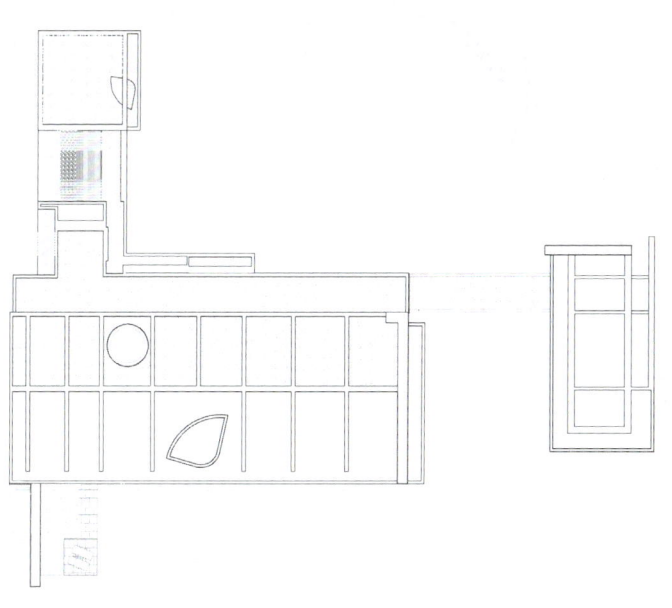

ROOF PLAN

LEGEND

1. CINEMA
2. SERVICE AREA
3. BEDROOMS
4. POND
5. GYM
6. KITCHEN
7. ENTRANCE
8. LOUNGE
9. STUDY
10. POOL
11. TERRACE
12. GARAGE
13. ENTRANCE GATE
14. GATE HOUSE

0   5   10   15 m

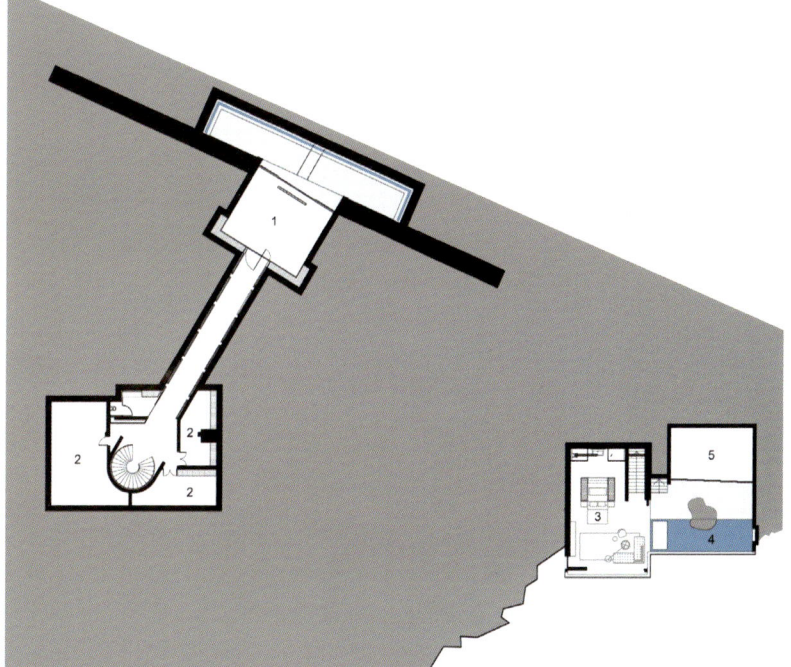

LOWER GROUND

LEGEND

1. CINEMA
2. SERVICE AREA
3. BEDROOMS
4. POND
5. GYM
6. KITCHEN
7. ENTRANCE
8. LOUNGE
9. STUDY
10. POOL
11. TERRACE
12. GARAGE
13. ENTRANCE GATE
14. GATE HOUSE

0   5   10   15 m

Cove 3

Architects
SAOTA

Architects Project Team
Greg Truen & Roxanne Kaye

Interior Design
Antoni Associates

Interior Design Team
Mark Rielly & Tavia Pharaoh

Building Area
1,005 m²

Location
The Cove, Pezula Estate, Knysna

Photography
SAOTA, John Devonport, Adam Letch

The primary idea driving the design was to create a single living space with a single roof element floating over it that responded to the slope of the site. The roof is set at a sufficiently high level so that it is out of one's line of sight from the living space, creating the illusion that one is sitting in the landscape rather than in a room looking out into a landscape.

A large triangular cut-out in the roof reinforces a connection with the sky. A very detailed solar analysis was done of the building to try and get direct sun (other than the rising east sun) out of the building. As a result, a midlevel horizontal sunscreen was added to the double height glass facade and the skylight is protected by a timber screen that hangs into the space to mitigate the scale of the double volume space. Care was also taken in selecting performance-glass that would minimise the impact of direct sun.

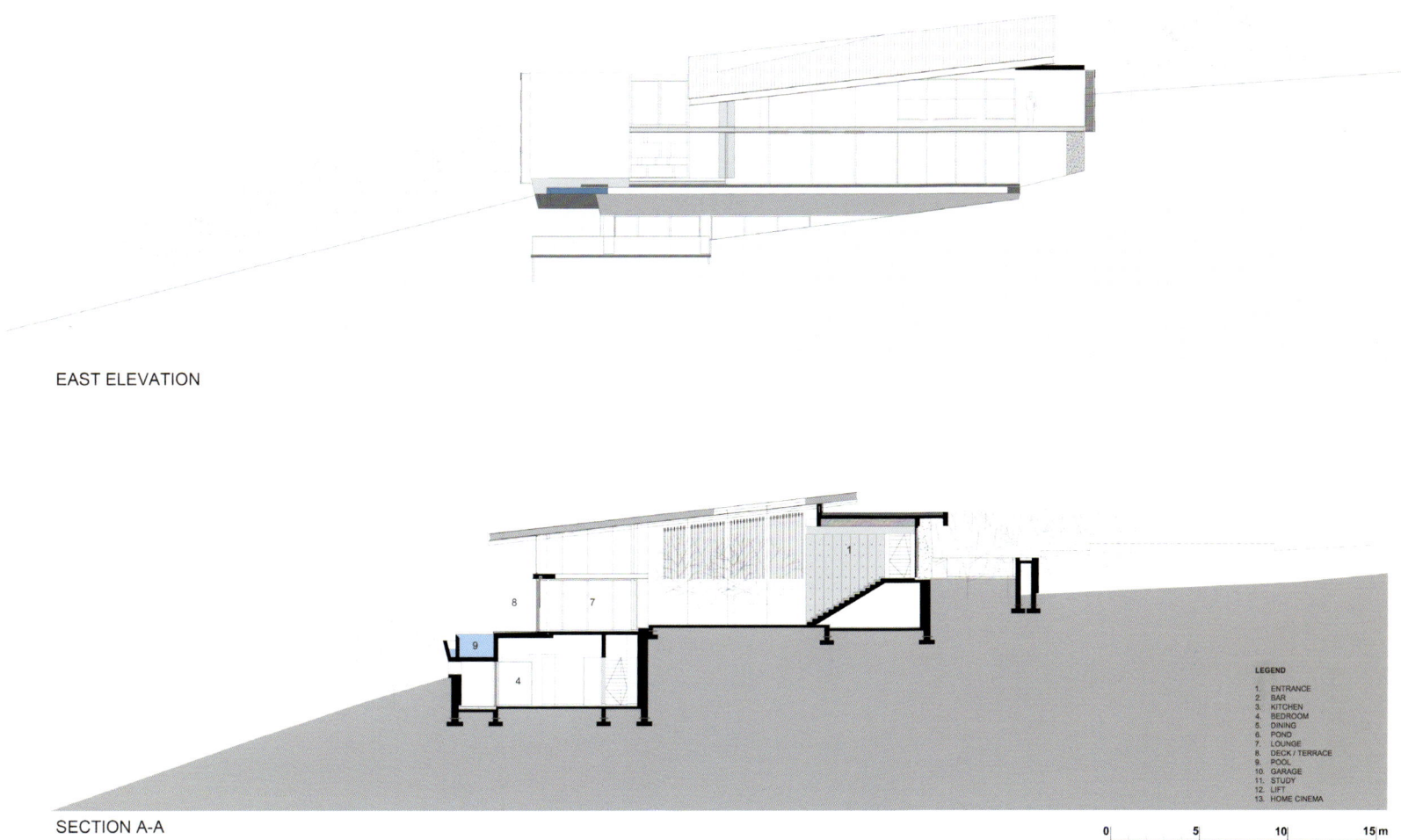

EAST ELEVATION

SECTION A-A

LEGEND

1. ENTRANCE
2. BAR
3. KITCHEN
4. BEDROOM
5. DINING
6. POND
7. LOUNGE
8. DECK / TERRACE
9. POOL
10. GARAGE
11. STUDY
12. LIFT
13. HOME CINEMA

0   5   10   15 m

The building is approached from the north west at the top of the site. The choice of materials, off-shutter concrete, Rheinzink roofing, timber cladding, stone and exposed aggregate will allow the building to fade into the landscape as it ages. The building is orientated towards the view; one enters at the upper level of the double volume looking towards the ocean. The contrast with the external approach is very powerful. A grand stair pulls on onto the living level which holds the kitchen, dining room and living room. To the right the landscaping is pulled into the building, blurring the distinction between the inside and the outside.

A spiral stair connects the living level to a private lounge and the master bedroom on a mezzanine level. This stair was conceived as a sculptural element in the large volume to again mitigate the scale of this space. This spiral drops through the floor to a lower level which houses a guest bedroom, a home theatre and a living room. An "L" shaped extension to the south west houses the two children's bedrooms. The bedrooms have curved curtain tracks that create very intimate sleeping spaces at night which contrast with the very open daytime character.

Water is a critical issue in this part of the world and a huge underground cistern was created under the garden terrace to harvest rainwater to minimise the houses' reliance on the municipal water system. A heat pump and water based under floor heating system uses less energy than would ordinarily be required for a house of this magnitude. The concept behind the landscaping was to reinstate the fynbos and let the building float over this restored surface.

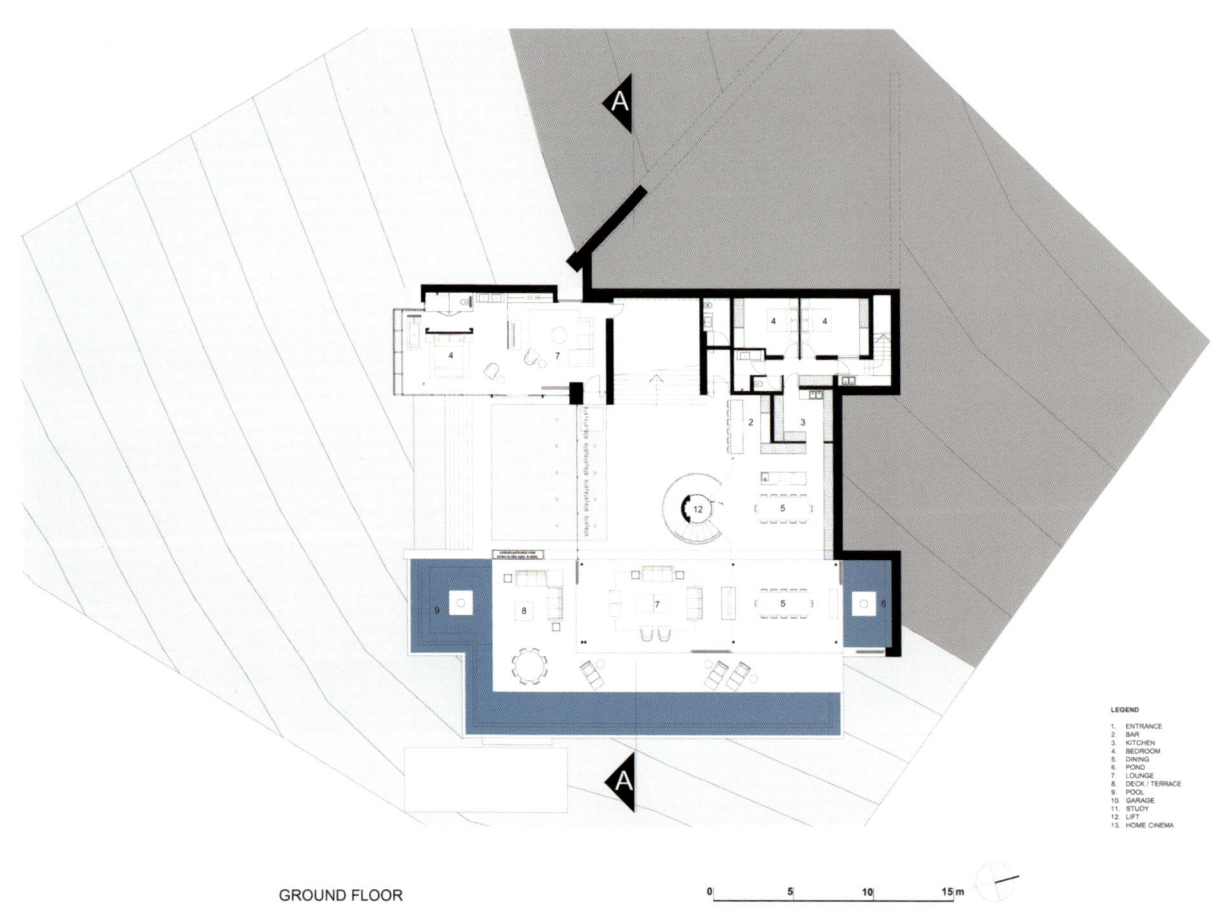

GROUND FLOOR

0   5   10   15 m

FIRST FLOOR

0   5   10   15 m

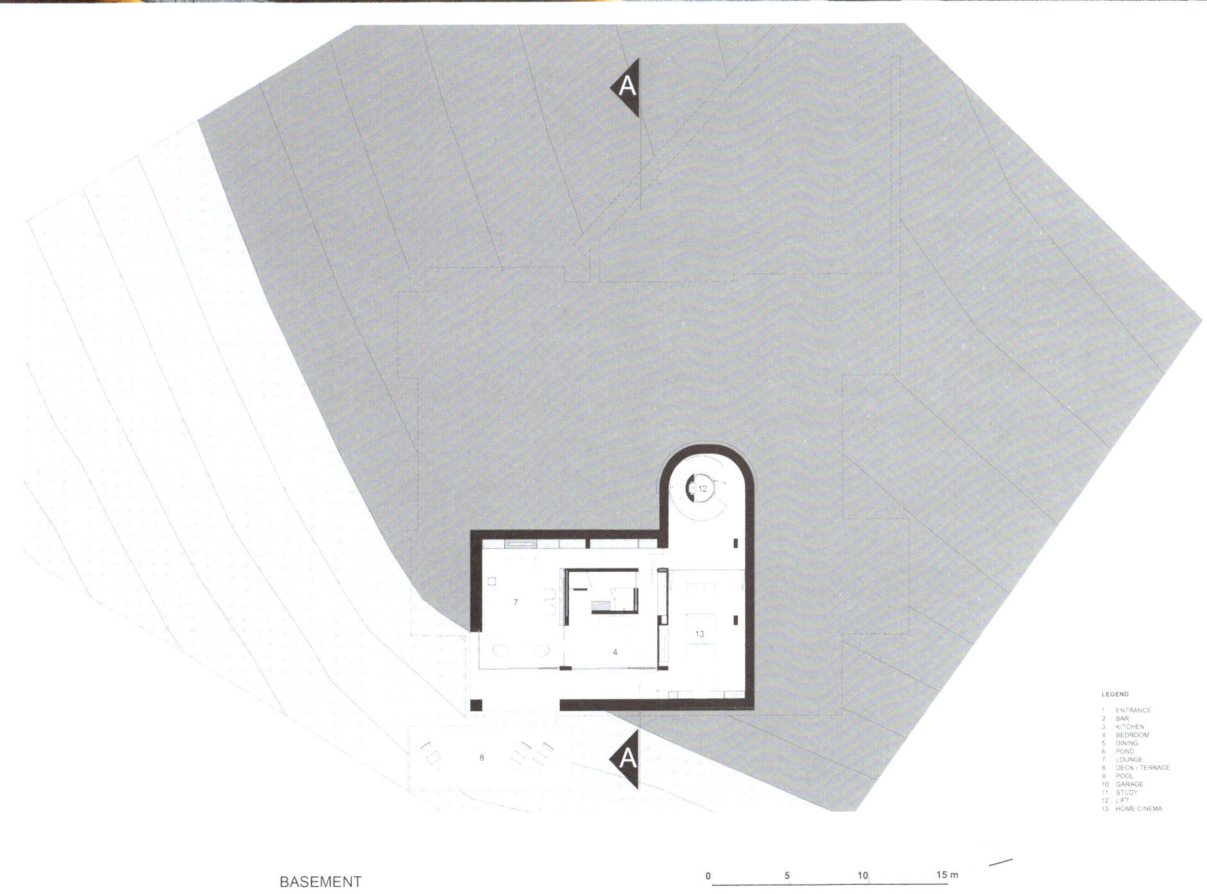

BASEMENT

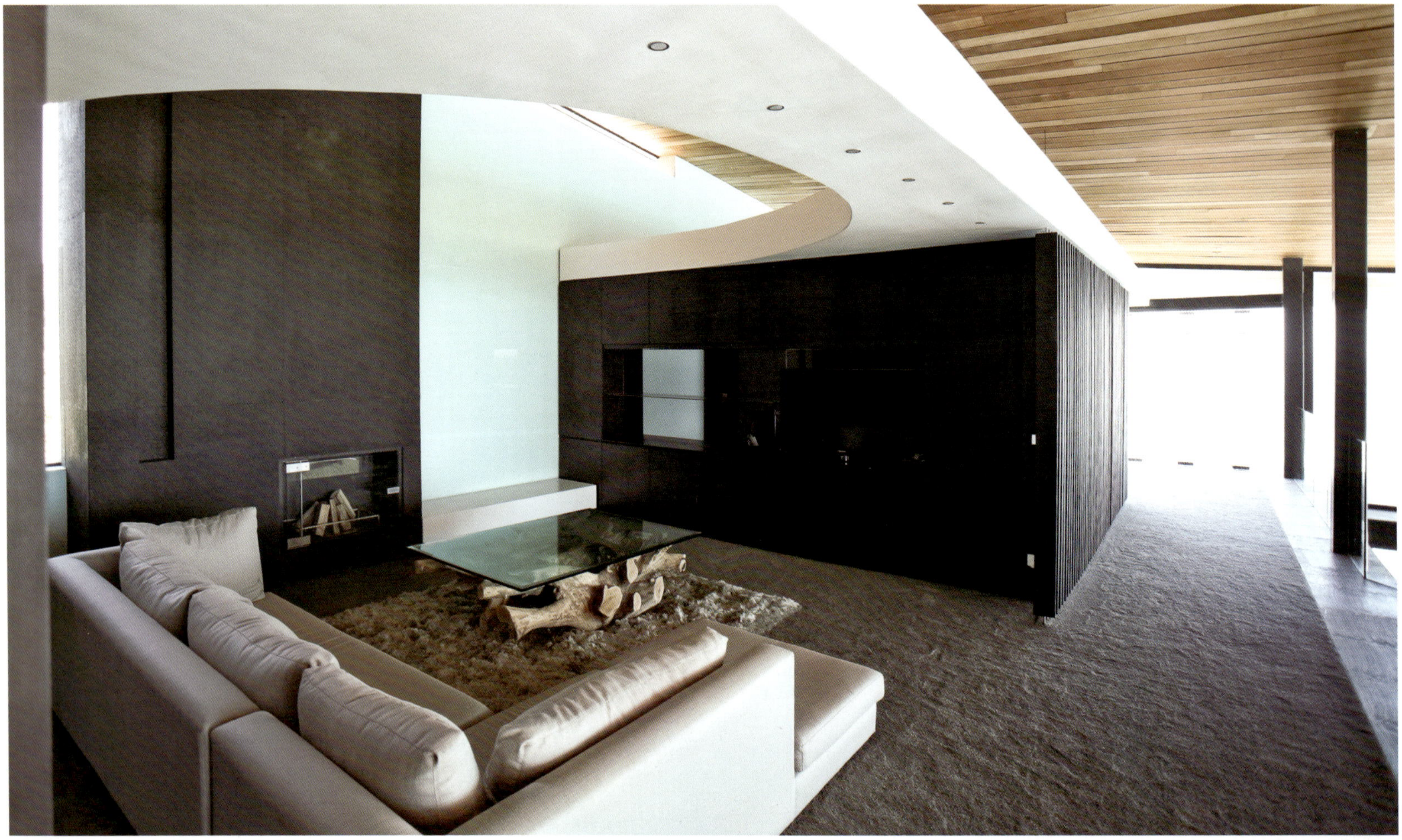

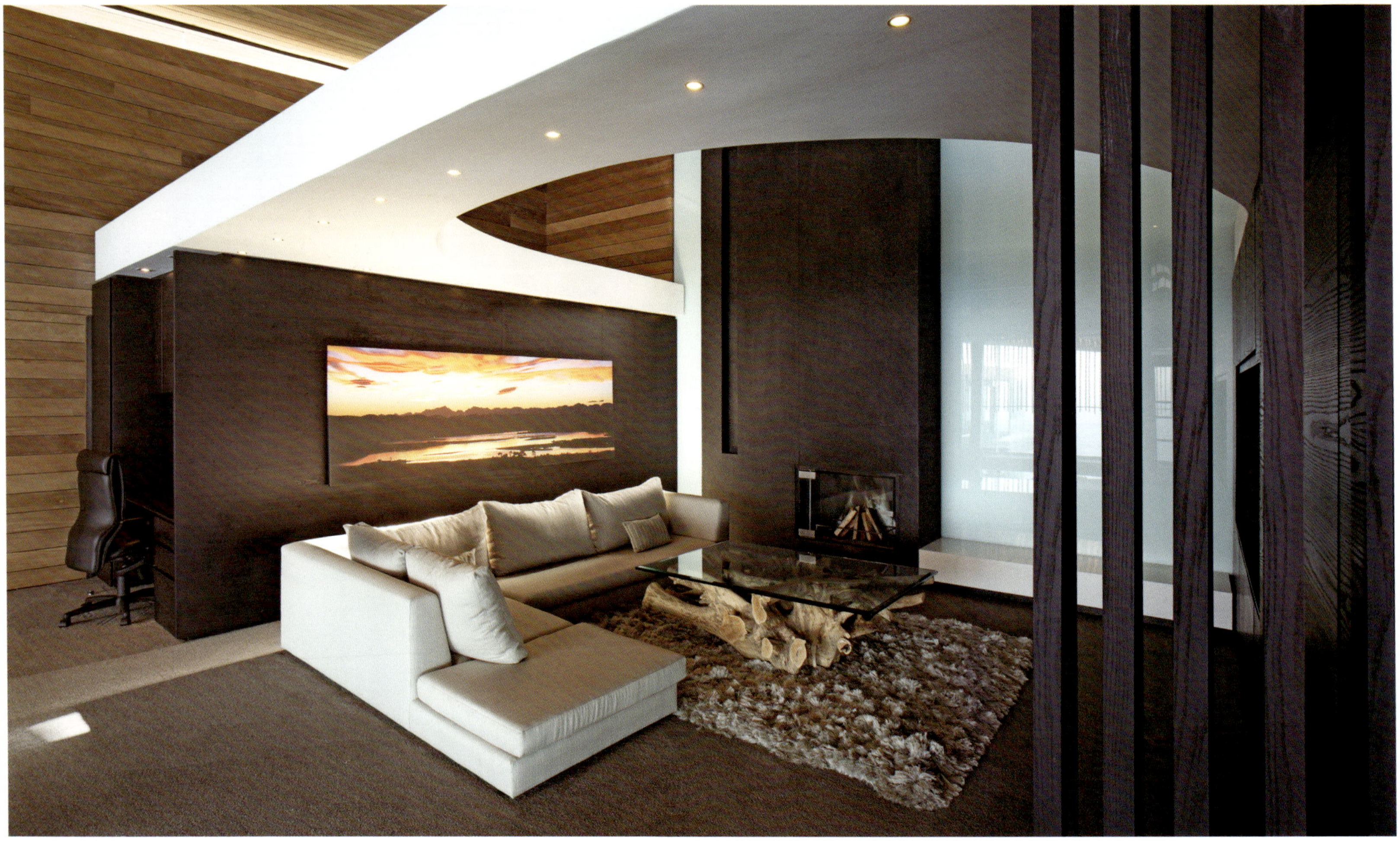

Head Road 1818

Architects
SAOTA

Project Team
Philip Olmesdahl, Stefan Antoni
& Mark Bullivant

Interior Decor
Craig Kaplan

Location
Fresnaye, Cape Town

Photography
Adam Letch

The clients acquired a steeply sloping site on Head Road and wanted to capitalize on the property in line with their lifestyle. Their focus was predominantly on a home that lived well on the site, with one great master suite, a number of guest rooms as well as ancillary rooms.

Whilst the site enjoyed great views to the ocean and back up to the mountain, Head Road has its own unique zoning which prescribed a large lateral boundary set back, and a height restriction aligned to the steep slope of the road. In addition to these restrictions, both lateral neighbours had built very large dwellings which towered over the narrow property. Fortunately due to the steep slope of the site, there was no

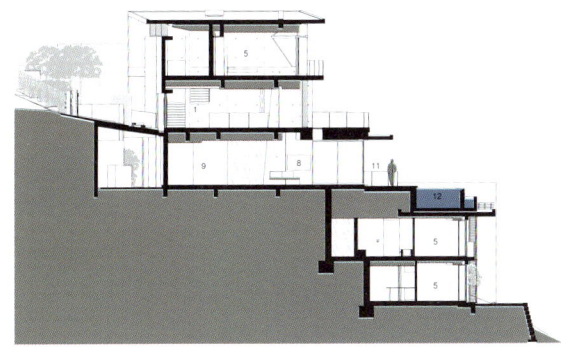

SECTION AA
HEAD 1818
1 : 200

LEGEND
1.   MAIN ENTRANCE
2.   GARAGE
3.   STUDY
4.   LIFT
5.   BEDROOM SUITE
6.   DRESSING
7.   DINING ROOM
8.   LOUNGE
9.   KITCHEN
10. DOUBLE VOLUME
11. TERRACE
12. POOL
13. BAR
14. LAUNDRY
15. GYM

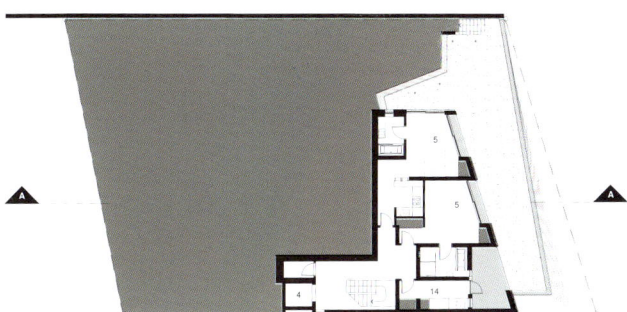

LOWER BASEMENT LAYOUT
HEAD 1818
1 : 200

LEGEND
1.   MAIN ENTRANCE
2.   GARAGE
3.   STUDY
4.   LIFT
5.   BEDROOM SUITE
6.   DRESSING
7.   DINING ROOM
8.   LOUNGE
9.   KITCHEN
10. DOUBLE VOLUME
11. TERRACE
12. POOL
13. BAR
14. LAUNDRY
15. GYM

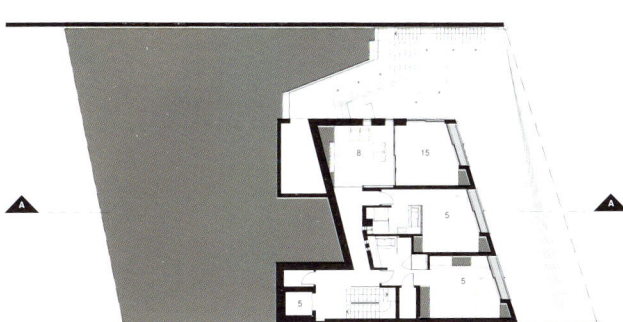

BASEMENT LAYOUT
HEAD 1818
1 : 200

LEGEND
1.   MAIN ENTRANCE
2.   GARAGE
3.   STUDY
4.   LIFT
5.   BEDROOM SUITE
6.   DRESSING
7.   DINING ROOM
8.   LOUNGE
9.   KITCHEN
10. DOUBLE VOLUME
11. TERRACE
12. POOL
13. BAR
14. LAUNDRY
15. GYM

negative influence on the house's outlook.

Effort was put into capitalising on views to the rear onto Lion's Head as well as across sea point and the Atlantic Seaboard. Such interesting dynamics impacted on the placement of accommodation, with the required levels of privacy. There is a clear vertical distinction between the living and bedroom accommodation. The upper-most level accommodates the master bedroom; a generous open-plan space inclusive of a dressing area and en-suite bathroom, which enjoys bidirectional views (i.e. a sea-facing terrace and raised clear storey views towards Lion's Head).

From the entrance, a timber staircase accesses the primary living and entertainment area through a double volume space.

This open-plan arrangement of dining, lounge, kitchen and breakfast area offers seamless connection to the terraces, garden and pool. The various functions within this versatile space are subtly defined through the ceiling plane, sliding doors which open dramatically.

The language of the house reflects bold contemporary lines and extended.

Challenges were turned into opportunities where screening elements ensuring privacy have become an integral component of the aesthetic. The juxtaposition of solid mass to large expanses of transparency is heightened due to the choice of materials and introduction of perforated panels. Emphasis was placed on a modern, contemporary aesthetic with a high level of comfort. The architectural language is bold and muscular with powerful, almost graphic facade layouts with glazed voids and planar walls that open up to create generous ocean views.

The angular nature of the site resulted in a number of complex junctions which were embraced, to emphasise the angularity of certain elements while capitalising on the valuable land. The tactile qualities of timber and the way it is used activate the senses — the sound and smell of the hardwood timber underfoot on the staircase sets a tone on entering the house. This is a remarkable site with amazing views; and it was critical that as large a living area was created with strong connections to the outside living spaces. Such a narrow, steep site often compromises the final outcome but here, with the seamless connection of indoor and outdoor spaces, the heart of the house was successfully extended from boundary to boundary.

The house has a clearly defined upper and lower portion. The upper three levels of the home consists of the living room / terraces level, topped by the entrance / garage level and the upper-most level is the master suite. The lower portion is two storeys, accommodating the pool structure, multiple guest rooms, staff quarters and plant rooms. All levels are connected by a lift.

Landscaping plays a key part of the design, with the landscaping undertaken by Franchesca Watson and characterised by architectural, robust planting. The scale of the various planted areas is varied through the scaling device of an interesting aluminium pergola. Planted areas add softness to the entrance area, and the pool terrace, as well as contribute to screening houses on the lateral boundaries as the house terraces down the property.

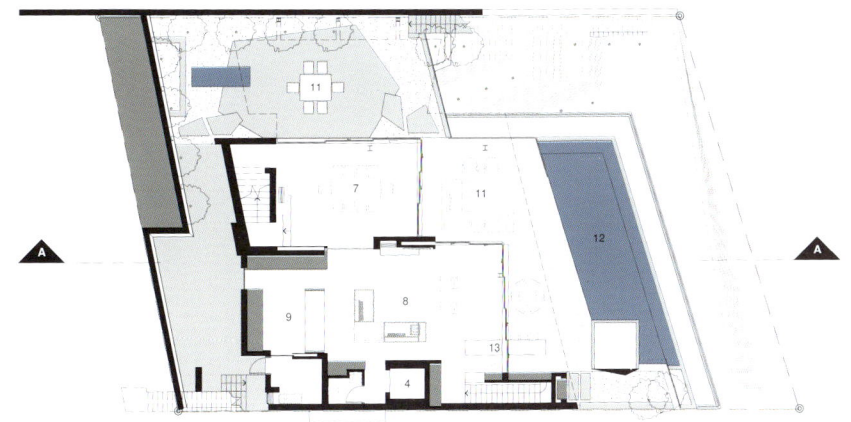

LEGEND
1.   MAIN ENTRANCE
2.   GARAGE
3.   STUDY
4.   LIFT
5.   BEDROOM SUITE
6.   DRESSING
7.   DINING ROOM
8.   LOUNGE
9.   KITCHEN
10. DOUBLE VOLUME
11. TERRACE
12. POOL
13. BAR
14. LAUNDRY
15. GYM

GROUND FLOOR LAYOUT
HEAD 1818
1 : 200

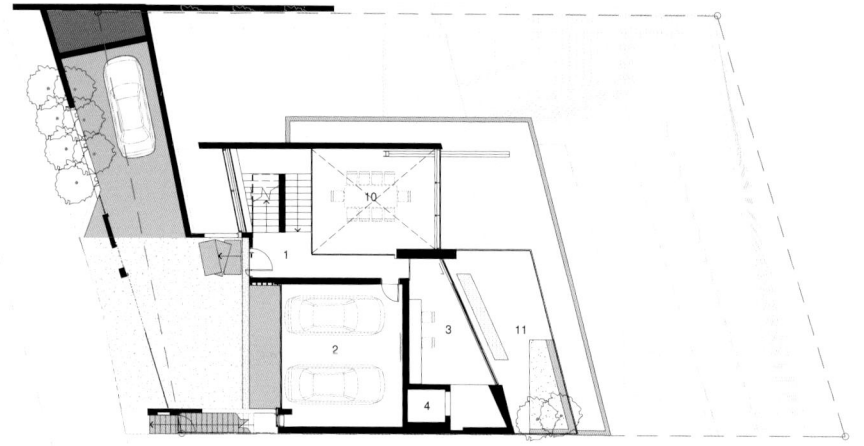

FIRST FLOOR LAYOUT
HEAD 1818
1 : 200

0   5   10 m

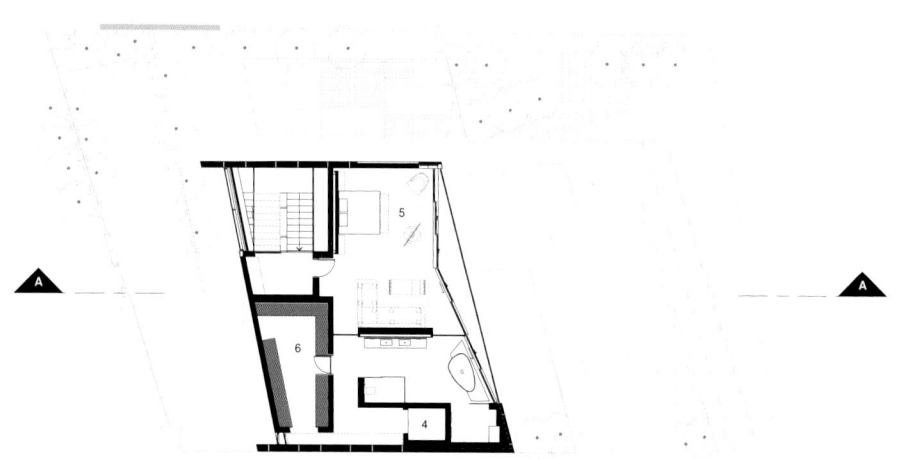

SECOND FLOOR LAYOUT
HEAD 1818
1 : 200

0   5   10 m

438 N. Faring Rd

Contributor
The Agency

Location
Holmby Hills, Los Angeles

Photography
Simon Berlyn

This spectacular new estate sits behind private gates on a lush property in Holmby Hills, Bel-Air, one of the most sought-after addresses in the world. Framed on all sides by mature trees and greenery, the contemporary 3-level, glass-encased compound boasts panoramic views of the Hollywood Hills, exquisite amenities and wonderful indoor-outdoor flow throughout.

The scale and proportions of this home are breathtaking. Secluded and utterly private, the 1,486 m² home was designed and built by renowned, London-based Quinn Architects and Estate Four, with a sophisticated sense of space. The main entrance is dramatic, offering an immense motor court and impressive 6.10 m high canopy. This leads you to the luxuriously spacious living room, with its earth-toned color scheme, floor to ceiling glass, and soaring 6.10 m high ceiling, tailor-made for displaying large-scale artwork.

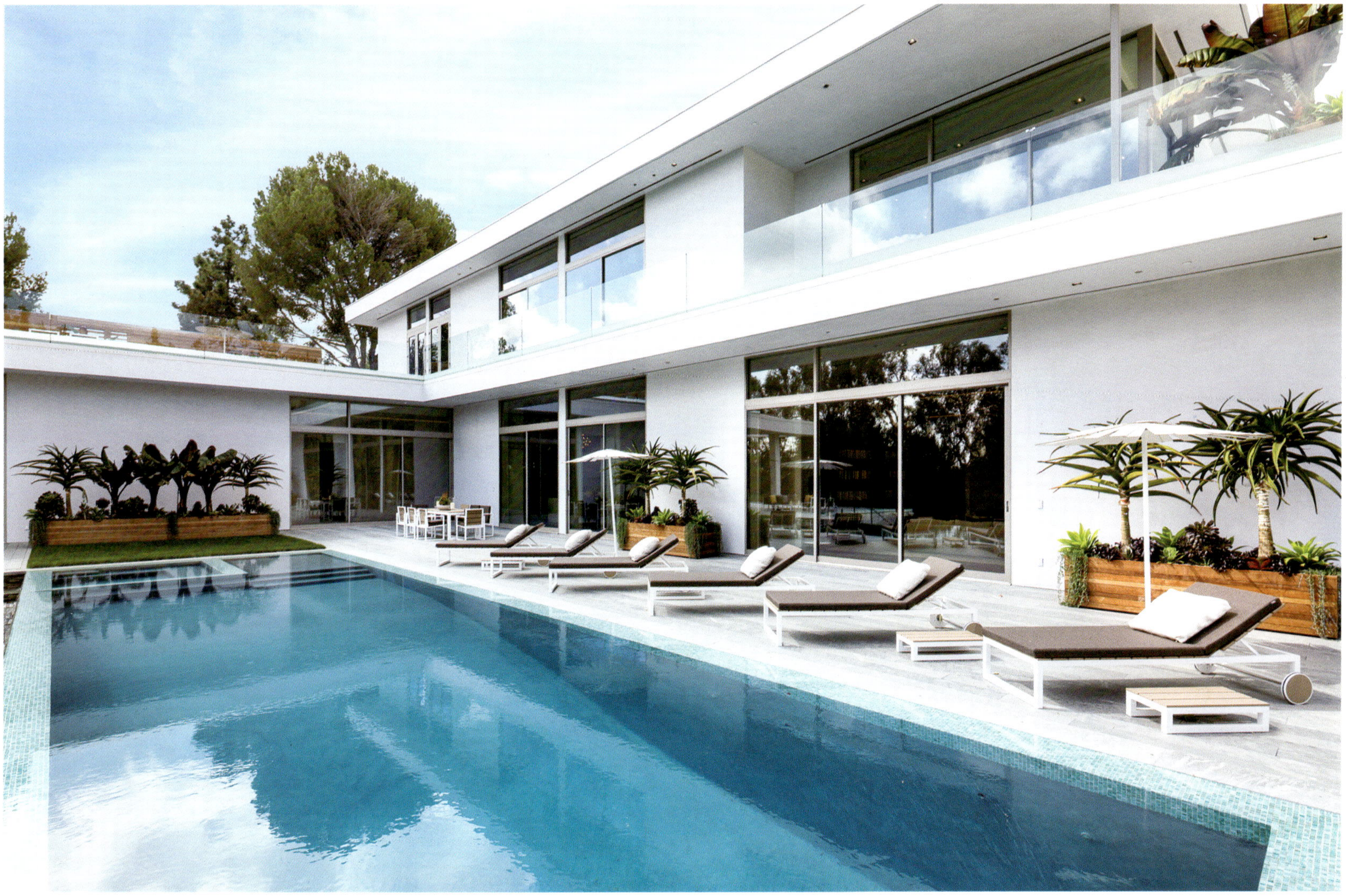

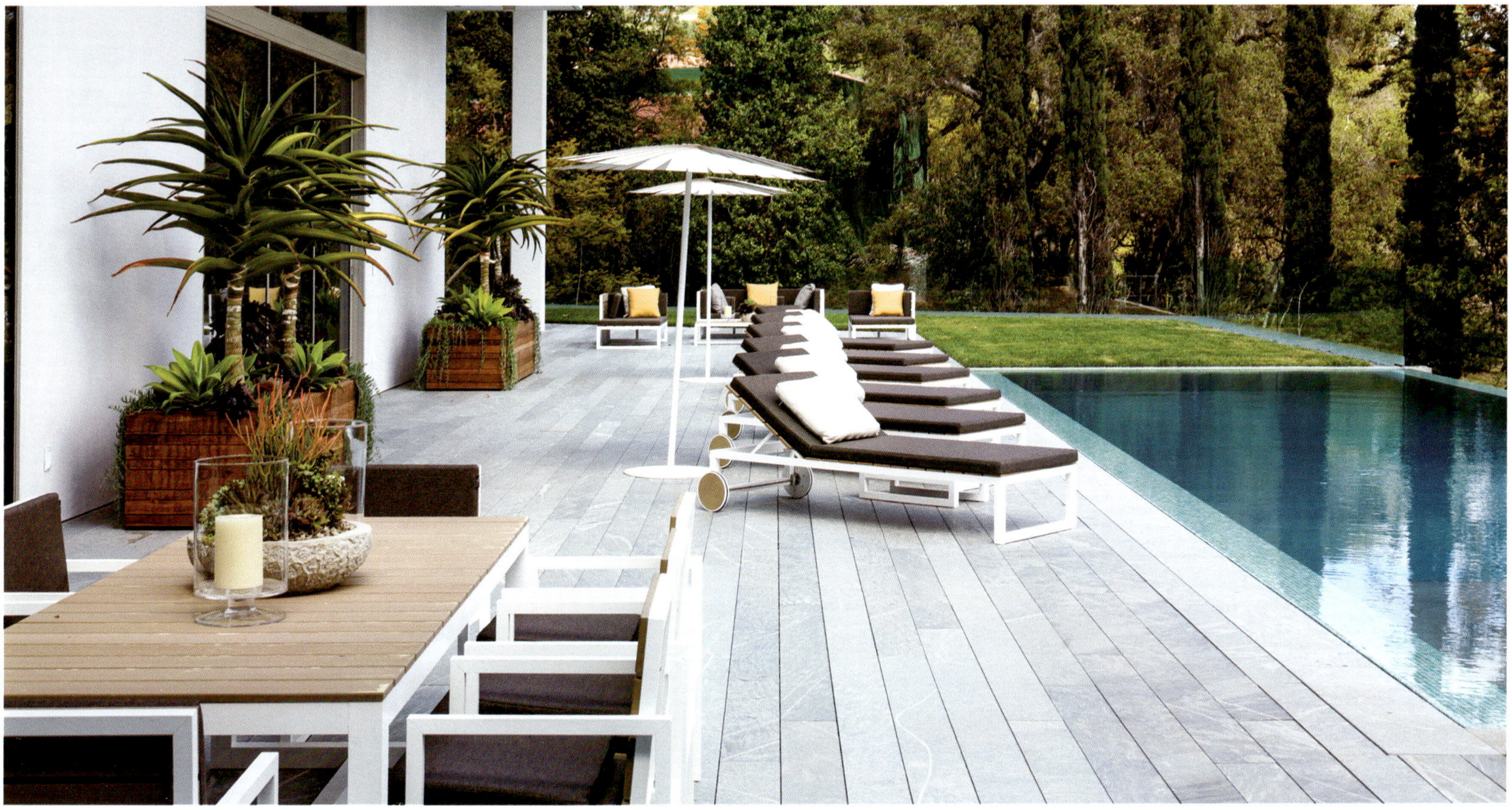

The home's interiors feature the highest quality materials throughout, from a marble-clad stairwell to custom recessed lighting to the American black walnut flooring. You'll enjoy an abundance of natural light and high ceilings in every room. Each space feels like a suite unto itself, and almost every room boasts its own outdoor patio or balcony with views. As you travel between rooms, dramatic vistas unfold. Transparent facades and sliding doors fuse indoor and outdoor living to exhilarating effect.

Off the 22.86 m central gallery — ideal for an art collector — the second living area boasts a 4.3 m high ceiling and direct access to the outdoor terrace and pool. An ultra-spacious kitchen features a state-of-the-art Molteni design with integrated lighting, Dada/Miele appliances and direct access to the terraces and custom-tiled infinity pool. The resort-like grounds are ideal for relaxing and entertaining, with 604 m² of terrace space in addition to the pool, landscaped gardens, outdoor kitchen, flat lower lawn and a gorgeous astro-turf tennis court with floodlights. Mature

trees provide a natural border of the property, and together with the tiered pool and gardens, it feels as if you are on a luxurious island looking out over your own private park.

Upstairs, the wide-open master suite combines a sophisticated master bedroom, huge master bath, 3 private walk-closets, powder room and separate offices. The master also boasts an extensive balcony looking out over the pool and tennis court.

The 3-level home also features 6 other elegantly appointed bedroom suites, 3 living rooms, formal dining room, 2 libraries/studies, double-height gallery, spacious fitness center, home theater, catering kitchen, elevator and wine cellar. The estate integrates a cutting-edge audio-visual system that uses an iPad interface, everything automated and with maximum security. This is truly an estate for the ages.

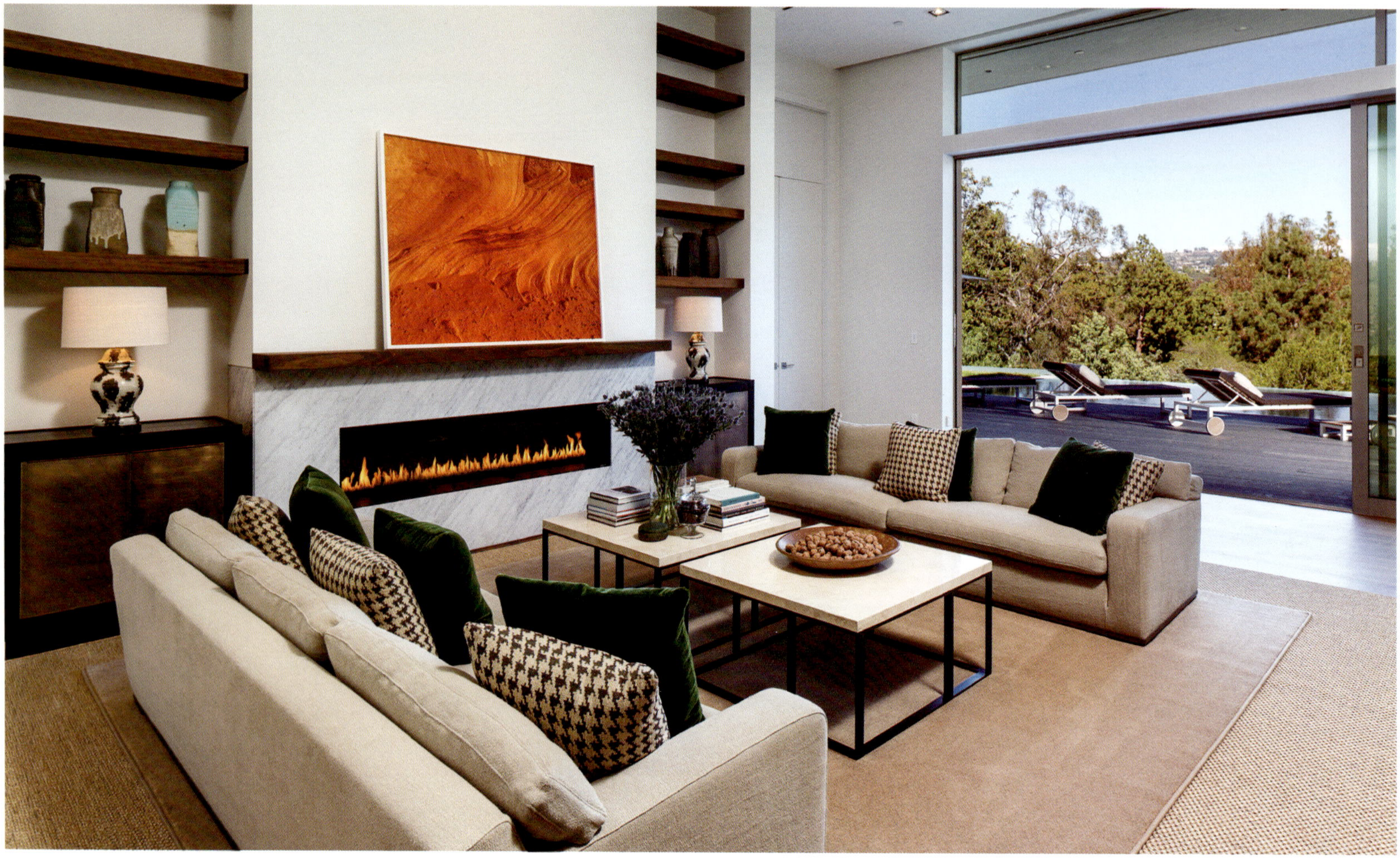

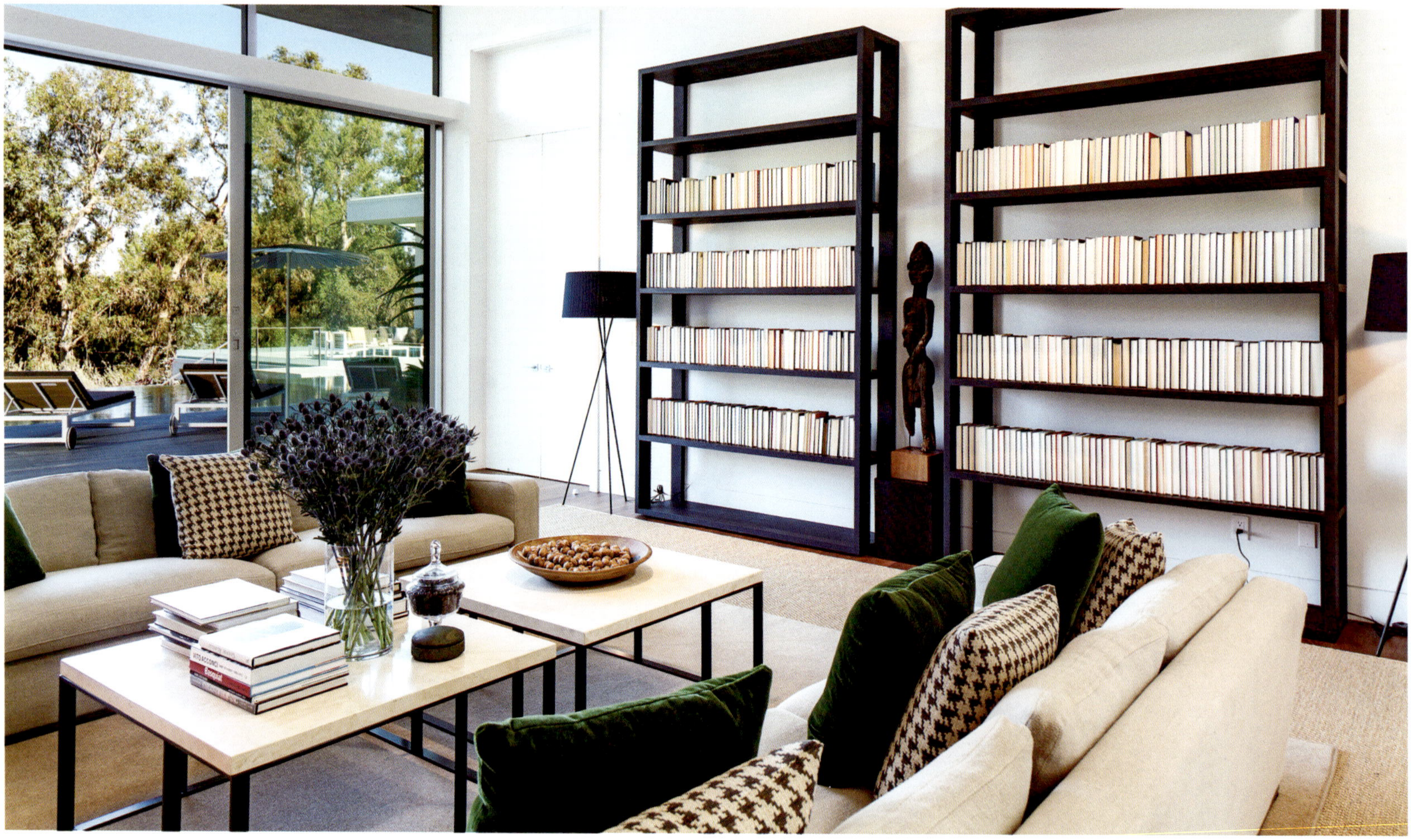

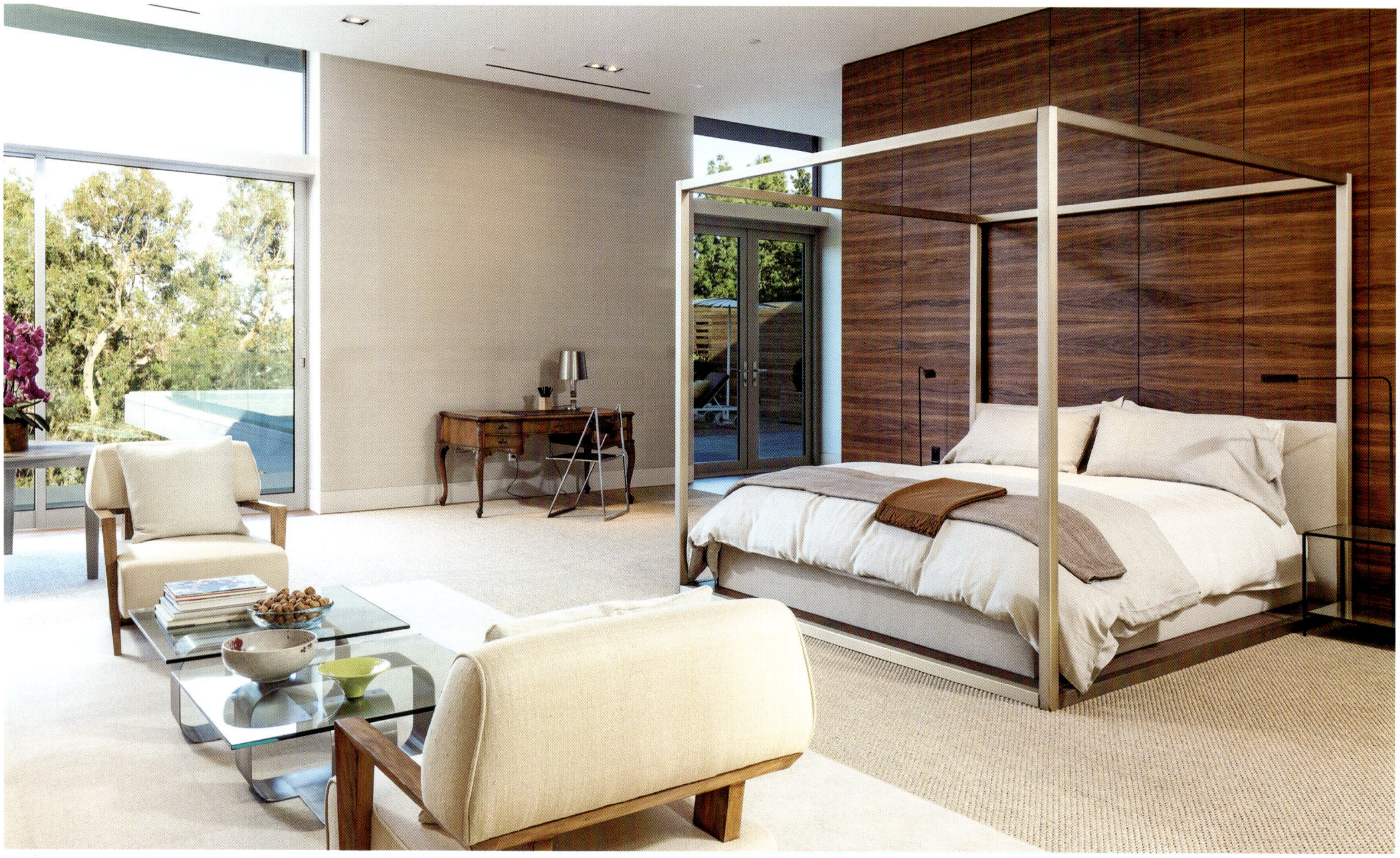

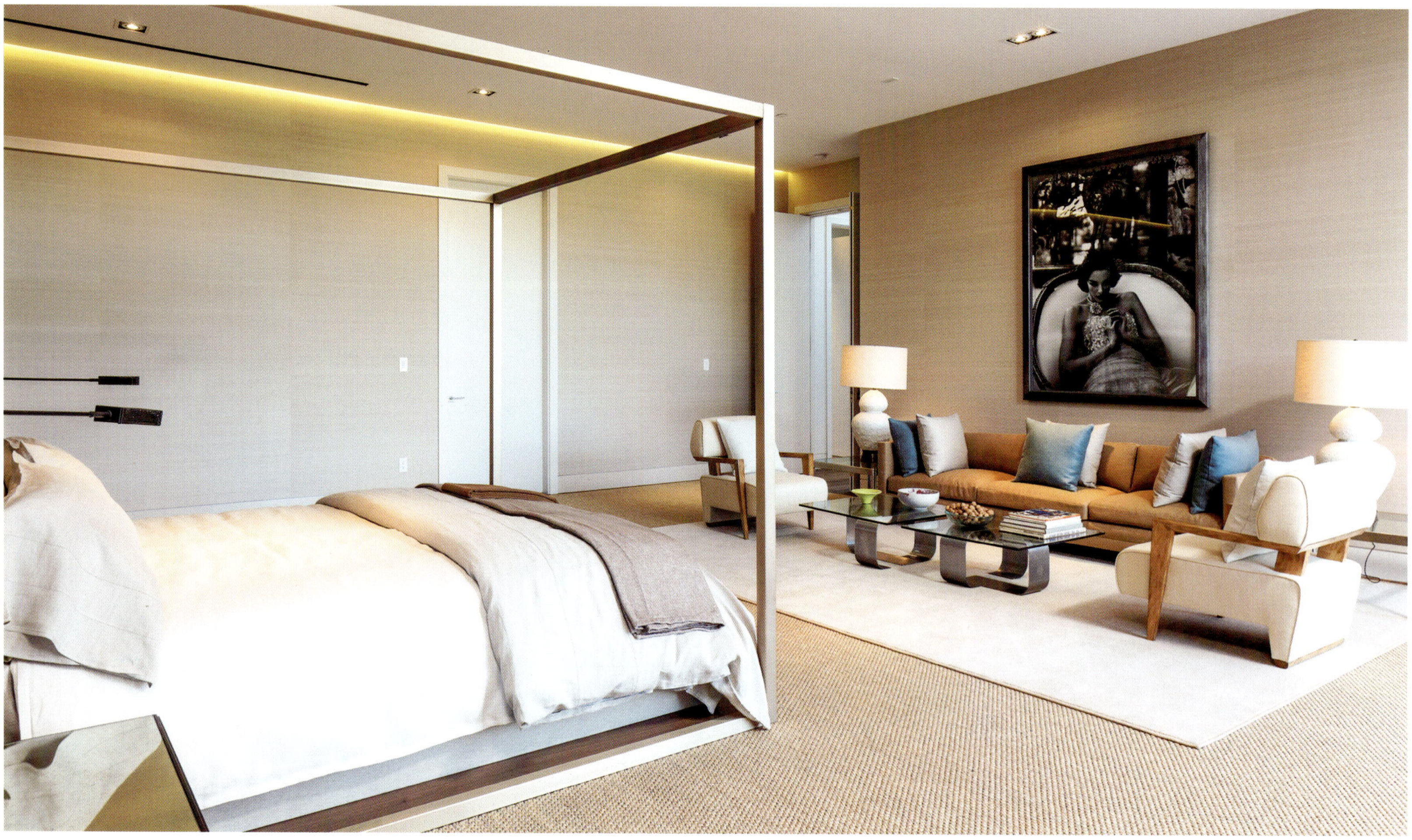

Winelands 190

Architecture & Interior Architecture
Antoni Associates

Photography
Adam Letch

Project Team
Mark Rielly, Sarika Jacobs,
Jon Case, Clive Schulze

Key Furniture Supplier
OKHA Interiors

Location
Stellenbosch, Cape Town

The clients' brief was to ensure that when they occupied the house on their own that it was not too big and empty, however at the same time it also had to allow for the whole family and grandchildren should they decide to stay over. The decision was made to keep all the entertainment spaces as well as the master bedroom on the ground floor, with three additional guest suites on the first level. As the

De Zalze design regulations only permitted a single story, the guests' suites were accommodated in the roof attics.

Two important criteria for the clients were that the project had to include a central courtyard and that the main living areas were to have double volume. At the front of the plot the concept of a traditional "Cape Dutch Langhuis" with gabled ends was

conceptualized. This part of the house was designed to contain the formal lounge & dining, informal lounge & braai room as well as the master bedroom and en-suite, giving all these areas direct access to the front pool terrace with spectacular views to the surrounding vineyards and mountains. In the "Langhuis" open trusses were used to give all the rooms a larger volume. To the rear of the "Langhuis", the two side wings and a linking lobby create a sheltered central courtyard which also visually links the kitchen to the family TV lounge. Identical feature stairs link to the guest bedroom suites located in the roof lofts of these back wings.

The owners of this home love to entertain and wanted the house to reflect their lifestyle. Key features of this include the bespoke wine cellar. Here the design team created a spectacular glass wine wall. The oak timber cabinetry encases frameless glass shelving which can house more than 400 bottles which are perfectly temperature controlled with concealed refrigeration. The wine wall also functions as a visual screen between the formal and informal family spaces. A dramatic double volume stone clad fireplace in the formal lounge is mirrored by a built-in braai in the informal lounge. These areas of the house flow out onto the outdoor entertainment deck and infinity pool. Linked to the terrace is a sunken outdoor boma (a typical South African outdoor enclosure). Here casual seating is arranged around an open fire.

For the interior architecture the design approach by Mark Rielly and Jon Case was to focus on the use of natural organic materials such as timber and stone. Limed oak flooring paired with honey coloured stone walls contrast with black charcoals and chalky white finishes. These tactile materials add a sense of homeliness and warmth to the contemporary architecture. A number of elemental forces are captured in the use of water features and fireplaces.

Werf walls and a pergola covered walkway lead to the front entrance which opens into the courtyard lobby overlooking the reflective pond and greenery. Glass pocket doors create separate entrances and lead into the side wings. Focal features of the entrances are the floating sculpture ledges. Here Angus Taylor sculptures are reflected in the fractured mirror wall

cladding. The same fractured pattern is again used in the smokey mirror cladding of the stairways. Limed oak cantilevered treads, timber cladding with white stone ledges and frameless glass balustrading add to the transparency and airiness of these spaces. Clear blown glass globes by David Reade are suspended and reflected in the double volume stairwells adding interest.

A combination of bold and discreet lighting was used to create a "wow" factor and the layering of lighting set various moods. Subtle lighting has been incorporated in all recesses and feature bulkheads to give a warm glow to peripheral edges. Concealed lighting has also been used to highlight and accentuate the organic natural finishes. In the dining room a customized crystal chandelier by Martin Doller is suspended

from the ceiling rafters. Other feature lighting includes a custom designed "ring" light by AA Interiors, over the informal braai room and a signature Willow Lamp in the main bedroom.

The interior furniture and décor were designed by Mark Rielly and Sarika Jacobs of AA Interiors. The furniture is modern and complementary to the experience of the home. Tactile finishes including timber, textured leathers and raw linens add a sophisticated sense of understated luxury. The clients' love for colour has been introduced with injections of bold prints and vibrant fabrics. Bespoke furniture from OKHA Interiors is featured throughout.

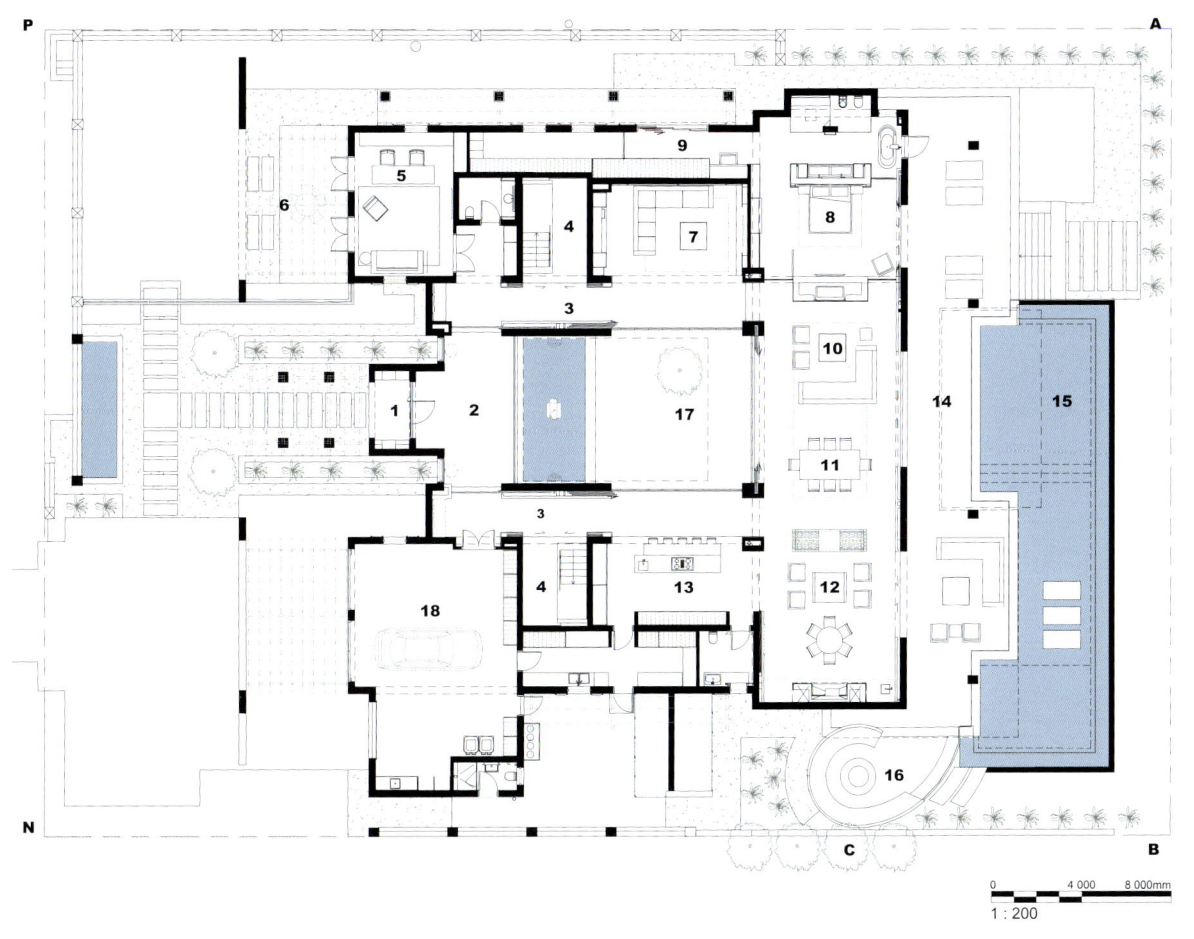

LEGEND

1. PORTICO
2. LOBBY
3. CIRCULATION
4. STAIR
5. OFFICE
6. OFFICE VERANDAH
7. TV LOUNGE
8. MASTER BEDROOM
9. DRESSING
10. LOUNGE AREA
11. DINING AREA
12. INFORMAL LOUNGE
13. KITCHEN
14. TERRACE
15. POOL
16. BOMA
17. COURTYARD
18. GARAGE
19. BEDROOM 2
20. BEDROOM 3
21. BEDROOM 4
22. FAMILY ROOM

PLAN NORTH

0   4 000   8 000mm

1 : 200

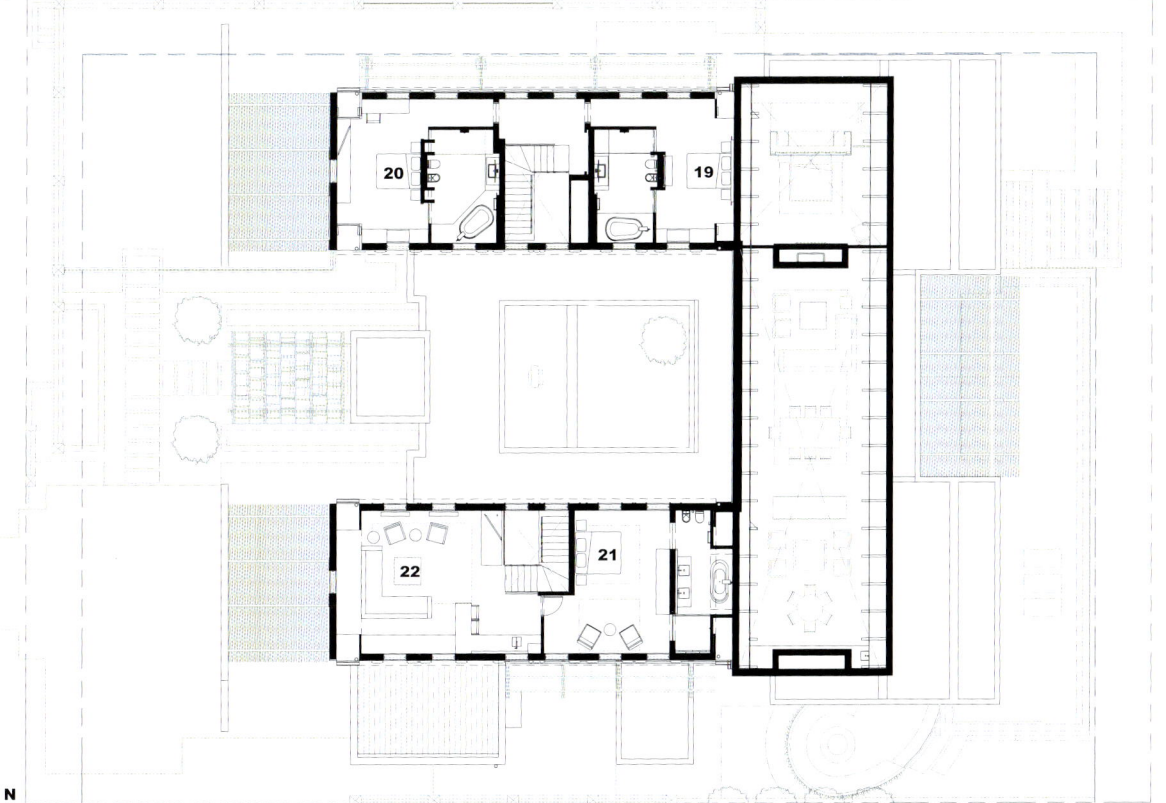

LEGEND

1. PORTICO
2. LOBBY
3. CIRCULATION
4. STAIR
5. OFFICE
6. OFFICE VERANDAH
7. TV LOUNGE
8. MASTER BEDROOM
9. DRESSING
10. LOUNGE AREA
11. DINING AREA
12. INFORMAL LOUNGE
13. KITCHEN
14. TERRACE
15. POOL
16. BOMA
17. COURTYARD
18. GARAGE
19. BEDROOM 2
20. BEDROOM 3
21. BEDROOM 4
22. FAMILY ROOM

PLAN NORTH

0   4 000   8 000mm

1 : 200

Expressing Views

Designer & Builder
Urbane Projects Pty Ltd.

Location
Perth, Western Australia

Photography
Joel Barbitta of D-Max Photography

Contemporary, timeless and spreading over three levels with a sparkling infinity edge pool to its elevated corner block, this Apple cross abode commands attention from first glimpse and allows its family of four to live the lifestyle they had always dreamed about.

The client shad lived for years in the older house on the block. When the chance arose to buy the house next door they took advantage of it to knock down both residences and build their dream home with Urbane. Now they have their "forever" home with a level of luxury finishes and a custom design that does justice to its market riverside location and makes the most of the site's panoramic river views.

A 3 m tall ebony-stained jarrah door opens onto the entrance foyer. A wall of

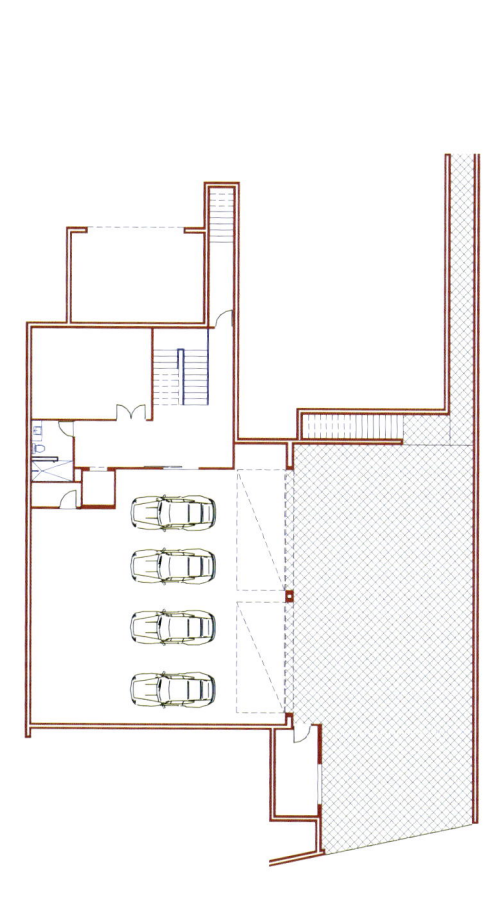

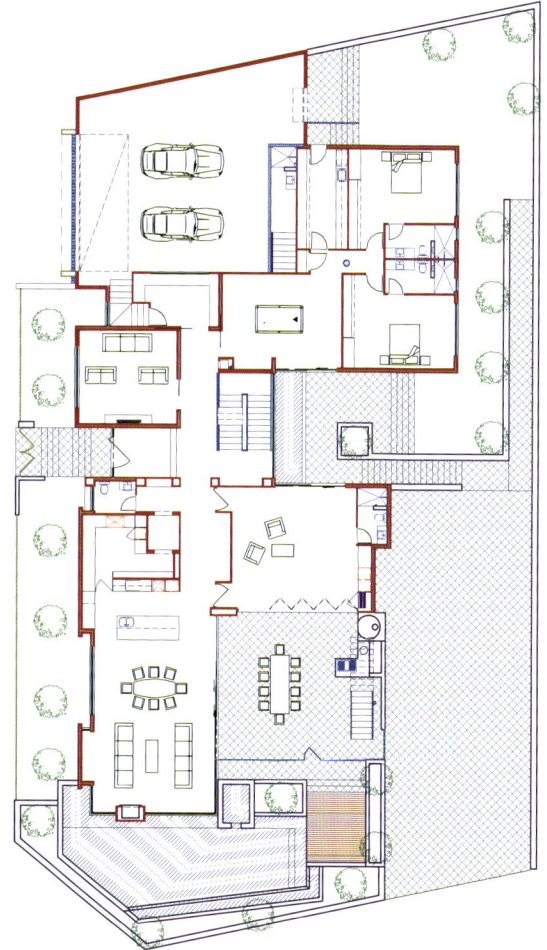

windows overlooks a reflection pond, mature frangipani tree and sculpture set against a backdrop of a glass face rendered wall. In the entry is one of the home's most spectacular features — the staircase. A feat of engineering, the staircase runs through all three stories and features a suspended steel structure with oak treads stained a rich Japan black that complement the honed limestone floors.

The clients wanted the design to have longevity and to cater for their teenage daughter and son for years to come. 5 bedrooms and 7 bathrooms encompass separate zones for the teenage children, as well as guest bedrooms for friends to stay over. A games room as well as a home theatre offer spaces for the children to entertain their friends, while parents have an upstairs bar and lounge, as well as a fully enclosable alfresco lounge and dining with its own bar, all set against river views. The hotel-like parents' retreat has a wraparound balcony and views from the bed and ensuite that stretch across the neighbourhood to the river and city beyond.

The open-plan kitchen, lounge and dining can also be opened up to the outdoors for effortless indoor-outdoor living and entertaining. The landscaped gardens include an infinity edge pool tiled in iridescent Bisazza mosaics that visually link the gardens to the sparkling Swan River beyond.

The clients said they were thrilled with Steve's work and loved the Urbane approach, encompassing everything from conception to the design of the custom-built cabinetry and selection of furniture. "Everything Steve picked, we loved." they said.

Laurel Way

Architects
Marc Whipple AIA

Project Manager
Andrew Takabayashi

Interior Designer
Michael Palumbo

Location
Beverly Hills, California

Area
931 m²

Photographers
William MacCollum, Art Gray Photography

One aesthetic idea driving the creation of Laurel Way was that each room or space should be a jewel box, an individually conceived, precisely functional and dramatic sensory experience with its own depth of architecture.

Central to the composition are many of Marc Whipple's signature elements, one being the use of texture; smooth next to rough stone, rich wooden panels against glass, and glass reflecting water. The immediate experience upon entering the house is its inherent weightlessness — the sense that the walls appear to float as panels and you are always connected to the outdoors. This is achieved with adherence to precise symmetry of beams, support panels, tiles, and sightlines, and also that walls do not meet the ceilings — a 1.3 cm gap is left that helps achieve the effect.

These elements play up the horizontals and verticals of the house while movement and curves come from the 3 tiers of greenery and 2 water channels that surround the house giving it the look of an island floating against the blue California sky. The moat-like water surround is more than a successful artistic inspiration; it adds the feeling of a protective boundary without obstructing the views in any way. It also provided an innovative water feature visible from the interior while adding a highly dramatic dynamic to the entire design.

The front entry steps lead to a 4.3 m wood pivot door flanked entirely by glass, and then into the main floor foyer. To the left, a section of glass flooring reveals a wine room below with storage for 1,000 bottles, and cantilevered wenge wood stairs float upward to the bedrooms.

The living and dining areas are a study in chocolate and creamy whites carried through to the exterior surfaces achieved with Texston's Lime based plaster, offset by rough split-faced stone and dark wenge wood. Lift and Slide German made Schuco windows and doors are state of the art offering dependable operation and drainage as well as thermal efficiency summer and winter. Glossy kitchen cabinets were custom designed and imported from Italy.

"Zero edge" and " floating" themes are echoed in the smallest details; kitchen cooktop venting is flush to ceiling.

With no use of molding all lines are visible, every element must be perfectly square and aligned. Minotii, Maxalto and B&B Italia furniture was selected or custom made for each living space. The main powder room's motorized sliding glass door opens up to a vanity and white glass rectangular column — the sink. A wall of small, mirrored black tiles, reflect a single chrome vertical water pipe suspended over custom made sink.

River House

| **Architects** | **Builder** | **Area** | **Interior Decoration** | **Structural Engineer** |
| MCK Architects | Alvaro Brothers | 530 m^2 | Scala and Romano Interiors | Simpson Design Associates + Luke Tsougranis |

| **Landscape Architect** | **Planning Consultant** | **Photography** |
| The Potager Garden | Mersonn | Steve Back |

The River House is essentially a home that integrates an informed assembly of clean lines, warm textured materials and daring structure on a difficult site.

The inhabitants now have a bespoke living vessel to live, work, and play within, and it has arguably created spaces that allow the members of the family to better congregate. The design allows the family and visiting guests to comfortably integrate or disperse for privacy as required. The house does not appear as a very big house through careful manipulation of the massing. The visual program is split into distinct objects which further breakdown the overall massing. Internally it has a series of clever buffers that separate distinct zones.

Ground Floor Plan

01 Entry
02 Hall
03 WC
04 Living
05 Kitchen
06 Dining
07 Terrace
08 Deck Area
09 BBQ
10 Study
11 Laundry
12 Guest Bathroom
13 Guest Bedroom
14 Bin Store
15 Garage
16 Lower Garden
17 Daybed below
18 Lower Pool Yard
19 Pool below

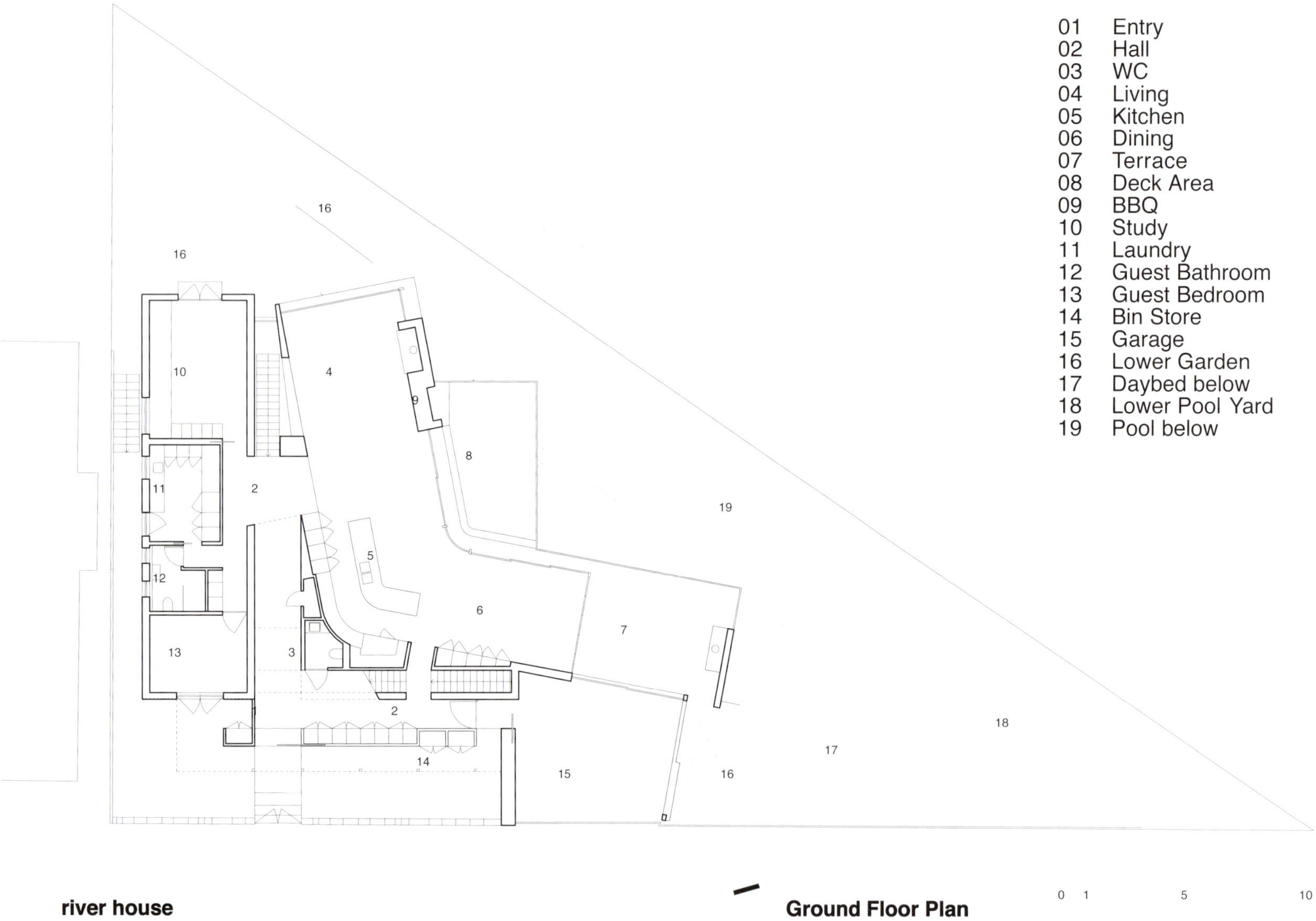

river house

Ground Floor Plan

0 1   5   10

The house takes on a schizophrenic nature by virtue of it's conservative, and private streetscape versus the more wild and open, cantilevered living zone. The streetscape adopts textures, colours and materials from the locality, specifically shingle, sandstone, and painted brick.

The functional performance of the design is wholly based on the clients brief busy lifestyles. The functions are split to 4 levels through the site being from top to bottom, parent's retreat, living/guest/work level, children's sleeping playing level and the pool/backyard level. The latter being newly constructed some 4.5 m above the existing yard, to eliminate an existing inaccessible space and better connect the "fun" parts of the design to the house proper.

The River House proved itself to be one of our greatest collaborative efforts to date. Between an incredibly enthusiastic and intuitive client, an innovative structural engineer, a master craftsman in a builder and ourselves, the design took shape and pushed everyone's imagination to their limits. At the end of the day this project would not have been achievable without the "integration" of such "allied disciplines".

There was a big push to retain a lot of the existing thick basement sandstone walls as they represented the original fabric of the building and a high quality of building stock. The decision to cantilever the main living level naturally increased construction costs however it allowed the design to be maximised on a smaller awkwardly shaped site, and effectively made the most of a smaller site. The abundance of controlled natural light also diminishes the requirement to use artificial lighting when the sun is shining.

Sustainable principles in design include retention of quality building stock like the 600 mm thick lower basement sandstone walls, implementation of a 20,000 L rainwater tank, retractable solar blinds to harness natural light as required, and means to enhancing cross ventilation. Laser cut security screens allow the house to breathe in the warmer months whilst providing adequate security, thus reducing the need to use air-conditioning.

The main living levels are constructed using thick concrete slabs creating excellent thermal mass qualities. General orientation of the plan enables best solar access.

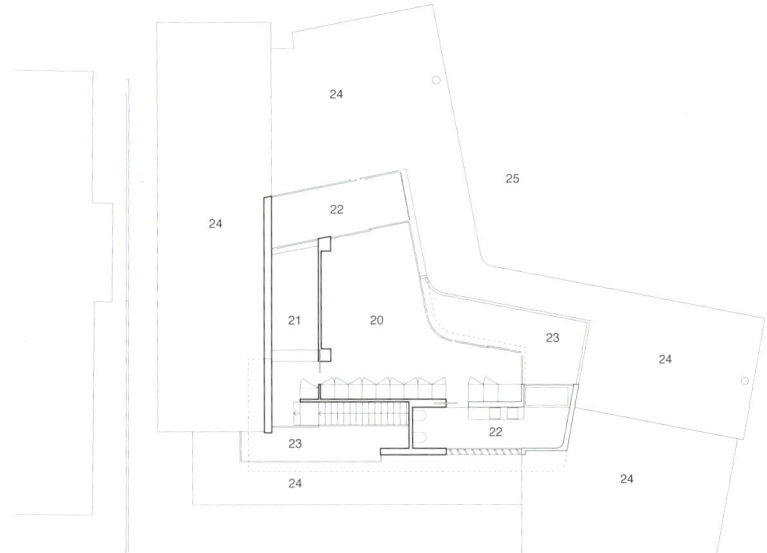

river house   First Floor Plan   0   1   5   10

Fieldview

Architects
Blaze Makoid Architecture

Area
372 m²

Located on a flat, one acre flag lot with neighbors close to the front and side yards, this 10,000 m² house is configured of 3 primary volumes arranged in an "C" that frame the expansive, southern view of an adjacent, agricultural reserve. This view serves as a backdrop to an interwoven composition of interior and exterior spaces.

Entry, through a glass void in the northern side of the house, is approached by a raised, stone walk, under an exaggerated uplighted canopy. The entry foyer, at the terminus of the outdoor pool, separates public space to the left and the private, 2-story bedroom wing to the right. An open floor plan contains living room, dining room and kitchen stretches along the length of the central outdoor patio. Large expanses of south facing glass help to dissolve interior/exterior relationships while a more

selective glazing strategy locates individual windows in the predominately solid north, east and west walls that create privacy while modulating temperature.

The arrangement, assisted by a series of pushed and pulled planes maximizes the ability to modulate the various sunlight requirements while creating more intimate indoor and outdoor functions that serve various functions as activities migrate throughout the day — swimming, breakfast, sunshine, lounge, sleeping.

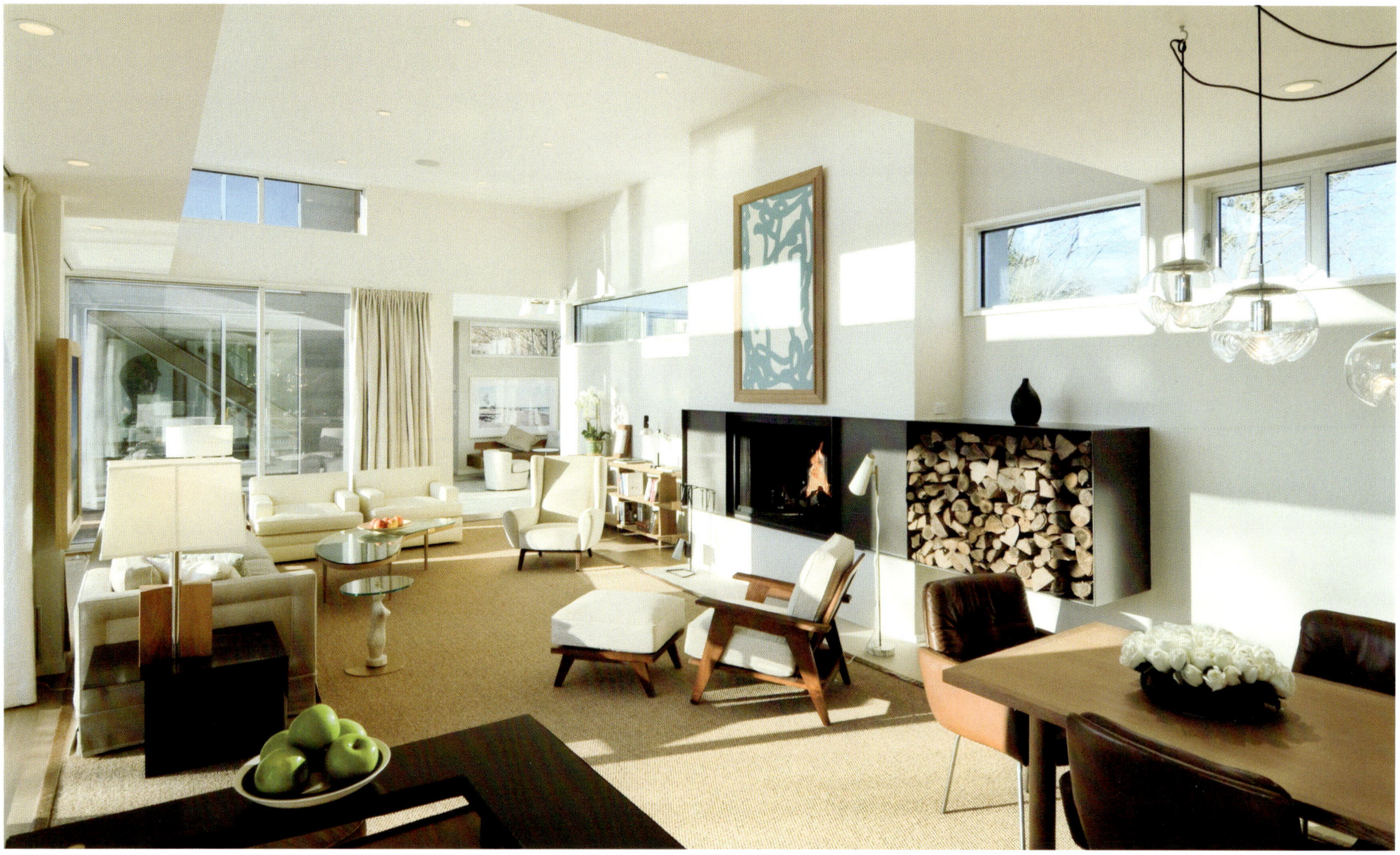

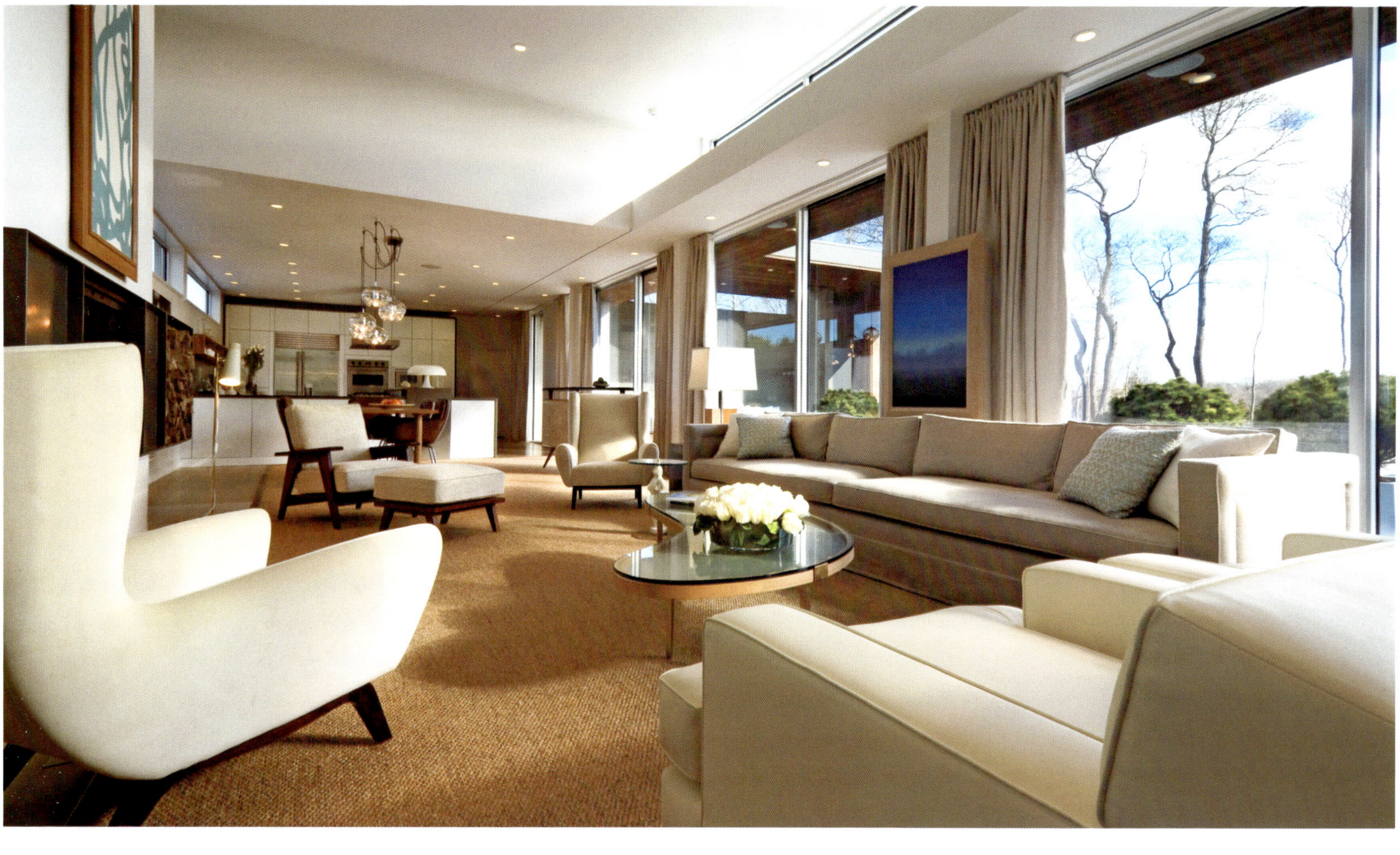

Wind House

Architects
OPENSPACE DESIGN Co., Ltd.

Scope of Works
Architecture and Interior Design

Location
Noble Residence, Bangkok, Thailand

Client
Janphim Sukumaratat

Gross Floor Area
675 m²

"Wind House" was created as "Resort Space" which was the owner's preference style regarding the site conditions. As it was located on the edge of the housing estate project's boundary, it gained the view of big natural green area beside and certainly, the atmosphere of tranquility.

The house planning started from the idea — "How to live comfortably with nature?" Therefore, the building orientation and the space of the house should allow the wind to flow through and allow natural light to shine in without too much heat. At the same time, the users inside could be able to see nice garden view outside as well.

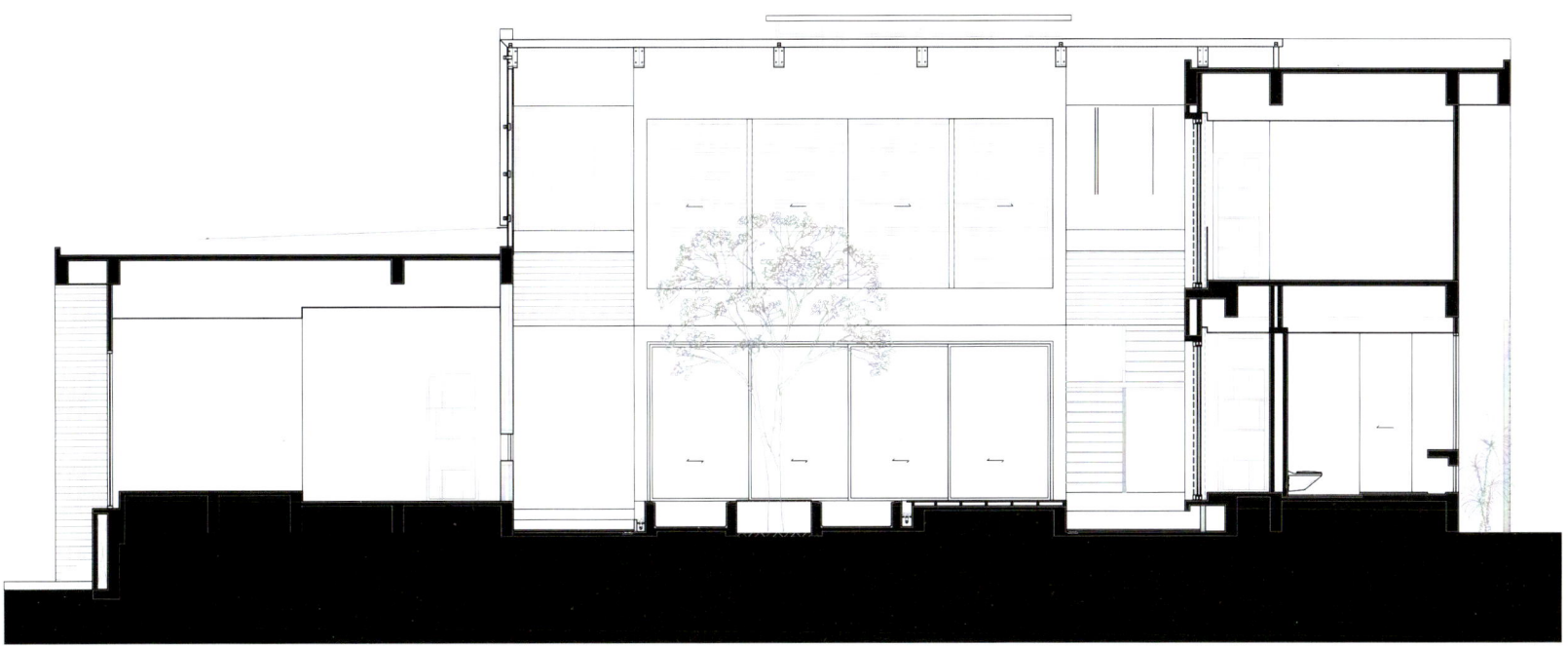

1st FLOOR PLAN

1 : CARPARK

2 : FOYER

3 : LIVING ROOM

4 : POWDER ROOM

5 : THE CORE

6 : DINING ROOM

7 : POND

8 : OUTDOOR LIVING

9 : PAVILION

10 : MAID ROOM

11 : GUEST BEDROOM

12 : THAI KITCHEN

13 : BUDDHA ROOM

14 : PANTRY

15 : WALK-IN CLOSET

16 : MASTER BATHROOM

17 : MASTER BEDROOM

The house was designed in "C" shape providing big courtyard on the right side, close to big green area beside, where every function from 3 sides could really share this pleasant courtyard together. The building itself could provide privacy to the users as neighbors would not be able to look into the center of the house. The technique to draw the wind flowing through the house perfectly was to provide some big voids of the building mass aligned to the courtyard which were also used as circulation core, stair and relaxation corner. Moreover, even some details such as doors, fences, sunlight screen patterns, etc. were meticulously designed to utilize the wind more efficiently for ventilation purpose.

One of the most significant design strategies was to create "Seamless Boundary" between building and nature, indoor and outdoor. All of the common area as well as circulation were treated as "Semi-Outdoor" space, under the roof but without walls, connecting to the courtyard harmoniously. In addition, some enclosed functions were still optional to get fresh air sometimes by sliding full-height partitions to the sides. These would enable the house space to look wider, more airy and definitely, to welcome the delightful wind to be "Wind House".

eat
pray
love

Always
listen to your heart
because even though
it's on your left side,
it's always right.

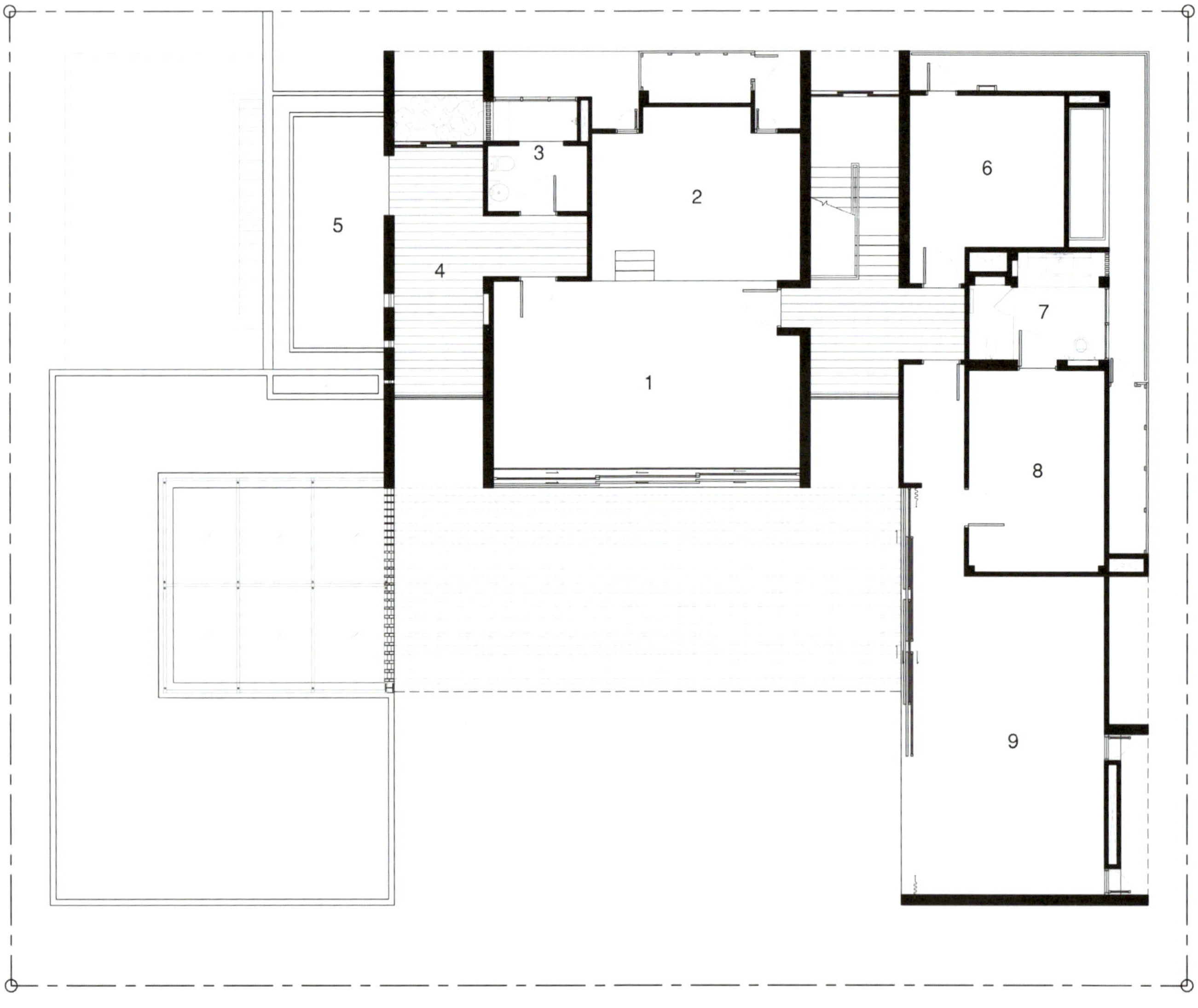

2nd FLOOR PLAN

1 : HOME THEATER

2 : WORKING ROOM

3 : BATHROOM

4 : RELAX CORNER

5 : TERRACE

6 : STORAGE ROOM

7 : BATHROOM

8 : WALK-IN CLOSET

9 : BEDROOM

Cadence Residence

Architects
Keith Baker, Keith Baker Design Inc.

Builder
Taran Williams, TS Williams
Construction

Interior Designer
Ashley Campbell, the Interior
Design Group

Photography
Mia Dominguez, Artez Photography

Completed in the Spring of 2014 "Cadence" was designed as a series of pavilions, nestled along the sunny shoreline of Lantzville on Vancouver Island British Columbia. This stunning home was an award-winner even while it was on the "drawing board". In 2012 it won a Gold Award for "Best Home Design Concept" at the annual Construction Achievements & Renovations of Excellence Awards. And now that it is built, it is a finalist in 7 prestigious categories in the "CARE Awards" including Best Custom House, Best Contemporary Kitchen, Best Master Suite, Best Interior, Best Millwork, People's Choice and Project of the Year. Finally, "Cadence" won 'Best Custom Home over $1M" at the Vancouver Island CARE Awards. It is also the finalist in four categories in the (provincial) Georgie Awards at the end of February, as well as it has won "Best Custom Home (in Canada) over $1M" at the National SAM Awards.

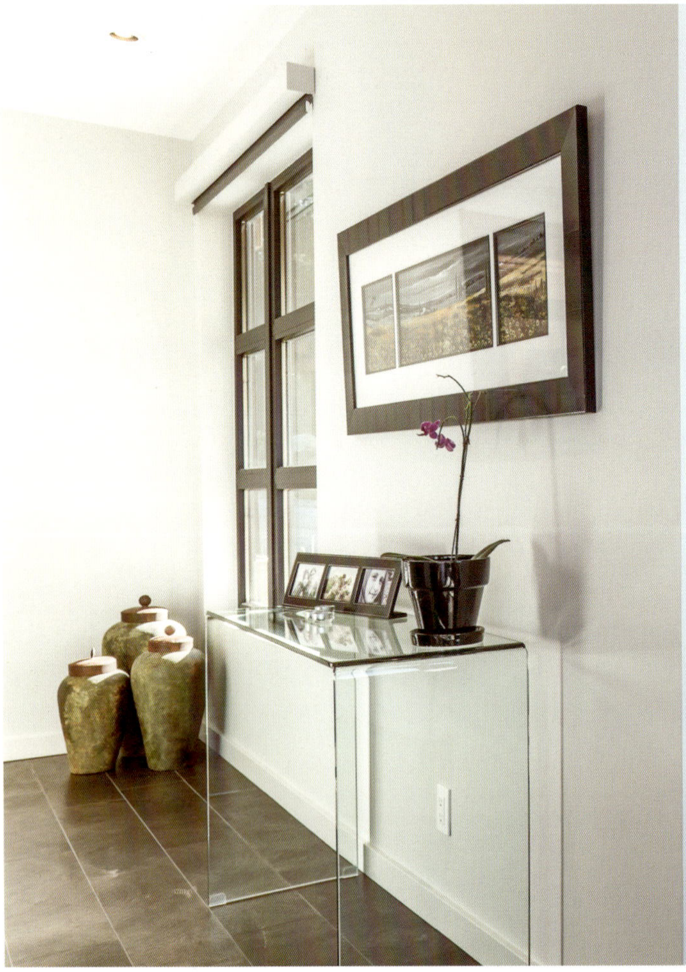

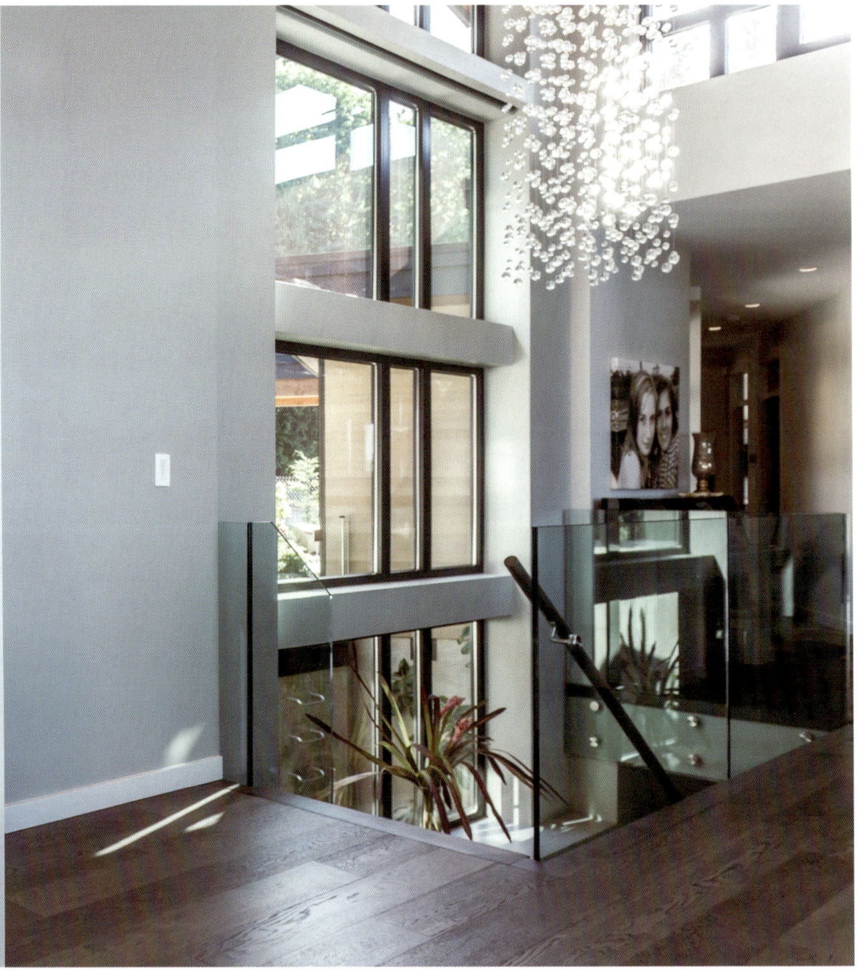

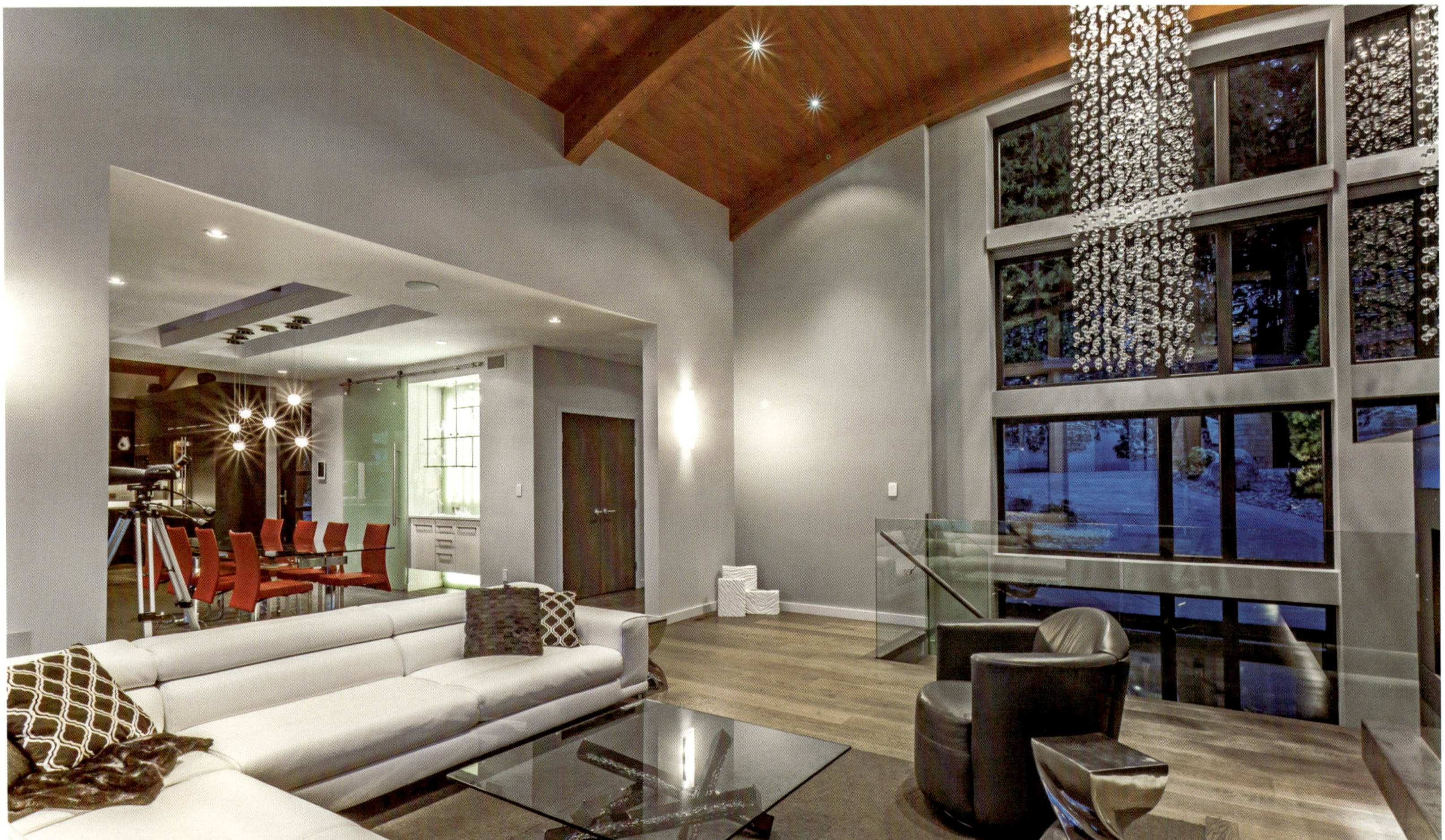

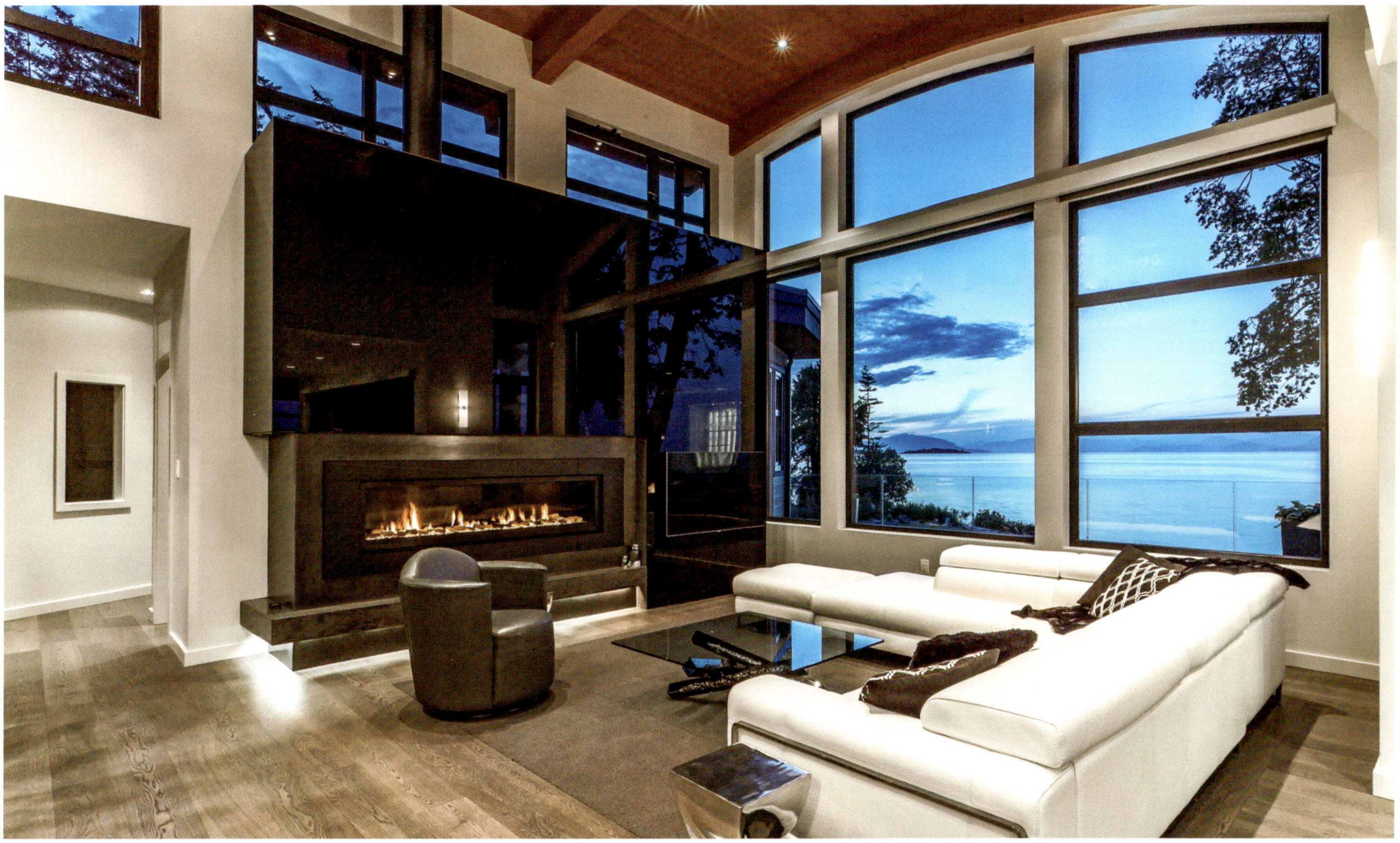

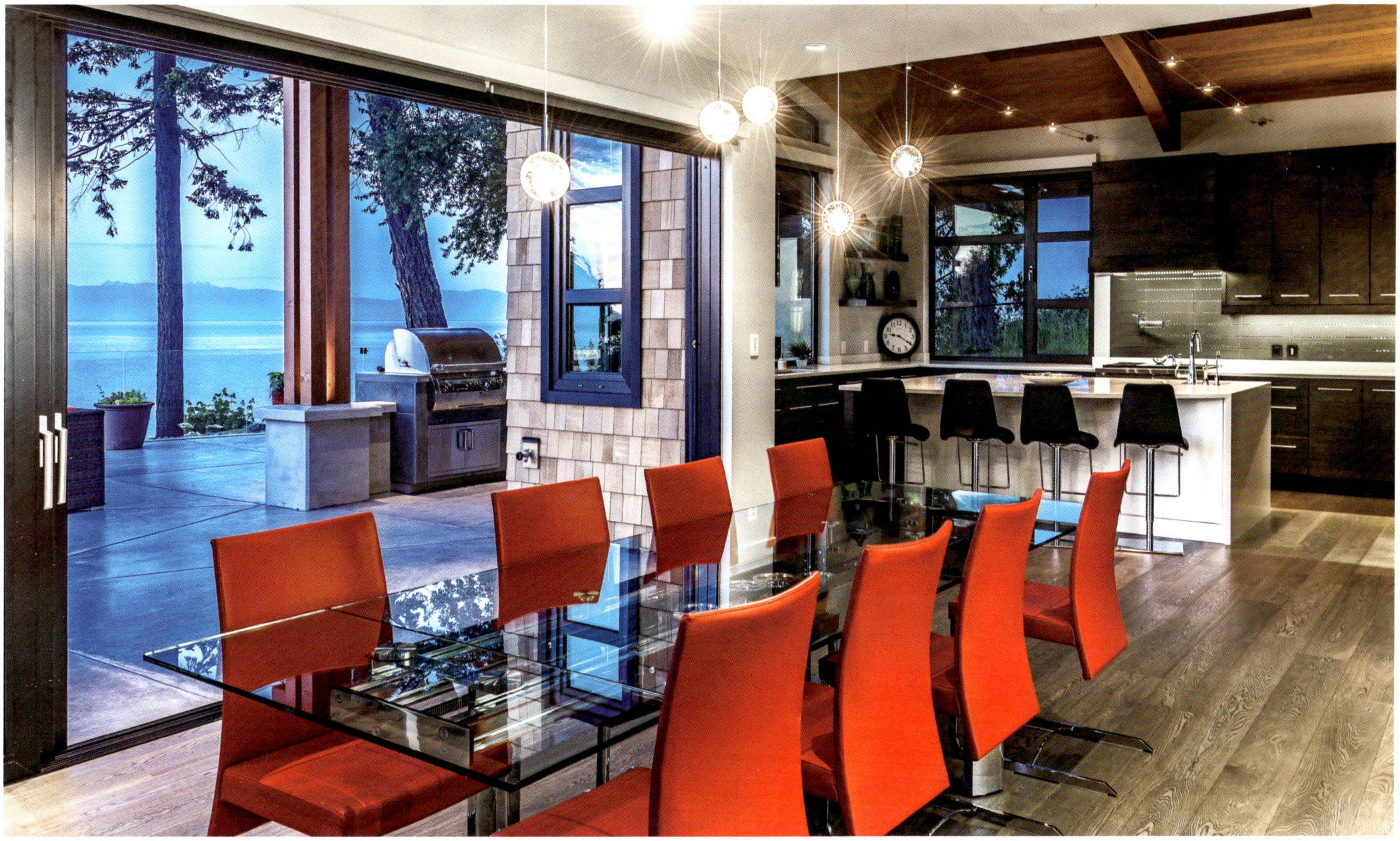

"The concept is such that the spaces should read as very open and create a flow without being too grand. The use of scale was very important by keeping the relative forms of a human size, which gives a very comfortable natural and relaxed feeling," said Keith Baker of Keith Baker Design Inc., the designer of the home. The radiused roof undulations are a subtle reference to the waves and the ocean environment. The light filled home feels very fitting in it's location resting comfortably along the sandy shore. The materials reflect a rooted modernism including extensive Douglas Fir clustered columns and grain-matched radius beams, Western Red Cedar siding rendered in both horizontal 2.54 cm x 10.16 cm T&G and the familiar 'cottage' texture of shingles. Concrete is used as a complement and underscore to ground the composition.

It's open plan is unusual in that it is not one large great room, but rather a series of open spaces interconnected and articulated between the 2 main pavilions of the kitchen and the living room. An 5.5 m wide 3 panel sliding glass patio door opens the dining room to the entertainment sized lounging patio, the ocean and the evening sunsets. As well the outdoor kitchen is well equipped with a wood burning fireplace, a gas fireplace for gathering around, a pizza oven, concrete countertops and BBQ.

One of the many standout features is the post and beam covered breezeway that offers a graceful transition from the triple garage to the mudroom entry and separate guest suite entry.

The Porte Coachiere lends a protective elegance for guests arriving at the front door. The home also features a master bedroom suite that at once is cocooning and cosy as well is expansive and connected to nature with stunning beach and oceans views. All in all an inviting open and intimate place to call home.

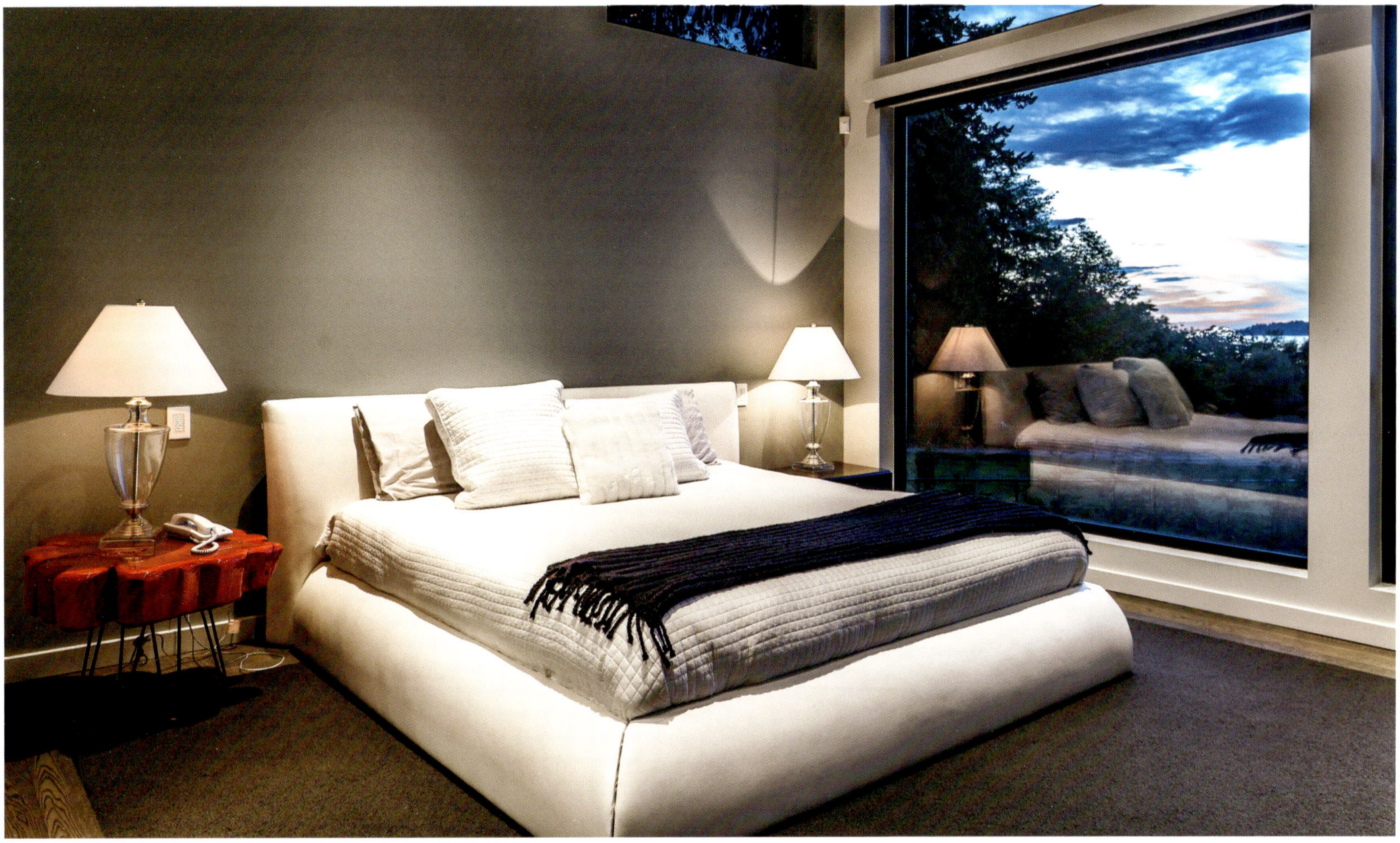

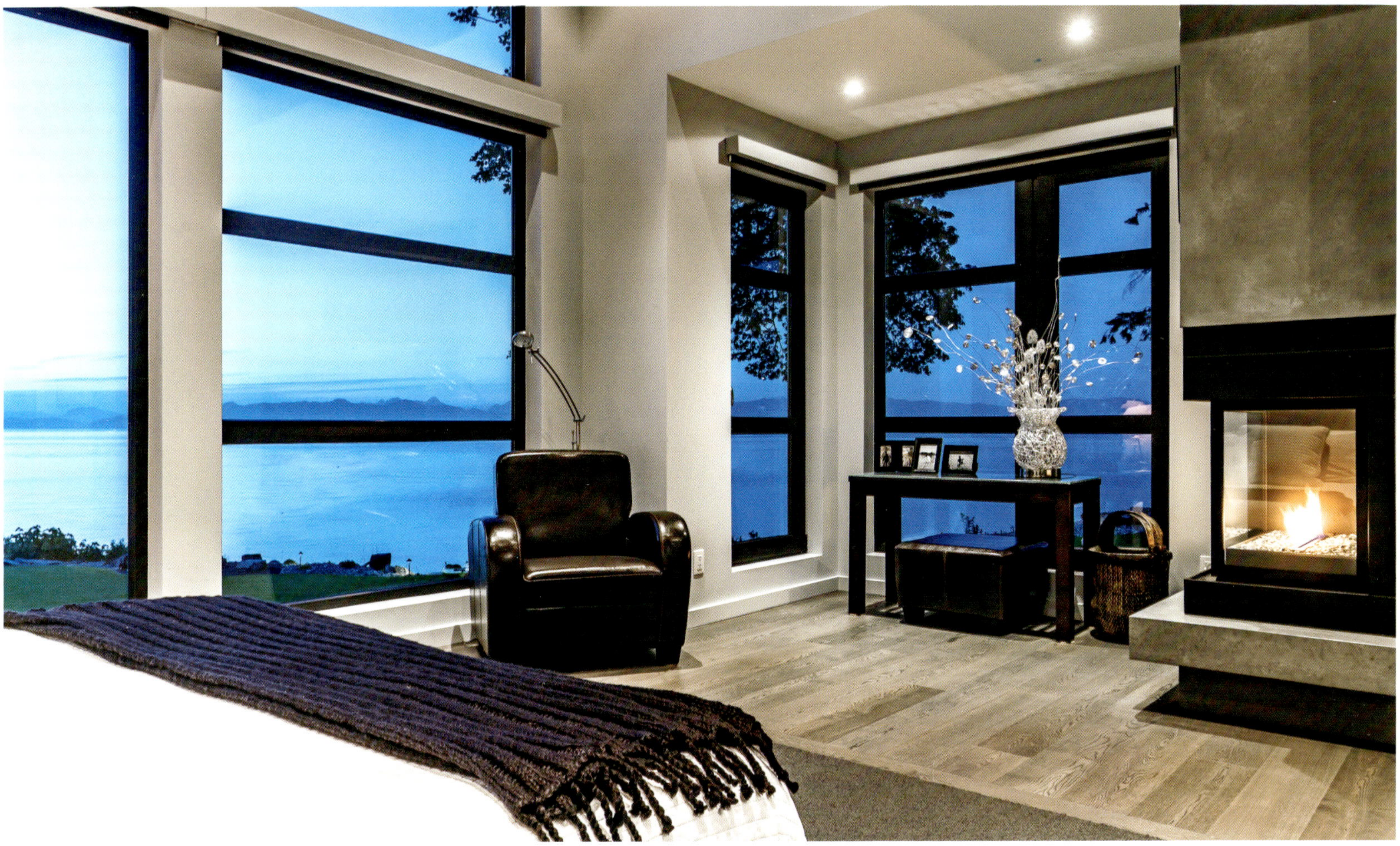

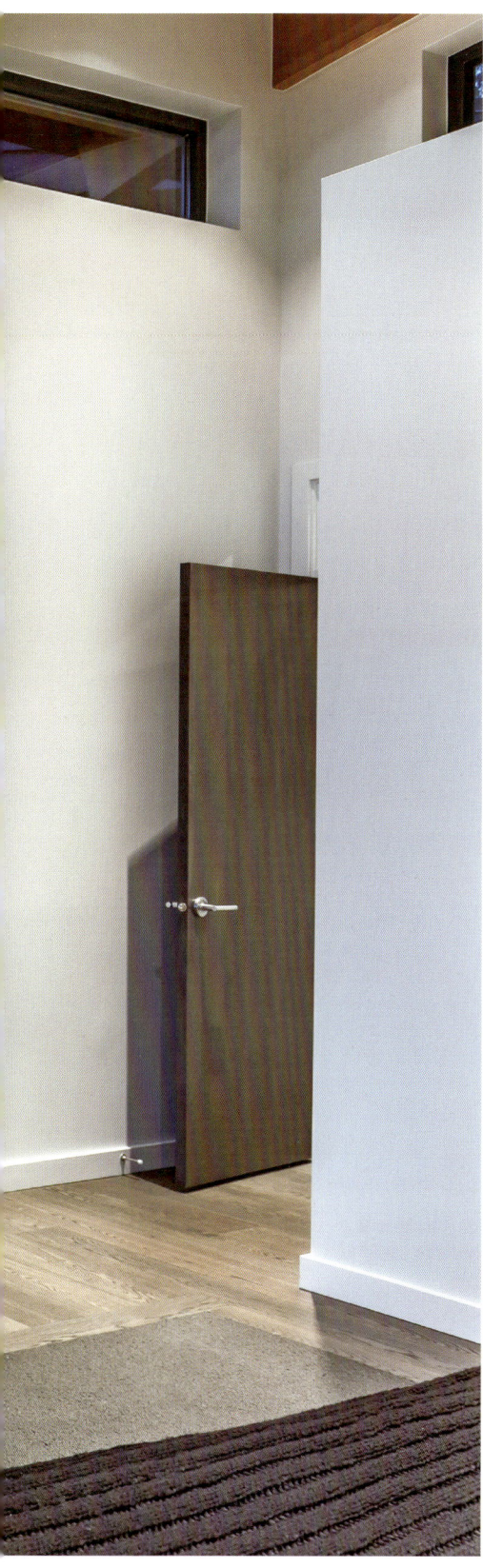

Aloe Ridge House

Architects
Metropole Architects

Design Architect
Nigel Tarboton

Project Architect
David Louis

Project Technician
Simon Wayne

Location
Kwa Zulu Natal, South Africa

Area
300 m²

Structural Engineers
DDR and Associates

Design Engineer
Pat Duffy

Project Engineer
Duran Rammanhor

Interior Designers
Dr. Gabriella Lachinger

Landscape Design & Implementation
Dr. Elsa Pooley

Main Contractor
IMB projects

Principal
Nic Moussouris

Site Foreman
Ernest Ramekwa

Photography
Grant Pitcher

Under the leafy canopy of an immense Albizia Tree nestles Aloe Ridge House, a 300 m² contemporary home in the Eden Rock Estate on Kwa Zulu Natal's South Coast of South Africa.

The planar estate road (public) facade is intentionally bold, minimalist and austere and hard up against the south western site building line. The result is a visually engaging architecture that makes efficient use of the small site, provides effective privacy to the inhabitants whilst at the same time acting as an efficient barrier to bad weather and prevailing strong winds coming from the south west. In addition a narrow linear plan form, maximizes openness and sheltered private space for living, entertainment and relaxation behind this to the north east, in close proximity to the wild natural bush and looking out towards the view beyond.

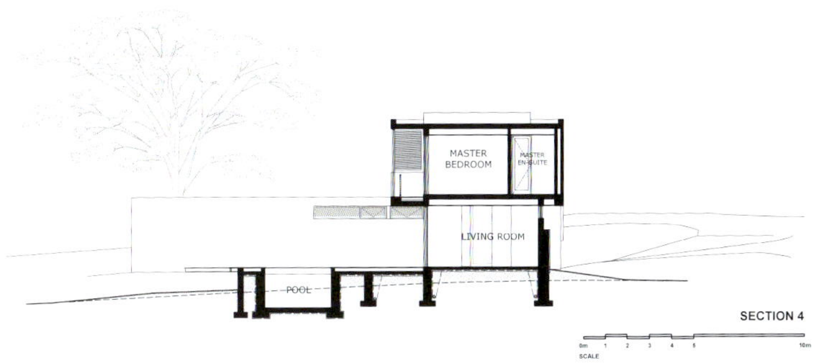

SECTION 4

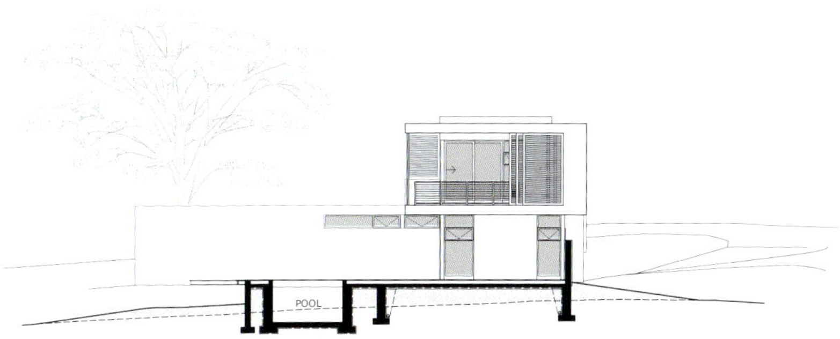

MASTER BEDROOM

MASTER EN-SUITE

LIVING ROOM

POOL

SCALE

SECTION 5

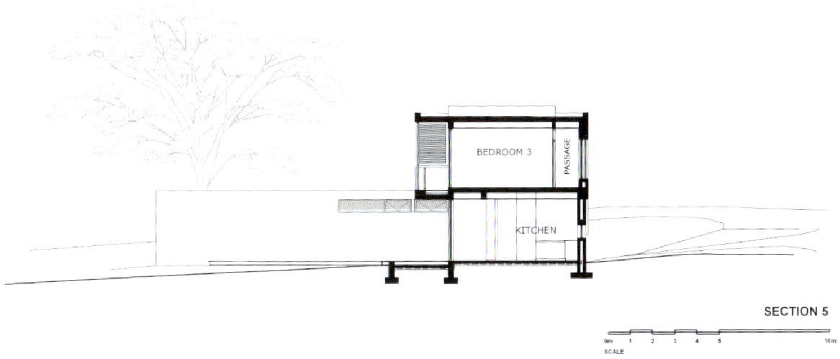

BEDROOM 3

PASSAGE

KITCHEN

SCALE

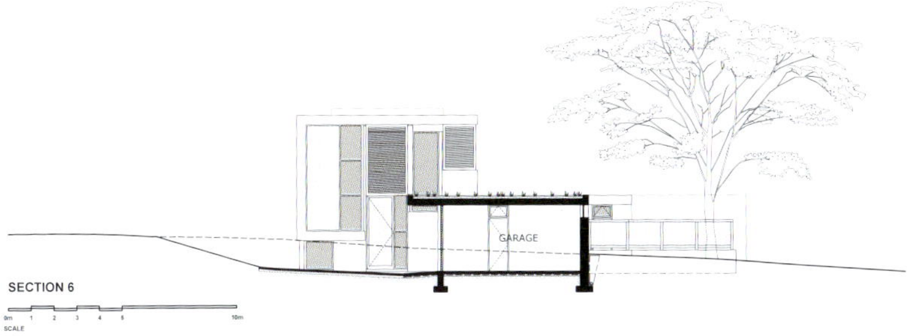

SECTION 6

GARAGE

SCALE

WEST SECTIONAL ELEVATION

POOL

SCALE

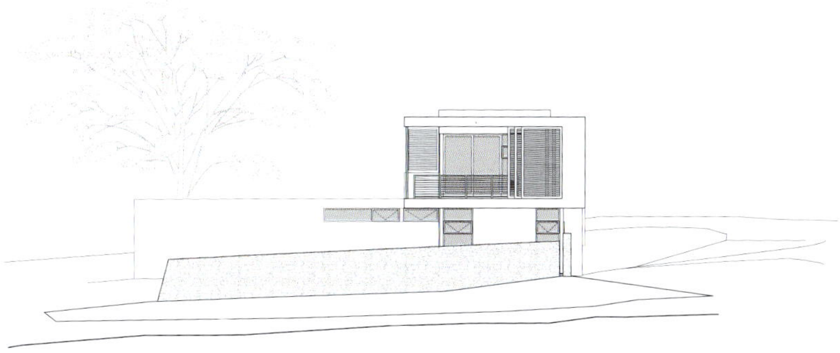

WEST BOUNDARY ELEVATION

SCALE

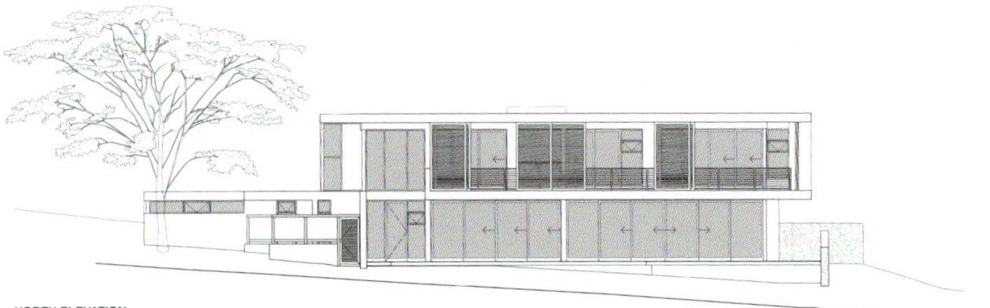

NORTH ELEVATION
SCALE

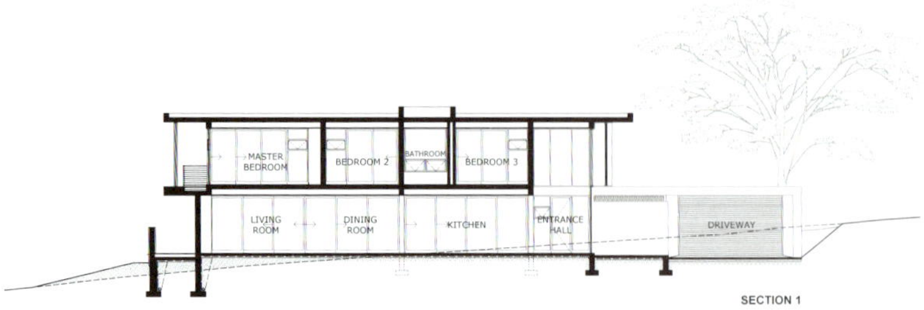

SECTION 1
SCALE

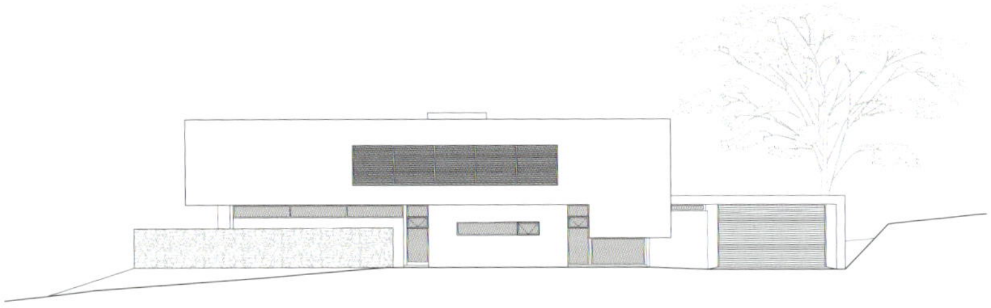

SOUTH ELEVATION
SCALE

SECTION 2
SCALE

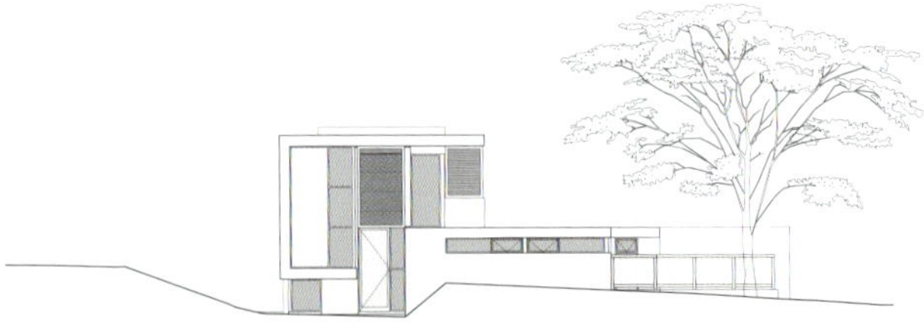

EAST ELEVATION
SCALE

SECTION 3
SCALE

SECTION 1

| MASTER BEDROOM | BEDROOM 2 | BATHROOM | BEDROOM 3 |
| LIVING ROOM | DINING ROOM | KITCHEN | ENTRANCE HALL | DRIVEWAY |

SECTION 2

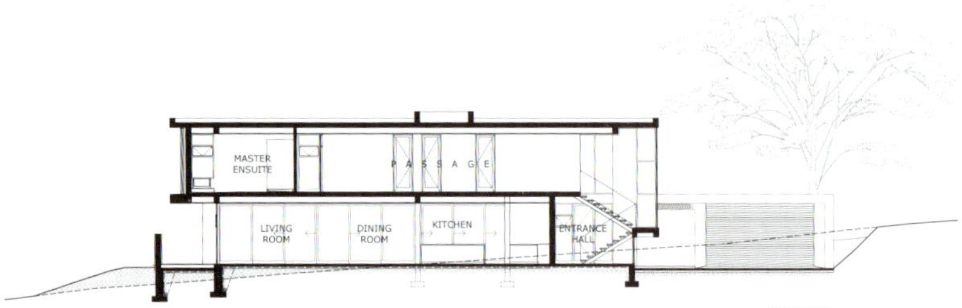

| MASTER ENSUITE | PASSAGE |
| LIVING ROOM | DINING ROOM | KITCHEN | ENTRANCE HALL |

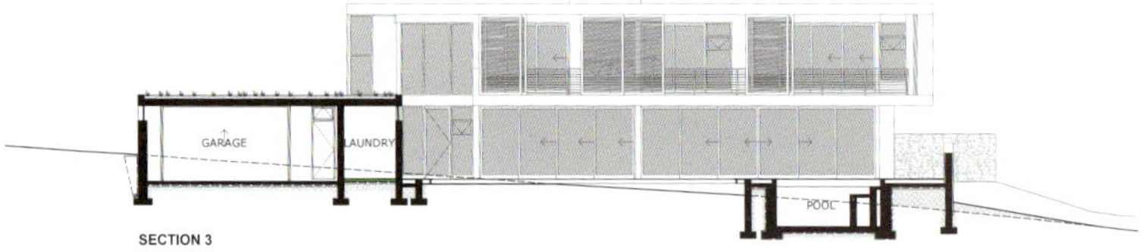

SECTION 3

| GARAGE | LAUNDRY |
| POOL |

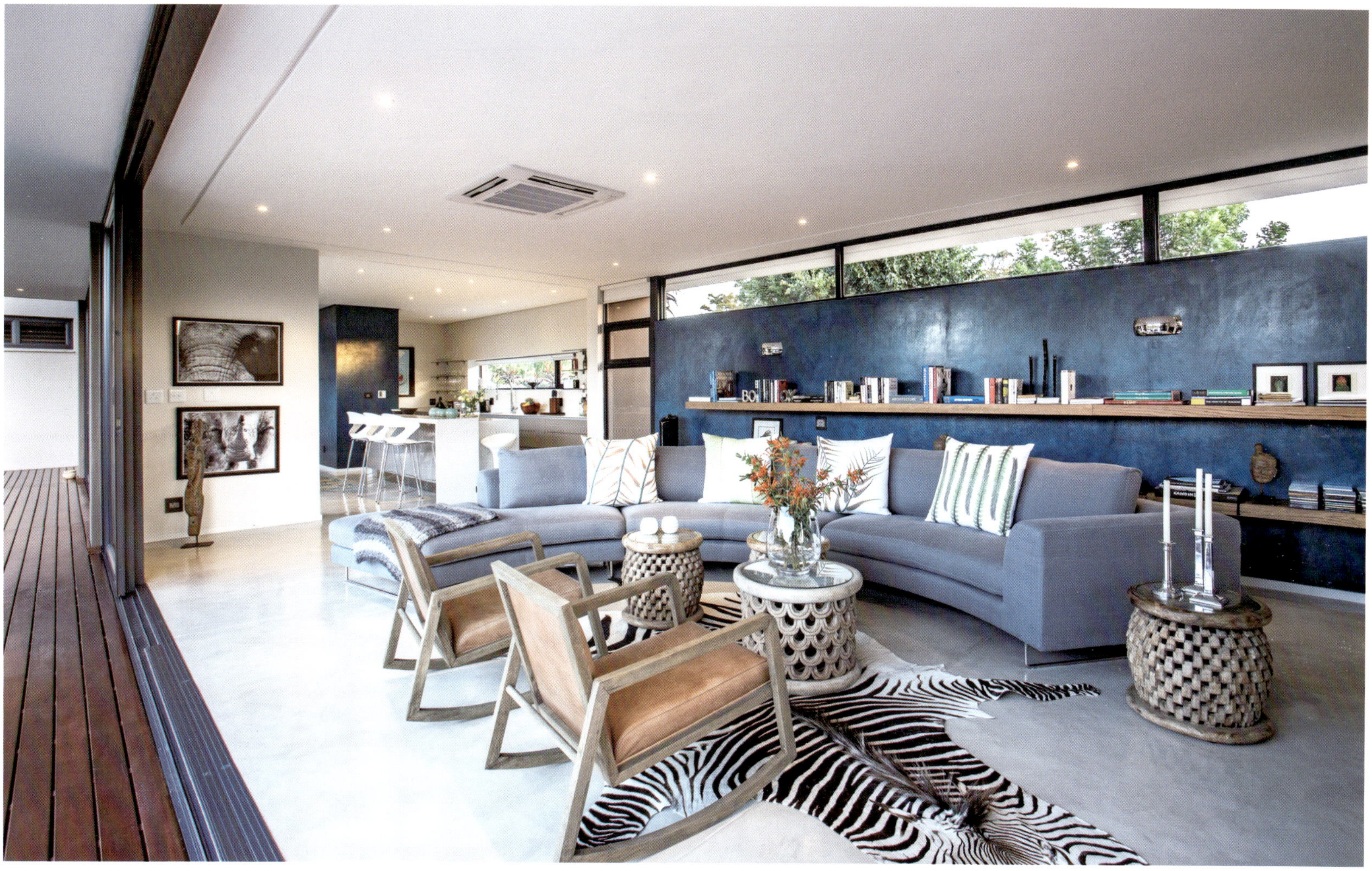

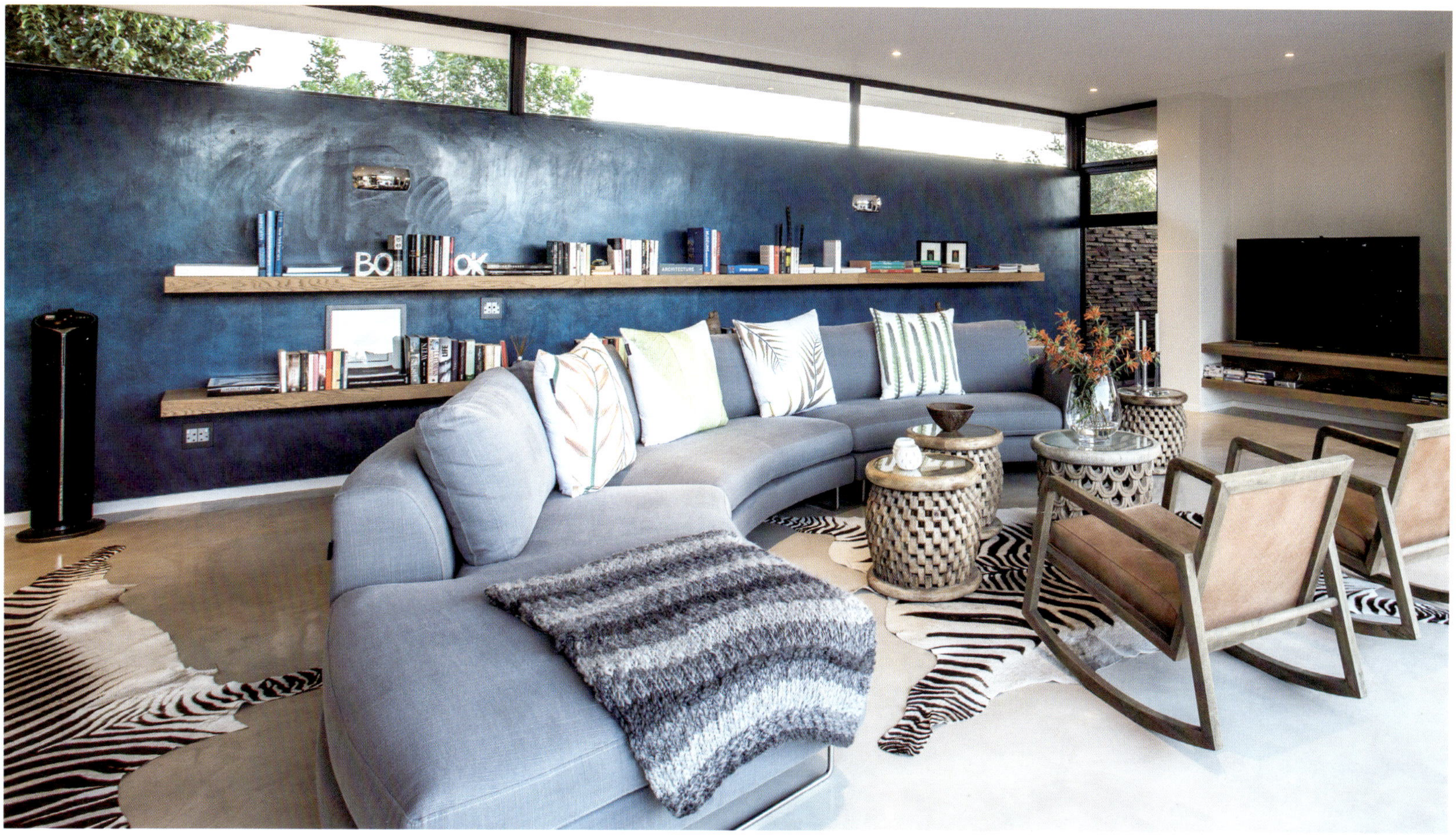

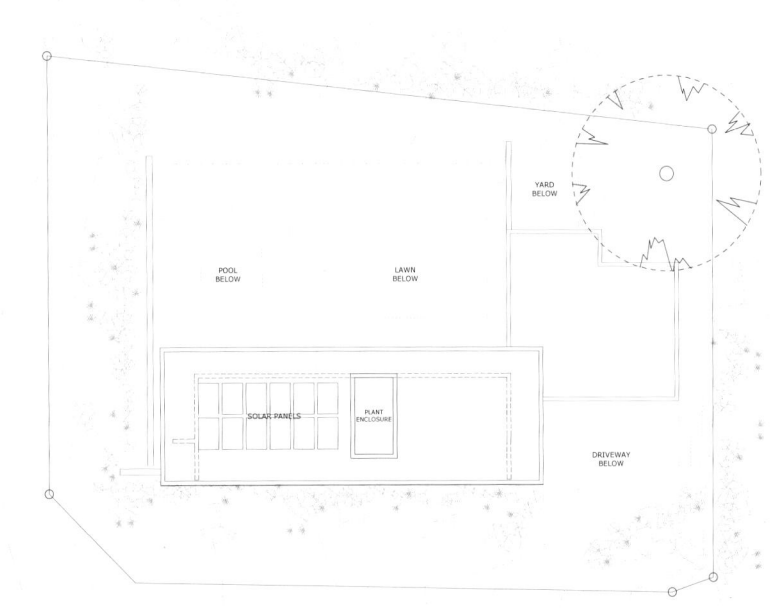

ESTATE ROAD

ROOF PLAN
SCALE

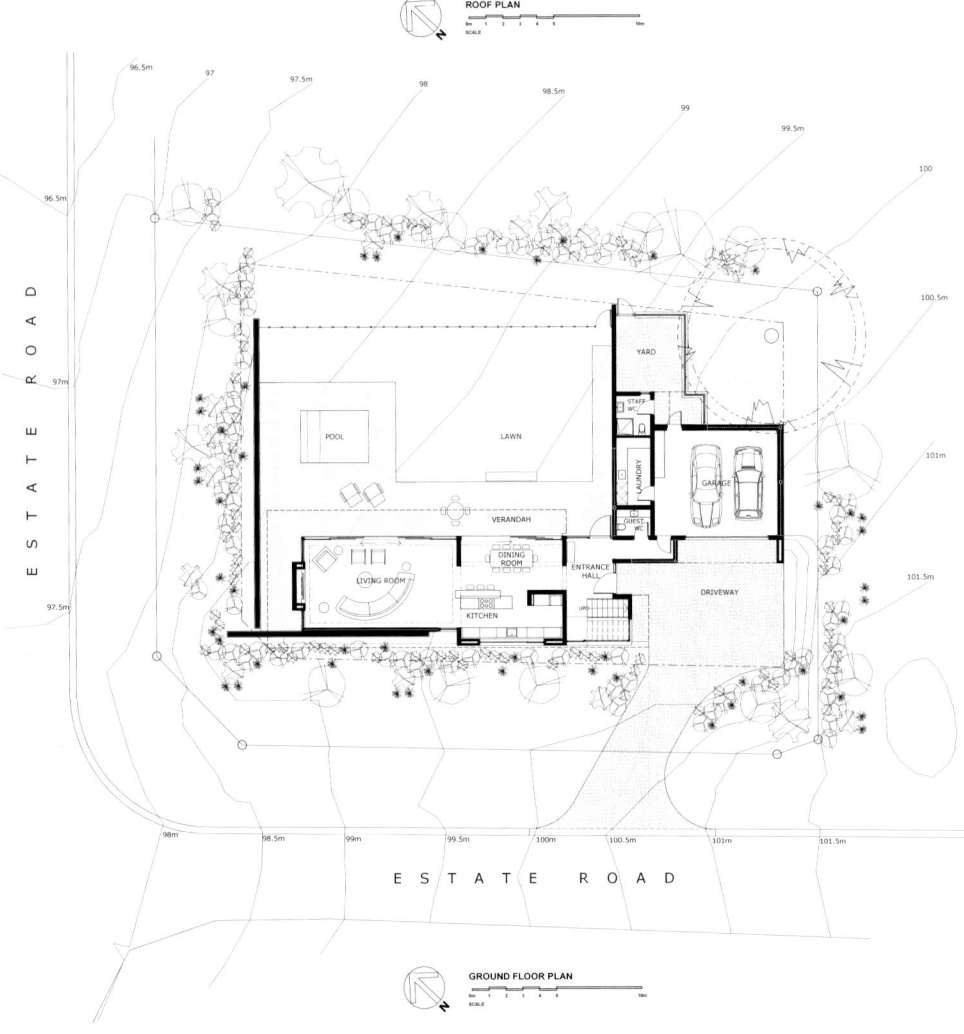

GROUND FLOOR PLAN
SCALE

The entrance to the house is a carefully considered grand, double volume arrangement of components in glass, timber and concrete and with "wrap around" form making, a signature characteristic of recent Metropole homes.

There is a sense of "big-ness" and "wow factor" right from the start.

The strong horizontal line created by the roof of the garage structure provides visual axial thrust to the point of entry, into a transparent double volume entrance area and through to the kitchen and living spaces beyond.

Internally, at ground floor level, open plan design with a minimum of dividing walls, no internal doors and level thresholds between inside and outside facilitate a user experience of a single large multi-use space that unconstricted, uncluttered and weather permitting, is able to open up and connect and extend to the outdoors.

High level perimeter strip windows visually lighten the experience of the first floor building mass overhead and enhance the experience of the vertical dimension of the living, dining and entertainment areas at ground floor level.

A generous external decked area with plunge pool and open lawn area beyond encourages the inhabitants to indulge in and celebrate an outdoor lifestyle of entertainment, play and relaxation.

At first floor level, once again the design focus was to promote a sense of openness with privacy and create a diverse, joyful place in a limited space. Whilst the need for privacy has dictated the use of doors, these doorways are full height at 2.6 m and when open allow continuity of space to be experienced through an uninterrupted ceiling plane.

The 3 bedrooms located at this level open out to an elevated balcony which allows distant views over the tree tops to the sea in the east and distant hills and the setting sun to the west. A series of movable Balau timber screens bring in filtered daylight to the clean, modernist interiors, without sacrificing privacy whilst adding a degree of detail and natural colours and texture to the modern facade.

In Aloe Ridge House there is a unity of opposites.

The clean, hard and straight lines of the man-made intervention meet the soft flowing irregular line and textures of the natural bush context in a respectful harmony.

The palette of natural materials including earthy colour tones, timber screens, decking stone cladding juxtapose with the bold and progressive architectural form making, creating a small home that packs a big punch and that is not only visually and spatially exciting, but also comfortable and intimate.

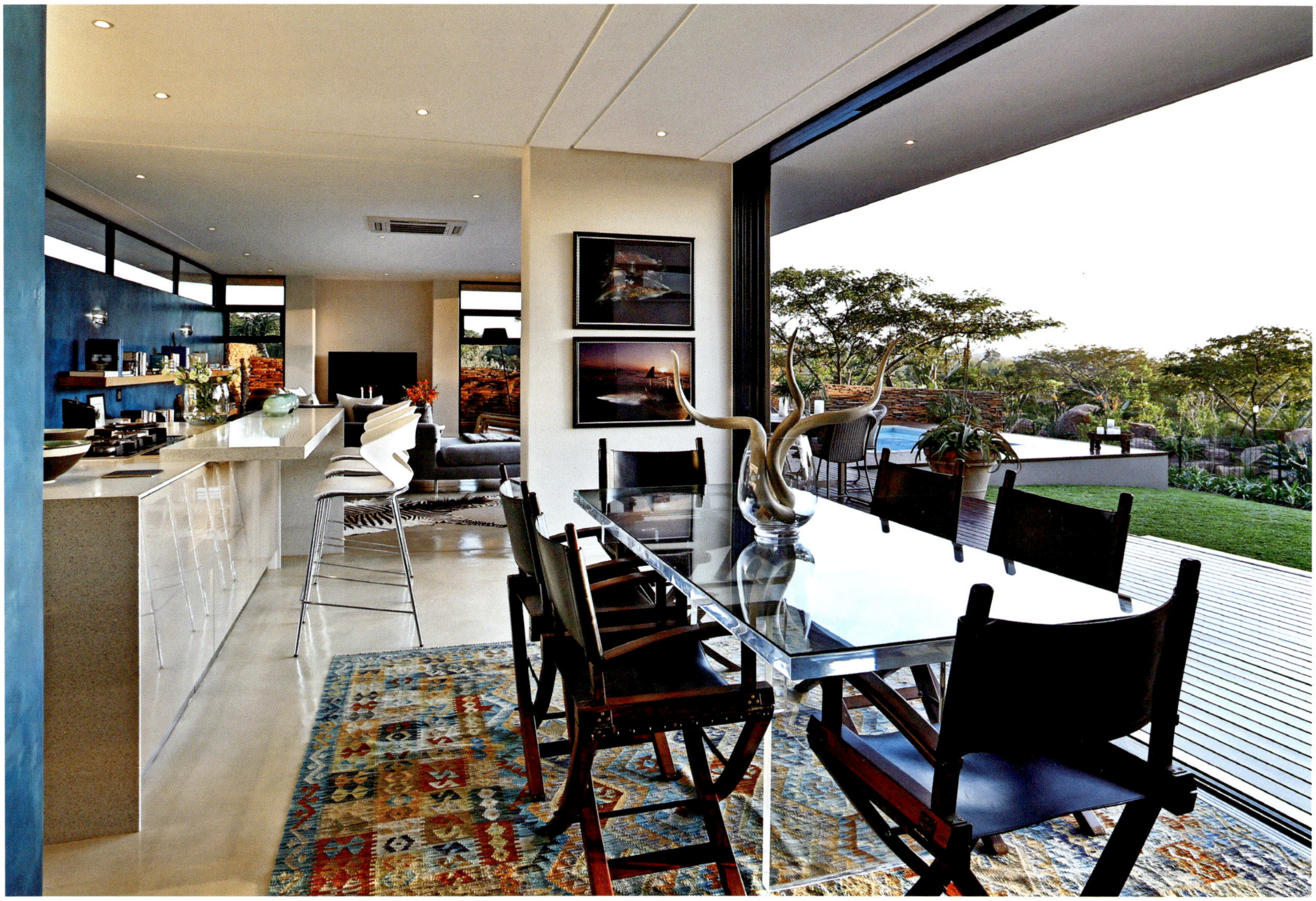

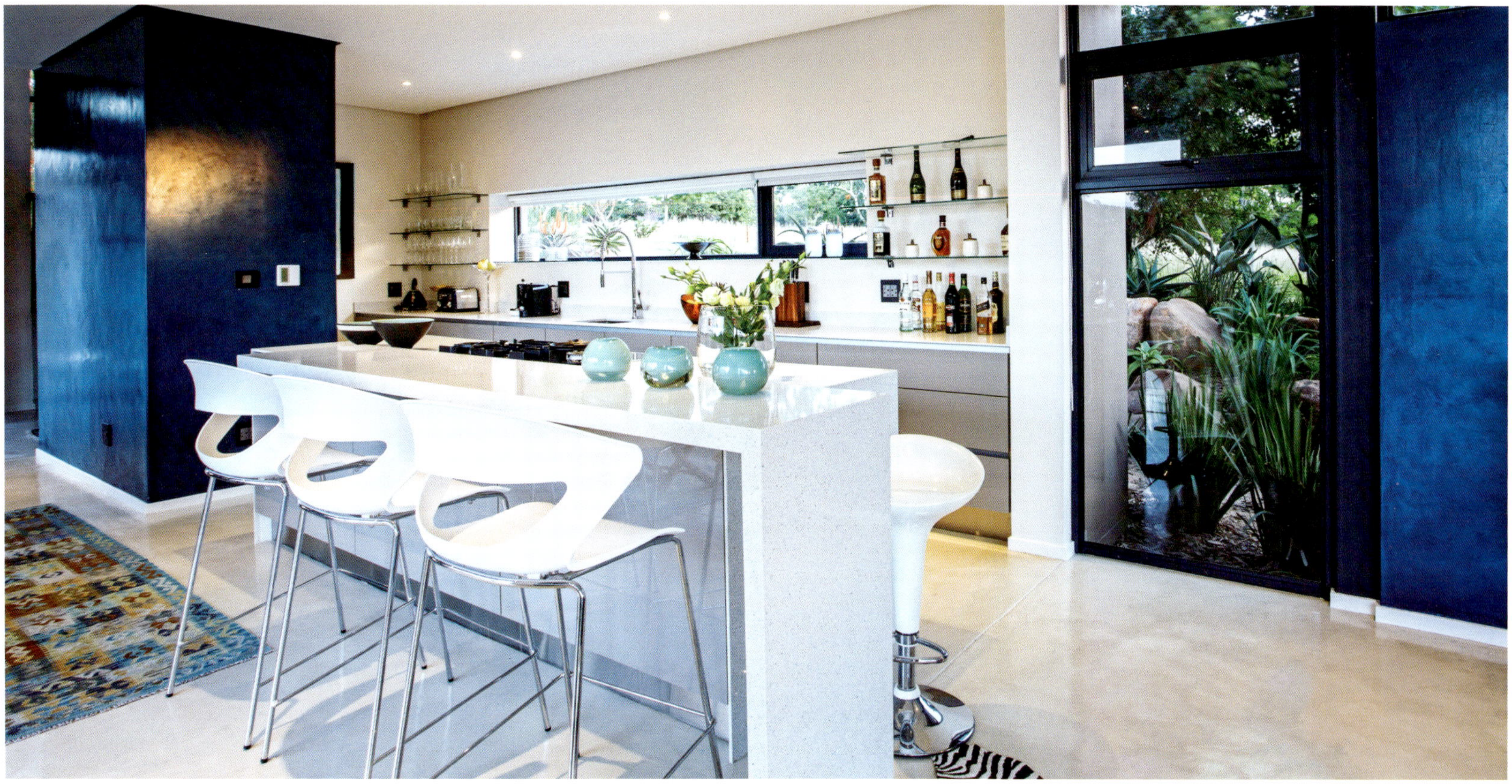

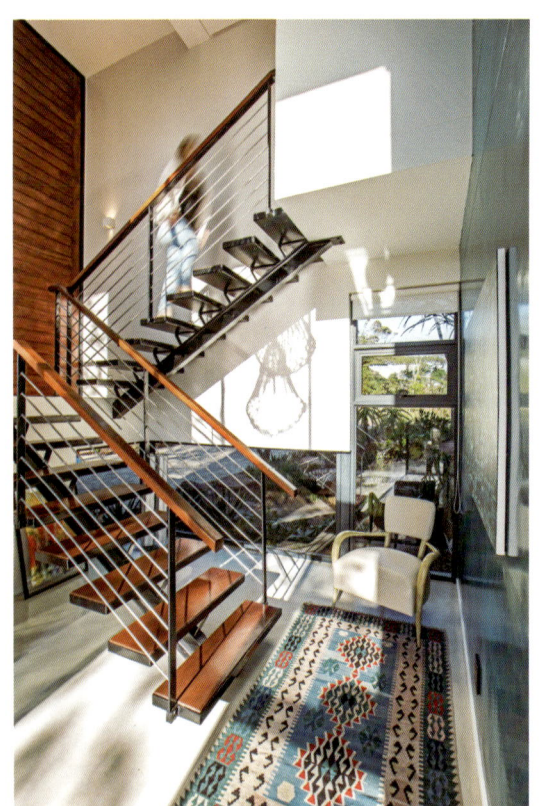

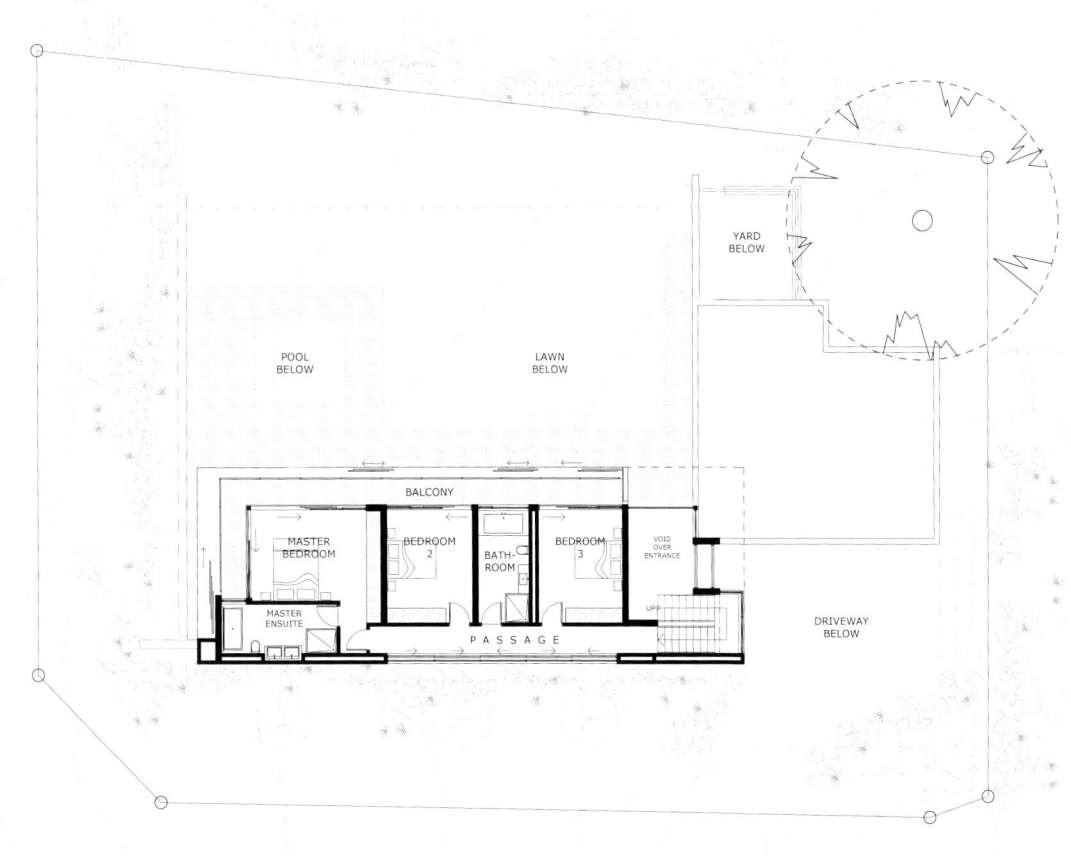

ESTATE ROAD

POOL
BELOW

LAWN
BELOW

YARD
BELOW

BALCONY

MASTER
BEDROOM

BEDROOM
2

BATH-
ROOM

BEDROOM
3

VOID
OVER
ENTRANCE

MASTER
ENSUITE

PASSAGE

UP

DRIVEWAY
BELOW

ESTATE ROAD

FIRST FLOOR PLAN

0m 1 2 3 4 5   10m
SCALE

Float House

Architects
Pitsou Kedem Architects

Design Team
Pitsou Kedem, Raz Melamed, Irene Goldberg

Photography
Amit Geron

A one storey, private residence in the center of the country. The architectural concept was to create a structure with a continuous, wide space, divided by internal courtyards and movable partitions into smaller spaces used for a variety of different functions.

The different spaces and internal courtyards are joined together into one structure by two, ultra-thin roofs supported at one central point so that seem to float in the air. The two roofs merge, one into the other and extend for 5 m over the building front walls. The entire roof is constructed from lightweight materials and, in order to provide a thin, wispy look at its edges, it is constructed with a moderate slop towards its center.

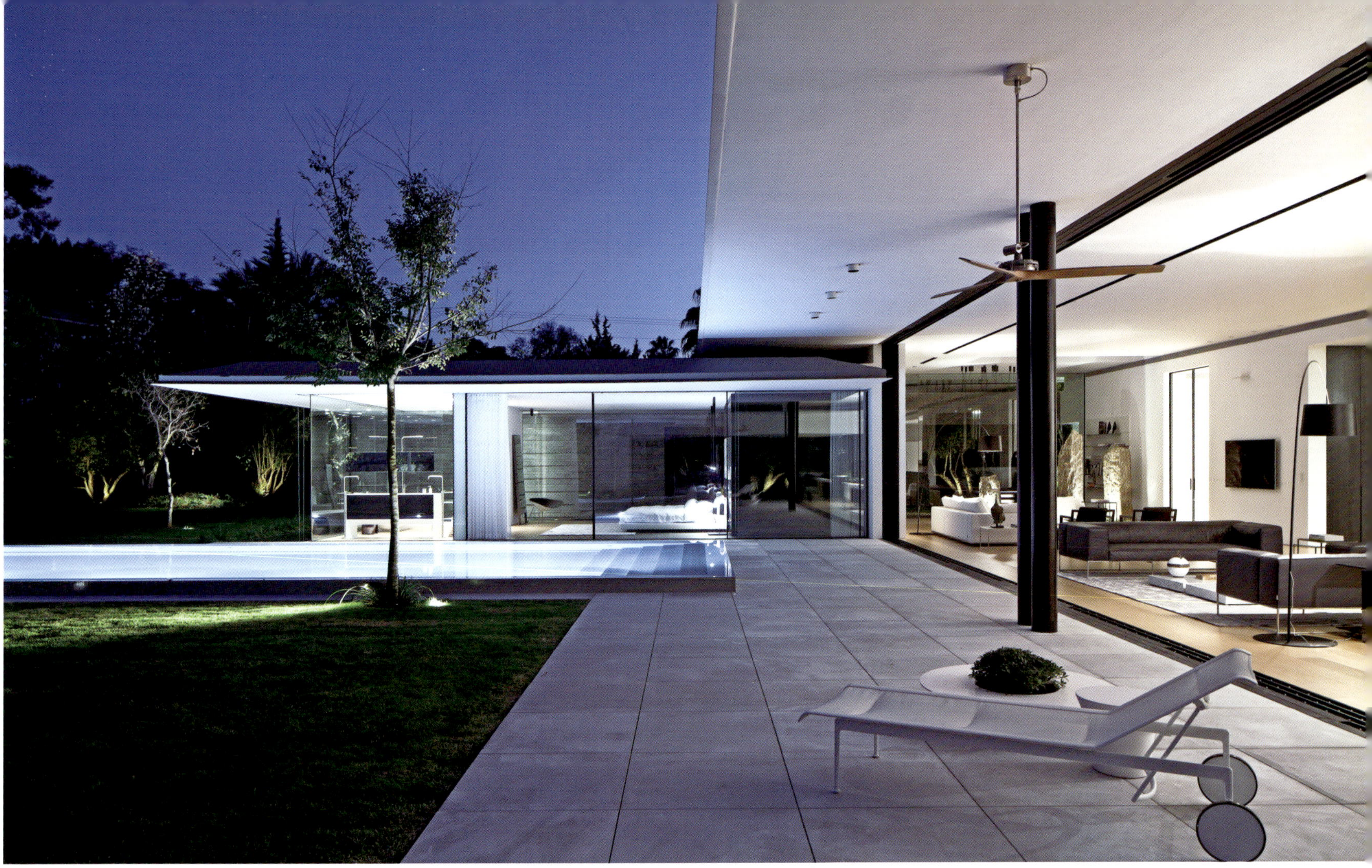
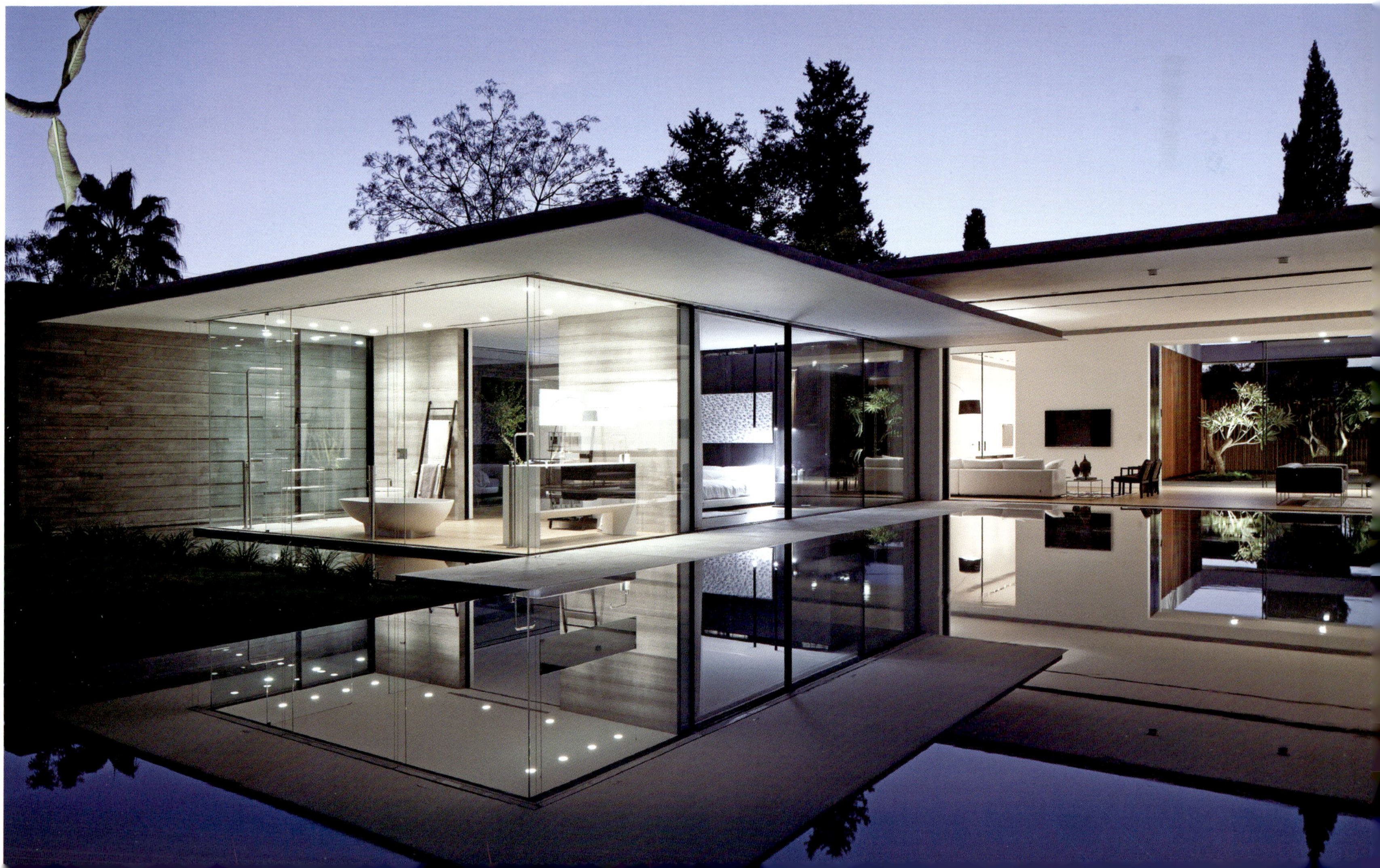

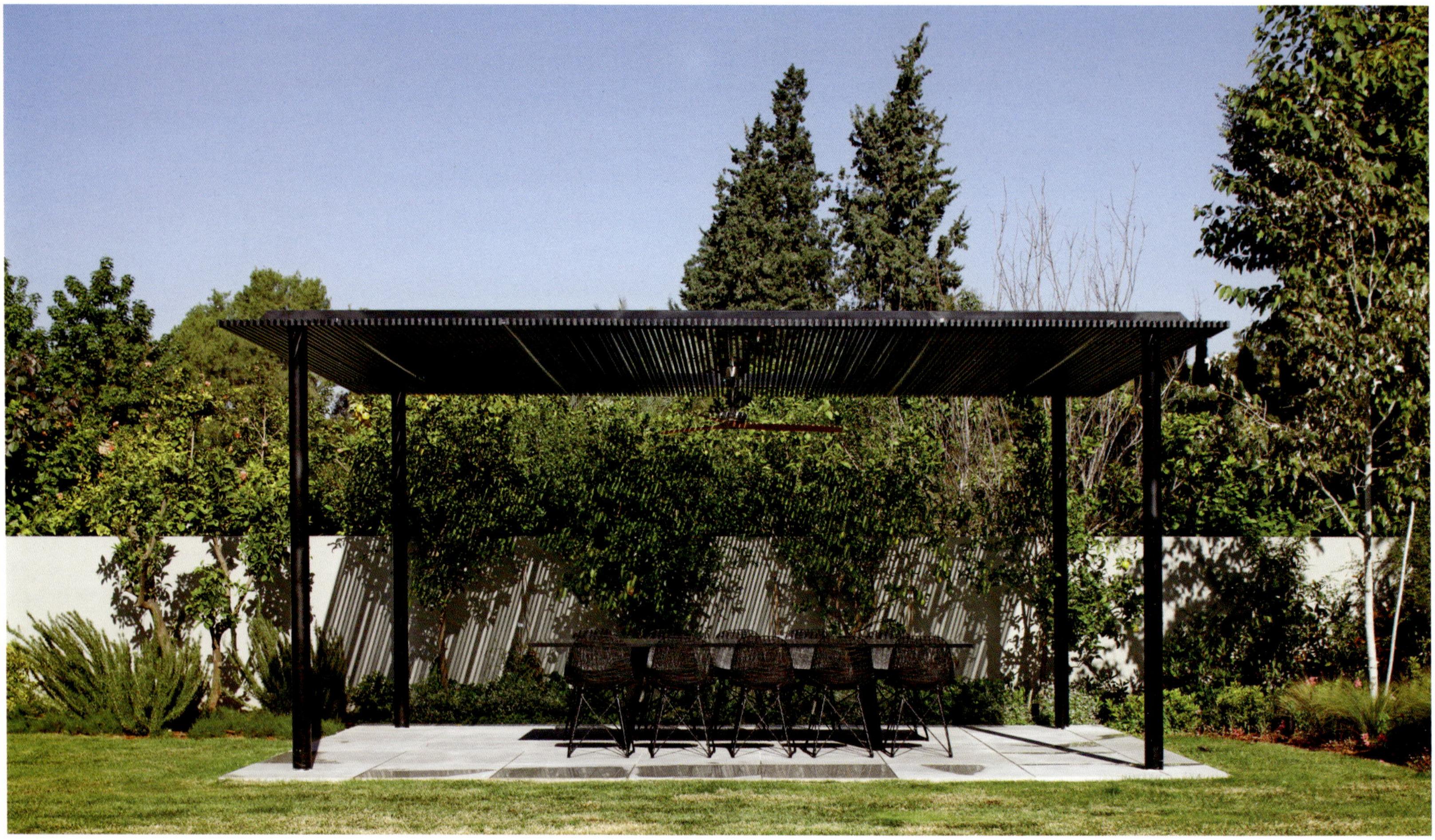

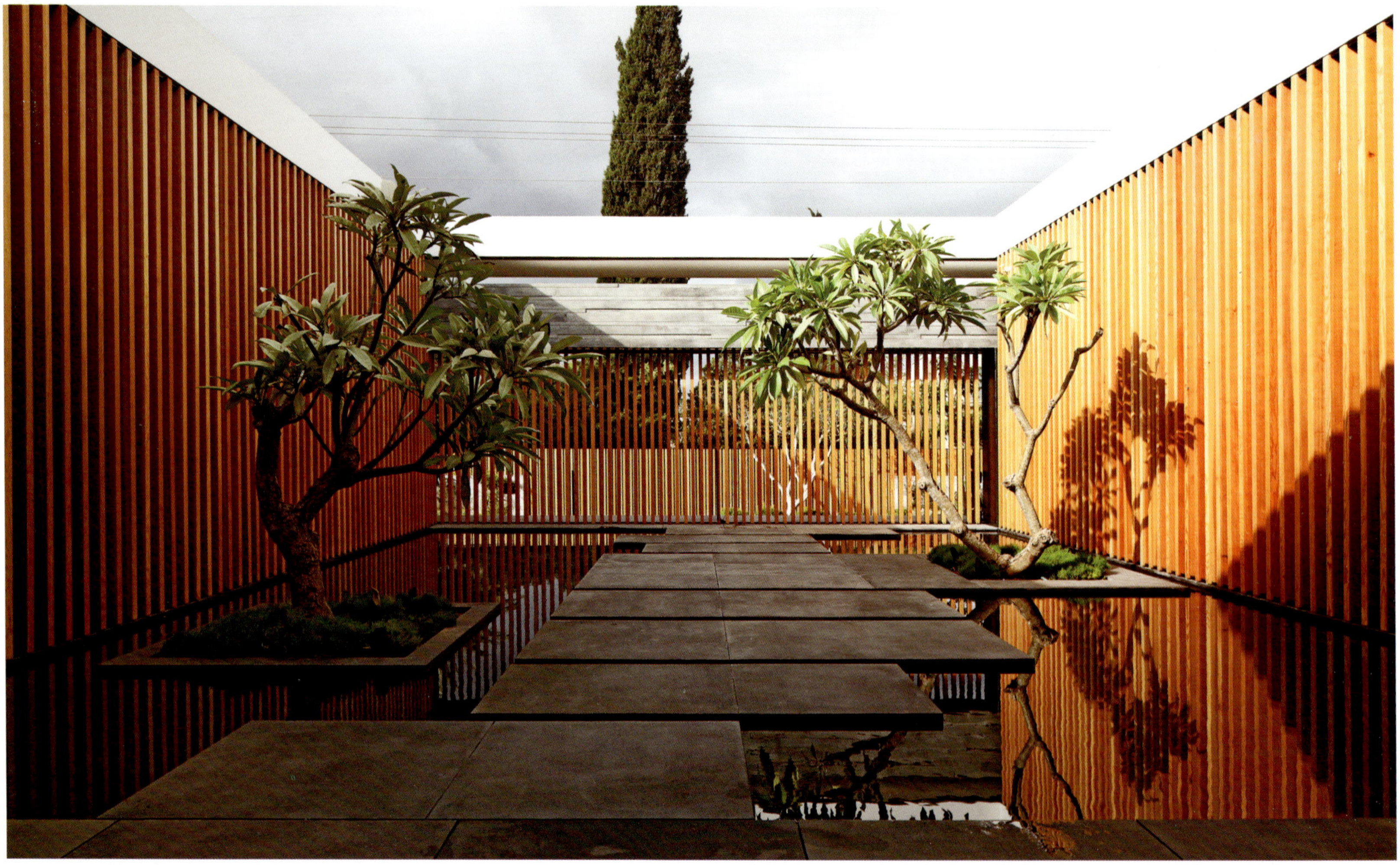

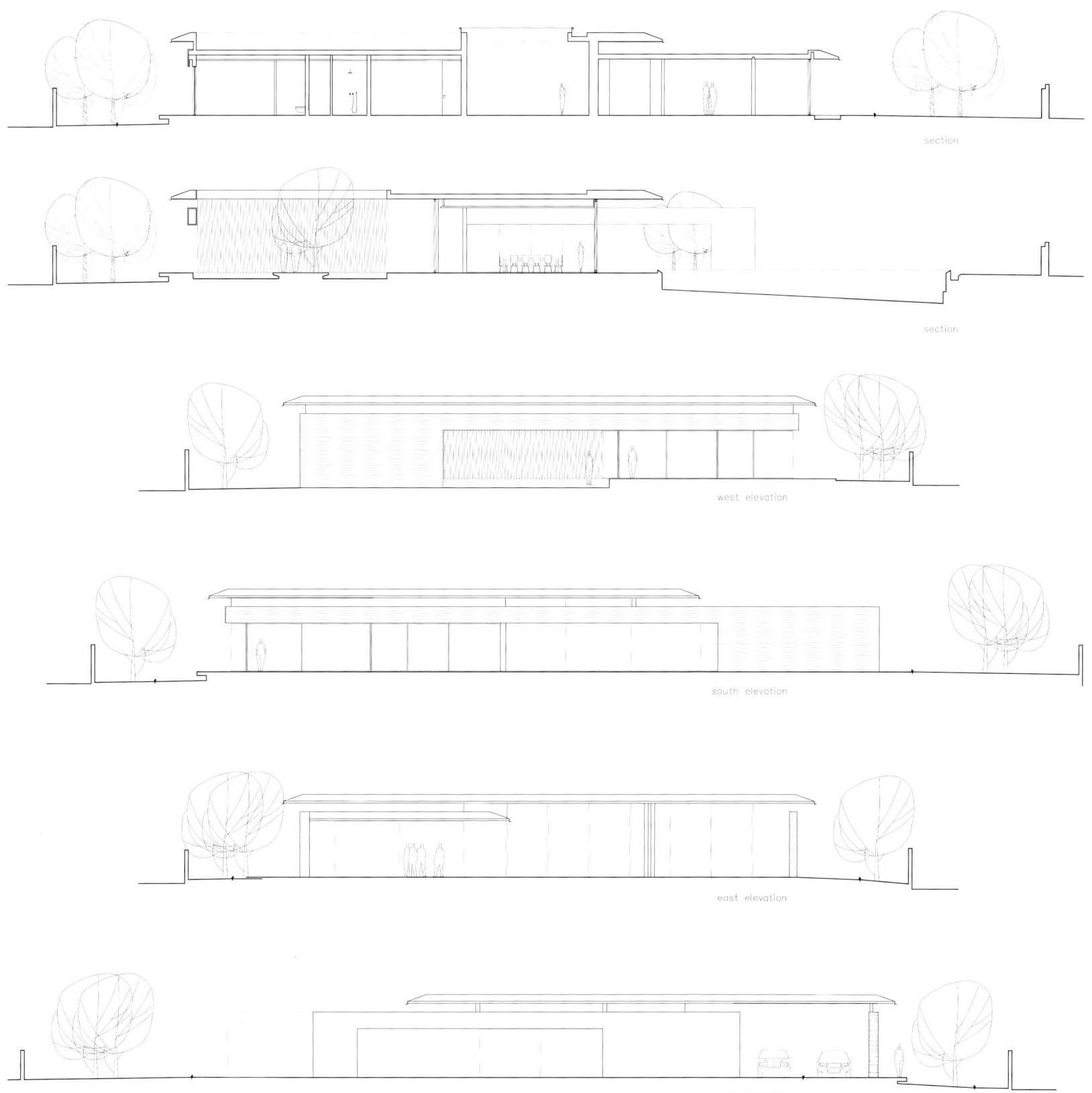

section

section

west elevation

south elevation

east elevation

north elevation

The structure itself is constructed from a series of spaces that are conceivably internal and conceivably external spaces. The entrance is framed with a wall of wooden slats which constitute what could be considered the initial boundary between the outside and the inside.

When entering the space, we pass through a space resembling an entrance lobby — again, conceivably internal and conceivably external — which embodies the soft seam between the outside and inside areas.

Whilst walking through the entrance lobby space, we cross a transparent pool,

studded with large basalt rocks and trees that seem to float on the water. As we enter the entrance lobby, we experience the illusion that the house is floating and being reflected, just as the roof appears to be floating above the structures walls.

A ribbon window running along the building's facades serves to emphasize the roof floating above the structure walls and cancels out the feeling of mass that its size suggests.

A long, narrow reflection pool follows the structure's walls, reflecting and emphasizing their covering and texture.

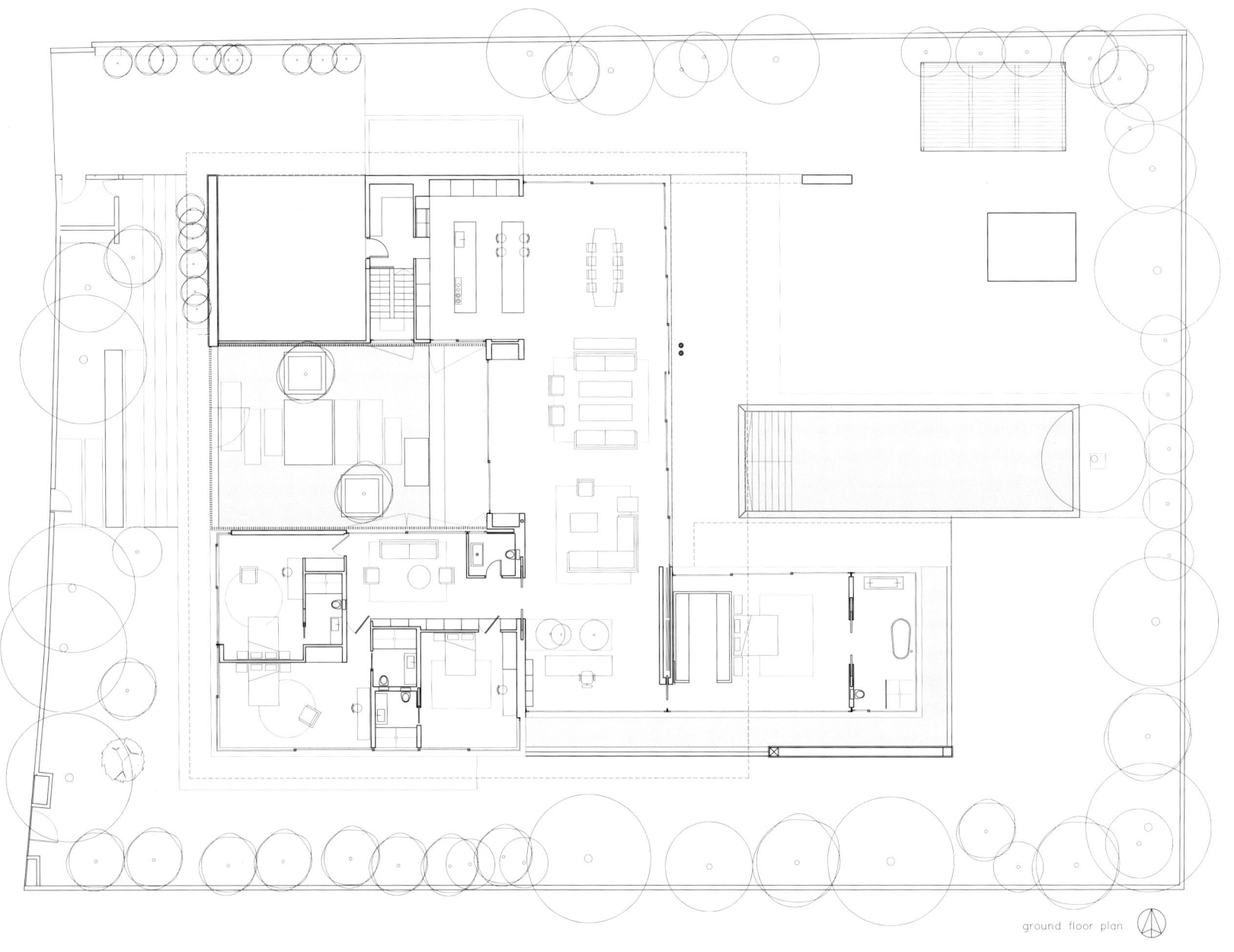

ground floor plan

Butternut

Interior Designer	Location	Area	Photography
Zimenko Yuriy	Ukraine, Kiev	200 m²	Andrey Avdeenko

The main planning challenge was to combine the two apartments into one. Consequently, the guest area, which occupies about a third part of the total useful floor area, is composed of a combined dining kitchen — drawing room, guest bathroom and a housekeeper room. The rest space is a private area, which is figuratively dimidiated: on the left are rooms of the boys and children's bathroom, across the corridor are: master bedroom, owner's bathroom and walk-in closet. On the right of the entrance room is a small laundry room. Herewith, such a matter, as the plenty of structural columns, the designer has met absolutely in a skillful way: now they are completely invisible. On the site of the balconies sprouted vast bathrooms with panoramic windows: sunniness and extent of overlook regulated by venetian blind.

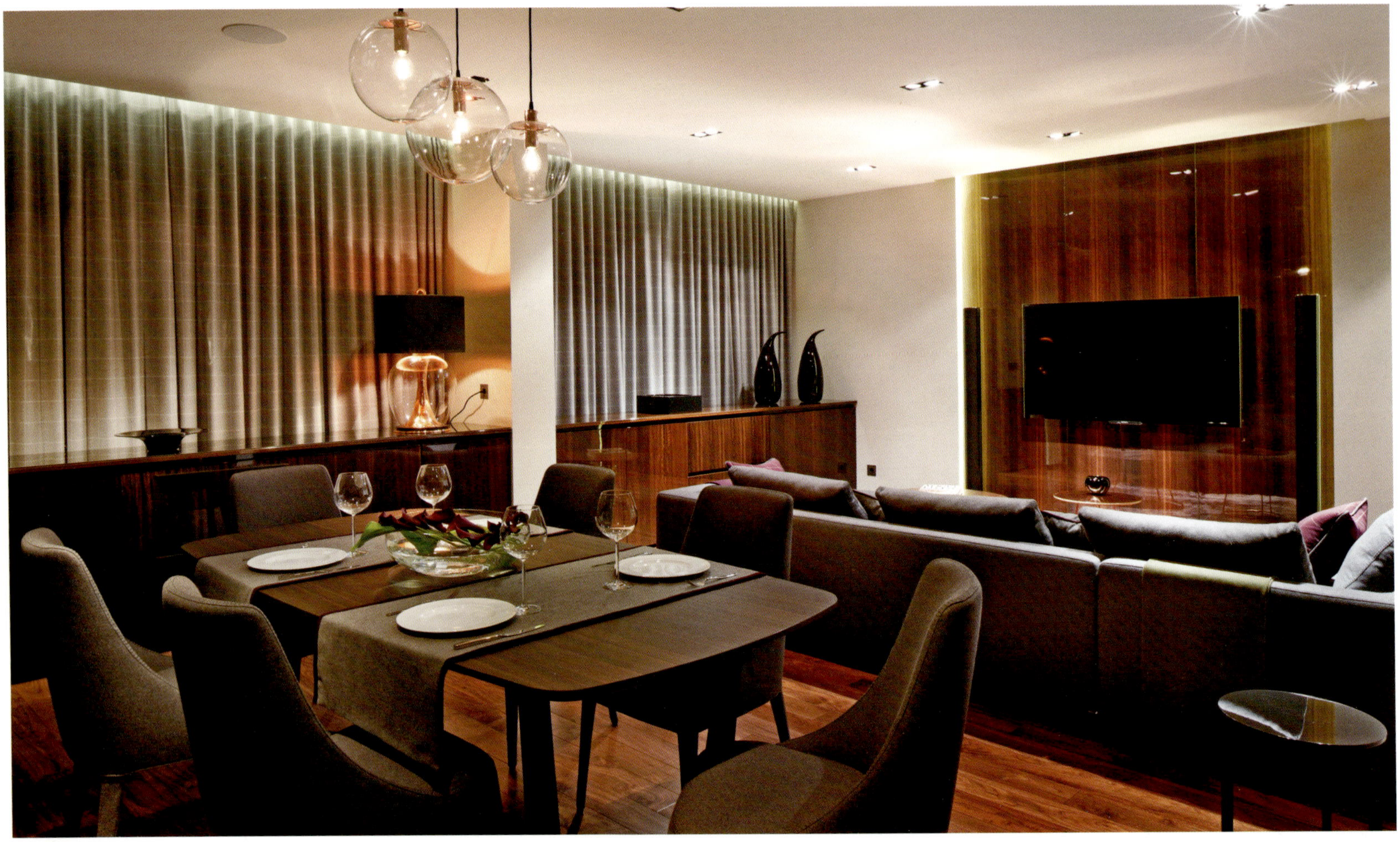

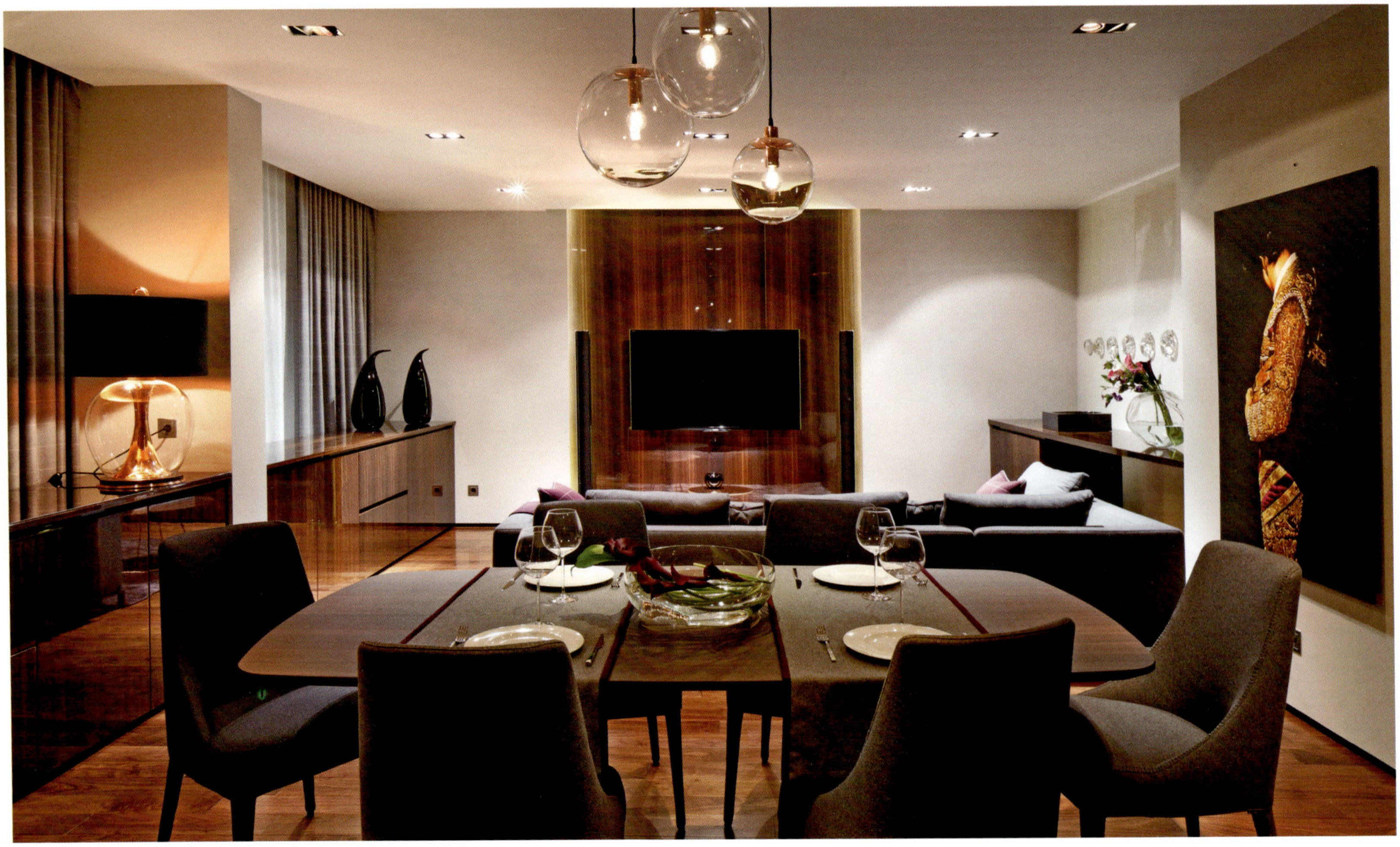

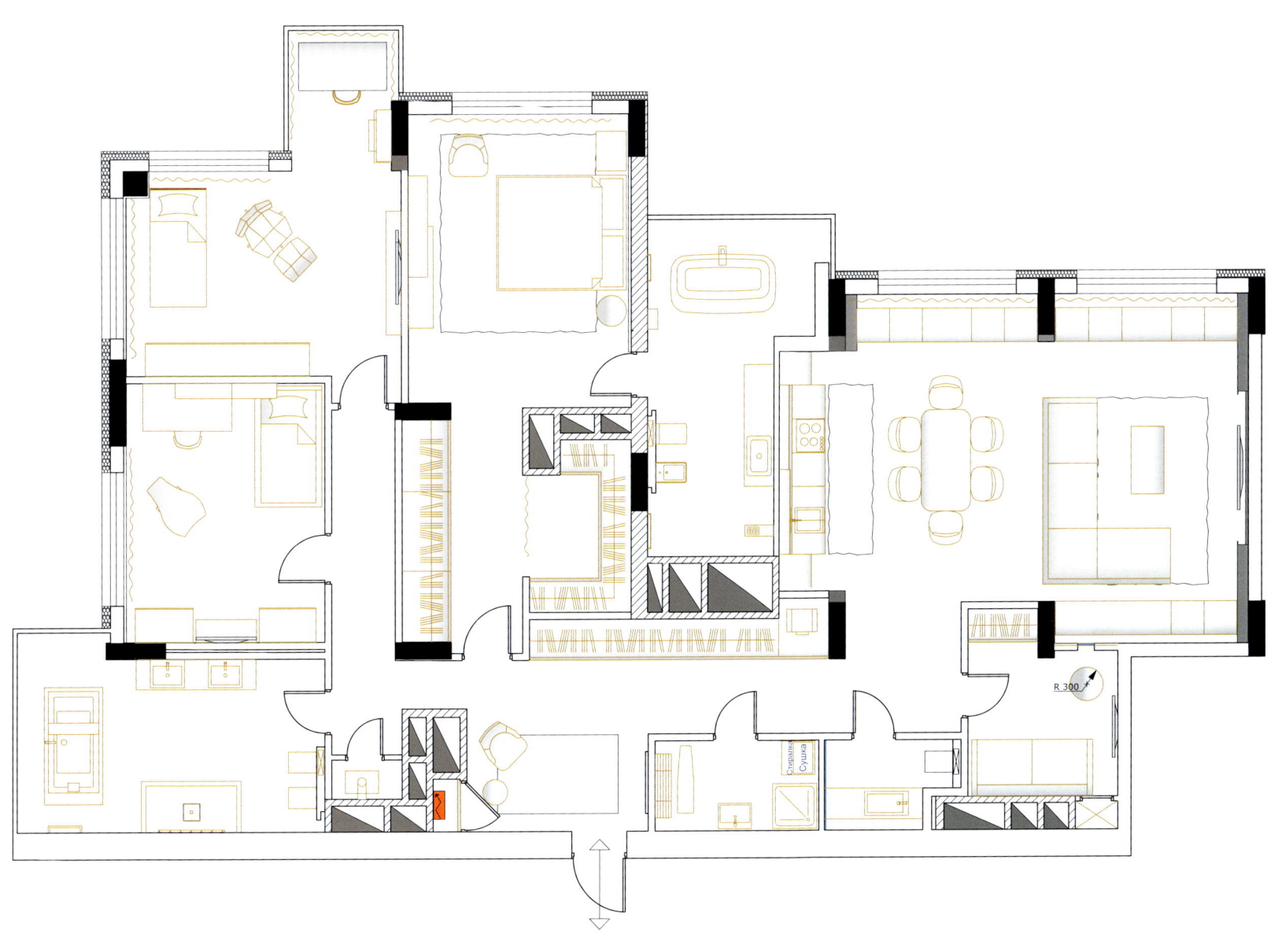

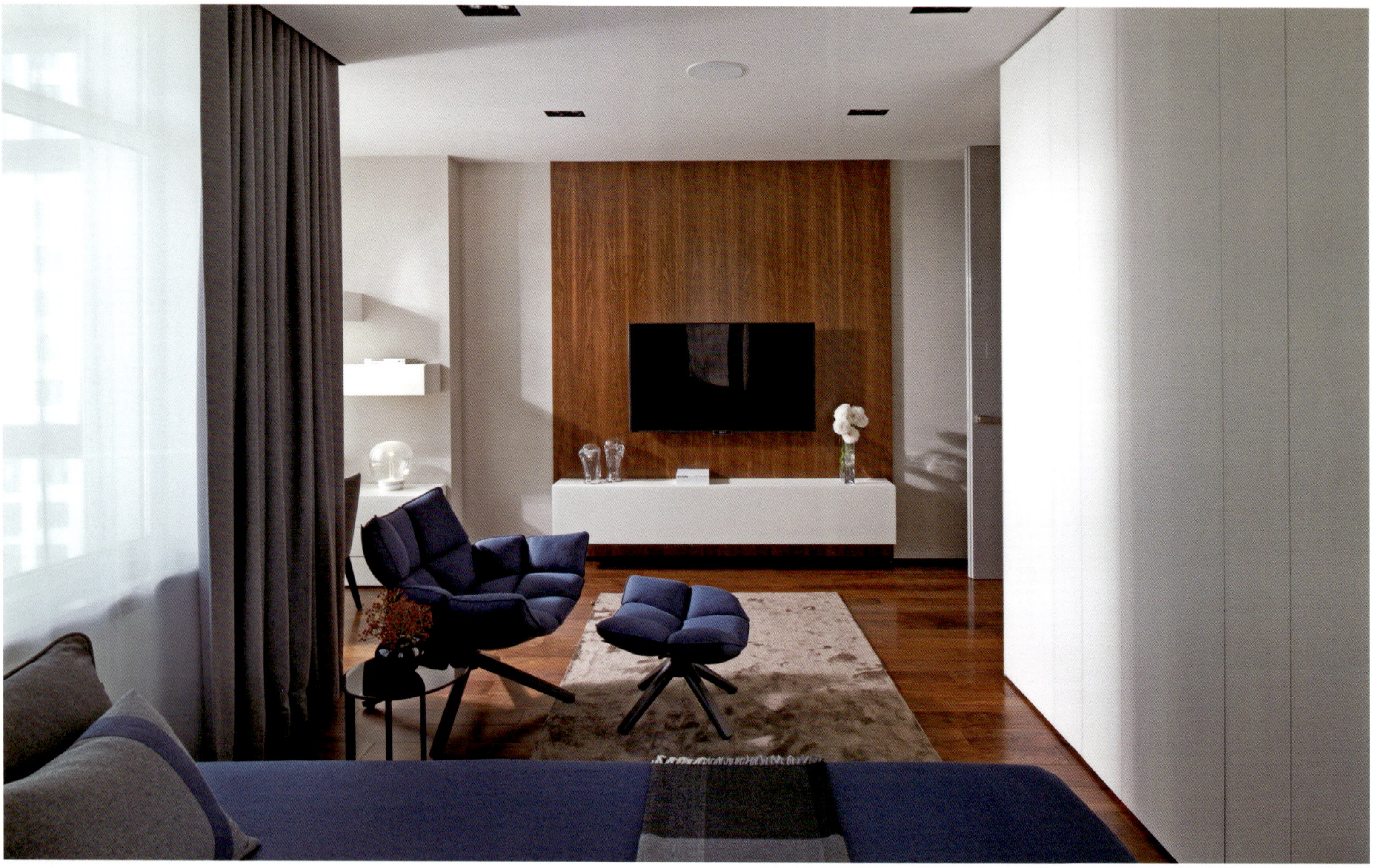

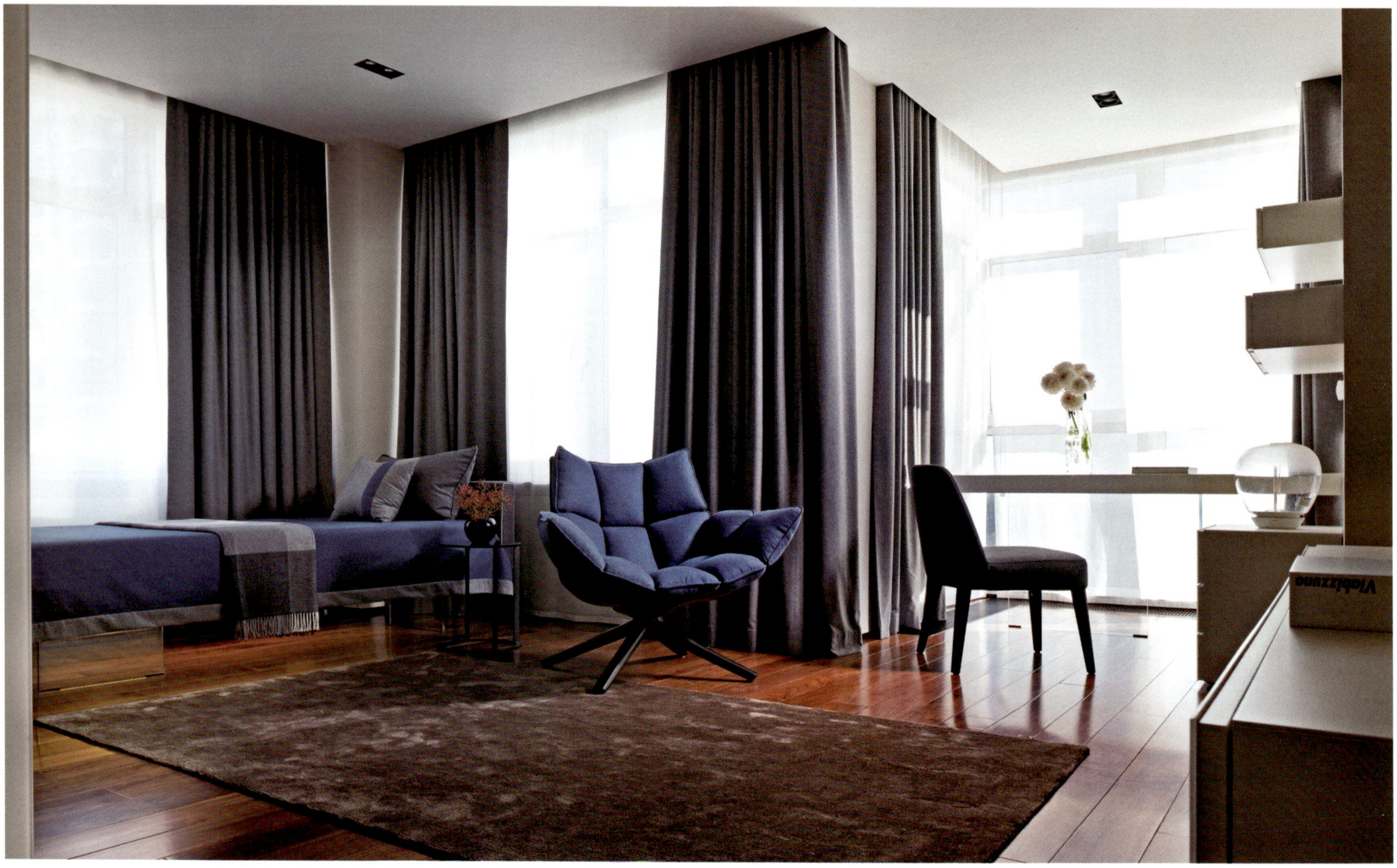

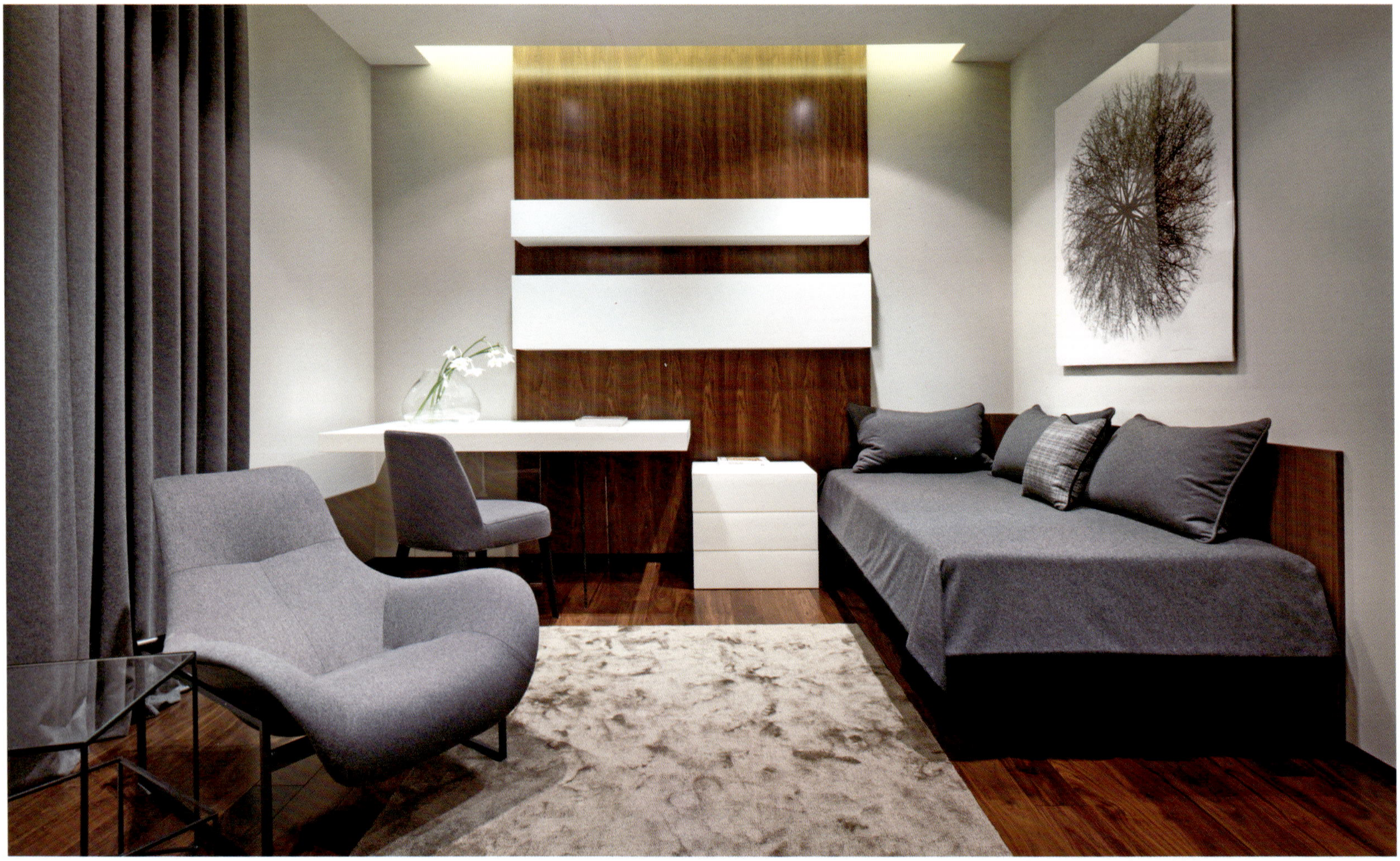

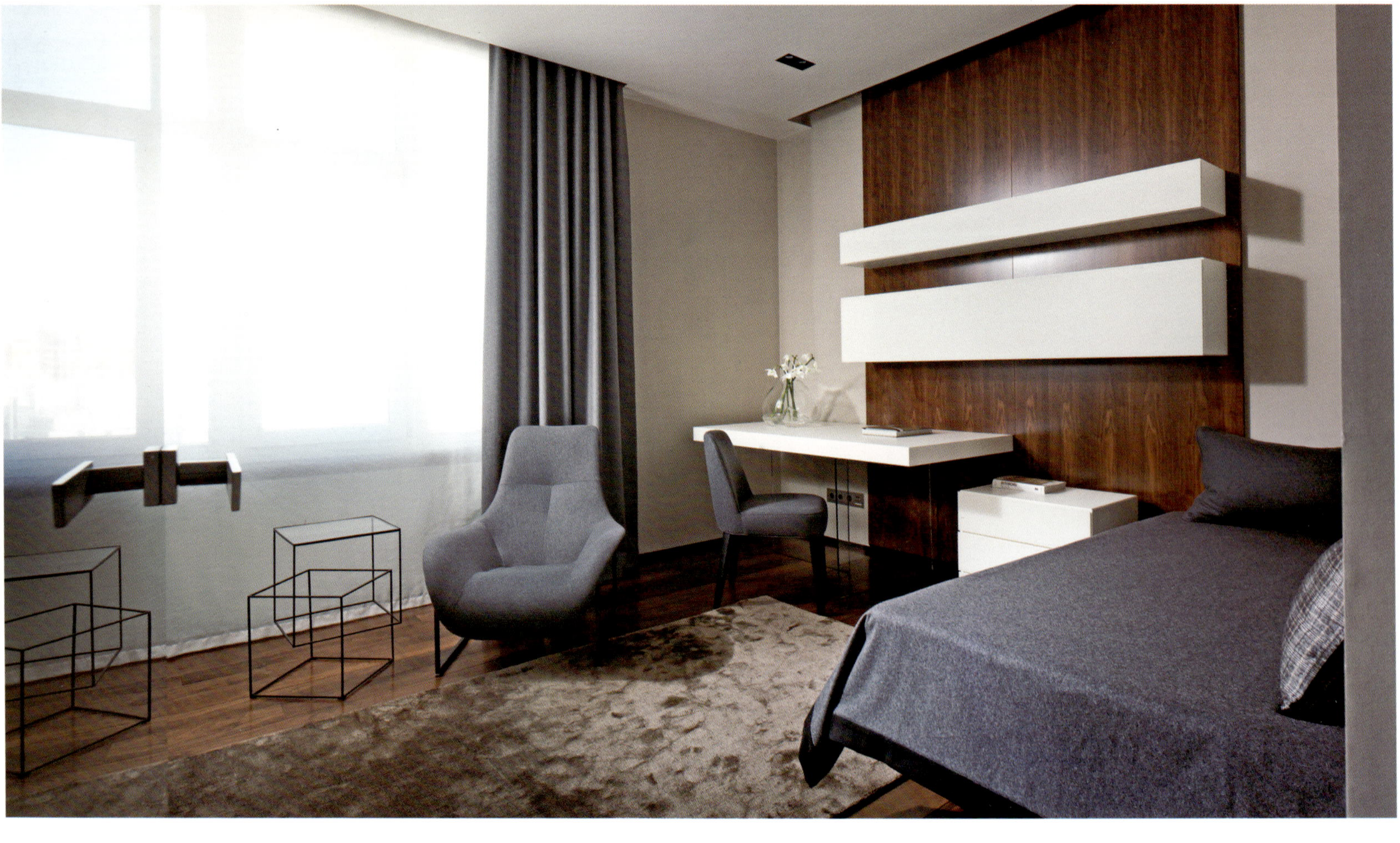

Oxford 49

Project Team
Adam Court & Tavia Pharaoh

Interior Decor
OKHA Interiors

Location
Johannesburg, South Africa

Main Furniture Supplier
OKHA Interiors

Photography
Else young

The JHB home of a French businessman with a love of art & fine entertaining. This 5 bedroom house was designed to be a multi-functional home for family, visiting friends and executive guests. The brief was to express an individual ambient character but maintain a calm and uncluttered elegance. Every vase, sculpture, artwork and furniture object is given enough meditative space to allow it to be seen and appreciated. Interiors by Antoni Associates.

Wallace Ridge

Architects
Whipple Russell Architects

Location
Beverly Hills, California

Area
622 m²

This project began with former clients' wish to move back closer to the city of Beverly Hills. They had found a potential property in Trousdale Estates and showed it to Marc for his advice on its possibilities. The property was in disrepair, had a choppy floor plan, and gabled roofs that did not fit the client's vision of a modern home. The goal, of course, was to maximize the views while creating fluid well-lit spaces that would both serve and reflect the lives of the inhabitants. Marc saw a way to stay within the Trousdale Estates' single storey 4.3 m height restriction and still provides spaciousness and a spectacular view.

The entire core of the house was redesigned to feature an open plan, high ceilings and a sleek flat roof. The front door, flanked by large glass panels opens to a wide entry a perfect stage for a piano and provides an open sight line across the living area, though 3.7 m high glass walls and 2.4 m high glass sliding pocket doors, to the patio and pool.

The clients do a lot of entertaining and required a kitchen that was open to the living and outdoor spaces. Rooms are minimally defined using tall panels, custom stained in a rich coffee bean brown, that contrast with the light walls, spaces suited to artwork. The warm modernism the clients wanted was achieved with a harmonious use of materials as kitchen, dining, entertaining and living room spaces flow easily into one another. In the living area a large screen television and fireplace are recessed into wall-sized expanse of Portico Slate tile by SOLI. In the kitchen, the island and countertops are Caesar stone in Lagos Blue and cabinets have an acrylic lacquered finish.

Large glass pocket doors open to the outside from both kitchen and living areas, where there is a patio bar, conversation areas and a tabletop fireplace all encircling the pool. The master suite also opens to the pool though large sliding glass panels. To create a vantage point for the best view, a roof terrace was built atop the master suite, accessible from the pool area. The master terrace provides space for entertaining, sunbathing, a game of table tennis, and a view all the way to the Pacific. Below, the master wing offers a library/sitting room, and a home theater.

Next to the bedroom, the master bath continues the use of brown with the tile in the master shower — a basket weave pattern from SOLI. Adjacent is a roomy closet/dressing area. As there is a musician in the family, the clients wanted to find space for a full music studio; Marc found it by digging down and locating the studio beneath the motor court. It includes a separate control room, sound booth for vocal recording, and tracking room, a soundproofed oasis for creation.

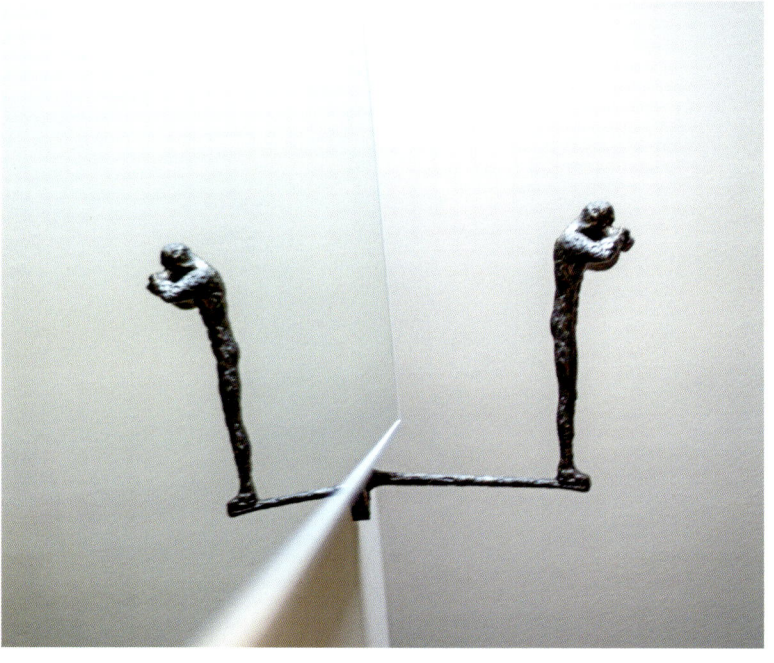

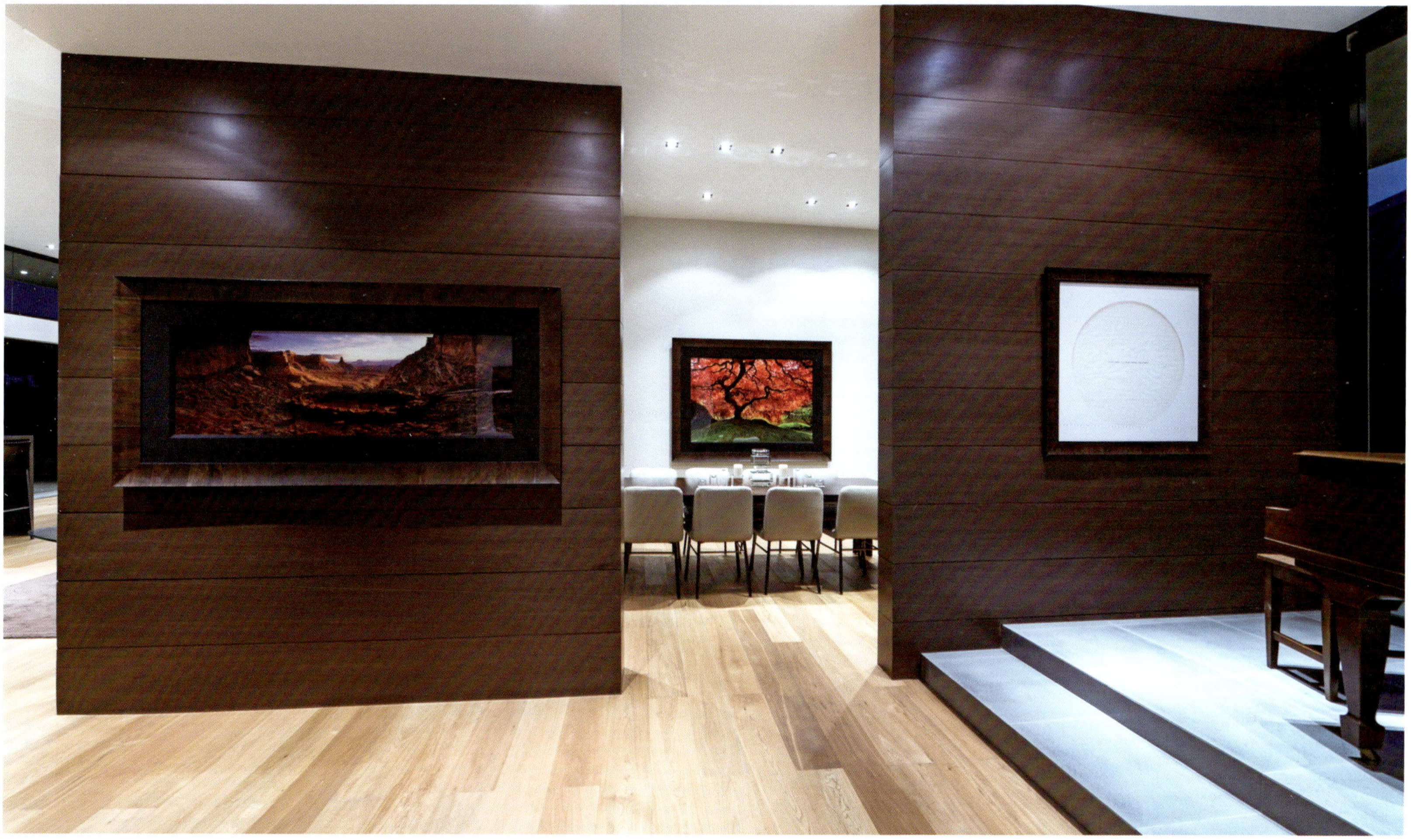

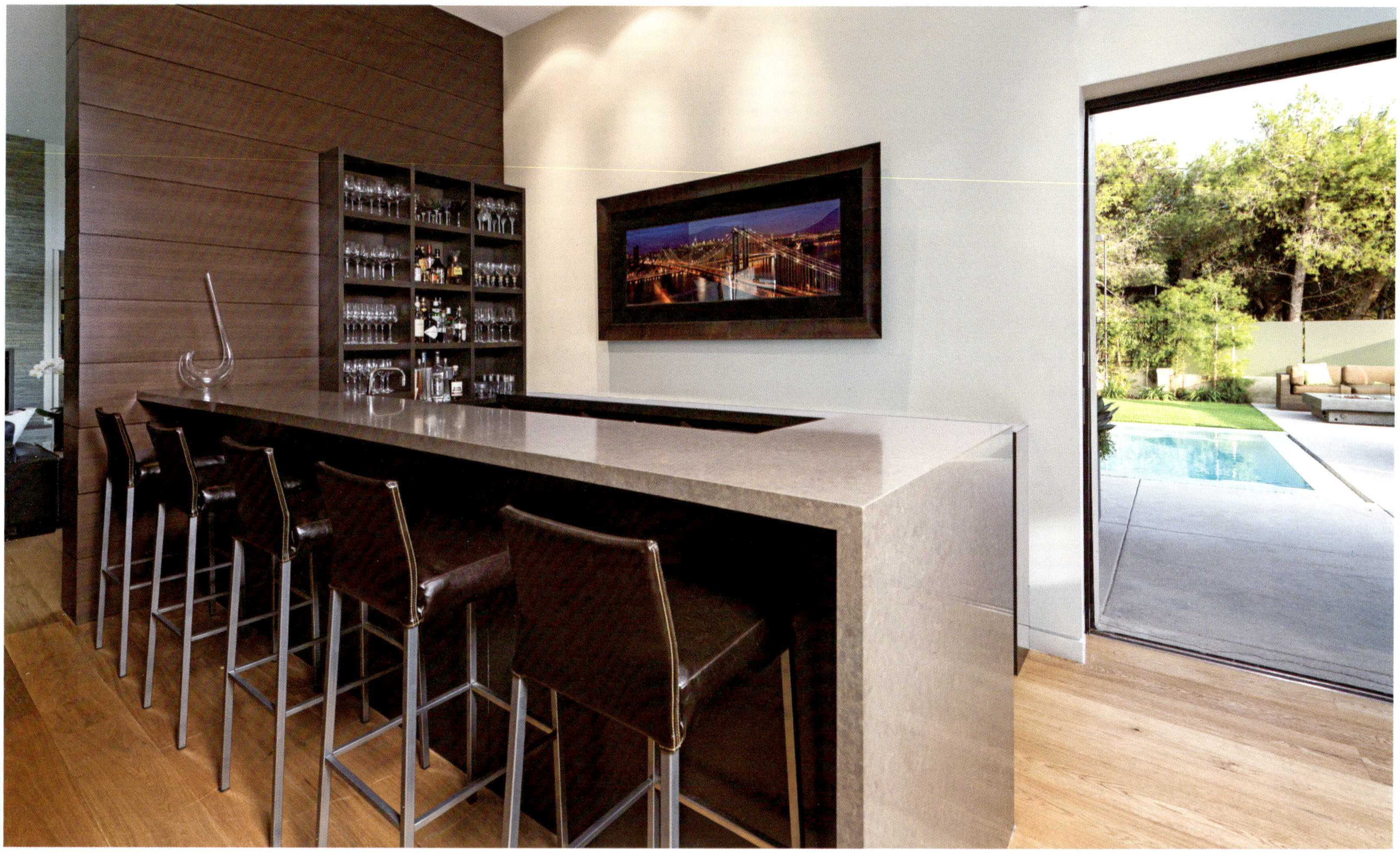

girl the right shoes
and she can
conquer the world.
Bette Midler

Clovelly House

Architects
Rolf Ockert Design

Location
Sydney, Australia

Client
Private

Builder
Tony Kerle - SL Wilson

Photography
Sharrin Rees

The design process, complex due to several defining key issues inherent to the site, ended up taking us through some radically different sketch options before settling on the one that was finally pursued.

These key factors together with of course countless smaller factors and decisions along the way shaped the house to what it is. The unusual but elegant roof shape allows sunlight in while still allowing neighbours to enjoy water views over the lower end. The expressive angled concrete wall mirrors the roof shape but in negative, resulting in complex facade geometry along the main face, enhanced by the movement of ever changing shadows over the shapes.

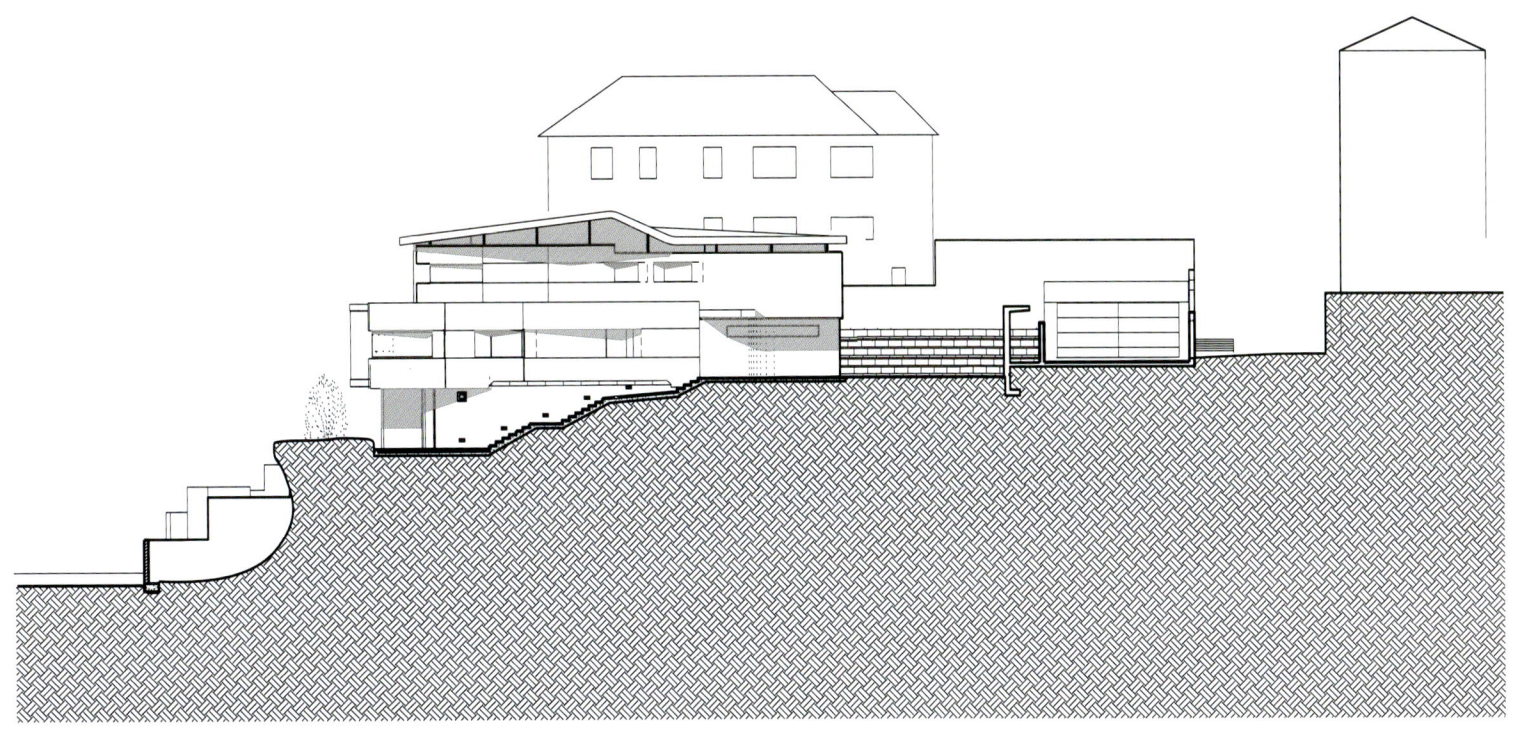

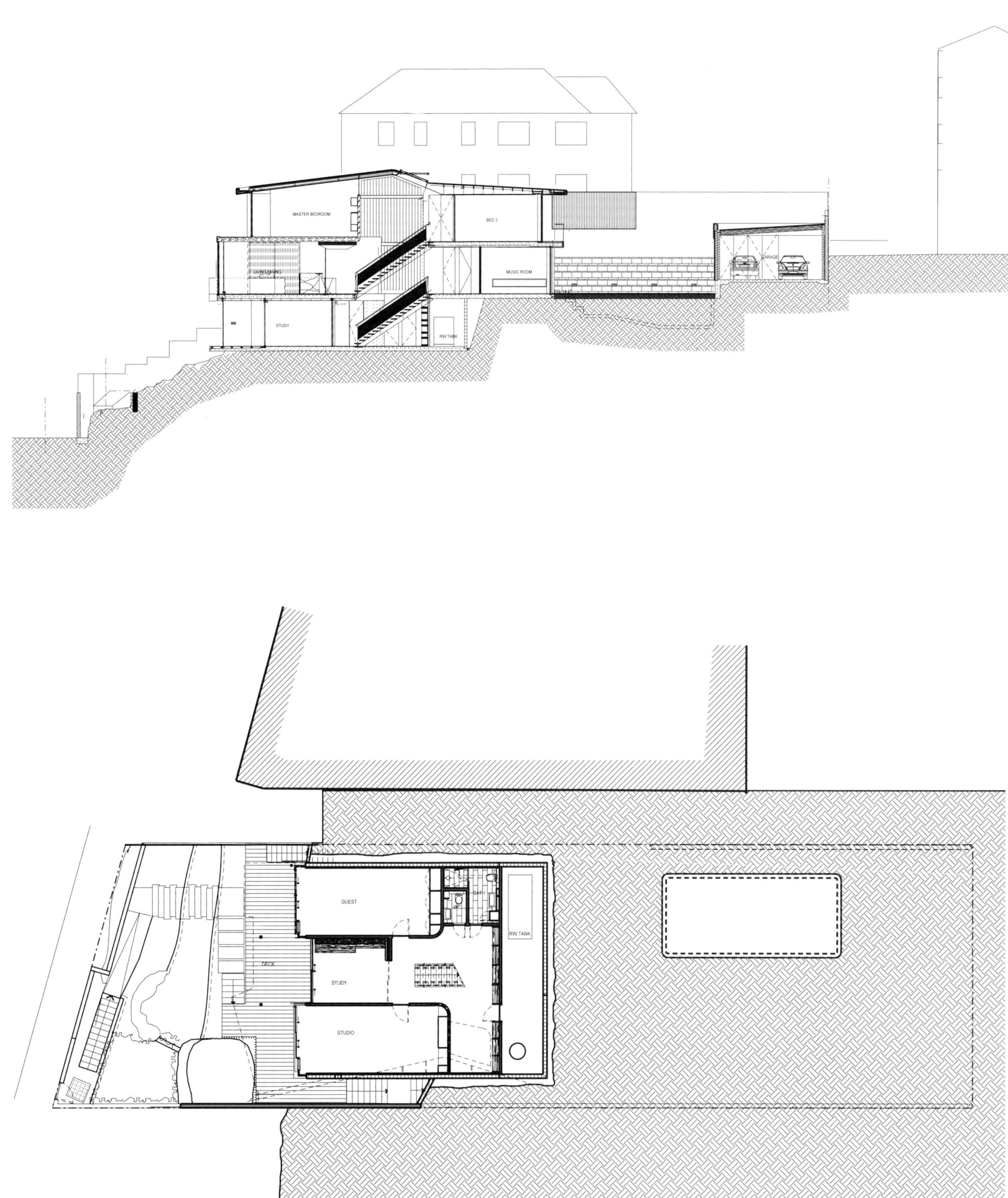

The light void also contains the central circulation, the stairs. These are light and airy without looking or feeling flimsy. To the north of are 2 levels, to the south 3, taking advantage of the natural slope of the site. The main living space is on the entry level, connecting it with the northern garden and pool as a very generous central family area. Upstairs are the bedrooms, on the southern lower level several areas for more individual activities, study, studios and library.

As a consequence of the relentless southerly winds the house was designed, unusually and against our original instinct, without any opening windows facing south. Instead large frameless floor-to-ceiling double glazed elements allow uninterrupted views over the Pacific and allow a more intimate visual connection than framed openable glazing elements would have afforded.

An outdoor deck is attached to the side of the living area, allowing outdoor activity on suitable days without interruption of the front row feel the house enjoys.

The original southern slope in front of the house was full of building rubble from some previous building incarnation. Once that was all removed several large natural sandstone blocks that had fallen eons ago and stood upright, affording us an unexpected, giant Japanese-style rock garden.

The materials for the house were chosen for a variety of reasons. First of all they had to be suitable for the harsh salt spray environment where everything gets a thick coating of corrosive salt within a few days. They were also desired to be suitable for the location, reminiscent of flotsam, rich but weathered. Finally, the rich natural palette of coastal colours, grey and red in the rocks, blues and greens in ocean and sky, provided already a magnificent canvas of hues and textures dominating large parts of the house. The rich geometry in the house as well as the resulting ever changing play of light in the interior and exterior spaces also meant that we did not feel the need for strong colour or texture, elements we often love to employ in other settings.

The resulting material palette relies on very few elements, the strong raw concrete, along the outside wall as well as to the living room ceiling. A dark Zinc roof, being allowed to weather. Dark timber in floors and joinery, both offset with white walls and joinery faces. And of course the ubiquitous glass. Both, outside floors and walls as well as interior benches are finished in the same, earthy grey stone. Having these few elements used in a diverse range of applications throughout the house also helped to tie the many different spaces of the house together to a coherent whole.

Environmental concerns also played a big role in the development of the design. The aforementioned central void allows natural light deep into the heart of the house, eliminating the need for artificial lighting during daytime.

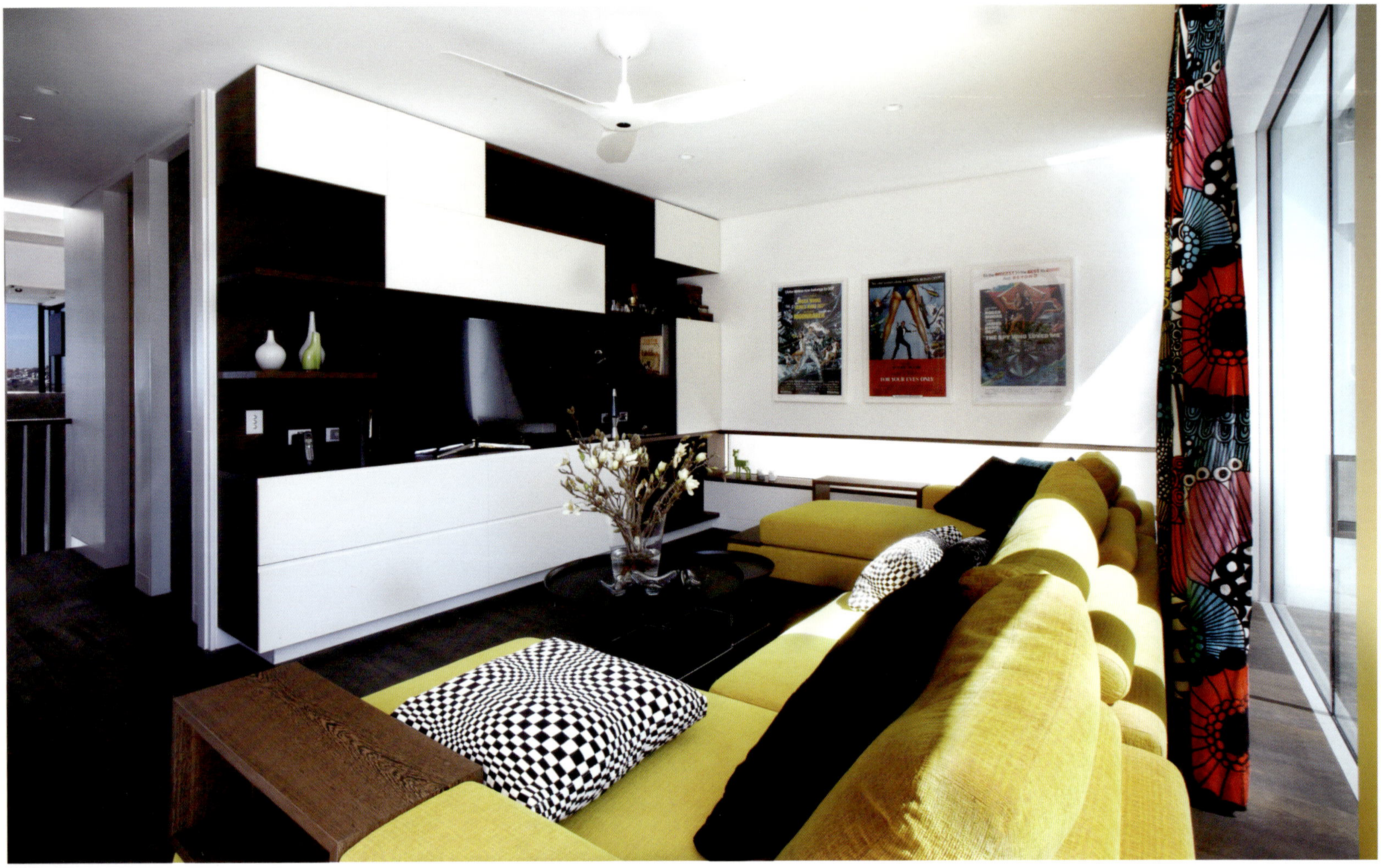
FOR YOUR EYES ONLY

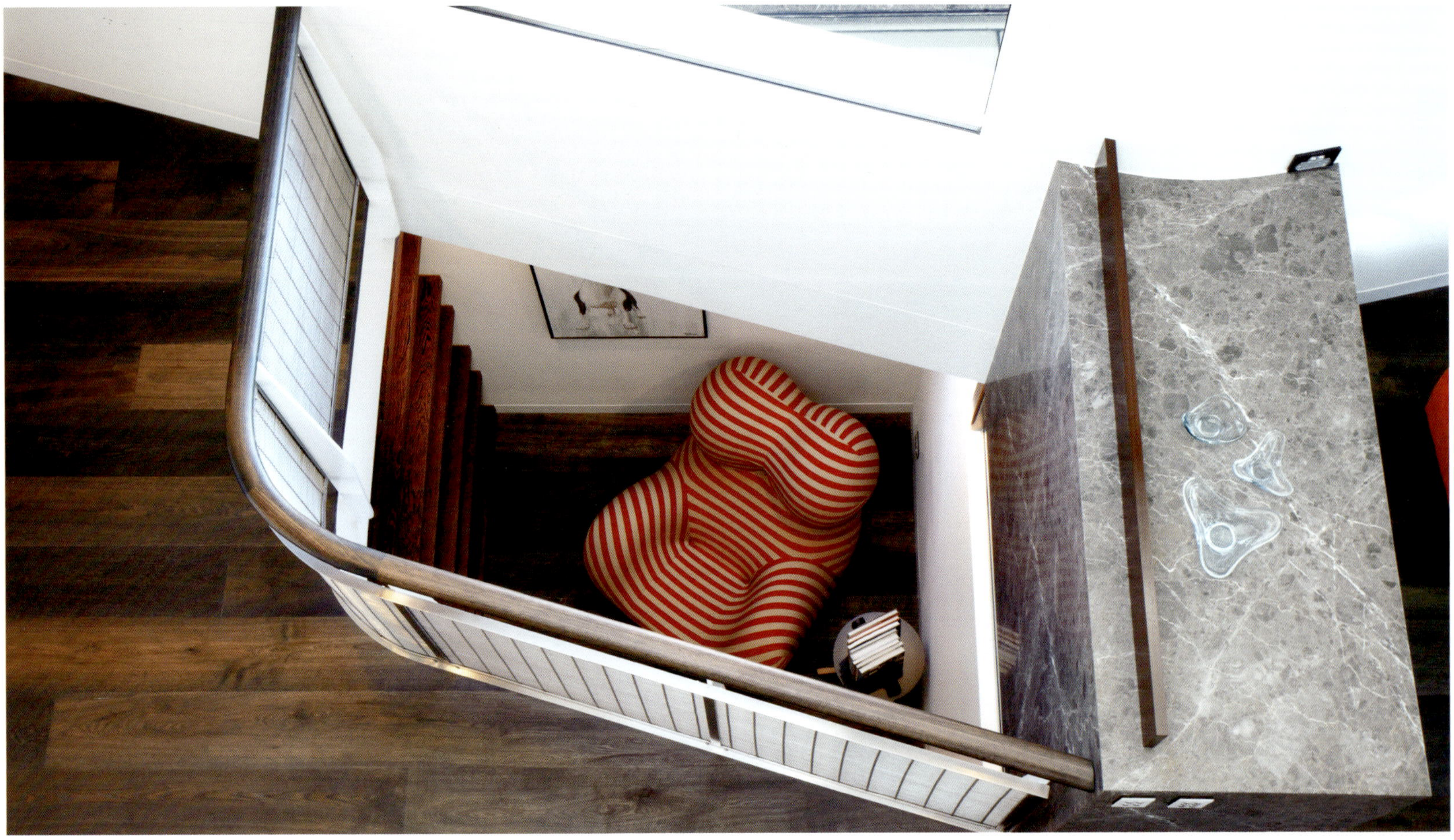

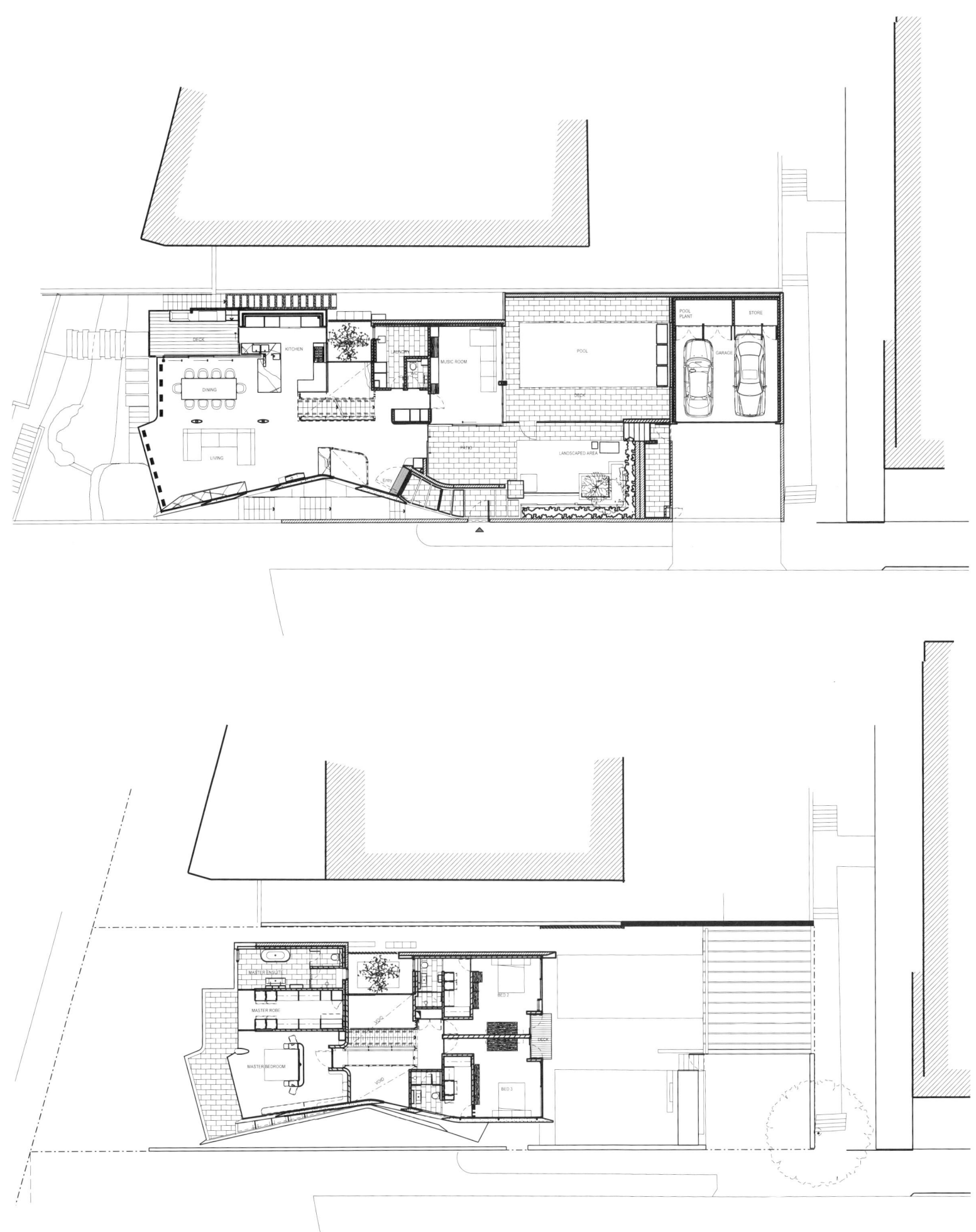

This void, supported by the roof shape in combination with the operable skylights, also helps to naturally ventilate the entire house as it allows the rising hot air to escape, drawing cooler air behind. Operable floor vents in the living area allow for the ubiquitous sea breeze to be let into the house in a controlled manner, all but eliminating the need for air conditioning.

High performance insulation and double glazing throughout in combination with the high thermal mass in the house allow for utilisation and storage of the northern solar heat gain in winter, keeping the house warm during the colder months.

Large rainwater storage tanks are sufficient to fill the pool and water the indigenous planting throughout the grounds.

All lights are low wattage LED type, reducing the electricity use significantly.

Kona Residence

Architects
Belzberg Architects

Interiors
MLK Studio

Principal
Hagy Belzberg

Area
725 m²

Project Manager
Barry Gartin

Location
Kona, Hawaii

Project Team
David Cheung, Barry Gartin, Cory Taylor, Andrew Atwood, Chris Arntzen, Brock DeSmit, Dan Rentsch, Lauren Zuzack, Justin Brechtel, Phillip Lee, Aaron Leppanen

Photography
Benny Chan (Fotoworks), Belzberg Architects

Nestled between cooled lava flows, the Kona residence situates its axis not with the linearity of the property, but rather with the axiality of predominant views available to the site. Within the dichotomy of natural elements and a geometric hardscape, the residence integrates both the surrounding views of volcanic mountain ranges to the east and ocean horizons westward.

The program is arranged as a series of pods distributed throughout the property, each having its own unique features and view opportunities. The pods are programmatically assigned as 2 sleeping pods with common areas, media room, master suite and main living space. An exterior gallery corridor becomes the organizational and focal feature for the entire house, connecting the two pods along a central axis.

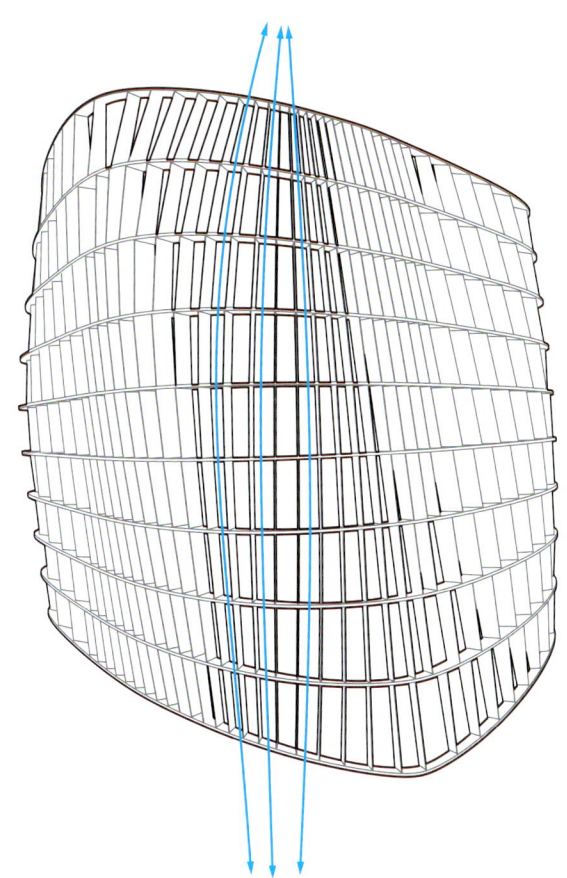

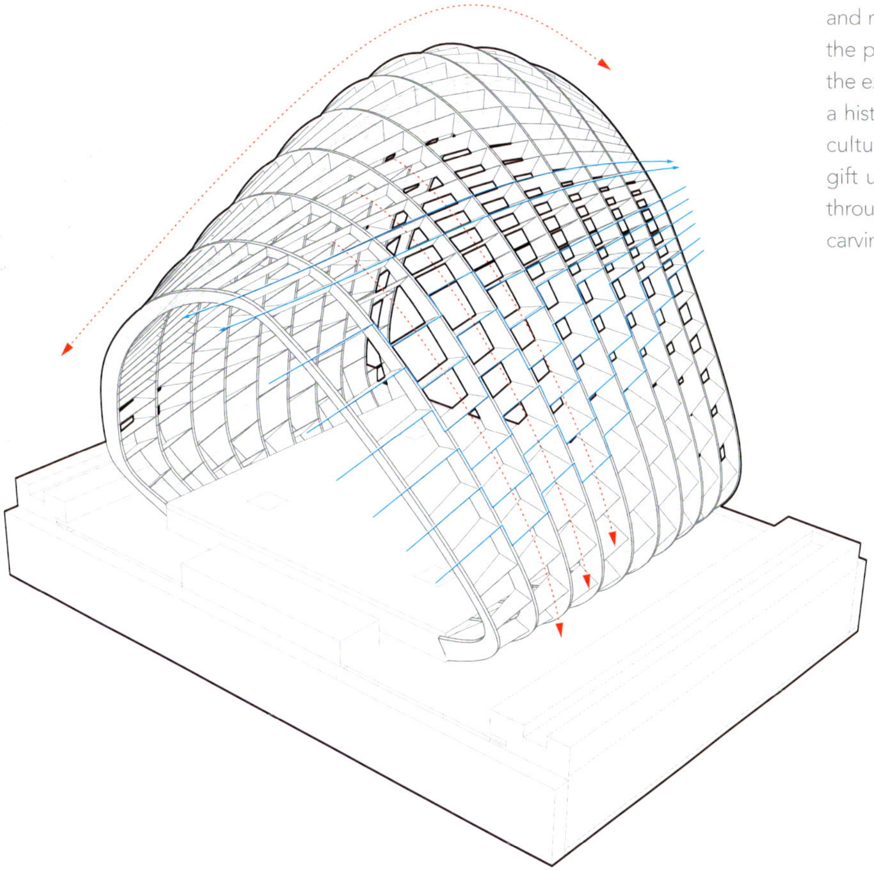

To help maintain the environmental sensitivity of the house, 2 separate arrays of roof mounted photovoltaic panels offset the residence energy usage while the choice of darker lava stone help heat the pool water via solar radiation. Rain water collection and redirection to 3 drywells that replenish the aquifer are implemented throughout the property. Reclaimed teak timber from old barns and train tracks are recycled for the exterior of the home. Coupled with stacked and cut lava rock, the 2 materials form a historically driven medium embedded in Hawaiian tradition. Local basket weaving culture was the inspiration for the entry pavilion which reenacts the traditional gift upon arrival ceremony. Various digitally sculpted wood ceilings and screens, throughout the house, continue the abstract approach to traditional Hawaiian wood carving further infusing traditional elements into the contemporary arrangement.

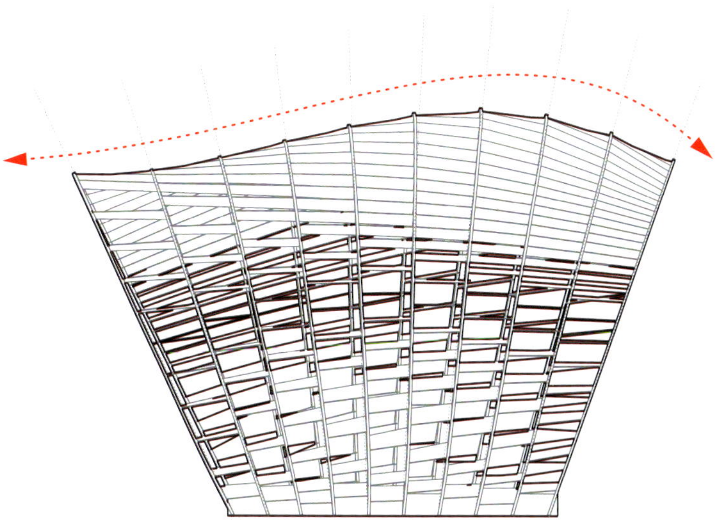

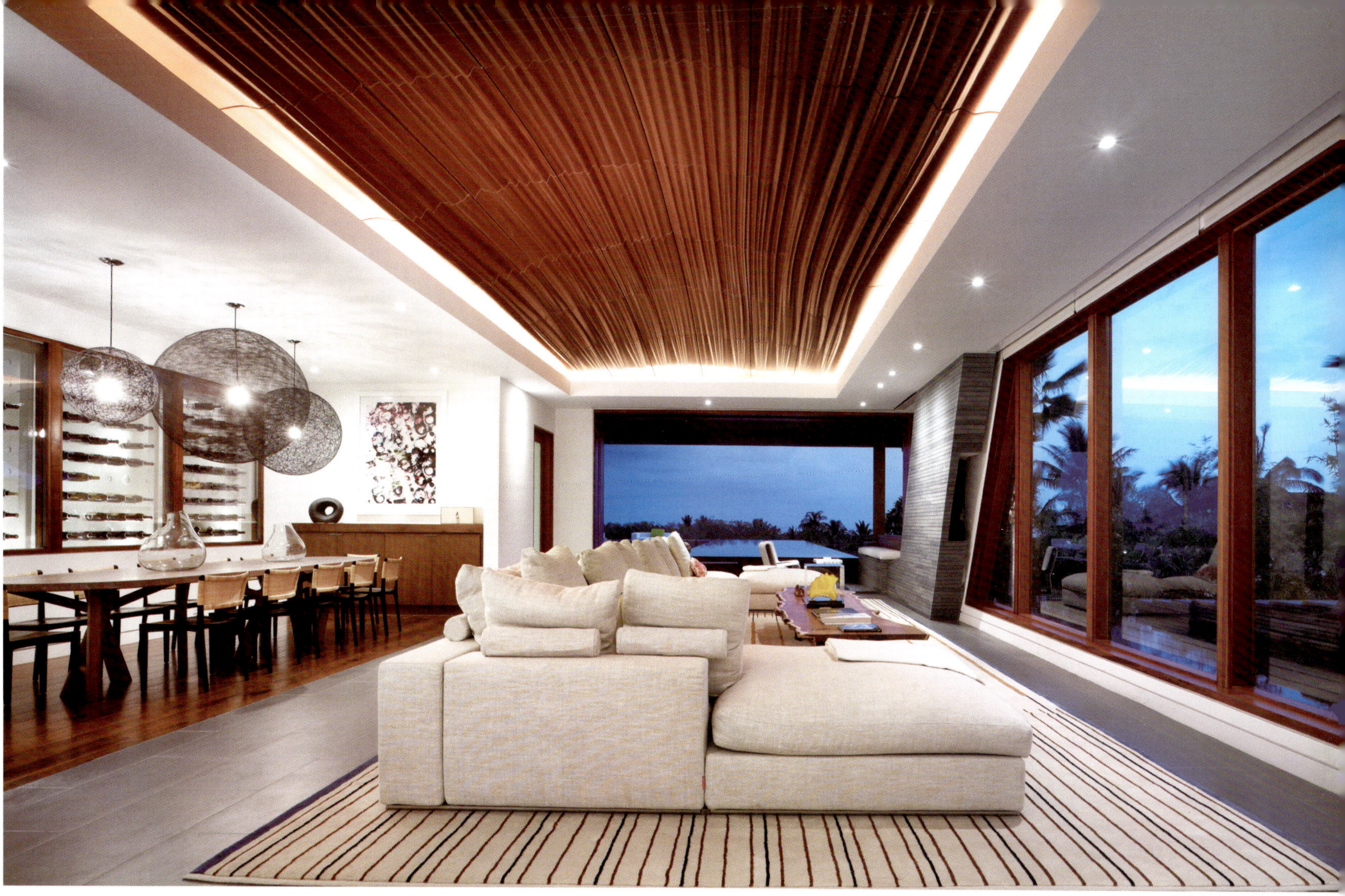

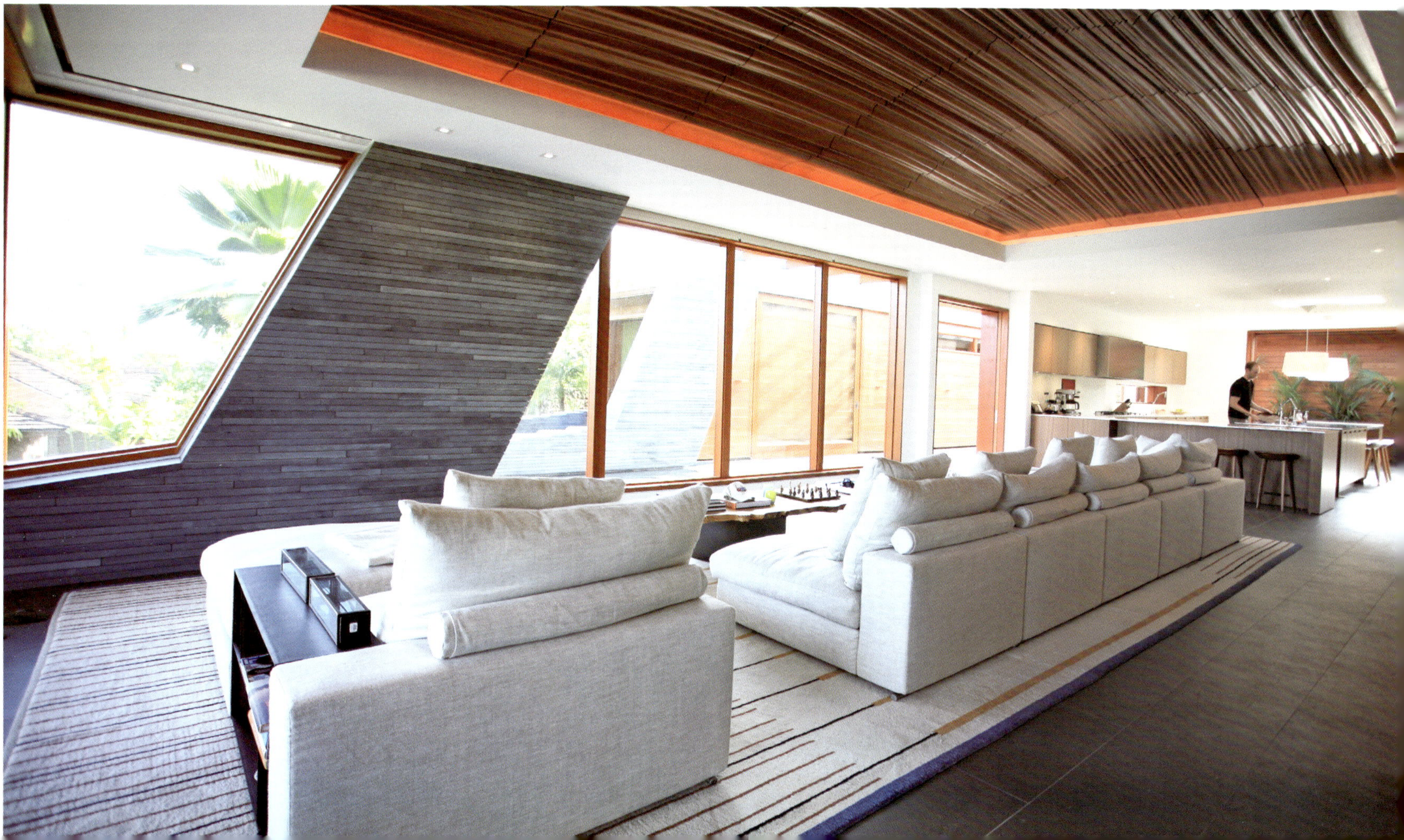

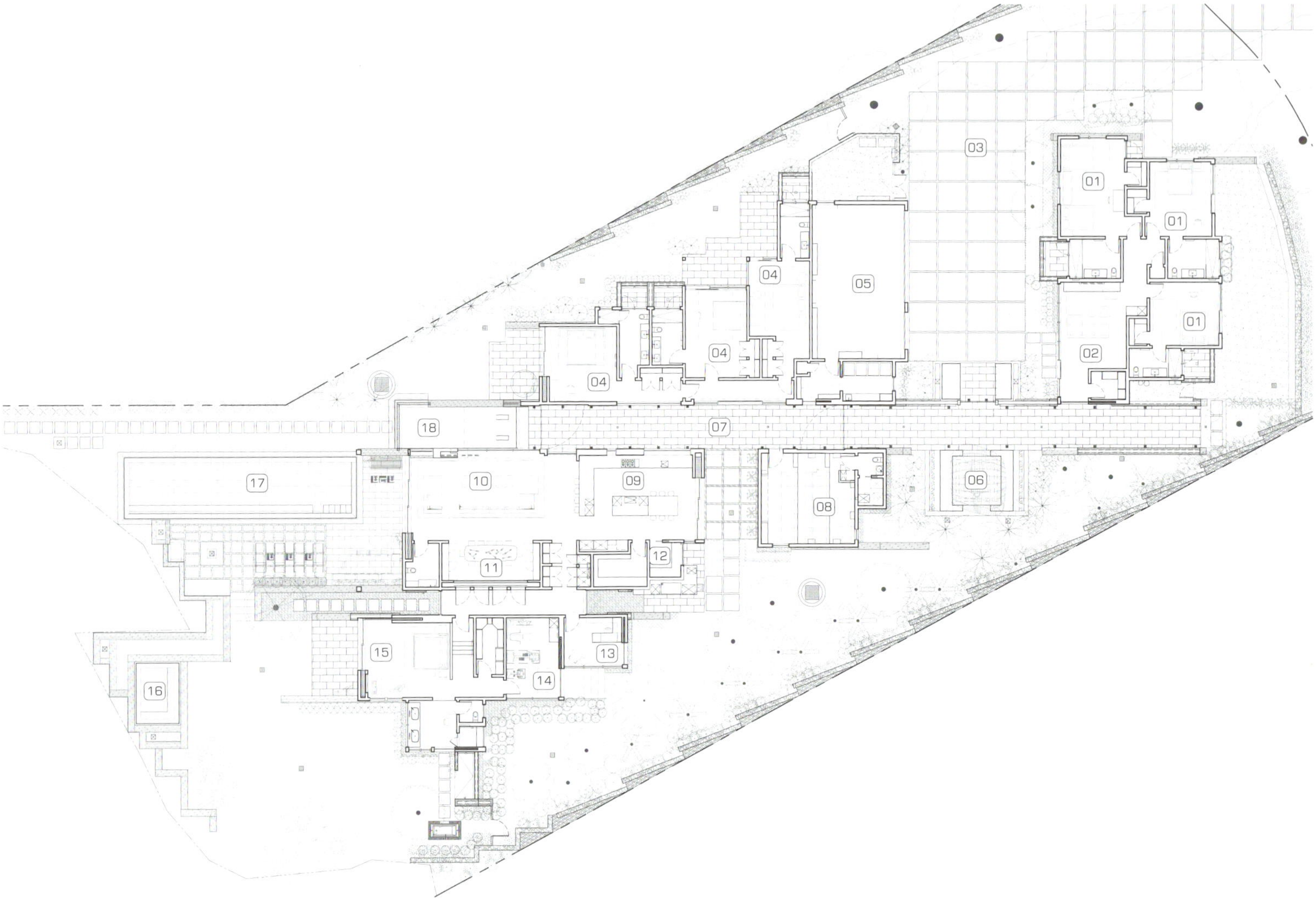

01 KID'S ROOM	06 ENTRY PAVILION	11 DINING ROOM	16 HOT TUB
02 KID'S COMMON	07 OUTDOOR GALLERY	12 OFFICE	17 POOL
03 MOTOR COURT	08 THEATER	13 OFFICE	18 REFLECTING POOL
04 GUEST ROOM	09 KITCHEN	14 GYM	
05 GARAGE	10 GREAT ROOM	15 MASTER BEDROOM	

House Boz

Architects
Nico van der Meulen Architects

Designer
Werner van der Meulen

Location
Mooikloof Heights, Pretoria, South Africa

Residence Size
777 m²

The client requested a spacious and luxurious four bedroom house with an emphasis placed on the design of the living rooms. Ensuring that the magnificent views were optimized was of utmost importance, the design of this 777 m² house not only responds well to the client's requirements but also to the context of the site.

Every design decision communicates and reinforces the concept, as can be seen in the selection of materials used and the way the internal spaces relate to the outdoors. With the choice of materials predominately natural materials and earthy colors, it is evident that even the smallest of details make reference to the concept in a very unique way. Initially the site revealed itself as a mound of quartzite rock which was excavated and hand cut for the gabion walls and the stone cladding used throughout the house.

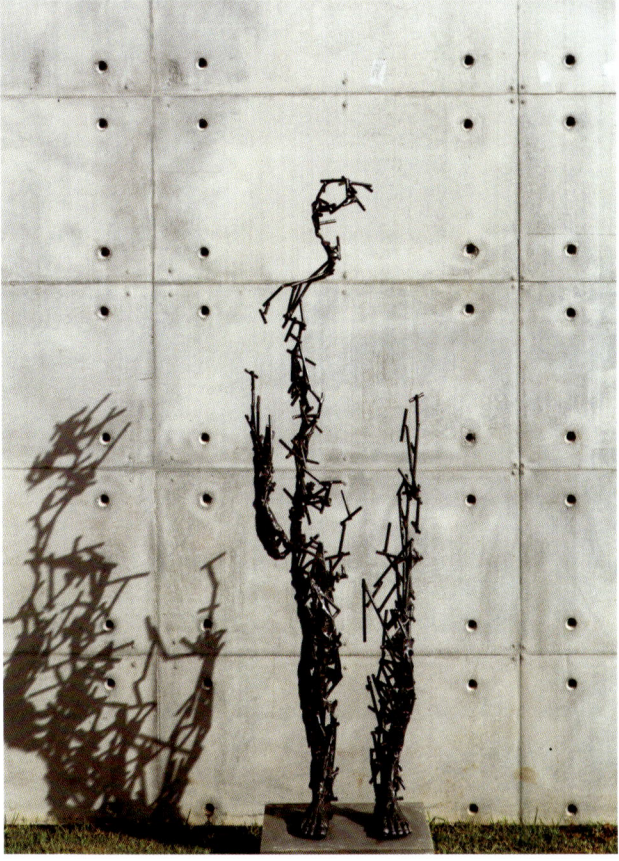

The entrance hall positioned between the double garages is distinctively located alongside a partially covered atrium that gently introduces you to several views through the house as you're welcomed in. The koi pond introduces water as you approach the front door while various podiums add depth and dimension to this space. An elevated sculpture podium and interlocking planters bring this atrium to life. This also makes it possible to sleep with the doors open as it is impossible to get into the atrium once the Mentis grating gate to the driveway is locked.

The double volume entrance hall is framed by a back-lit perforated skin of scaffolding boards bolted to a wall, creating the perfect backdrop for the sculptural looking concrete staircase with steel inlays. Underneath the staircase is a sculpture by Regardt van der Meulen.

The kitchen overlooks the lanai and garden while the frameless folding doors create an invisible threshold between the inside and out. These doors, when completely open, allow for the kitchen and dining room to overflow onto the lanai and bar, making entertaining effortless and enabling adults to keep an eye on children in the pool, a mere meter away.

The lanai with a sunken jacuzzi is snugly positioned between the pool on one side and a stone-cladded wall on the west which screens the afternoon sun to ensure the lanai's temperature remains moderate. It is these design decisions that truly set this house apart from the rest.

All four en-suite bedrooms are situated on the first floor with all of the bedrooms having their own private balcony. The 3 children's bedrooms are situated on the western wing of the house while the main bedroom is located on the eastern wing. A suspended walkway with steel sheeting as floor tiles overlooking the atrium links the 2 wings and creates a sense of privacy for the main bedroom.

Phia van der Meulen and the M Square Lifestyle Design team strategically linked spaces through their use of various natural materials in the interior spaces. In situ-concrete, quartzite cladding and rusted mild steel were incorporated into the design.

The interiors feature linear and monolithic forms that complement the architect's vision for this house. Many of the functional elements were designed to become beautiful features that visually connect the spaces and create links throughout the house rather than just remaining purely functional. An example of this would be the way the staircase relates to the aluminum ceiling which features in both the main living room as well as in the main bedroom.

Regardt van der Meulen's original steel sculptures were chosen for the project, as they fitted perfectly with the steel theme of the project. The selection of furniture pieces once again continued this theme where splashes of orange were used in the living room making reference to the orange seen in the rusted metal cladding. The overall charcoal colour range used in this house complements the shades of grey of the concrete walls.

Residence Amsterdam

Architects
Robert Kolenik

Area
450 m²

This project, a 450 m² villa, is located in the north of the Netherlands. With the owners throwing a house warming party to welcome everybody in their new home, the villa is now definitely ready. Robert placed a few outstanding eye catchers in the interior. The Maretti "Dream" chandelier designed by Kolenik for instance. Situated in the basement are a wellness room and a bar. De master bedroom has a view on the "Dream" Chandelier. Simply pushing a button can easily blind that view. Innovative privacy glass makes this possible.

Seacliff Residence

Designer
Paul McClean

Location
Los Angeles, CA

Photography
Nick Springett

A long and difficult planning process added to the challenge of designing this home. A restrictive height limit plus views from neighboring properties that needed to be preserved on all sides limited the location and size of the upper floor. This resulted in a 3-level home with primary living spaces on the top floor, entry and master bedroom at the ground floor and additional bedrooms below with views out over a steep slope in the rear yard. Because space was limited, the main living area was streamlined into one useable area with the kitchen separating dining from living. The kitchen itself consists of a full height cabinetry wall in white glass with a glacier white marble island with ample seating and cooking space. The room is wrapped in glass on 3 sides to increase the feeling of volume and sliding Fleetwood doors fold back to reveal a large entertainment deck with lounge and BBQ areas.

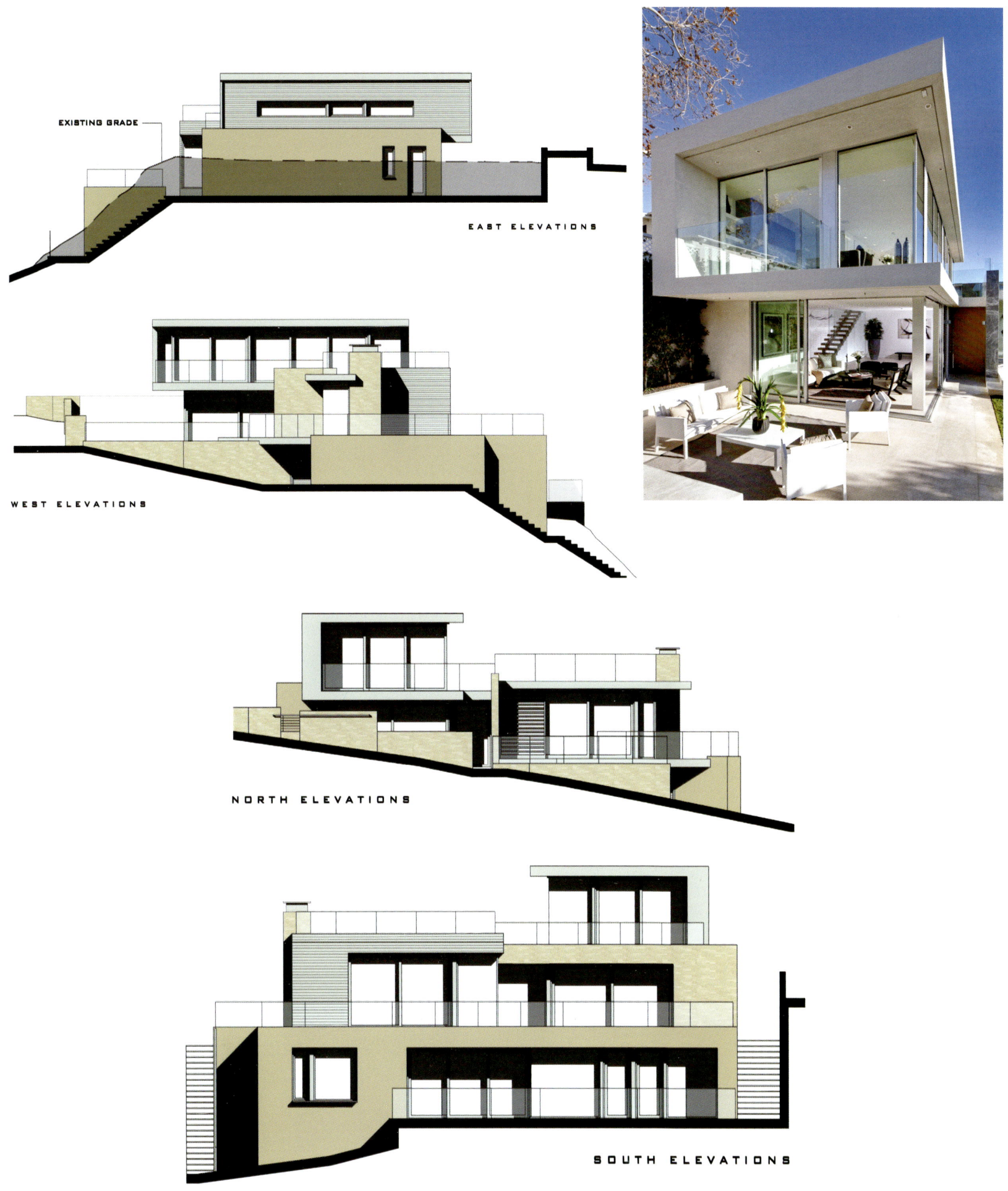

EAST ELEVATIONS

EXISTING GRADE

WEST ELEVATIONS

NORTH ELEVATIONS

SOUTH ELEVATIONS

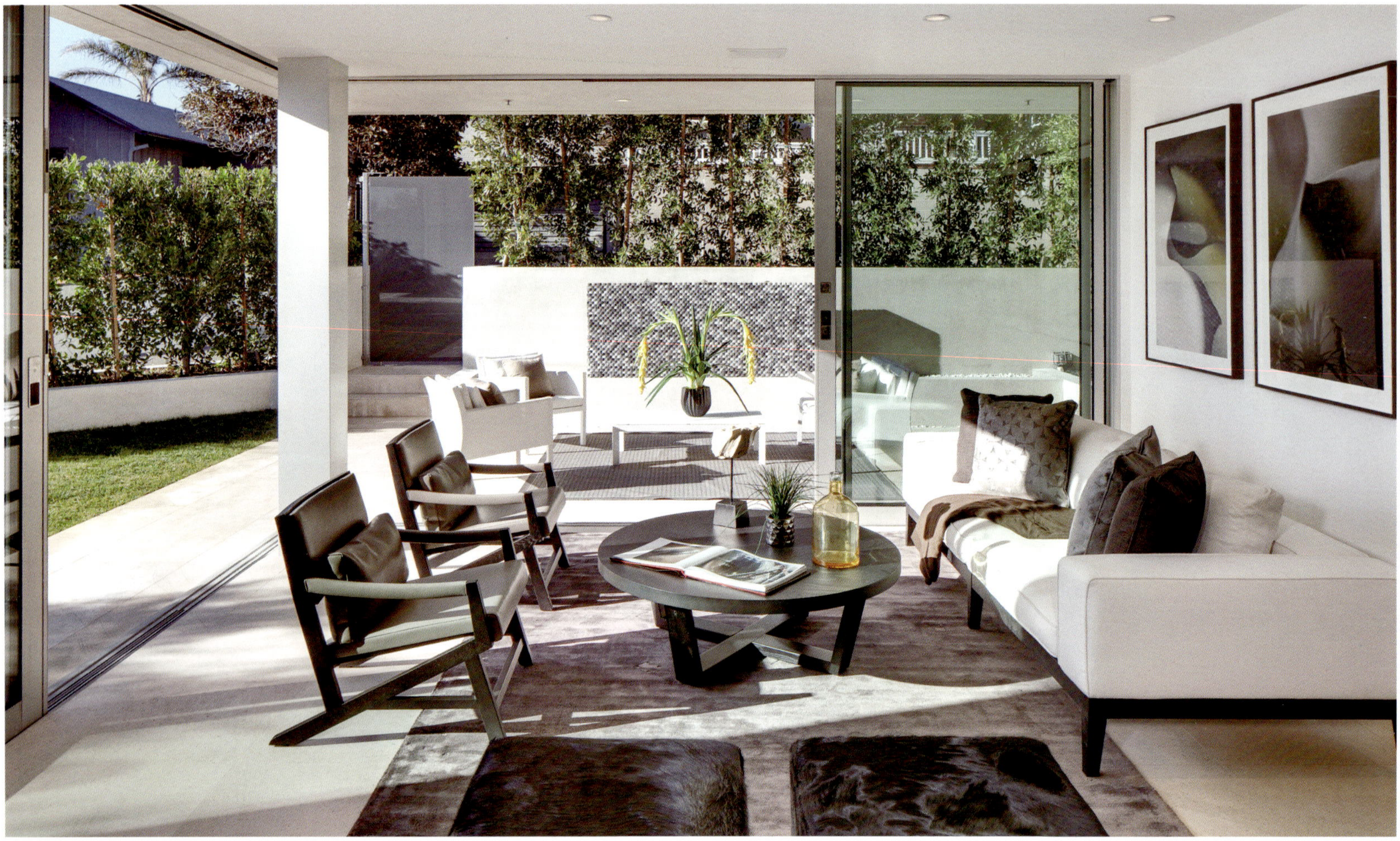

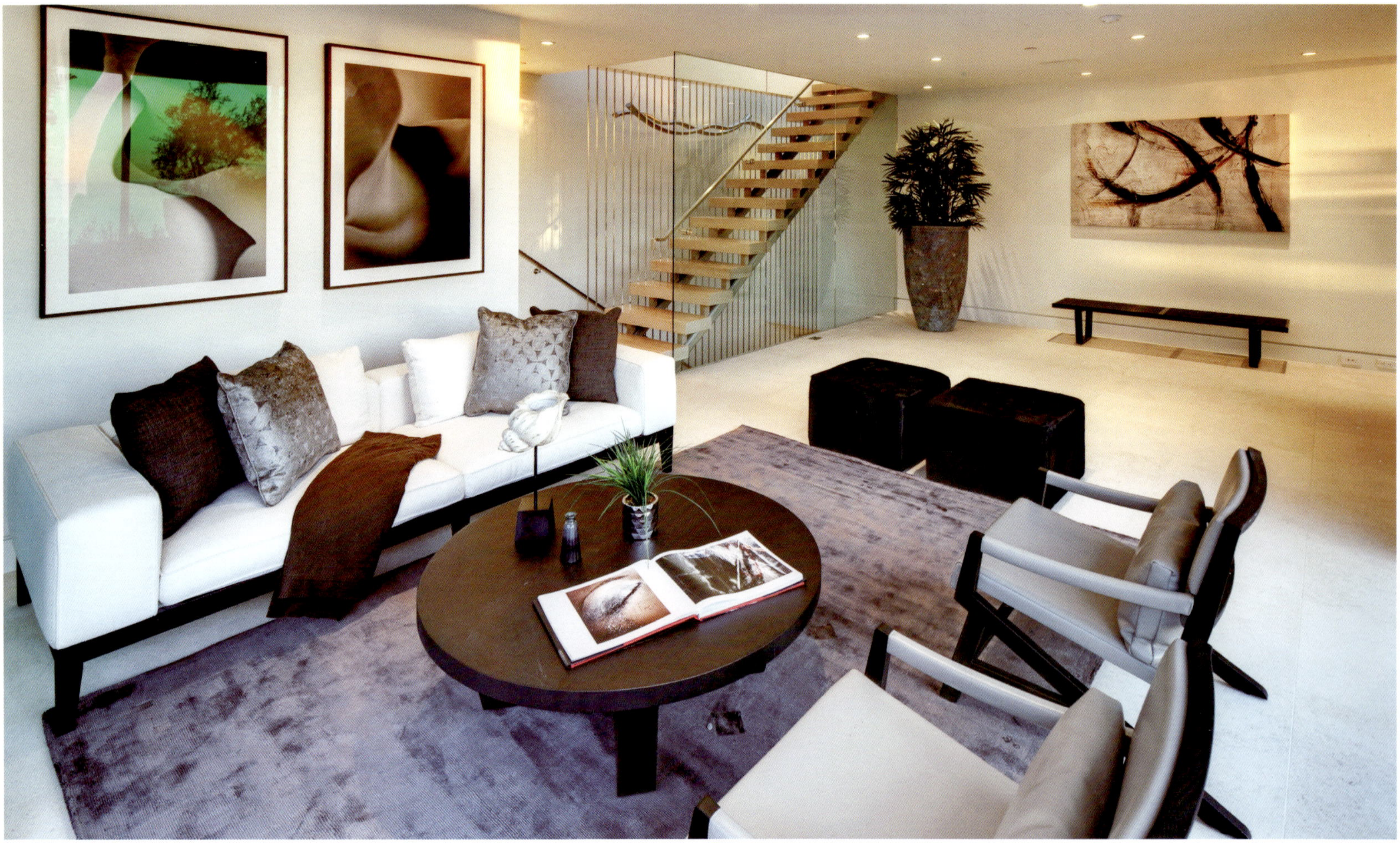

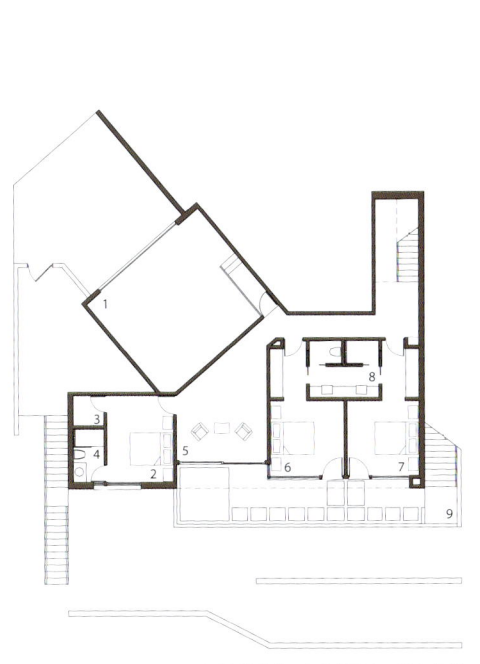

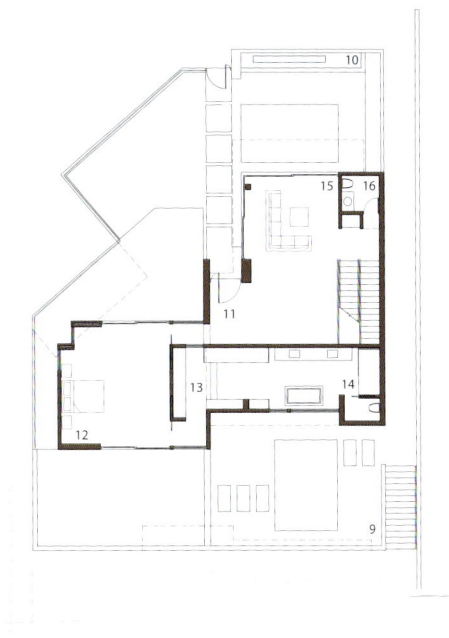

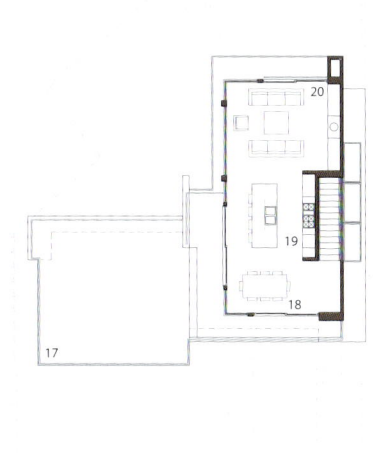

LOWER LEVEL PLAN   MAIN LEVEL PLAN   UPPER LEVEL PLAN

LEGEND

GARAGE	1	PATIO	9	DECK	17
BEDROOM 1	2	WATER FEATURE	10	DINING ROOM	18
CLOSET 1	3	ENTRY	11	KITCHEN	19
BATHROOM 1	4	MASTER BEDROOM	12	FAMILY ROOM	20
LOUNGE	5	M. CLOSET	13		
BEDROOM 2	6	M. BATHROOM	14		
BEDROOM 3	7	LIVING ROOM	15		
BATHROOM	8	POWDER	16		

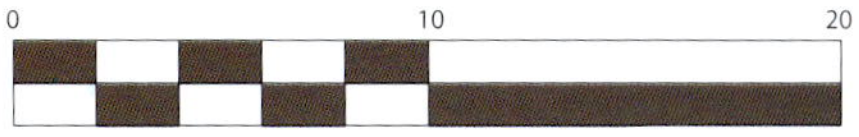

0   10   20
SCALE IN METERS   NORTH

The entry is approached through a walled off courtyard and leads directly into a family room focused on the courtyard and its water feature. The master bedroom has views to the waves below and a unique combined closet and bath with beautiful Italian closets and fixtures. At the lower level the 3 bedrooms and family area open onto a terrace with views of the garden below. The palette of the house is designed to reflect its beach side location, light walls and soft limestone and oak accented with glass.

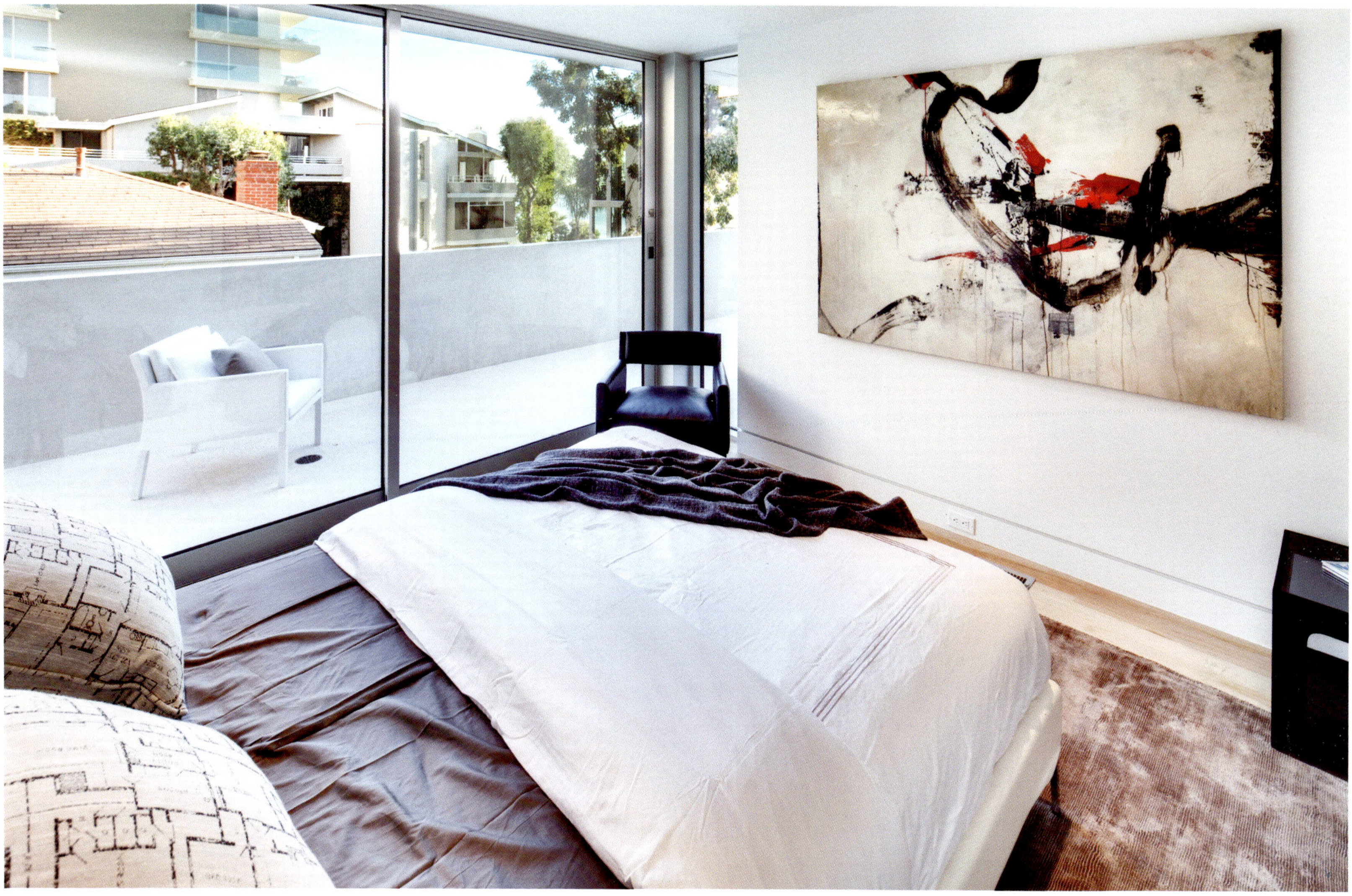

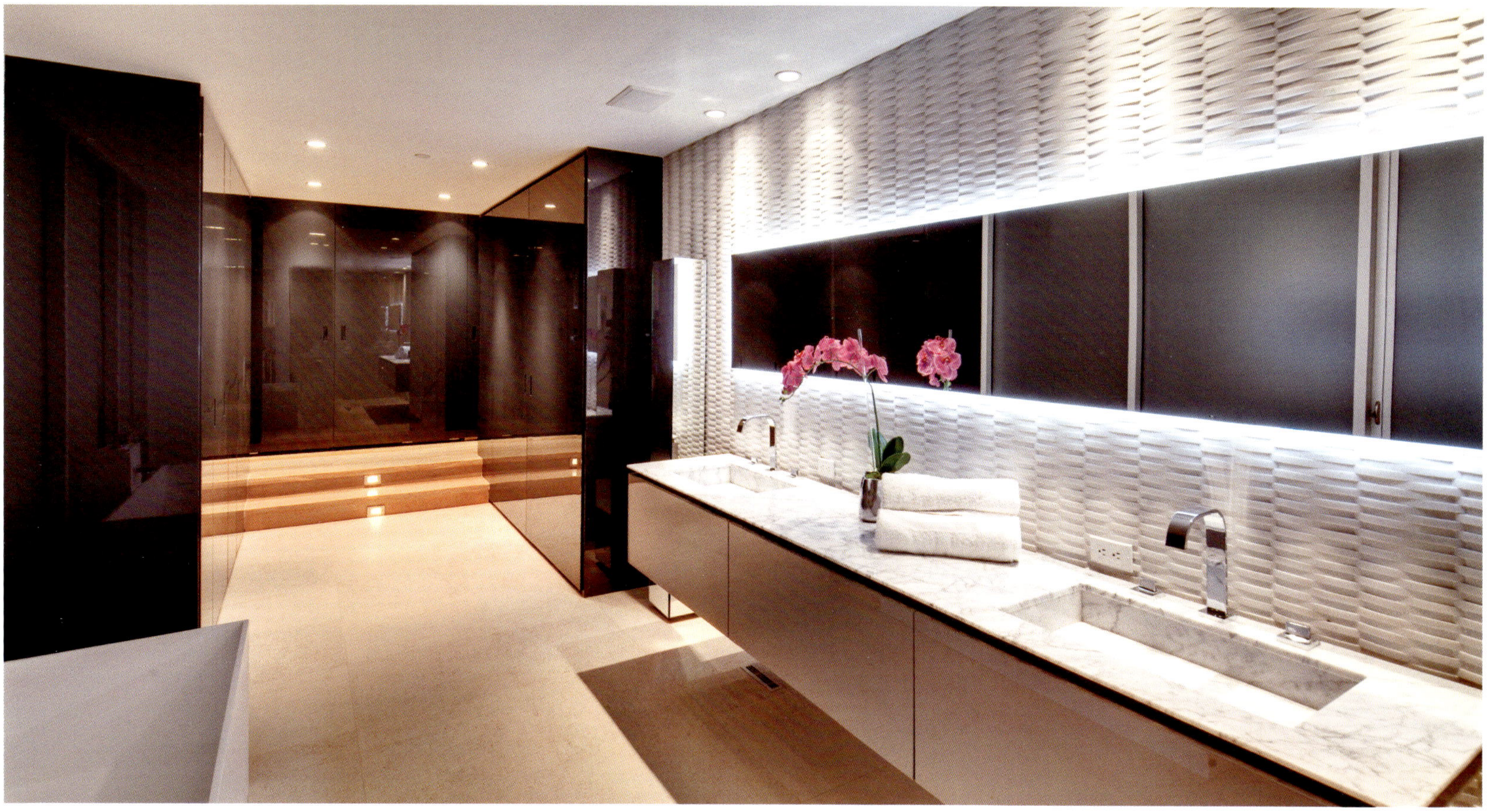

Albizia House

Architects	**Design Architect**	**Project Architect**	**Project Technician**	**Structural Engineers**	**Design Engineer**
Metropole Architects	Nigel Tarboton	Tyrone Reardon	Chris Laird	Young & Satharia	Rob Young

Structural Technician	**Interior Designers**	**Main Contractor**	**Principal**	**Project Manager**	**Site Foreman**
Terry Schubach	Union 3 Clifton Smithers	East Coast Construction	Justin Rosewarne	Benno Terblanche	Tony Moodley

Site Area	**Building Area**	**Photographer**
4,360 m^2	1,000 m^2	Grant Pitcher

We were commissioned to design a contemporary family home on a one acre site, situated at the end of a spur, in Simbithi Eco-Estate. The clients brief called for a home with an overriding sense of simplicity but with a high degree of sophistication.

All the living areas and bedroom suites face onto a panoramic vista, which includes a dense forest down-slope from the house.

The palette of natural materials including timber screens, decking and cladding, off-shutter concrete and stone cladding juxtapose with the aggressive architectural form making, creating a home that is not only visually and spatially exciting, but also comfortable and intimate.

The extensive use of water in the design of the home includes a 25 m lap pool with a

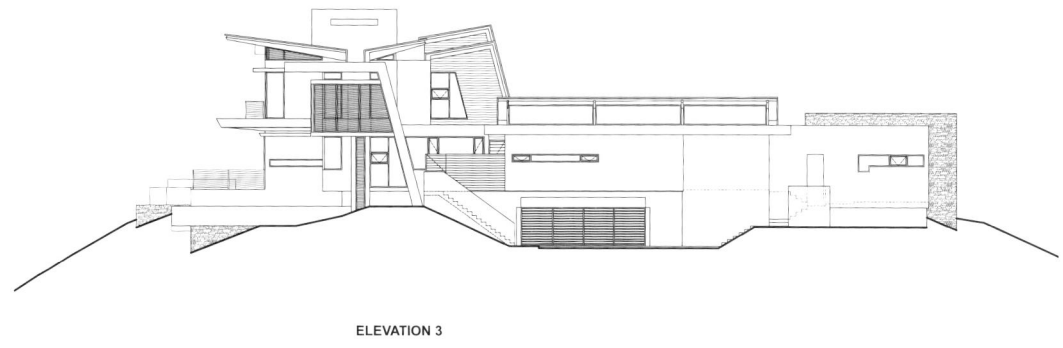

ELEVATION 3

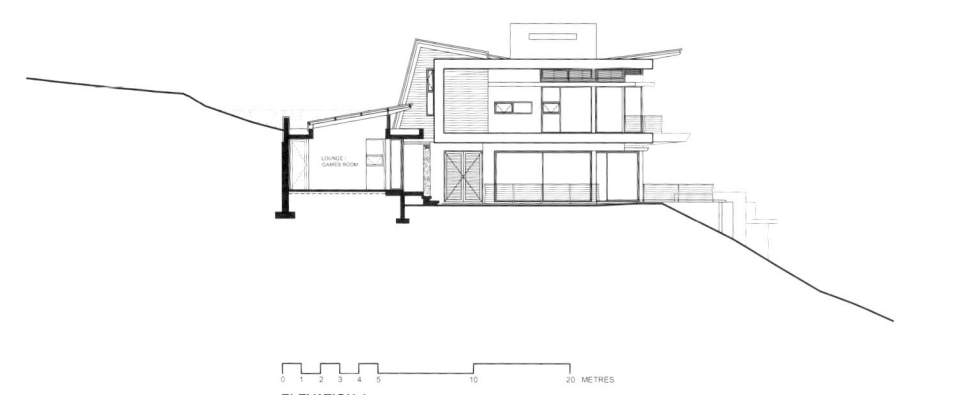

ELEVATION 4

glass panel between the water and the basement cinema room, and a shallow but expansive reflective pond on the approach side, which mirrors the building day and night, and evokes a sense of tranquility.

The architectural style of the home is heavily influenced by the "Googie" architecture of the American architect John Lautner. The origin of the name "Googie" dates to 1949, when architect John Lautner designed the West Hollywood coffee shop, Googies, which had distinct architectural characteristics.

"Googie" architecture is a form of modern architecture and a subdivision of futurist architecture with stylistic conventions influenced by, and representing 50's American society's fascination and marketing emphasis on futuristic design, car culture, jets, the Space Age, and the Atomic Age.

"Googie" was also characterized by design forms symbolic of motion, including upswept roofs, curvaceous geometric shapes, and the bold use of glass, steel and neon, the spirit of which is embodied in Albizia House.

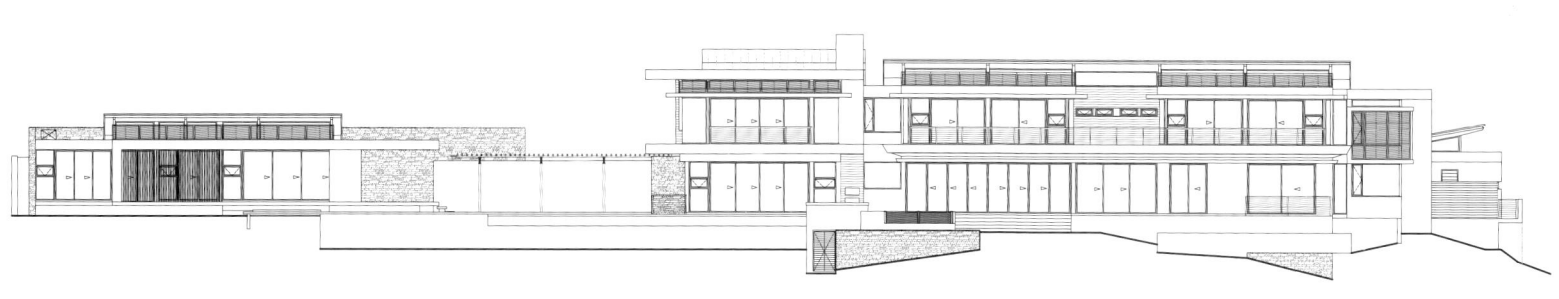

ELEVATION 1

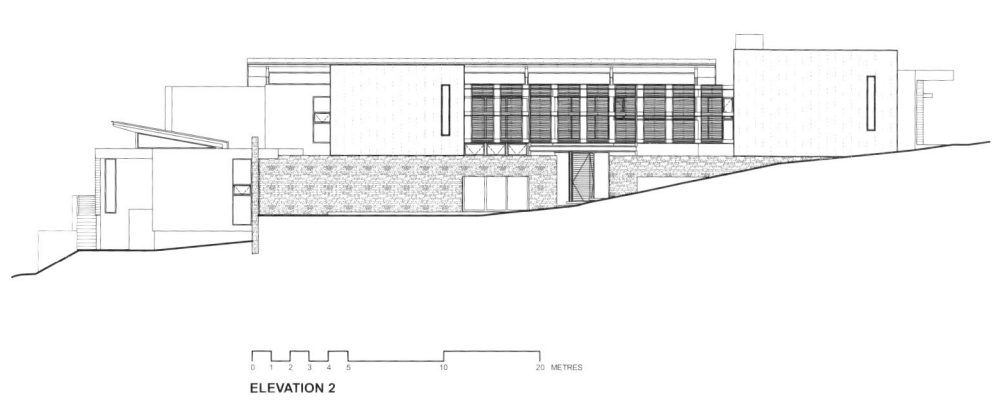

ELEVATION 2

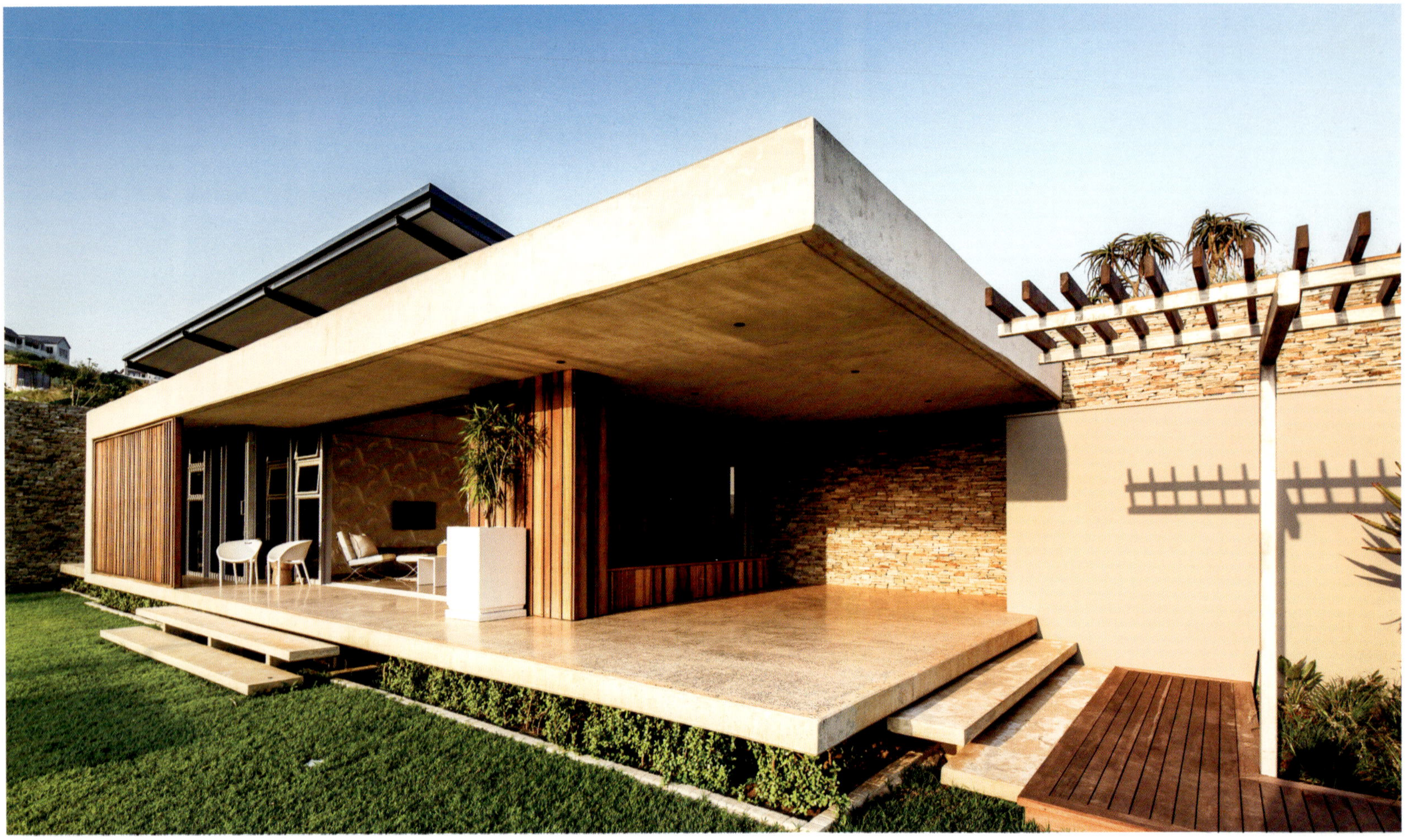

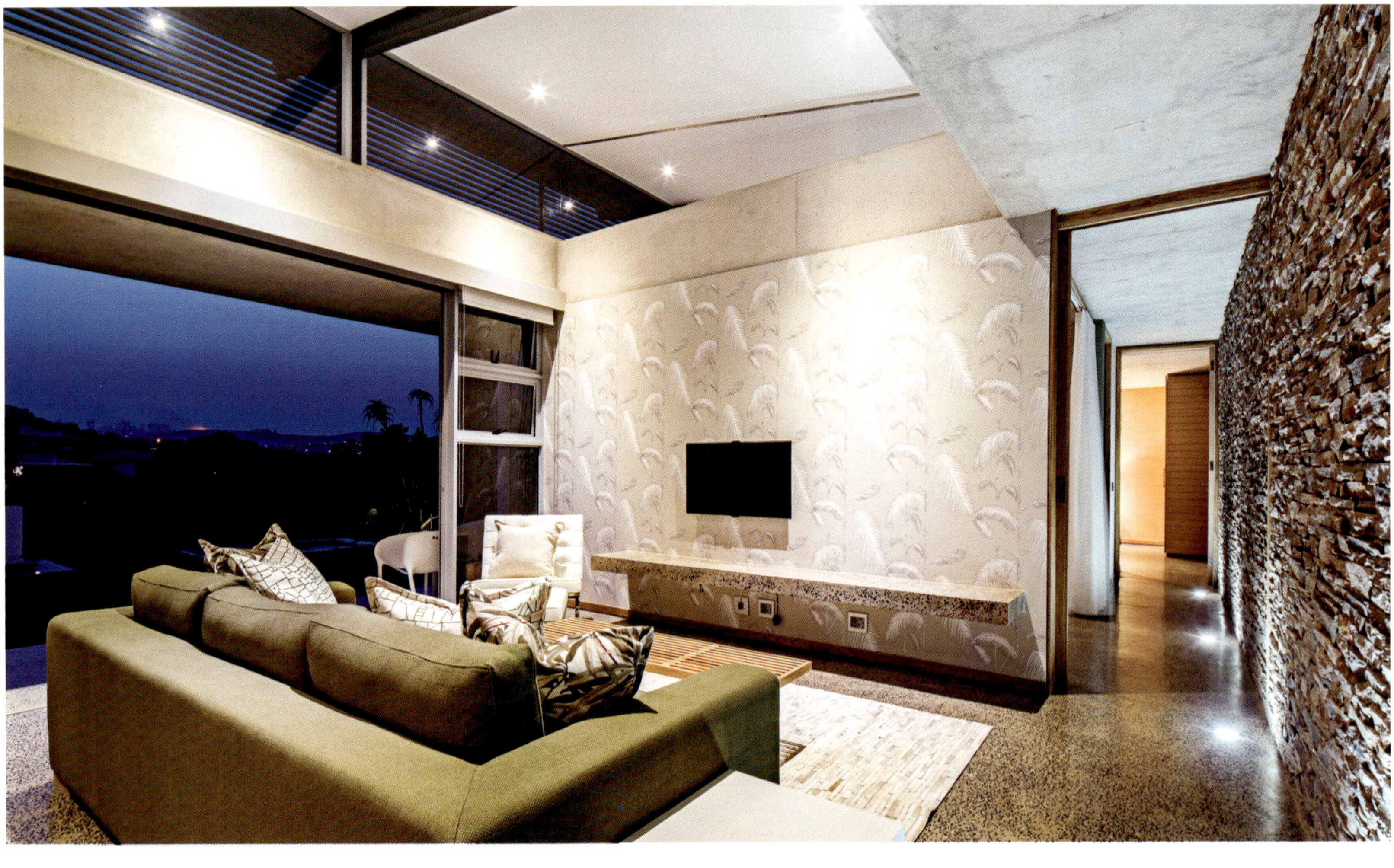

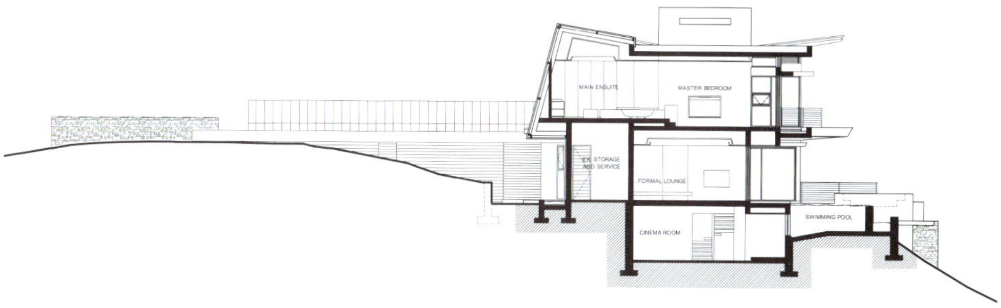

SECTION 1

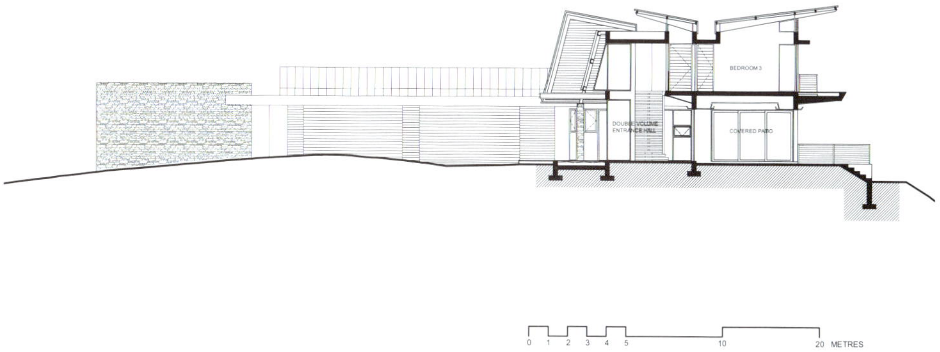

SECTION 2

0 1 2 3 4 5   10   20 METRES

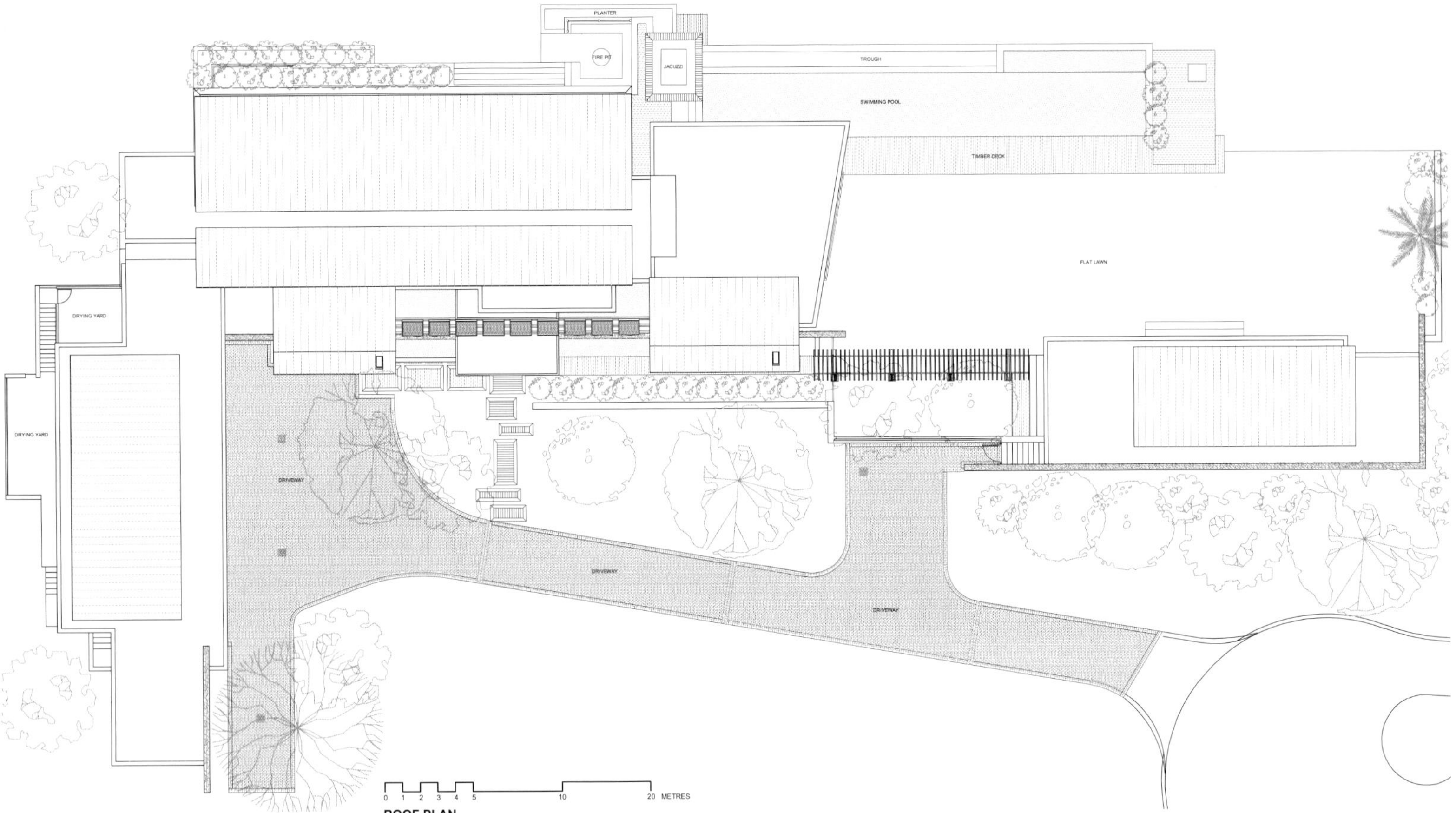

ROOF PLAN

PLANTER

FIRE PIT

JACUZZI

TROUGH

SWIMMING POOL

TIMBER DECK

DRYING YARD

FLAT LAWN

DRYING YARD

DRIVEWAY

DRIVEWAY

DRIVEWAY

0 1 2 3 4 5   10   20 METRES

ROOF PLAN

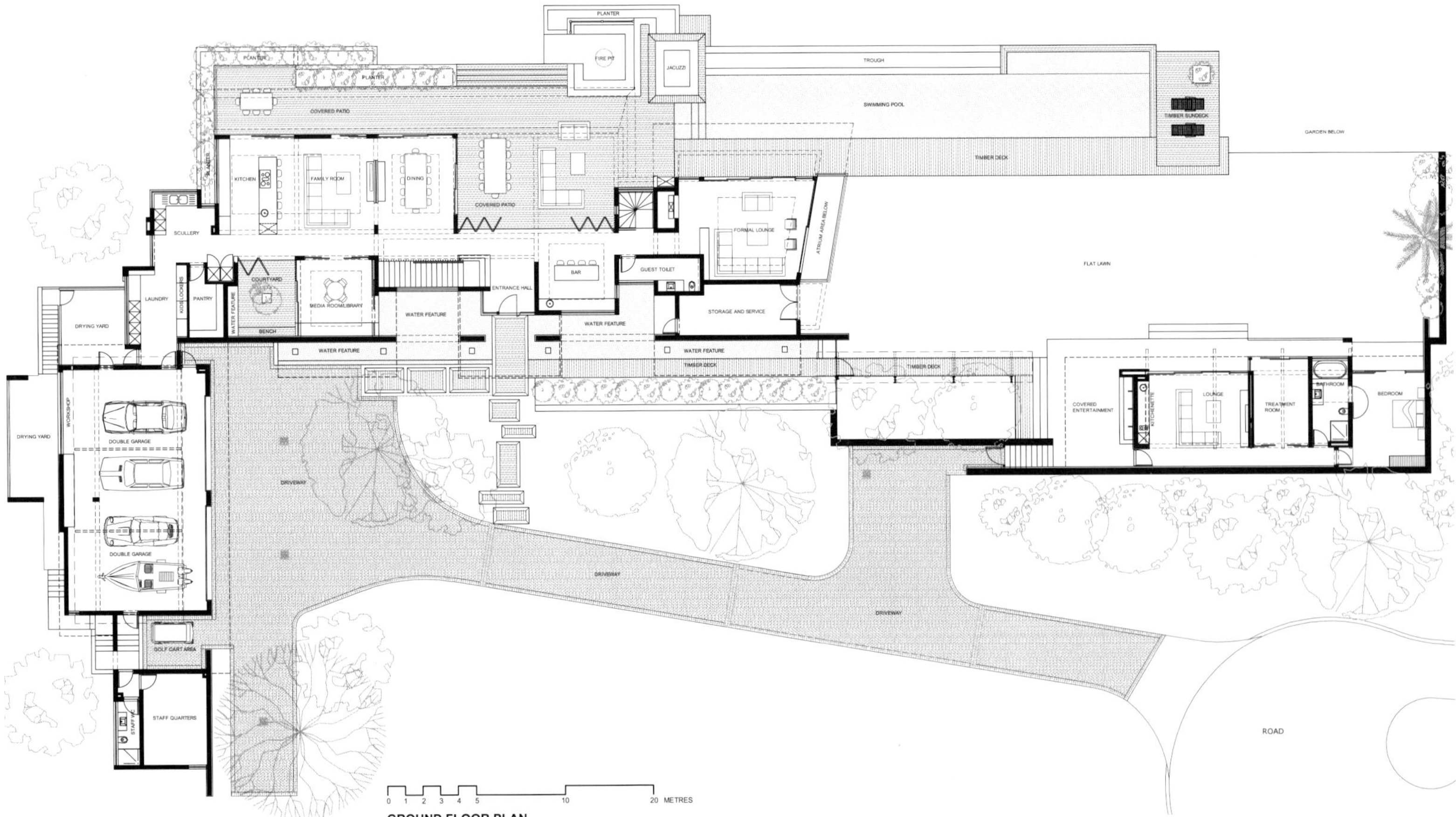

GROUND FLOOR PLAN

PLANTER

PLANTER

PLANTER

FIRE PIT

JACUZZI

TROUGH

SWIMMING POOL

COVERED PATIO

TIMBER SUNDECK

TIMBER DECK

GARDEN BELOW

KITCHEN

FAMILY ROOM

DINING

COVERED PATIO

FLAT LAWN

SCULLERY

LAUNDRY

PANTRY

COURTYARD

MEDIA ROOM/LIBRARY

BENCH

WATER FEATURE

WATER FEATURE

ENTRANCE HALL

BAR

GUEST TOILET

FORMAL LOUNGE

ATRIUM AREA BELOW

STORAGE AND SERVICE

DRYING YARD

WATER FEATURE

WATER FEATURE

WATER FEATURE

TIMBER DECK

TIMBER DECK

COVERED ENTERTAINMENT

LOUNGE

TREATMENT ROOM

BATHROOM

BEDROOM

DRIVEWAY

WORKSHOP

DOUBLE GARAGE

DRYING YARD

DOUBLE GARAGE

GOLF CART AREA

STAFF QUARTERS

DRIVEWAY

DRIVEWAY

ROAD

0 1 2 3 4 5   10   20 METRES

GROUND FLOOR PLAN

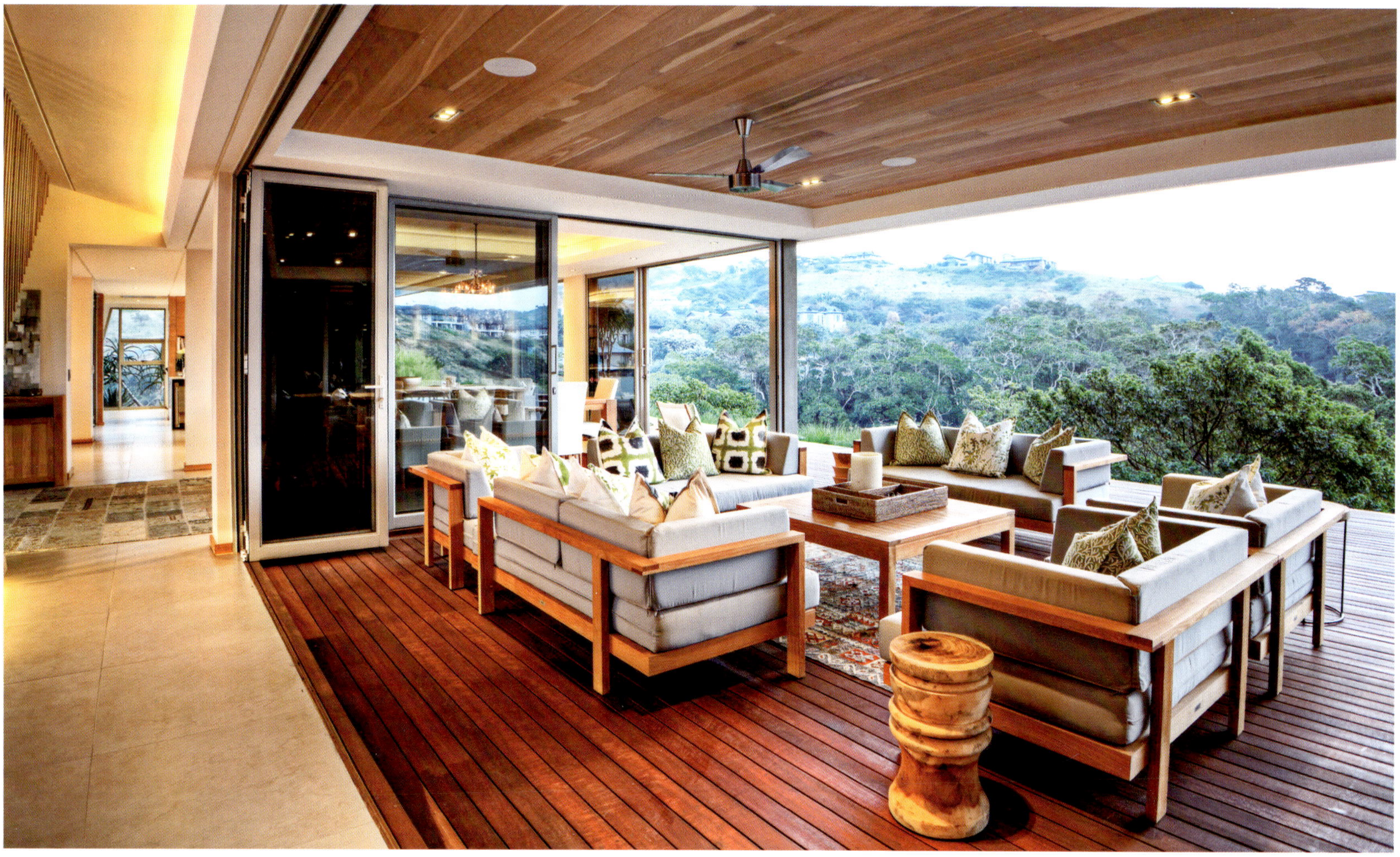

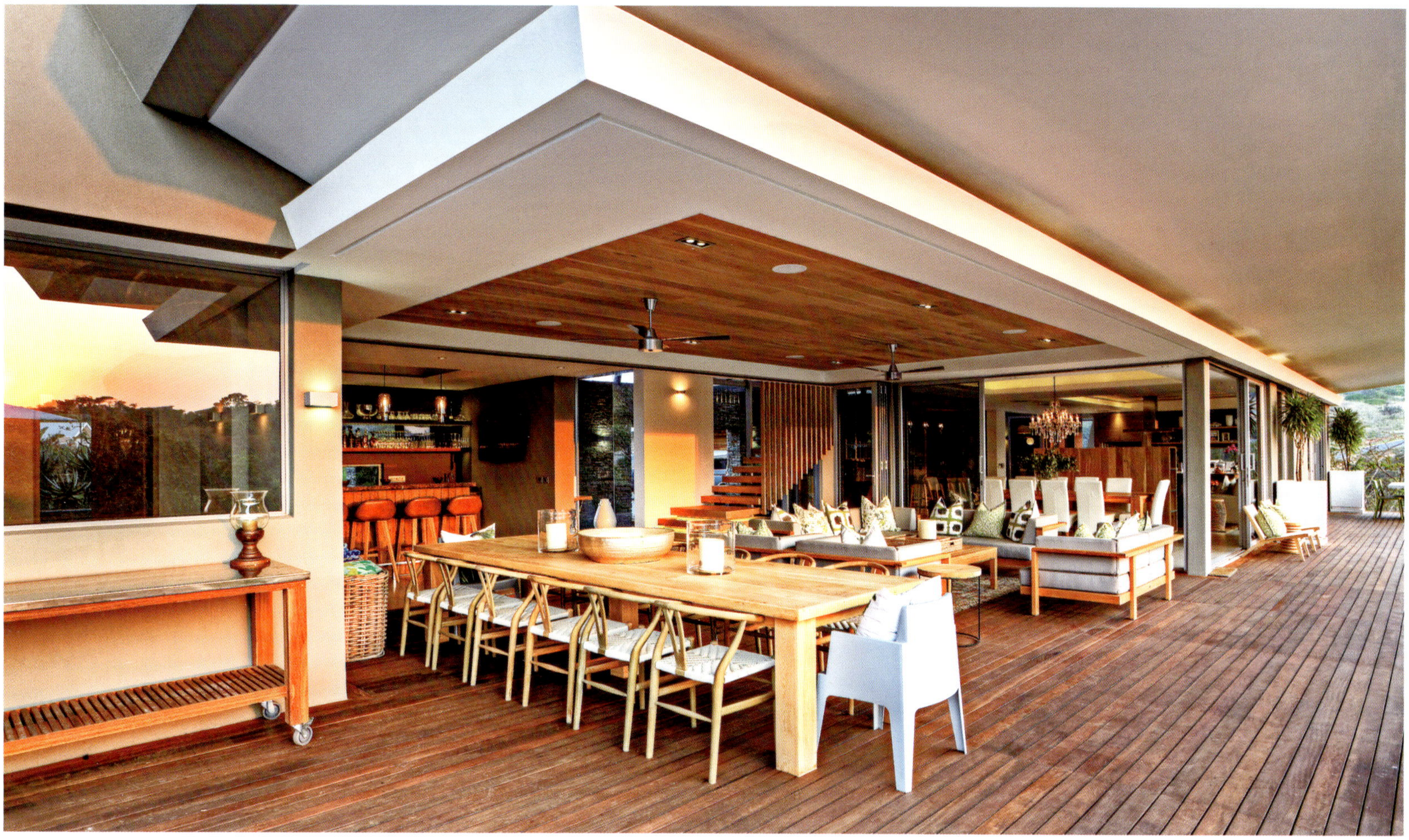

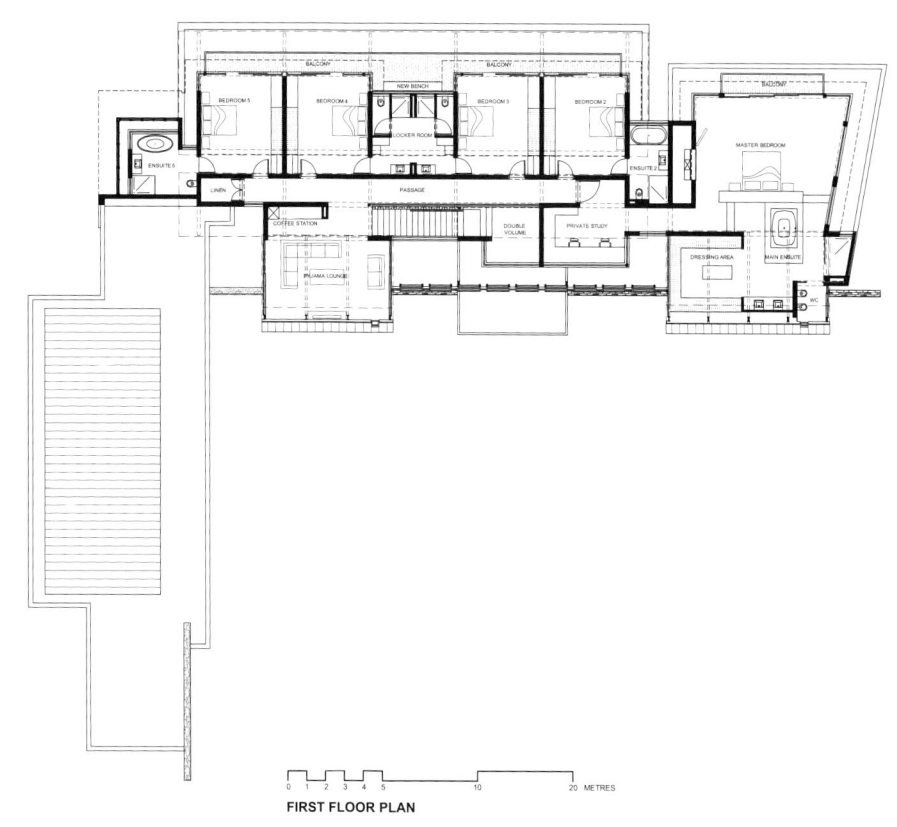

FIRST FLOOR PLAN

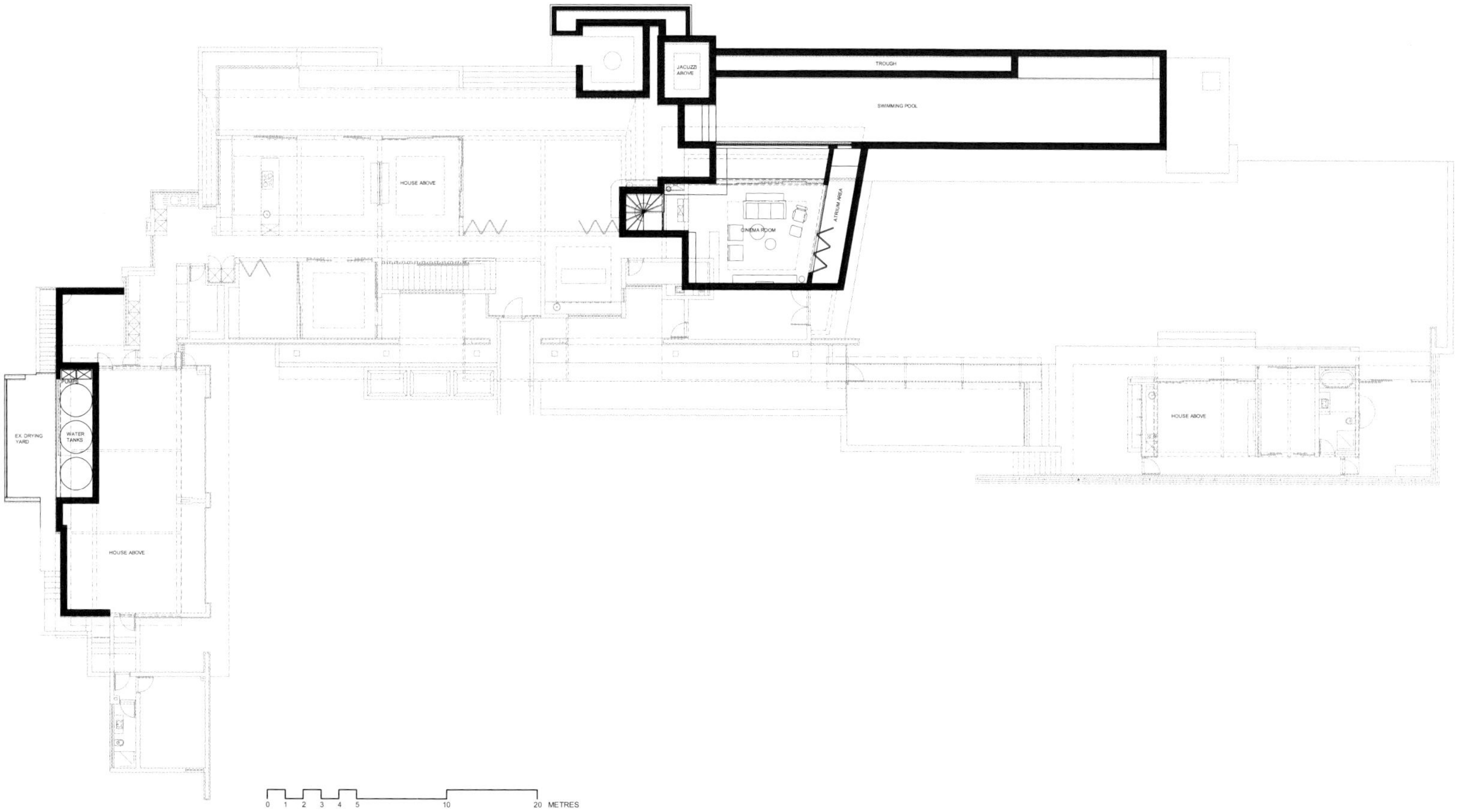

LOWER FLOOR PLAN

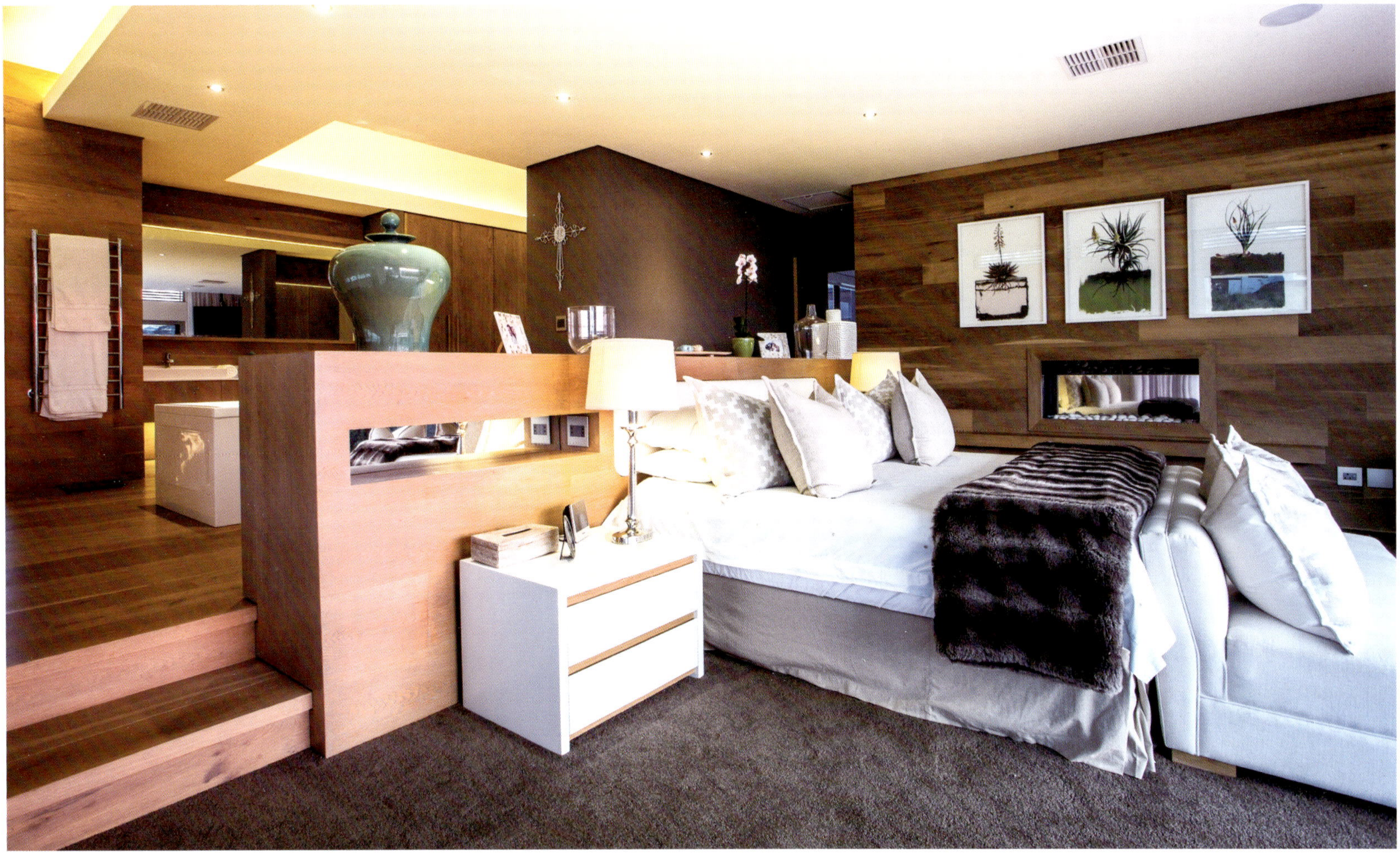

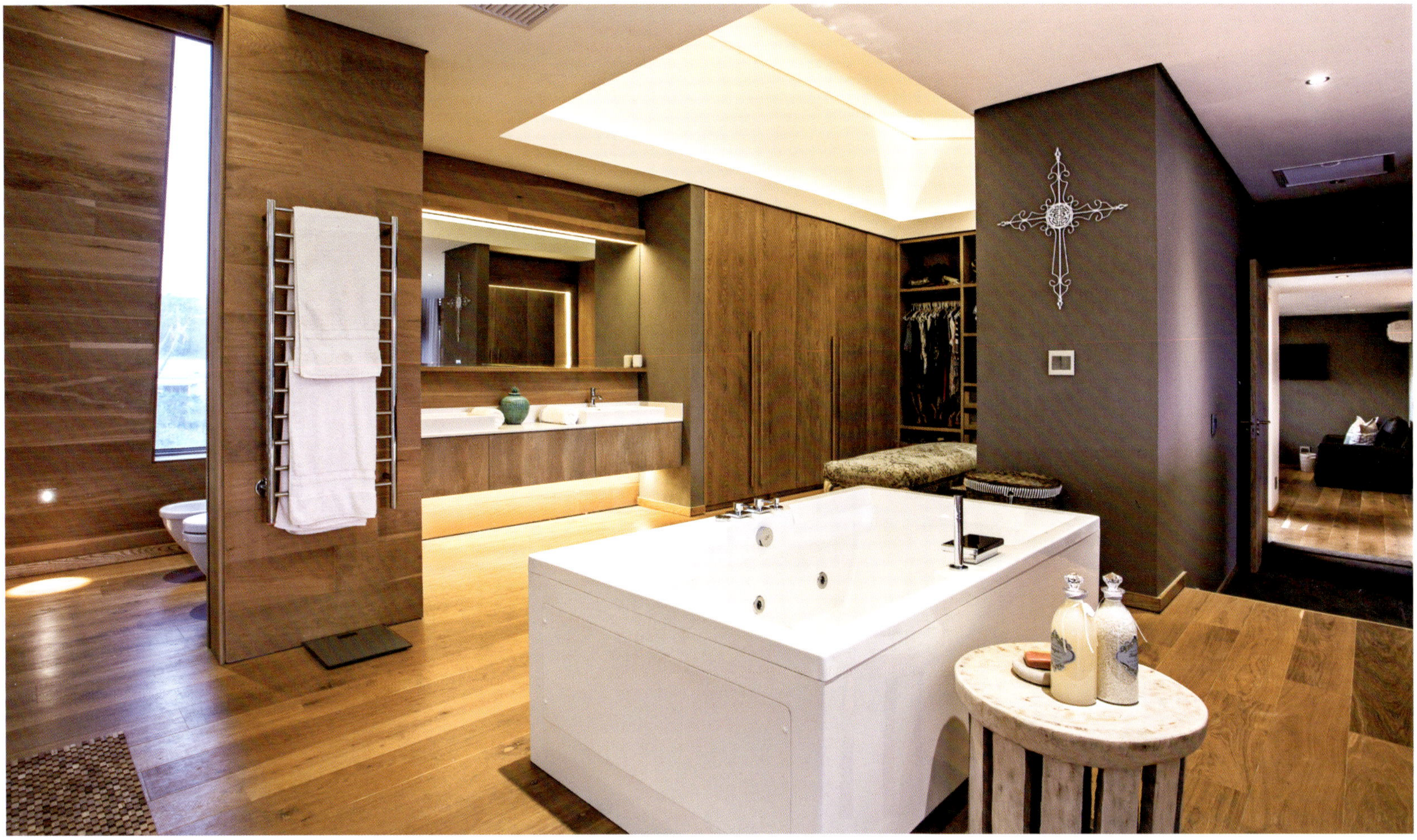

Daniel's Lane Overview

Architects
Blaze Makoid Architecture

"Our work focuses on creating total built environments that are a modern reflection of our clients while striving for a timeless product that remains fresh, exciting and inspiring."

The residence Blaze Makoid Architecture created for a father with three children in Sagaponack on the Eastern Shore of Long Island was inspired by the iconic architect Norman Jaffe's Perlbinder House(1970) and Tod Williams' Tarlo House (1979) but with his and his firm's signature of designing residences that have a quiet elegance that are uniquely suited to each client. As in all of Makoid's work, there is a cohesiveness that unites the architecture with its interiors and the site. The lines between indoors and out blur as they become the greater part of the whole.

The client put his trust in Makoid's ability to find the property and design a residence devoid of anything extraneous. His only mandate — he wanted a house that wasn't "busy".

Sited on a narrow, 4, 047 m^2, oceanfront lot, the design of this house was one of the first projects in the Village of Sagaponack to be affected by the 2010 revision to FEMA flood elevations, requiring a first floor elevation of approximately 5.2 m above sea level with a maximum height allowance of 12.2 m. All construction was required to be located landward of the Coastal Erosion Hazard Line. The location within a high velocity (VE) wind zone added to the planning and structural challenges.

Makoid wanted the structure to appear simple and clean upon arrival. The 2-storey travertine entry facade is highlighted with a single opening accentuated by a cantilevered afromosia stair landing that hovers off the ground. A "cut and fold" in the wall plane bends to allow for one large glass opening, from which an over scaled wood aperture containing the main stair landing cantilevers. A layer of service spaces run parallel to the wall plane creating a threshold prior to reaching the horizontal expanse of the open plan living room, dining area and kitchen that stretches along the ocean side of the house. 4.6 m wide floor to ceiling glass sliding panels maximize the ocean view and create easy access to the patio and pool beyond.

The second floor is imagined as a travertine and glass "drawer" floating above the glass floor below. 3 identical children's bedrooms run from west to east, setting a rhythm that is punctuated by a master bedroom with balcony. It is clad in the same afromosia wood as the stair landing. The quiet elegance and clean lines of the house are accentuated by the materials that also include poured-in-place concrete floors, Calcutta marble cladding and afromosia millwork.

Balcony House

Architects
A-cero

Location
Madrid, Spain

Area
952 m^2

The architecture studio A-cero, led by Joaquin Torres and Rafael Llamazares, presents one of its latest projects, Balcony House in Madrid.

This single family house has an area of 947 m^2 arranged on 3 levels and located on an individual plot of 2100 m^2 with a moderate slope and a prime location with natural surroundings, just 14 km from the center of the capital.

You access the house by the main door that stands out for its high altitude, settled in black glass and black gloss steel. On the ground floor (entrance floor), you enter through a hall with double height which separates the house in two main parts. On this floor, on the left wing, is located the most public and service area. The kitchen with pantry, living room area and stairs which connect all floors. On the right wing, you can find the master bedroom with dressing room and bathroom, and the guest bedroom.

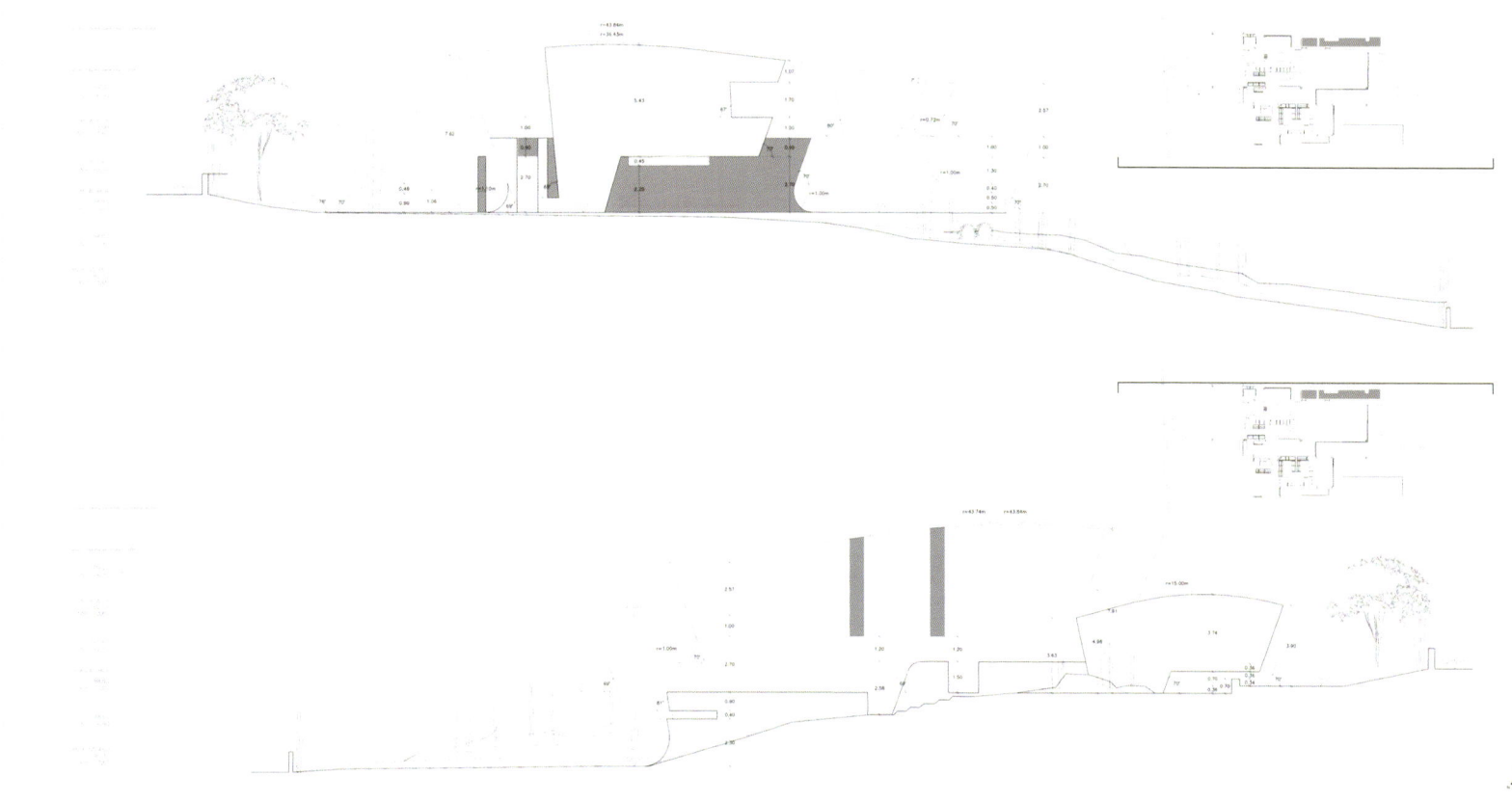

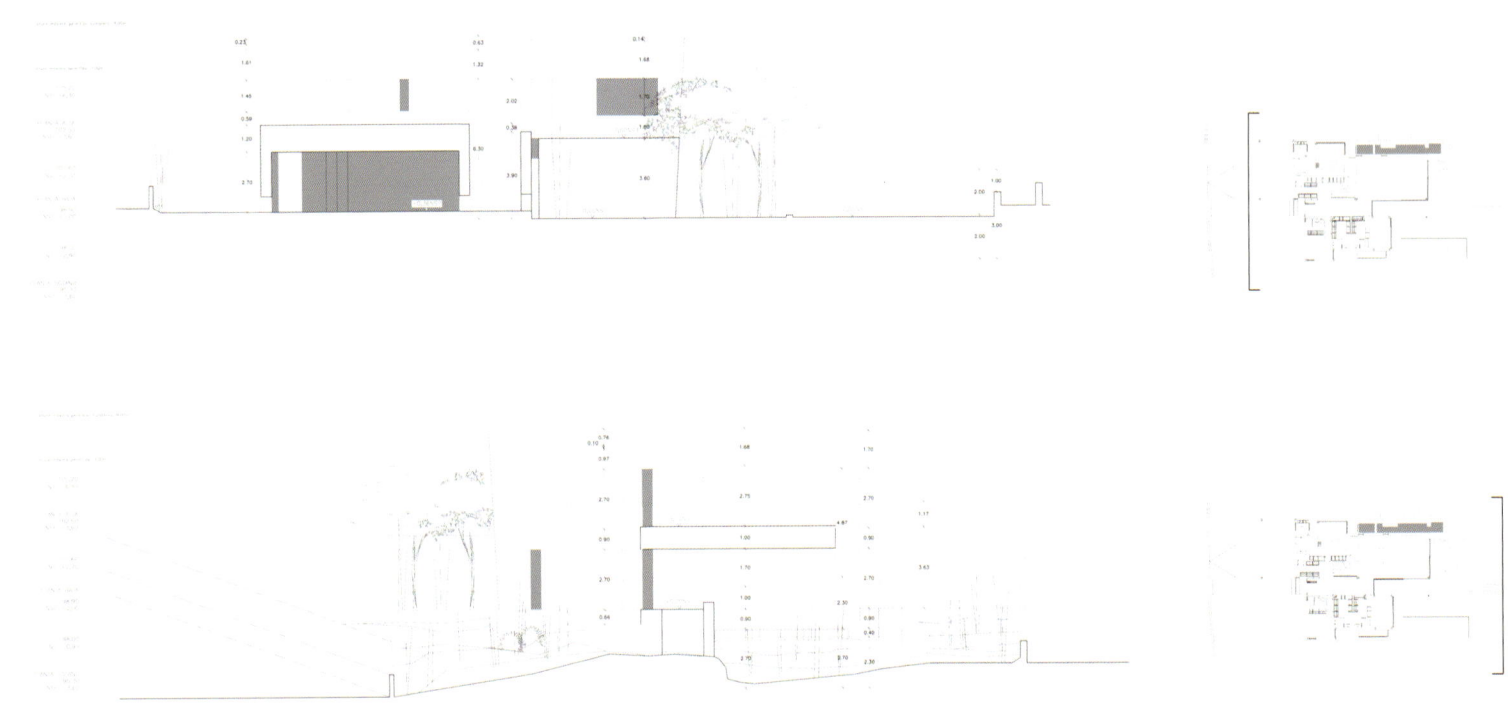

The living room features a great height that gives a sense of spaciousness. A central wood block runs through the ceiling to the wall and becomes television container with hinged panels in the same finish that ends in a fireplace.

This element also acts as a separator item for the dining room which has 2 tables for 8 people which can be combined into a table for 12. The whole room turns towards to the porch and pool area with large glass windows in black with openings, that allows a perfect interior – exterior communication.

The bedroom involves a practical and comfort philosophy and has the particularity that the windows open directly to the outside pool. They have the same views to the extensive wooded area that sets up the environment of the plot.

At the back you will find 2 generous closets open to a bathroom that stands out for its breadth, quality of finishes and elegant elements like the rest of the house.

Upstairs, the same double height foyer extends with a glass walkway that ends up in a bookstore. On one side, there are a study area, office, a cinema room and the two children bedroom suites.

The basement is reserved for installation rooms, utility rooms and iron, wine cellar and a large gym with a play area which

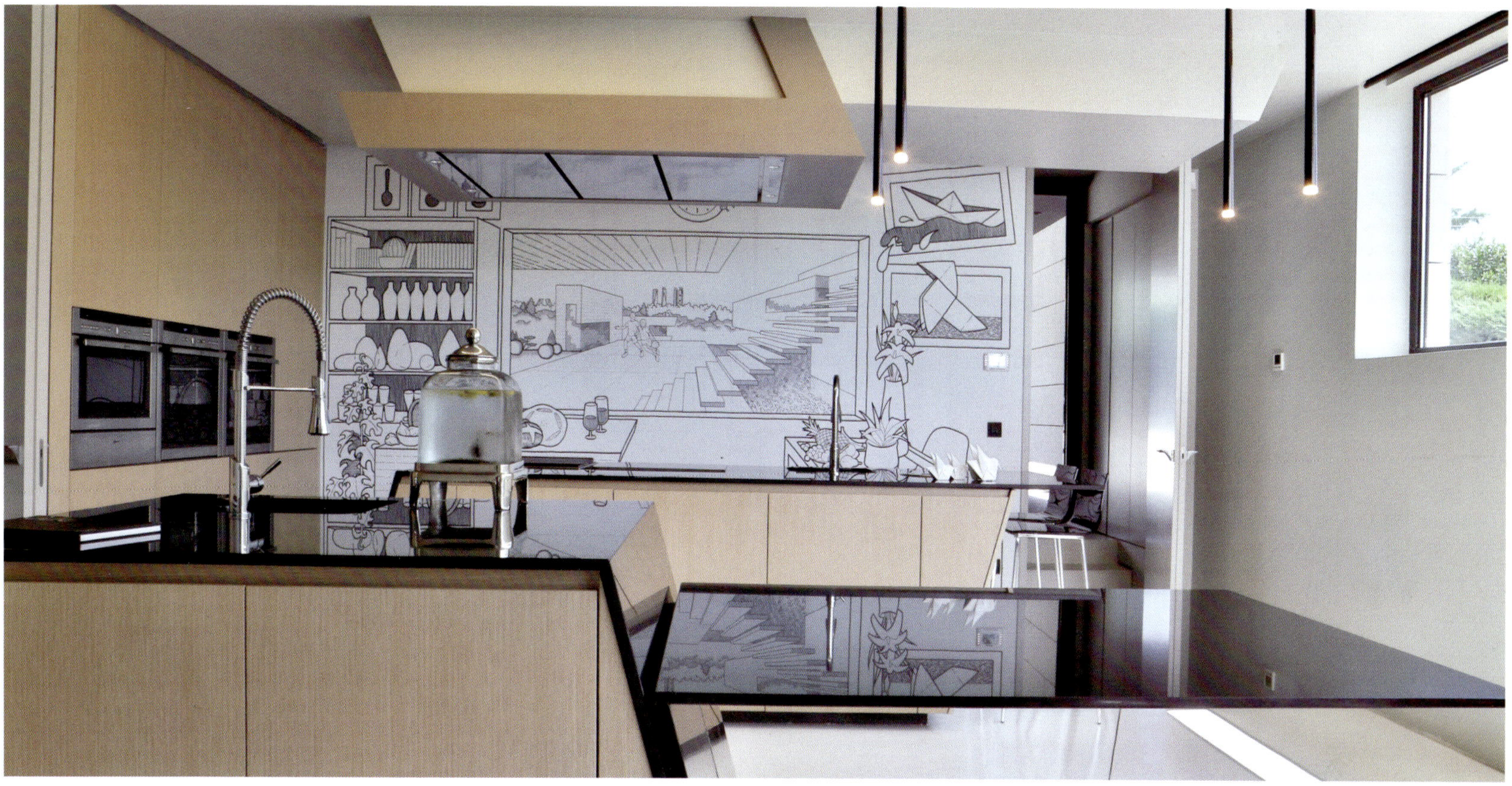

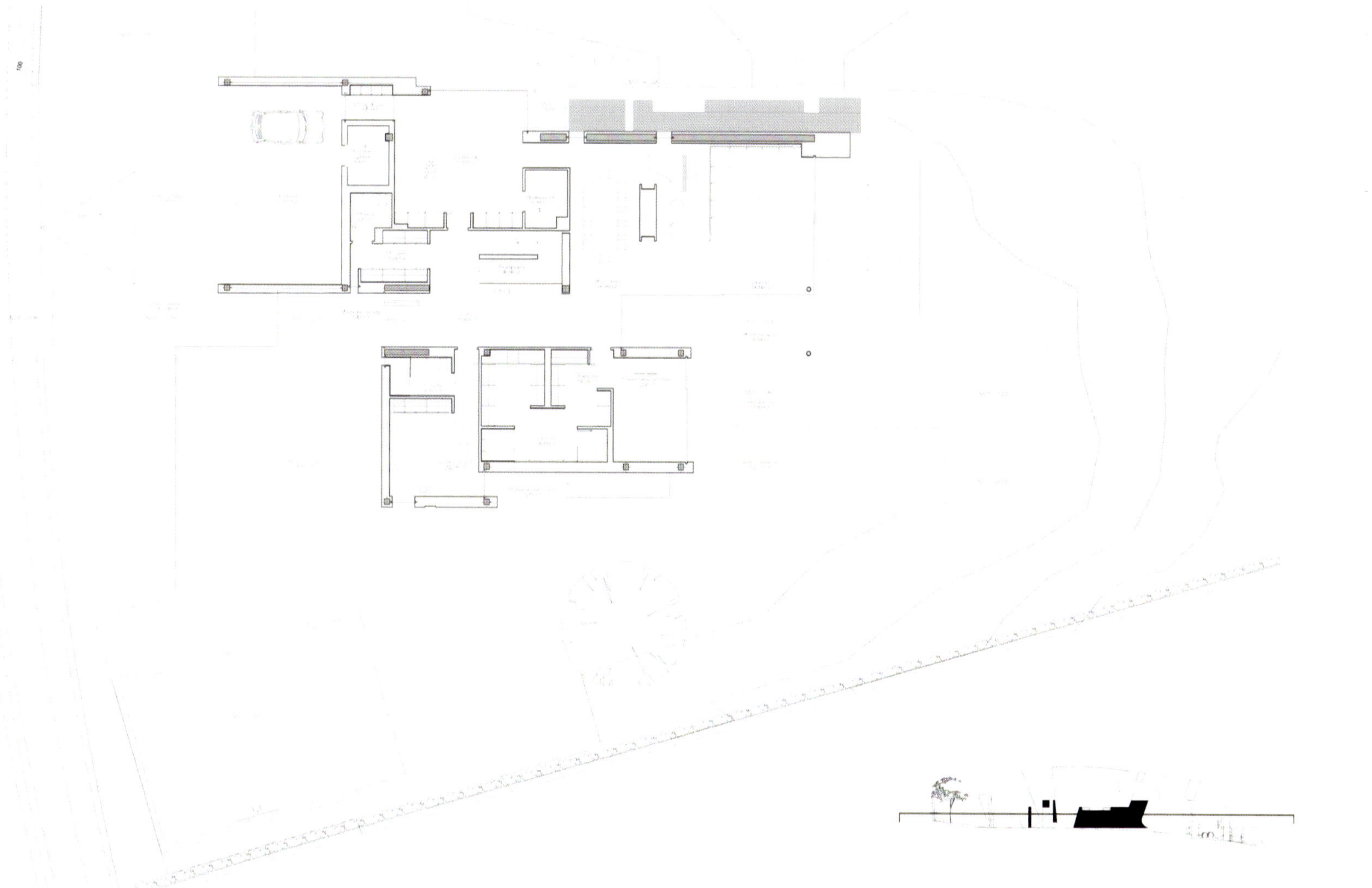

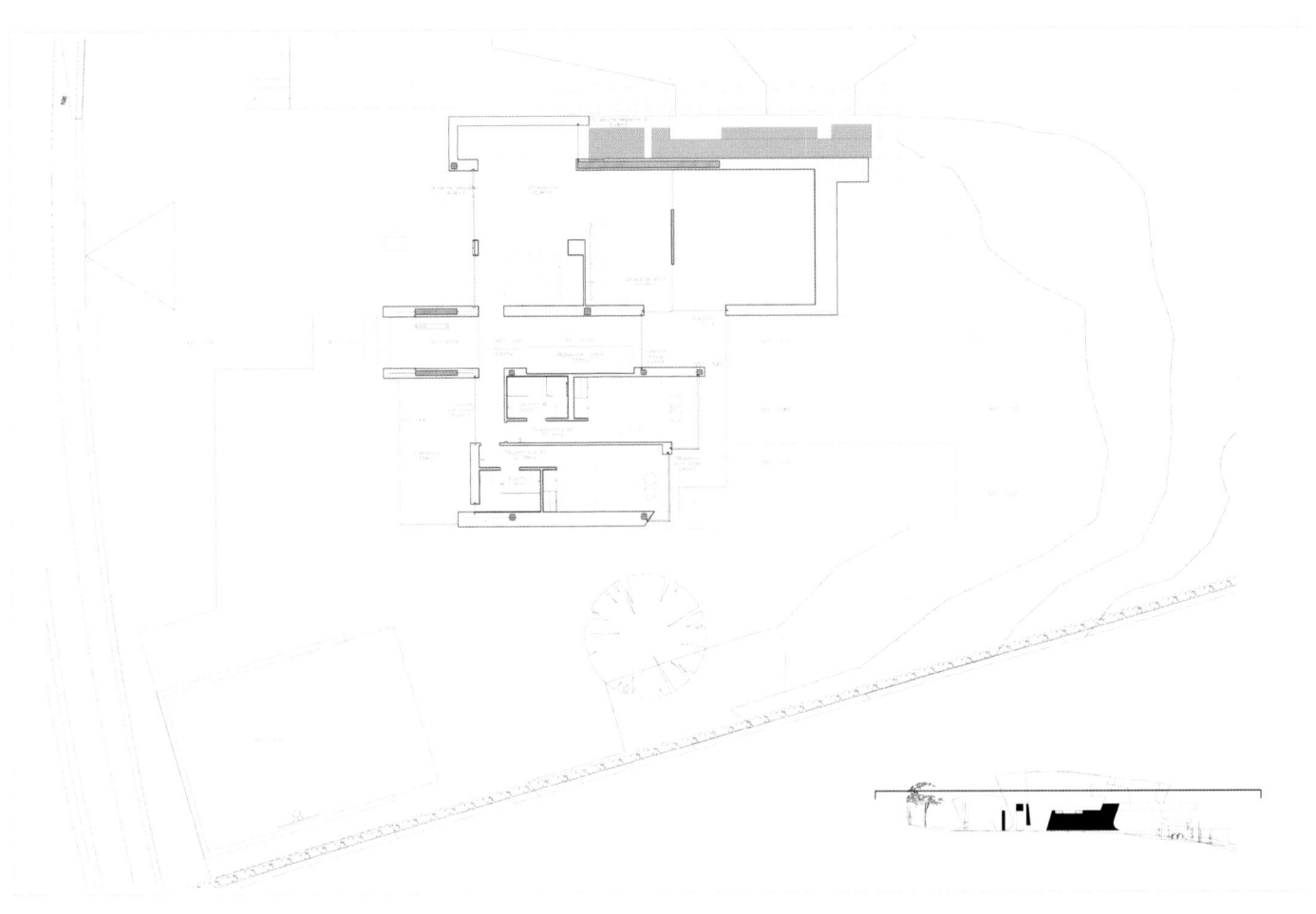

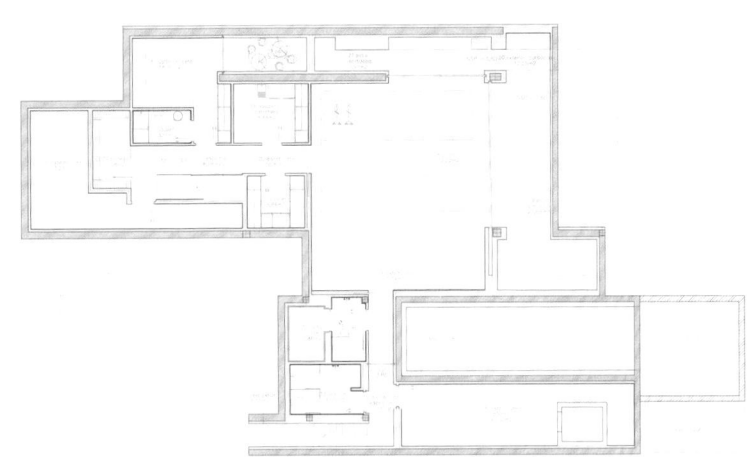

connects directly to a porch with a sliding windows also connecting this area with the garden. This porch is developed as a dining area, barbecue and outdoor kitchen, visually connecting the inside of the pool with the top floor.

The exterior of the house is designed with a curved sculptural image to add an organic value integrated with the environment, clad in white limestone and black glass. It represents an architecture rich in volumes, flat cuts and other aesthetic solutions which give meaning to the internal layouts and to the abundant light that floods into the house.

Private Residence

Architects
Robert Kolenik

A recent example of Eco Chic can be seen in the monumental villa in the south of Holland. The serene atmosphere of materials like wood and leather give a peaceful feeling of coming home. This big living is dominated by a stairway like we know from castles. As a soft tapestry in wood it unfolds itself into the room. In the kitchen area a splendid bar in rock crystal becomes a splendid eye catcher as it is lighted. In the living itself Kolenik designed a special fire that seems to float and which divides the room in a very natural way. The theatrical feeling increases with the stairs, now as a central monument in the room, with bending walls that high above split up in two symmetrical parts. The wooden steps make a very good contrast with the dark tiled floor in leather look. That makes a natural link with the rich leather furniture that invites to sit down. The open fire from Dofine in a crusted finish seems to float. It breaks the space with a look through from a cosy second sofa.

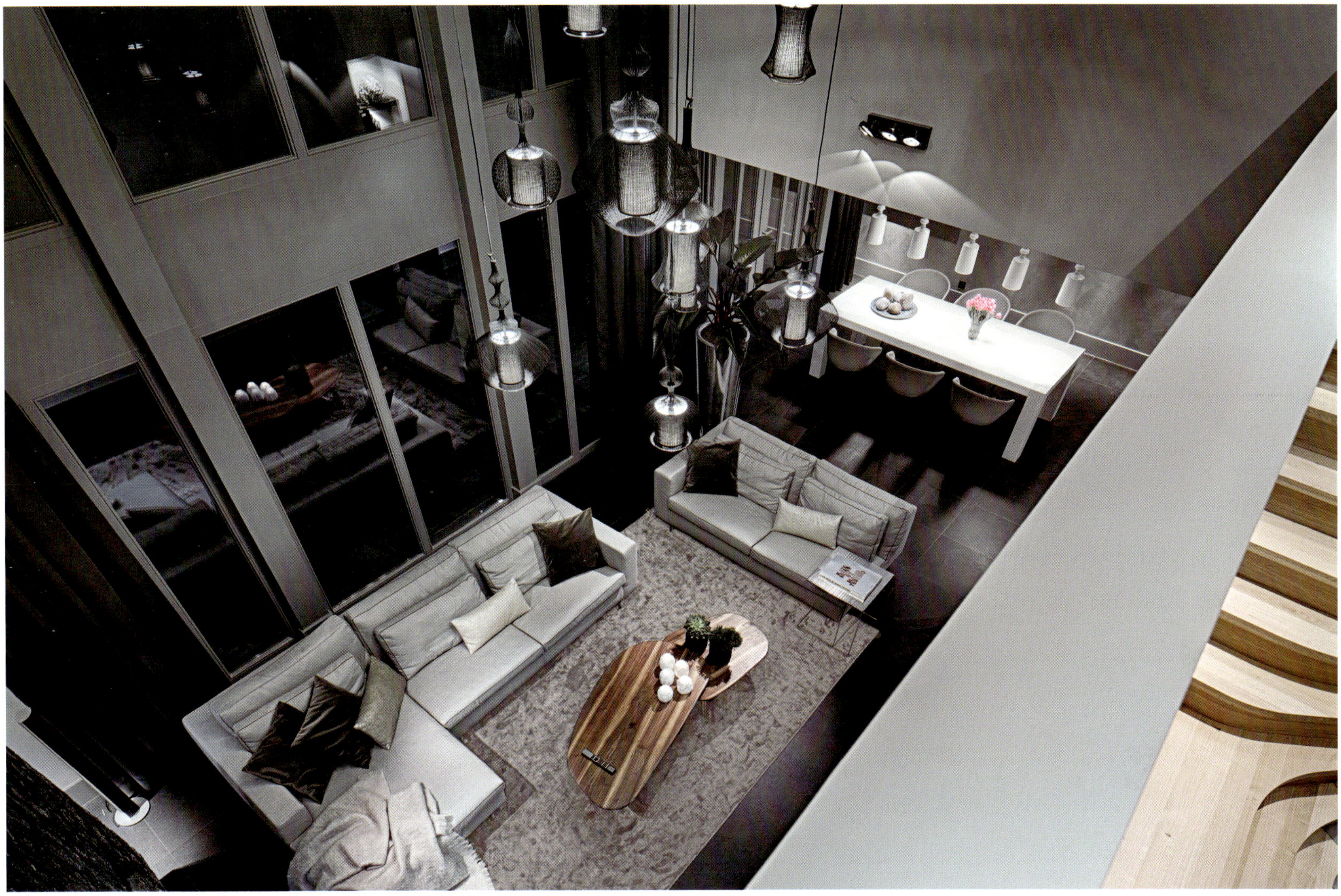

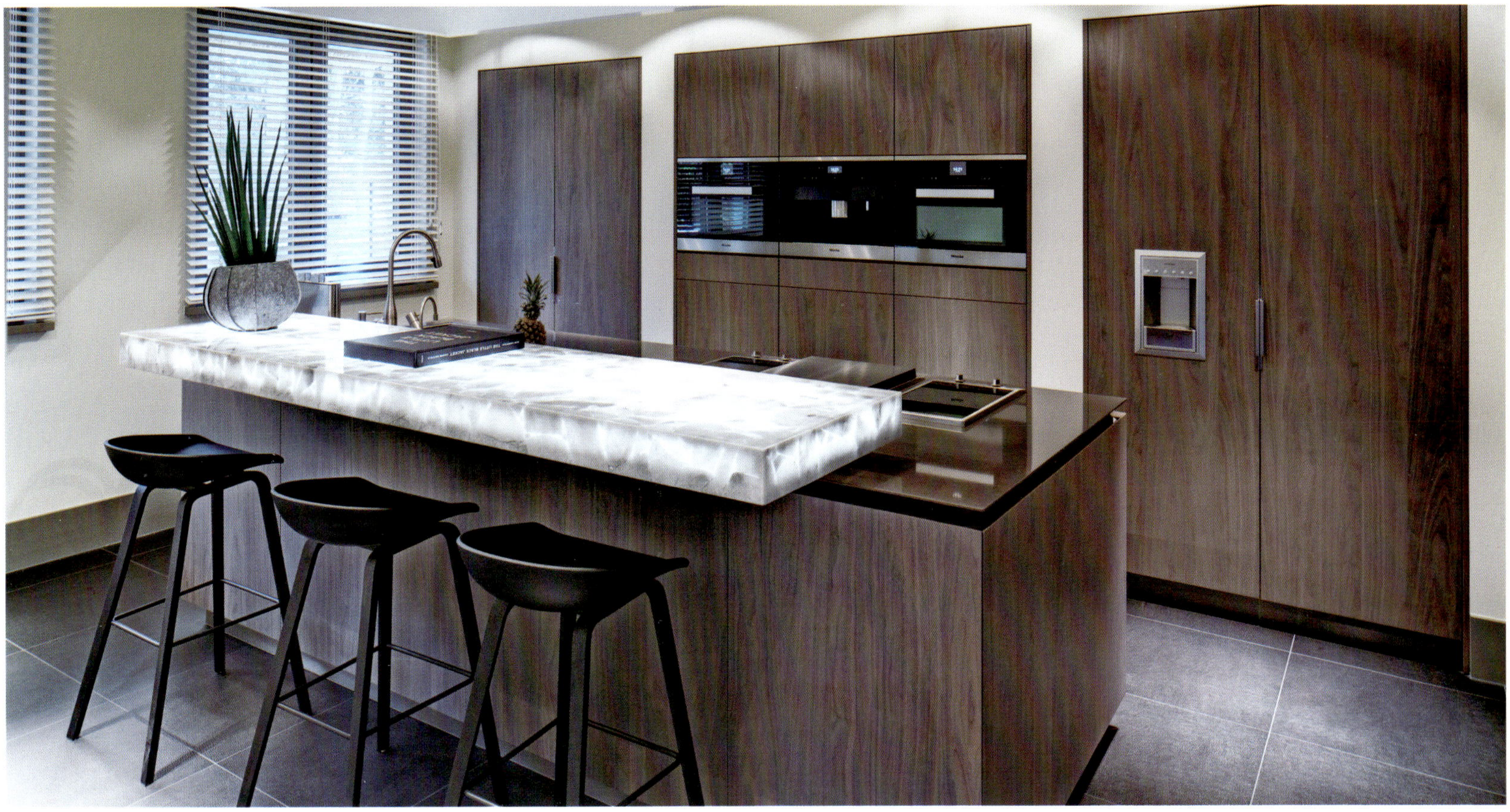

With a long experience in design of professional kitchens Robert Kolenik knew exactly how the cooking area could be practical and beautiful, with most garments behind wooden doors in brush painted nut. There the beautiful lighted bar in smoked pebbles offers the intimacy of a pub without an association with cooking. If the cook is ready for it he or she finds everything in this custom made area. The newest appliances of Miele, an icecrusher, a wine storage and all the luxury to feel guest in your own house. In the cellar this estate did get a second bar where visitors can get a drink in privacy.

Taking the beautiful stairs brings us to the master bedroom and bathroom with stunning make up table. In a former cupboard het integrated the toilet in eucalyptus wood. The door handles in leather underline the soft feeling of the room and of the whole surrounding. Like in nature itself the combination of serene and special effects of lighting makes the owners every day happy as here they never have a dull moment.

Russian Hill

Architects
jmA

Principal
John Maniscalco

Project Architect
Kelton Dissel

Project Team
John Maniscalco, Kelton Dissel, Mick Khavari

Location
San Francisco, CA

Area
542 m²

Photography
Paul Dyer

This certified LEED Platinum new 4-storey home establishes an understated but dignified urban presence on an atypically wide San Francisco site. A transitional 2-storey glass-walled entry hall draws users to an airy and open living level. An increasingly light stair element transitions from floor to floor ultimately arriving at a roof deck enjoying panoramic views.

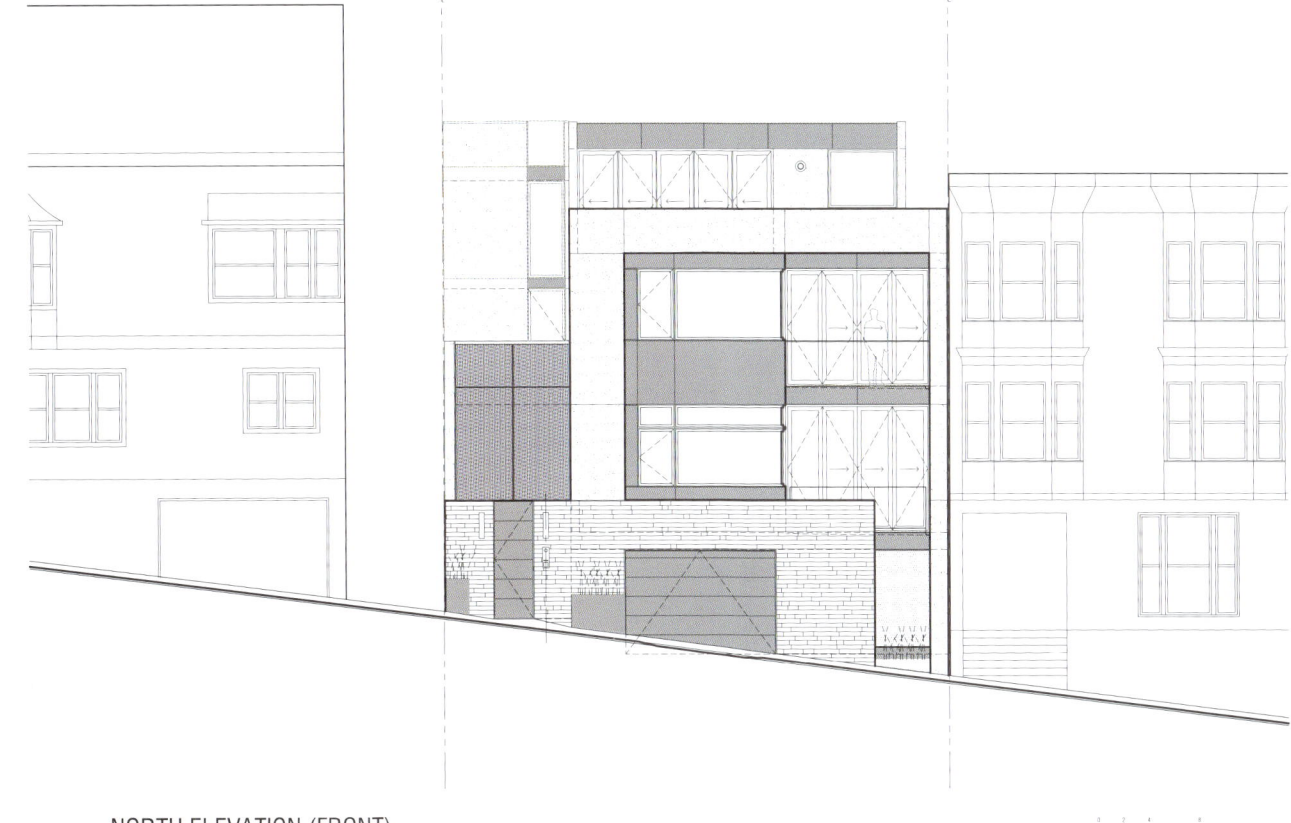

NORTH ELEVATION (FRONT)

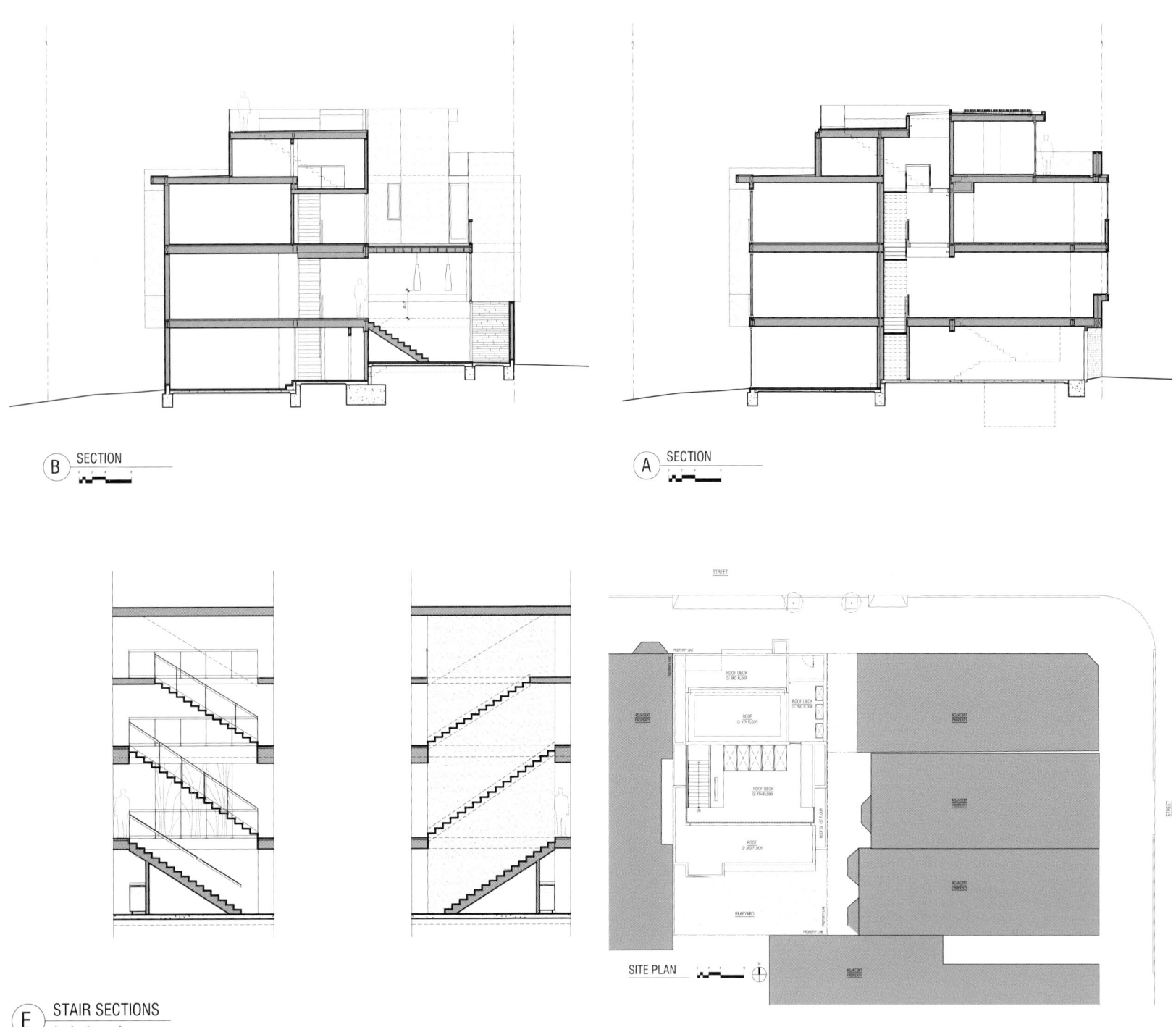

B ⊙ SECTION

A ⊙ SECTION

E ⊙ STAIR SECTIONS

SITE PLAN

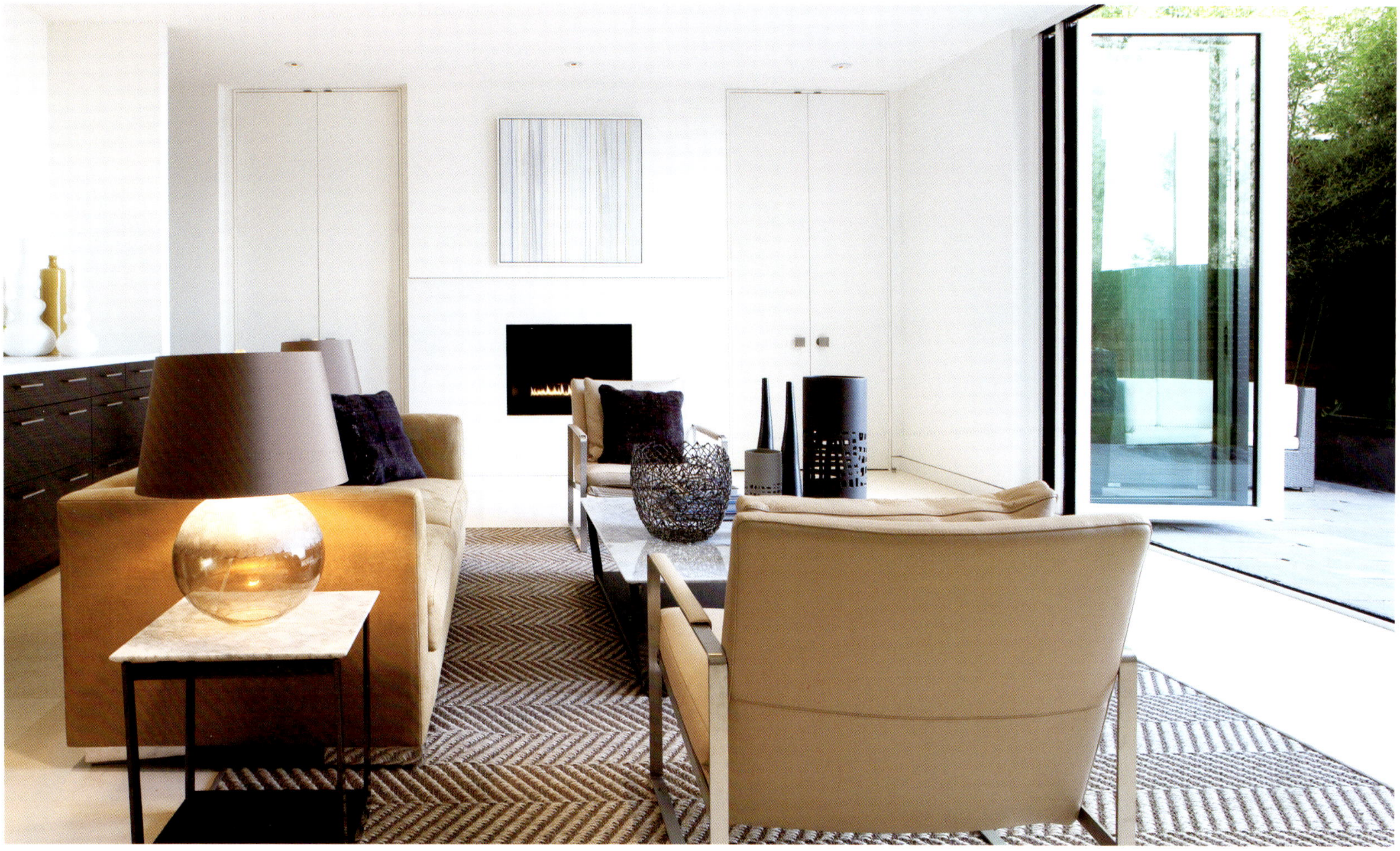

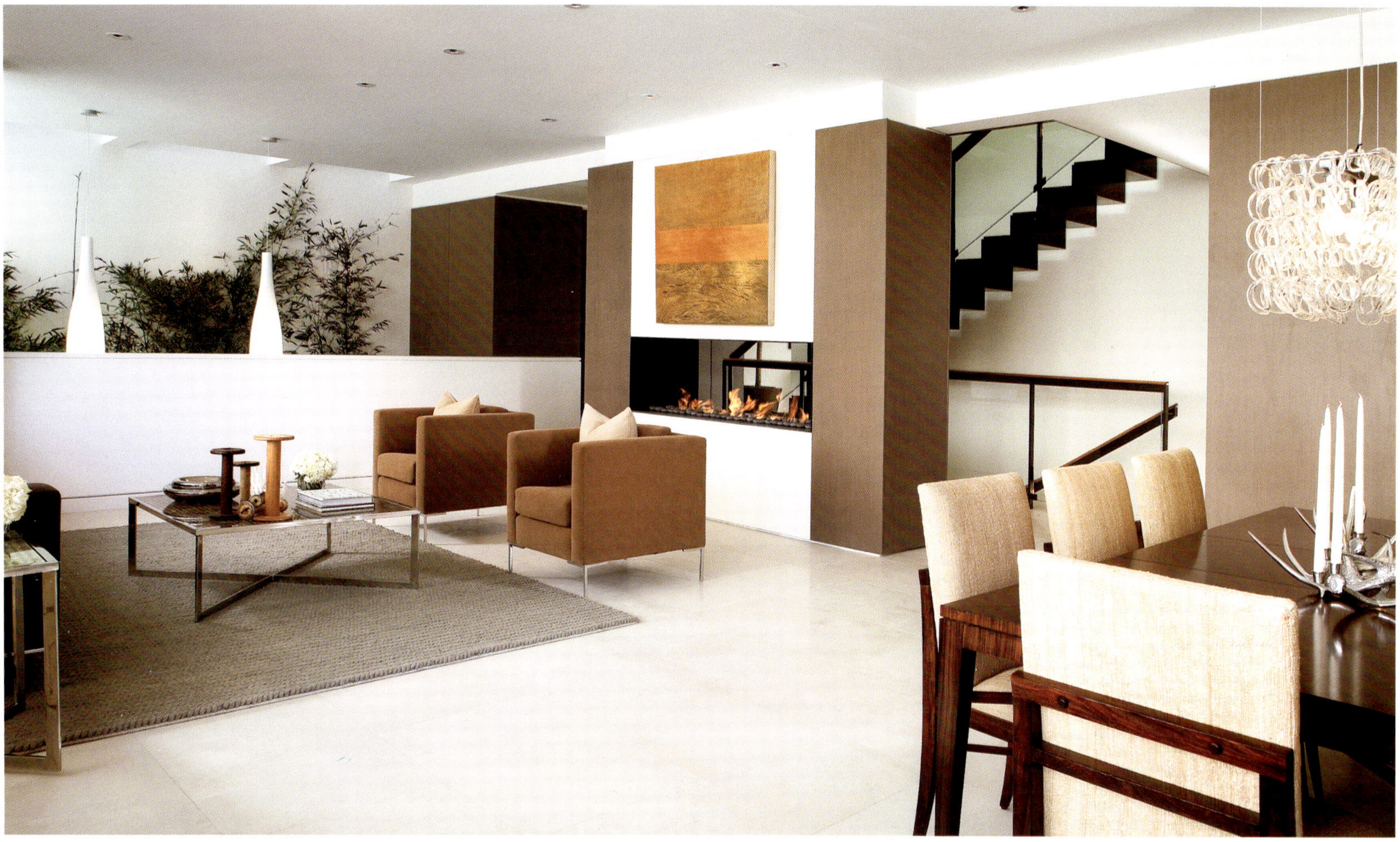

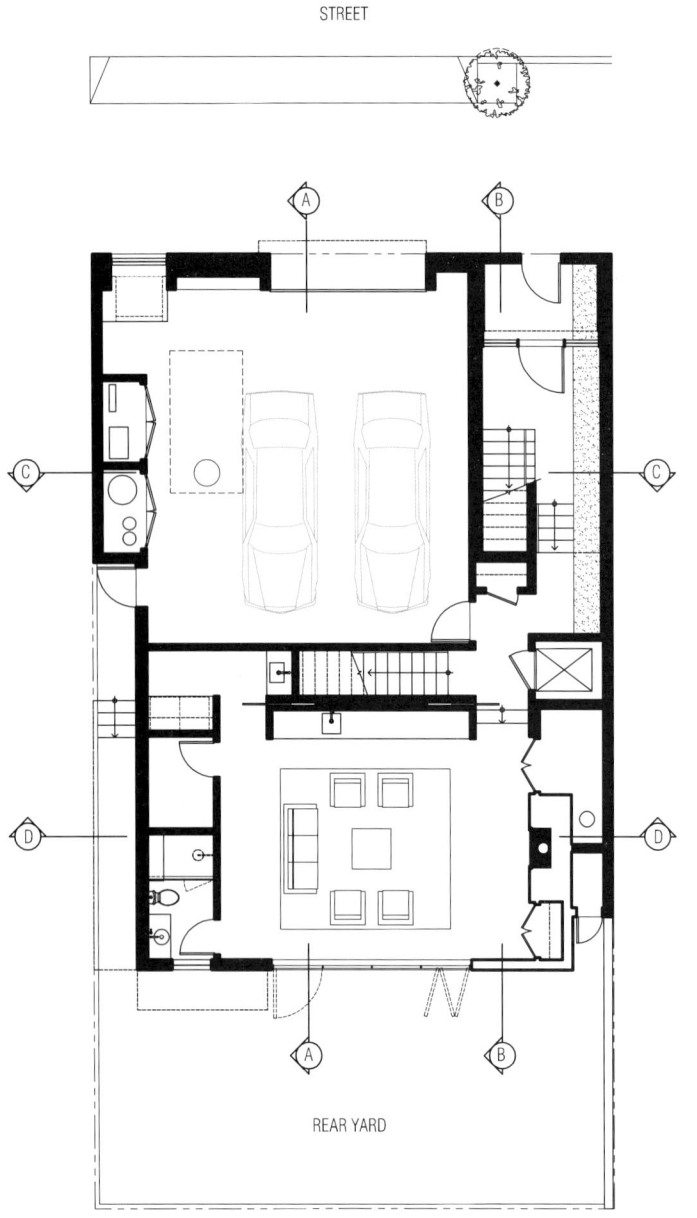

STREET

Ⓐ Ⓑ

Ⓒ　　　　　　　　　　　　　　Ⓒ

Ⓓ　　　　　　　　　　　　　　Ⓓ

Ⓐ Ⓑ

REAR YARD

FIRST FLOOR PLAN

N

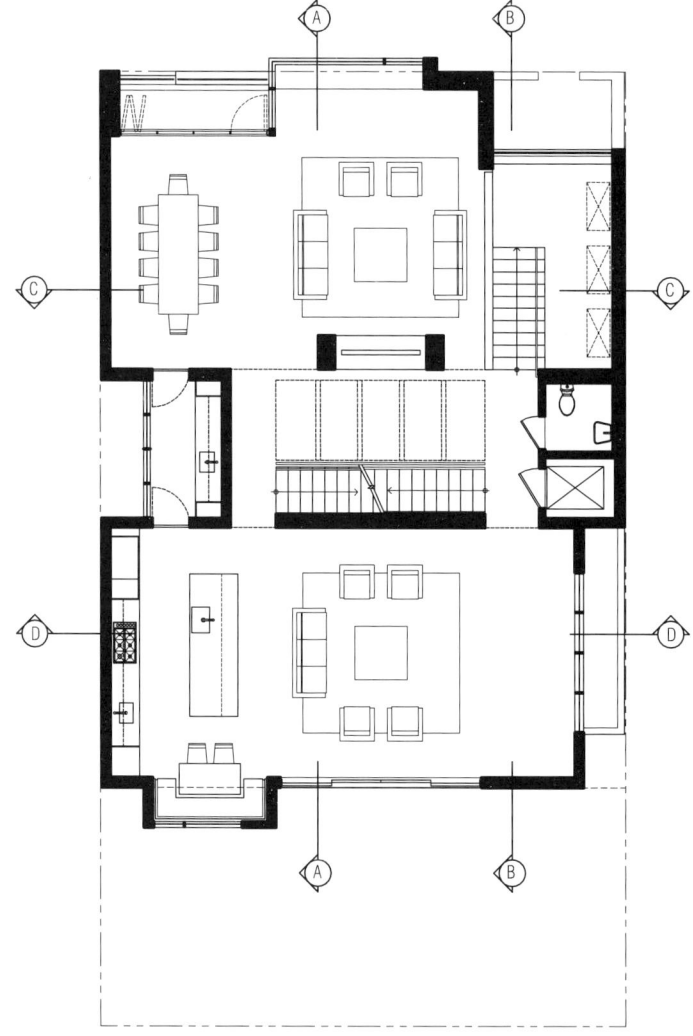

Ⓐ Ⓑ

Ⓒ　　　　　　　　　　　　　　Ⓒ

Ⓓ　　　　　　　　　　　　　　Ⓓ

Ⓐ Ⓑ

SECOND FLOOR PLAN

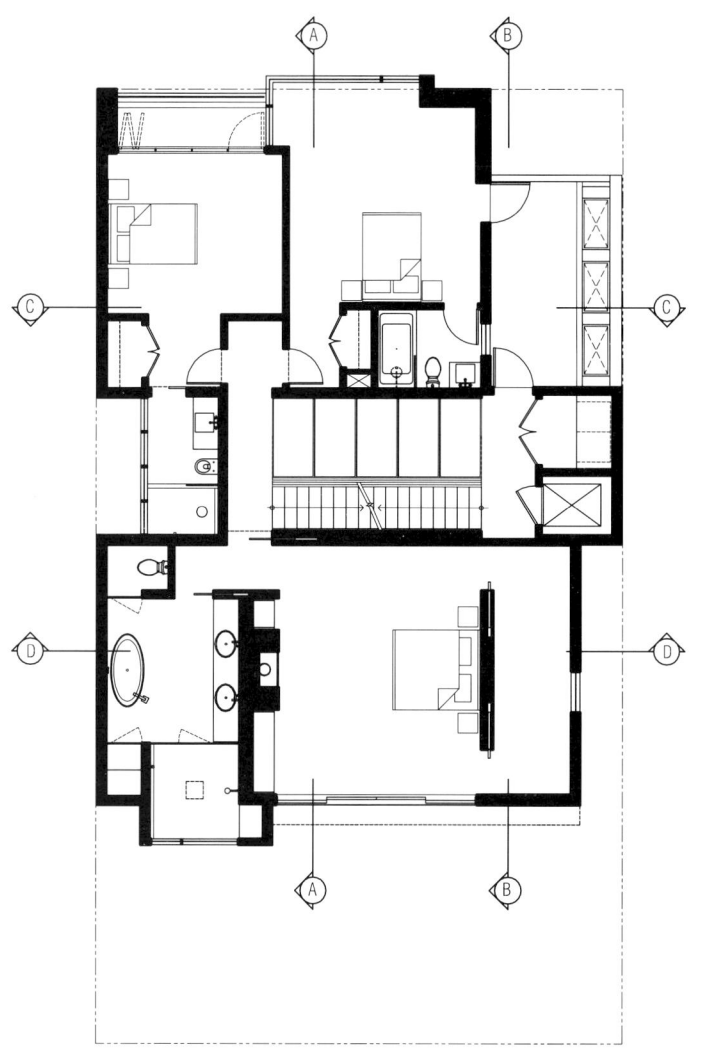

THIRD FLOOR PLAN

FOURTH FLOOR PLAN

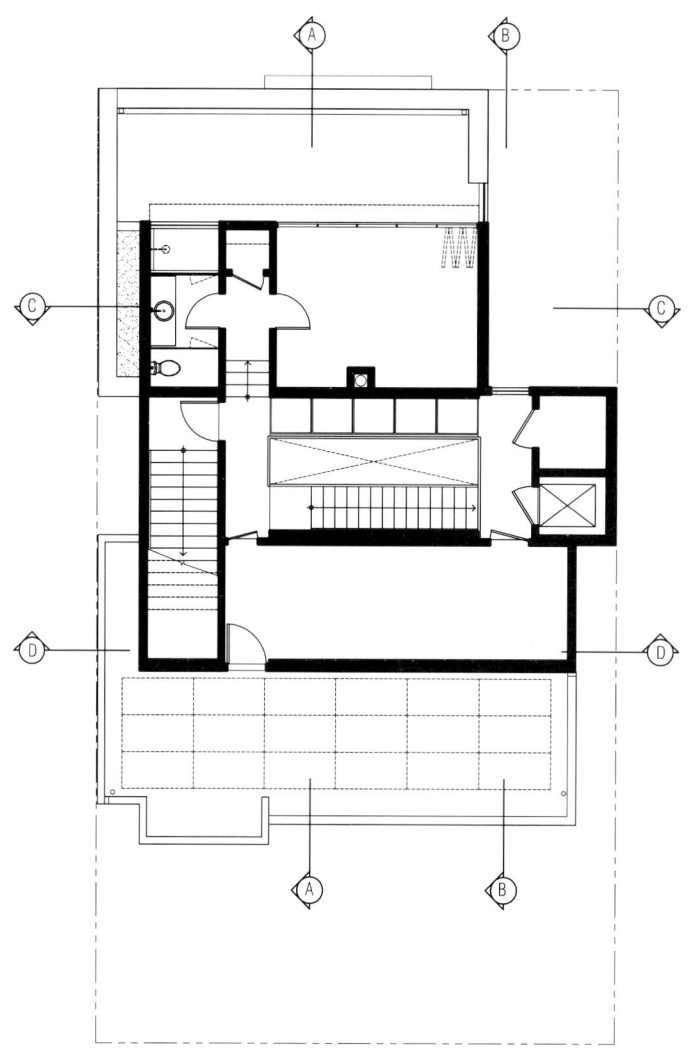

Casa Sorteo Tec 191

—

Designer
Arq. Bernardo Hinojosa

Location
Monterrey, N.L., México

Area
750 m²

Photography
Francisco Lubbert

The design reflects strong heavy materials which perfectly blend with the landscape that surrounds the house.

Steel and stone make an excellent material for décor and design of the property.

The pool and terraces make a relaxing environment and adding palm trees to the mix creates a resort like atmosphere.

The mezzanine library is a feature Arq. Bernardo Hinojosa likes to encourage, is one of many signature styles he has.

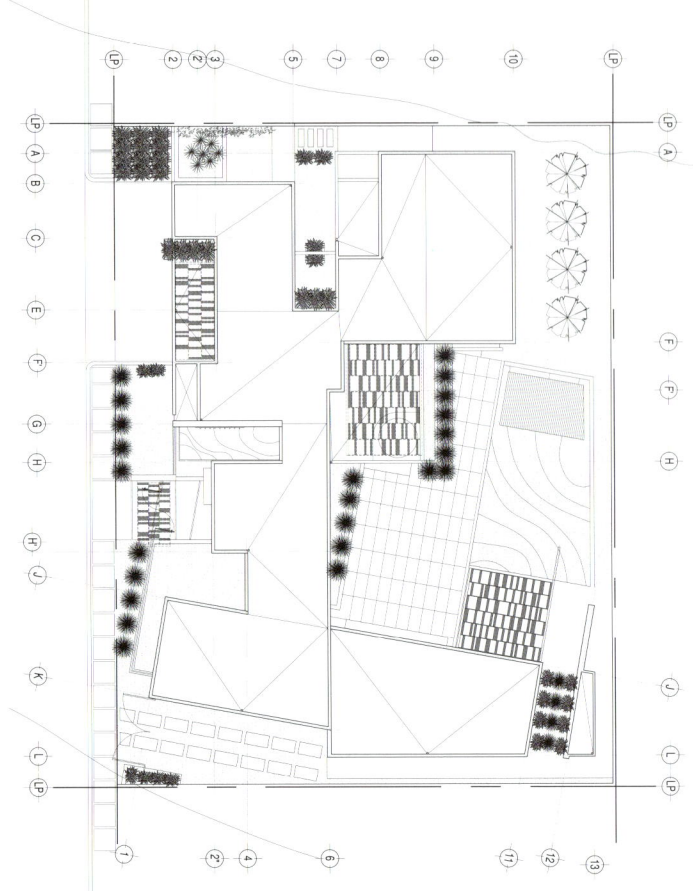

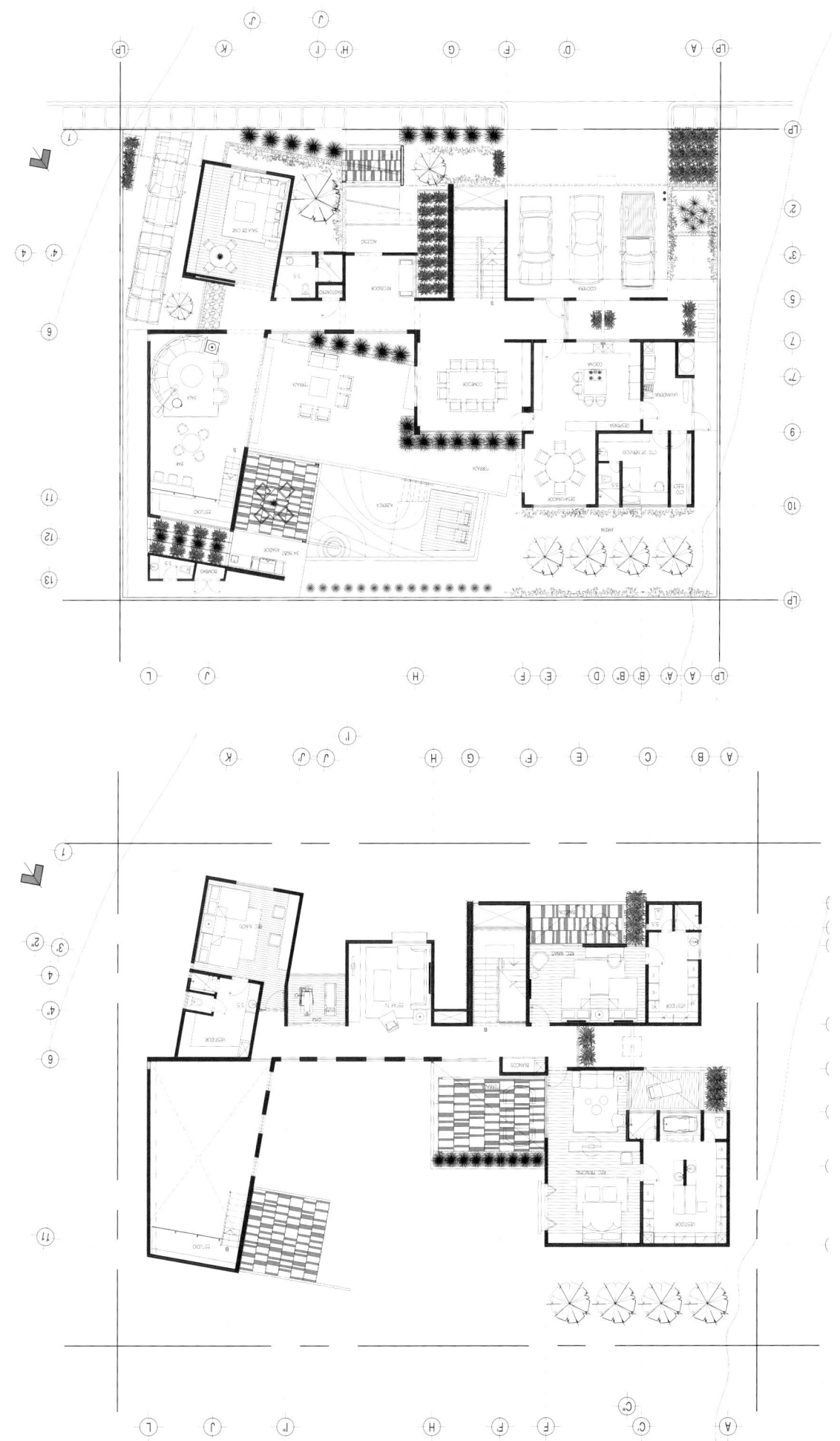

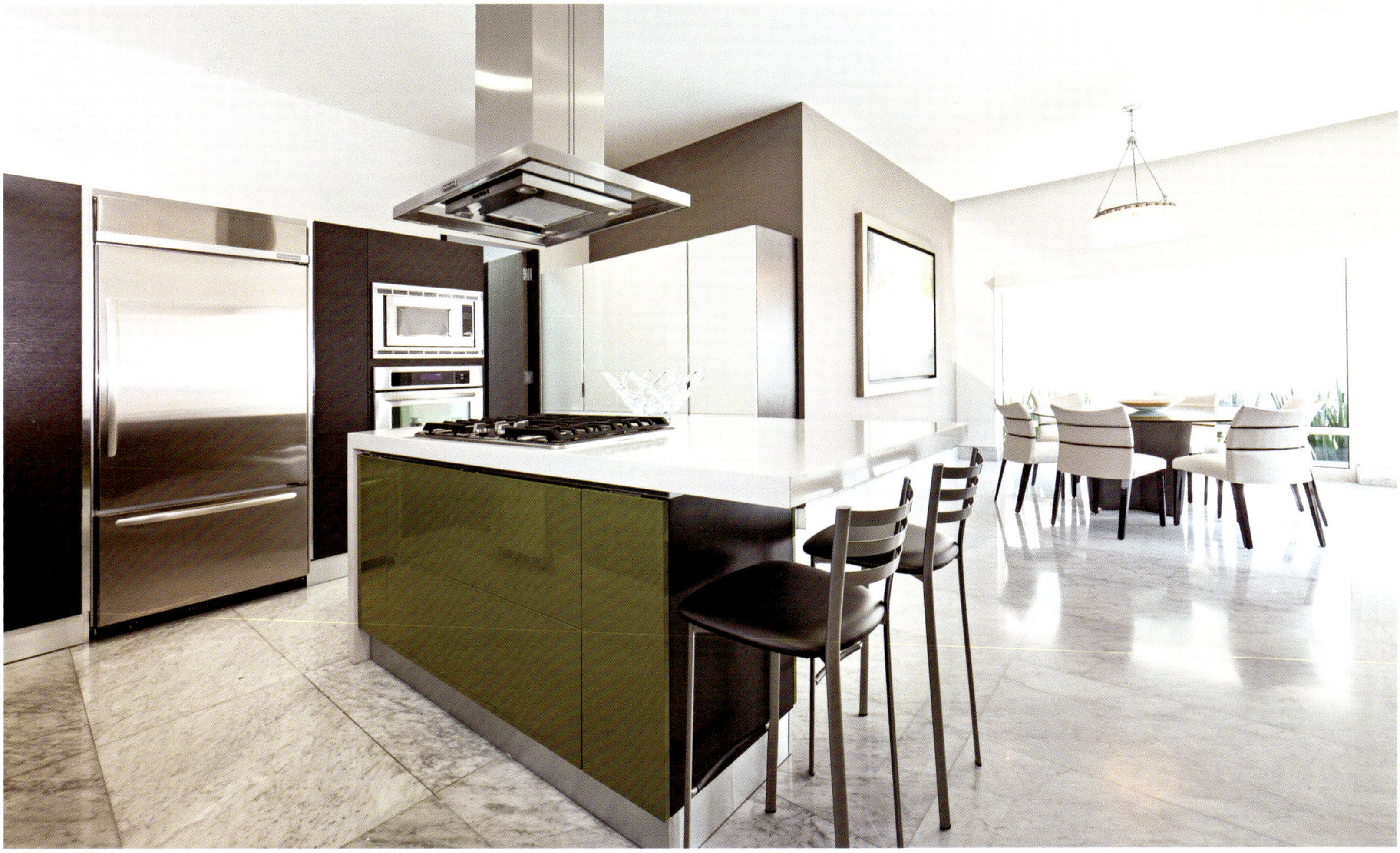

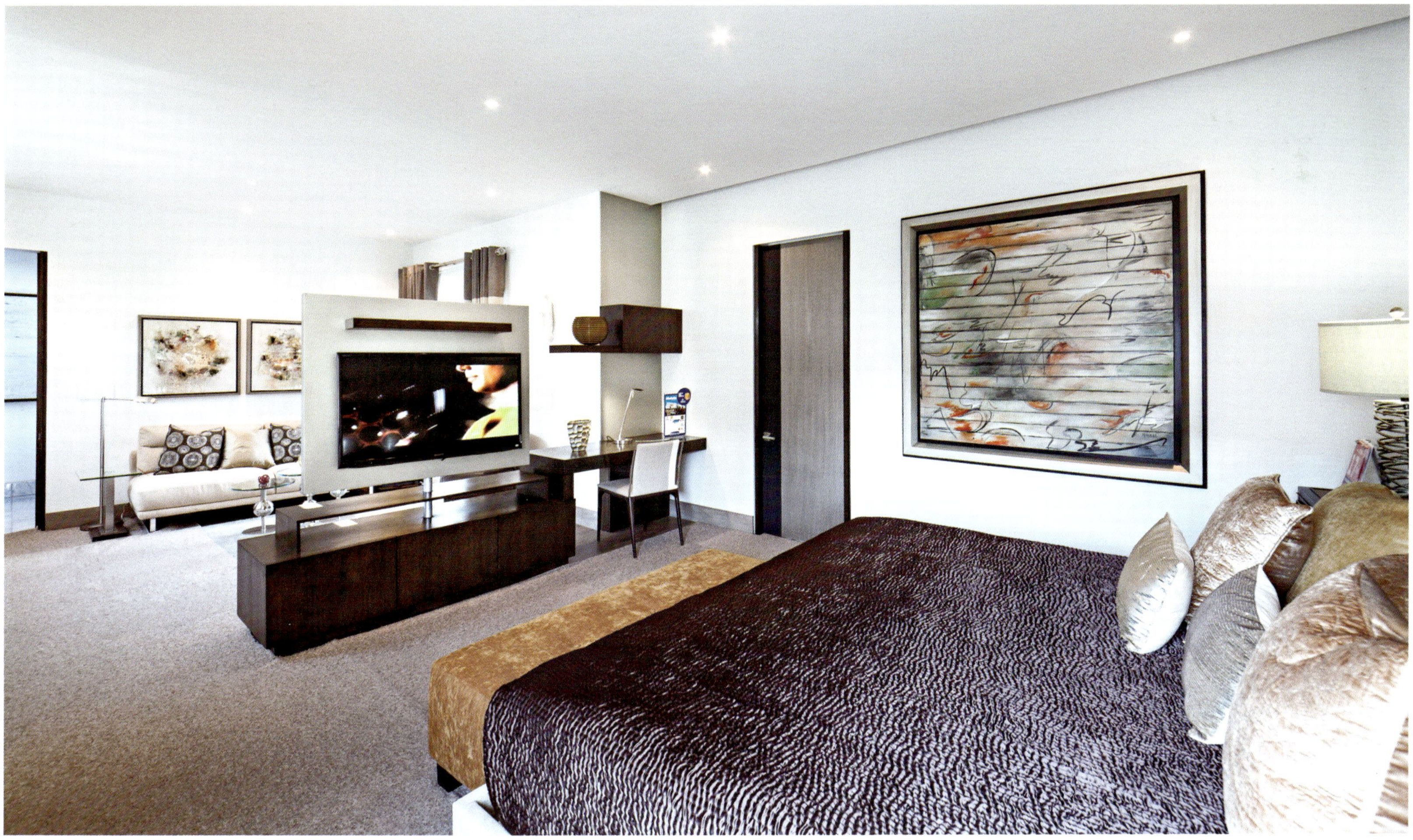

Villa Escarpa

Architects
Mario Martins

Project Team
Sónia Fialho, Rita Rocha, Rui Duarte, Rui Saavedra, Sara Glória, Sónia Santos, Fernanda Pereira, Ana Filipa Santos, José Cabrita, António Caçapo

Technical projects
Nuno Grave, Engenharia, Lda

Client
anonymous

Location
Luz Algarve, Portugal

Photography
Fernando Guerra [FG+SG]

Villa Escarpa is located near the village of Praia da Luz, in the district of Lagos, Algarve, in the south of Portugal.

A condition of the planning permission was that the new house be constructed in the space occupied by a previous building. This had little architectural or technical merit, but was located in an exceptional position on an escarpment overlooking the Algarve

coastline and village of Praia da Luz.

The footprint was therefore predetermined: on a very steep slope, and exposed to the prevailing winds. Paradoxically, it is these constraints and difficulties that underpin the conceptional basis of the project.

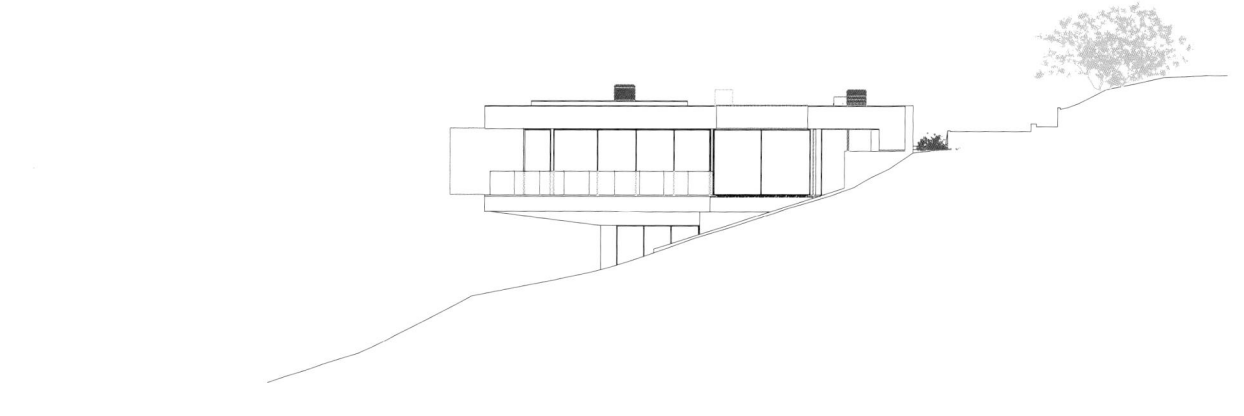

ALÇADO SUL

ALÇADO POENTE

0 1 2   5m

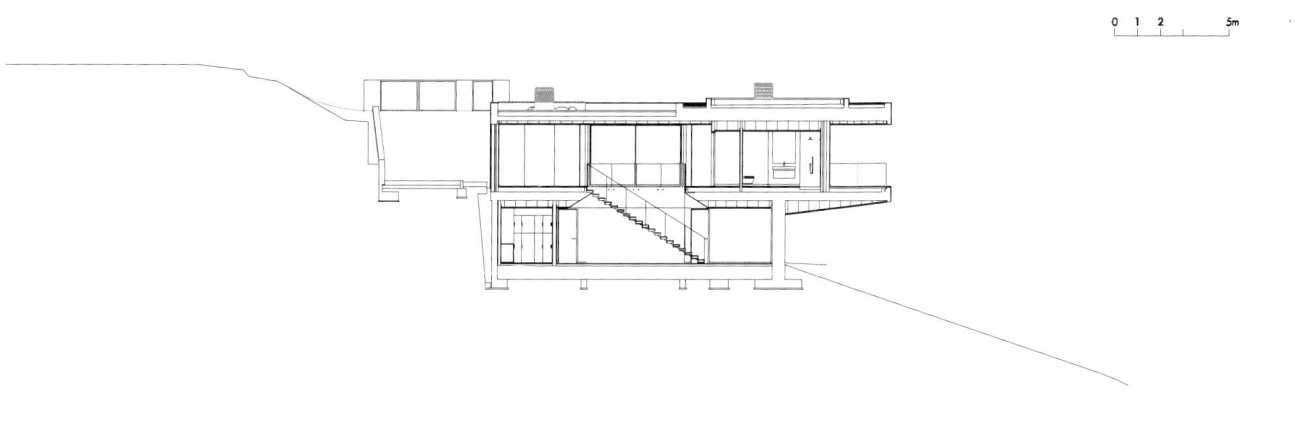

CORTE 1

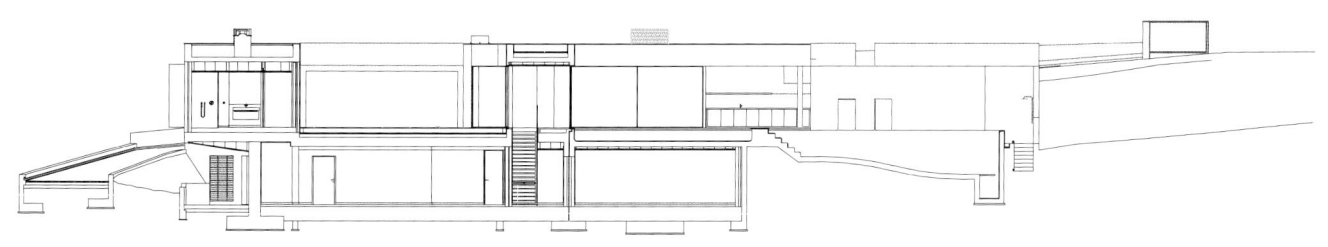

CORTE 2

0 1 2   5m

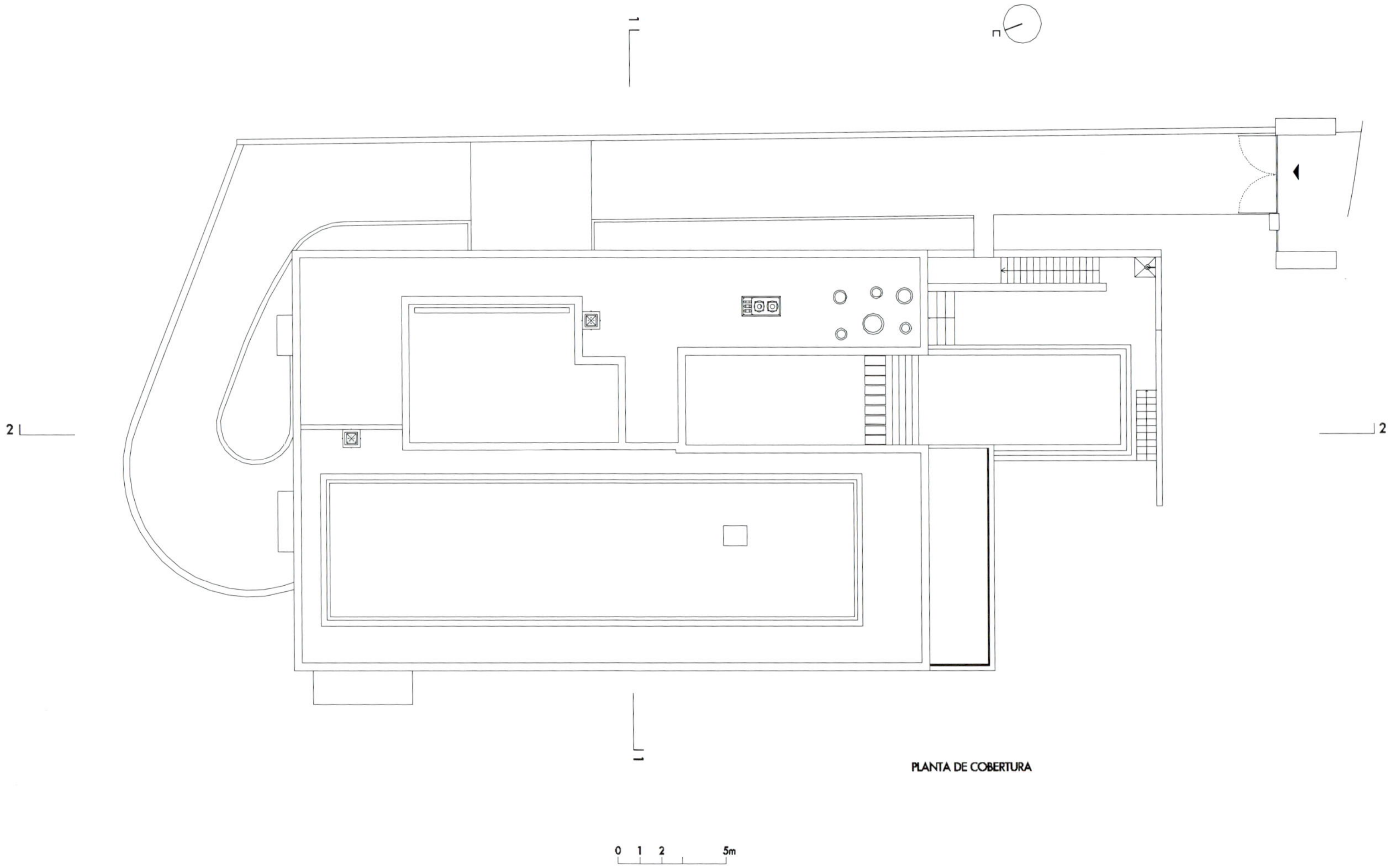

PLANTA DE COBERTURA

0 1 2   5m

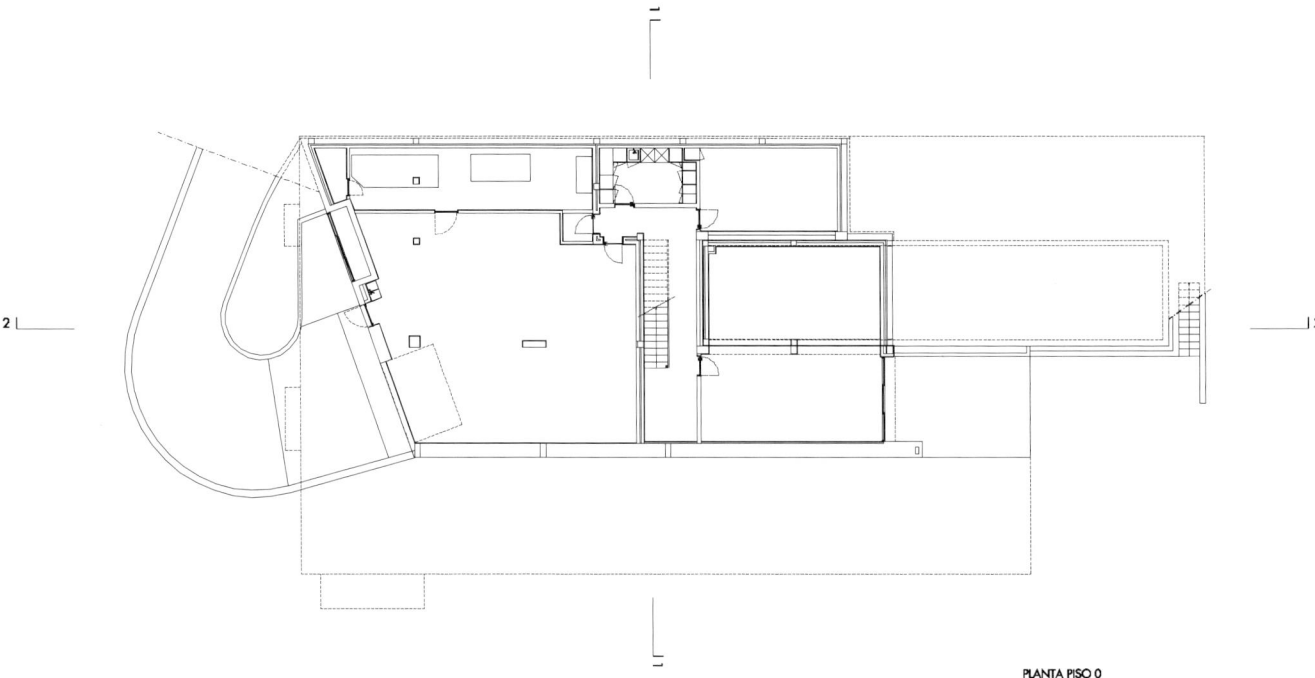

In an architectural language, pure and contemporary, we created sheltered terraces and courtyards for outside living. These are cut from the horizontal volume which is white and highly transparent. This volume gently sits upon an exposed concrete support giving the appearance of the house floating above the landscape. The touch on the environment, which we want to preserve, is minimized and resolves the difficult balance of the building with its physical support. This ensures a desirable visual lightness.

The house merges with a long water surface which dissects the wide living and kitchen spaces. These spaces are complemented by terraces, open to the sun and impressive views. This is the social area of the house, open and fluid.

4 bedrooms are located in a private area with access from a corridor that runs alongside a central courtyard. In this private courtyard the natural light is filtered, creating an intimate and desirable space.

The lower area provides garaging and technical support.

The roof terrace accentuates the visual lightness of the floating building in its environment.

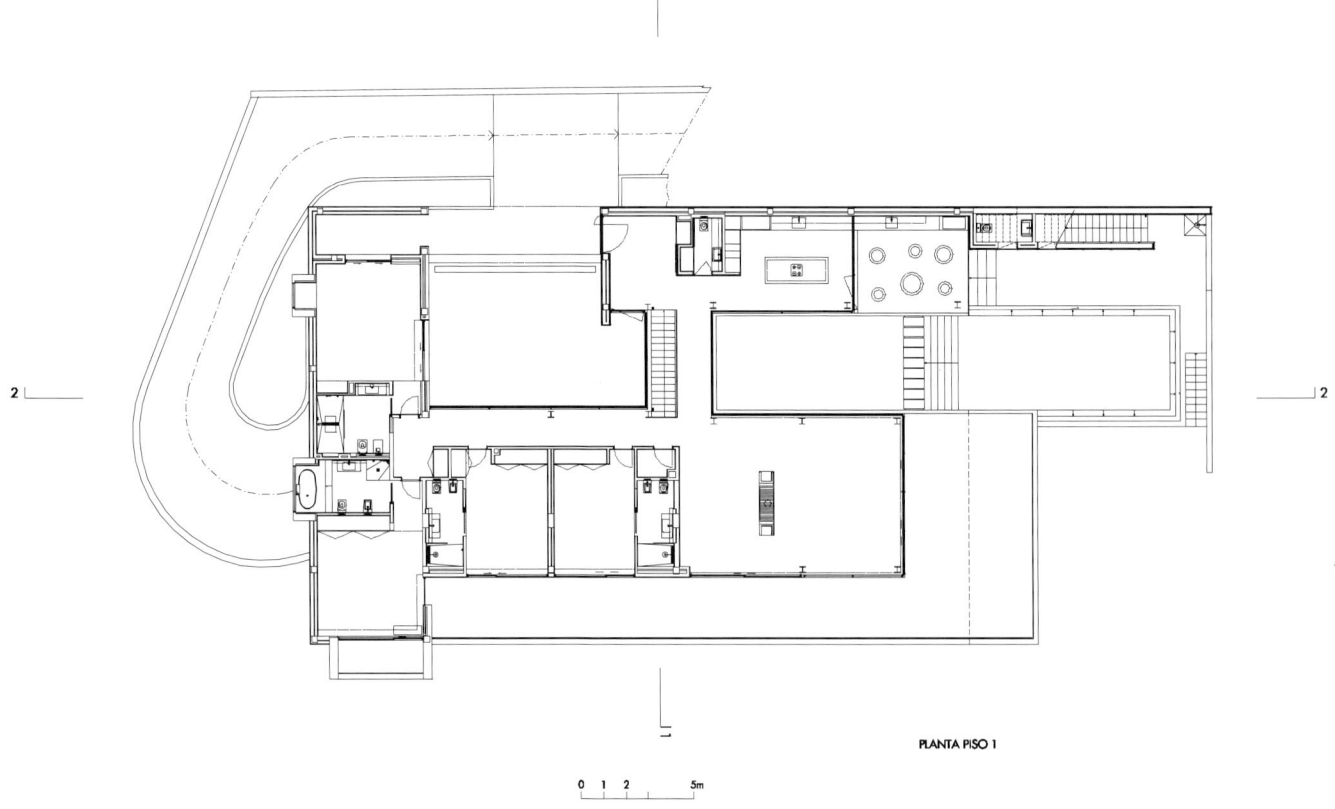

PLANTA PISO 1

0 1 2   5m

Oceanique Villas

Architects
MM++ architects / MIMYA .co

Project Architect
My An PHAM THI

Location
Mui Ne, Phan Thiet, Vietnam

Building Area
1,014 m^2

Photographs
Hiroyuki OKI

This project is a small real estate development located in Mui Ne, a seaside holiday destination in Vietnam's south east coast.

The site has a trapezoidal shape 110 m deep between the ocean and the road and 42 m along the beach. The sea front view is amazing and unusual for a private residential project in this area, usually occupied exclusively by resorts and hotels. The idea was to maximize this potential with semi-detached sea front villas and keep a large part of the land as a "buffer" landscaped area to prevent noise from the road.

The construction is composed of 3 units: Two 3 bedrooms villas, and one 4 bedrooms villa, each with a private 10 m x 3 m swimming pool. The construction was raised to 1.8 m from the beach level in order to keep a good privacy from the public beach, maximize the sea view and prevent from site erosion.

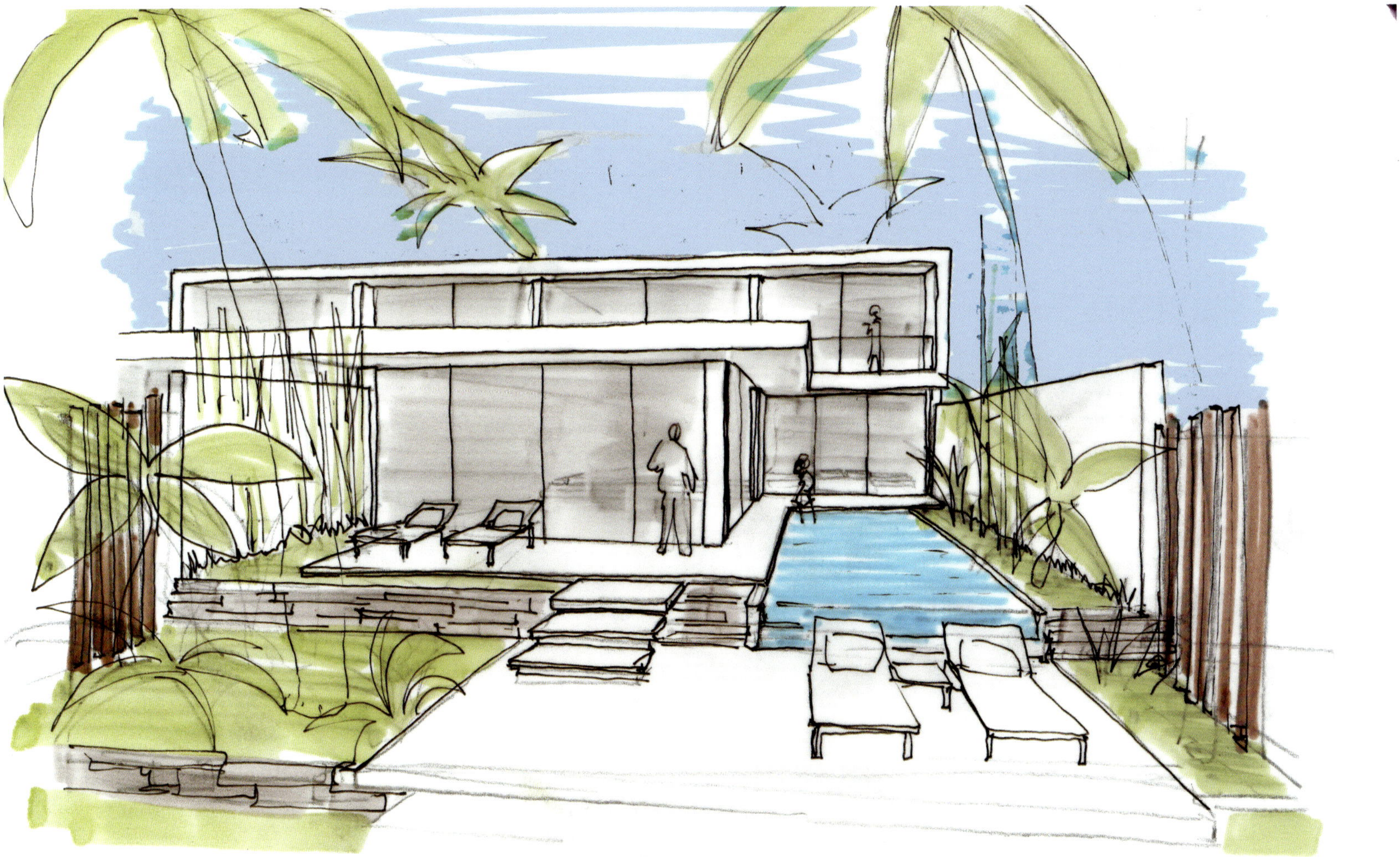

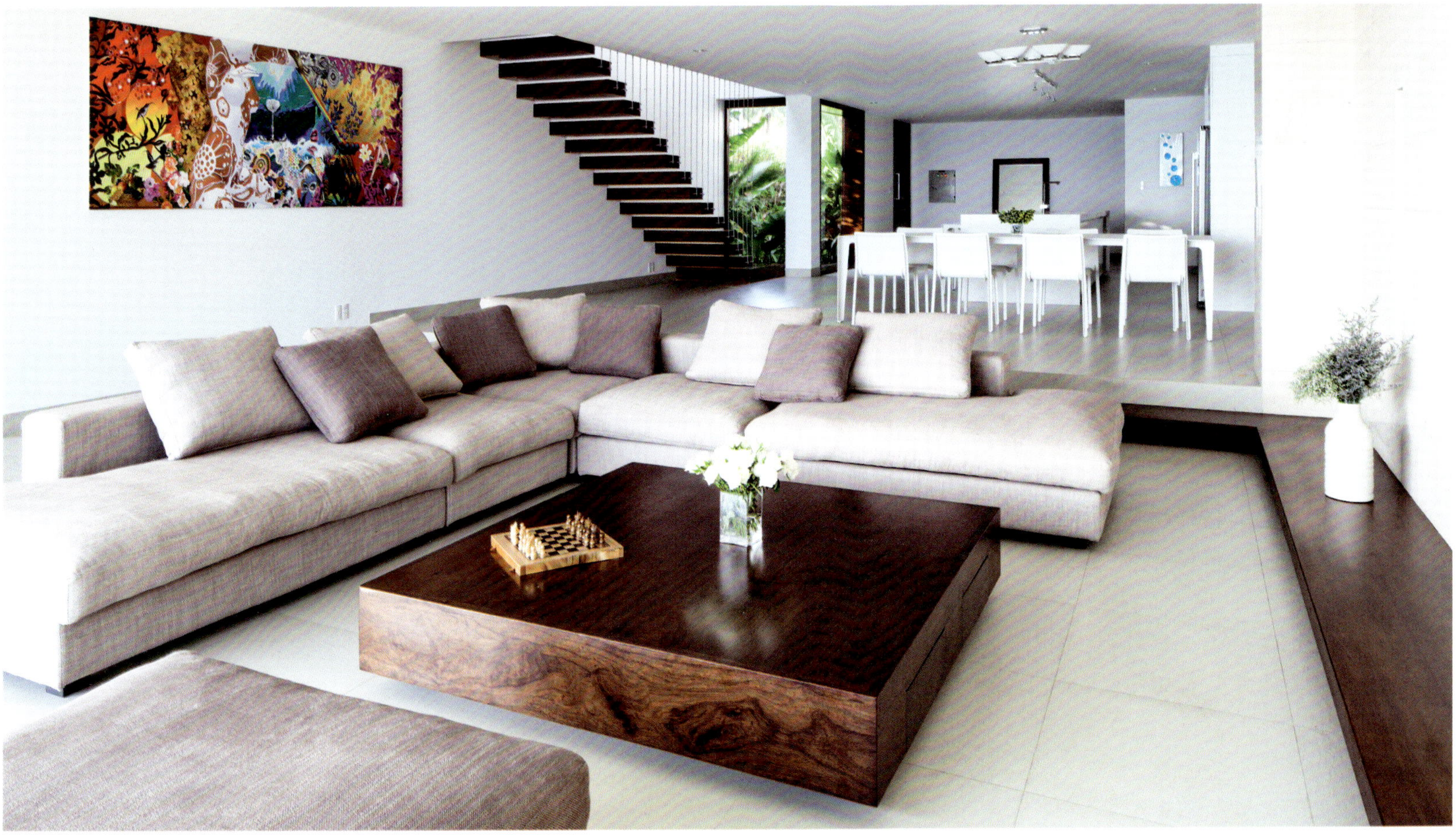

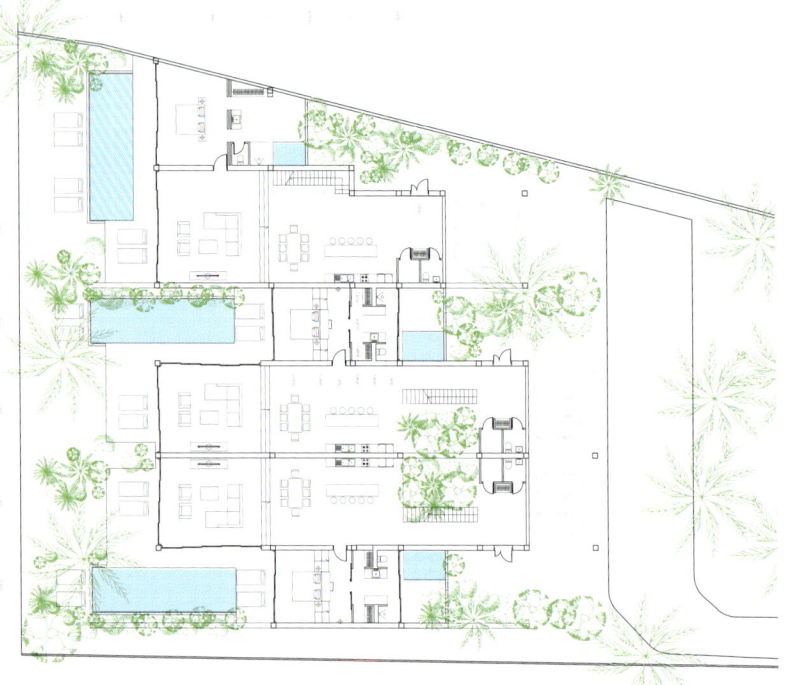
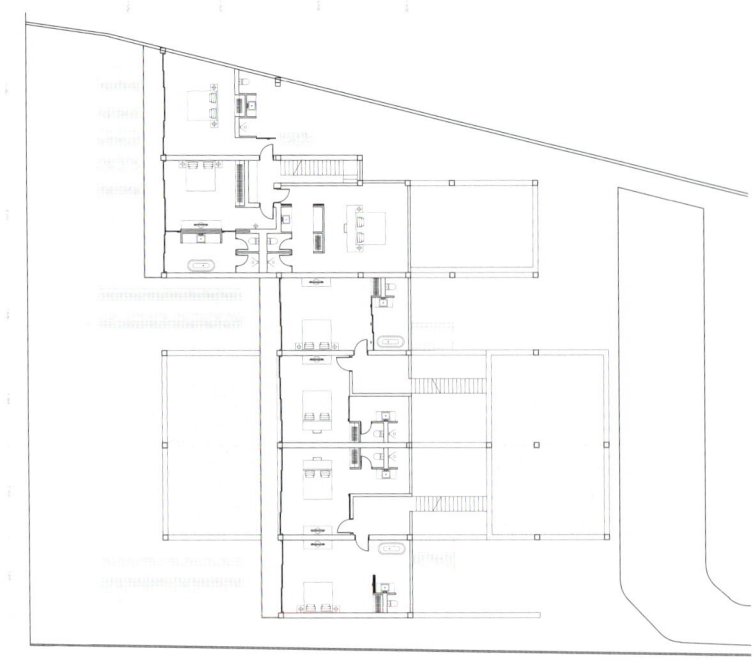

The interior layout offers a generous sea view for each space:

On the ground floor the kitchen, dining and living rooms are merged in one single space mono-oriented to the beach front while the back has been designed with a patio open to the sky to bring sunlight, natural ventilation and a nice sequence for entrance and staircase with the pond and the interior tropical garden.

Master bedrooms are open to the infinity swimming pool and by extension to the sea. In the back, each bathroom has a private garden with Jacuzzi, bringing light, ventilation and strong outdoor/indoor connection.

On the first floor, all bedrooms have a large ocean view with floor to ceiling windows recessed in the concrete structure providing enough shadows. On the front, the flat roof becomes a huge timber decking terrace, extending possibilities to contemplate the ocean.

In the back, are located the bathrooms, naturally ventilated through timber louvers.

Elevations are simple, following the layout strategy. The beach front elevation is widely open with large aluminum frame windows while the back elevation has no windows but timber louvers only. Therefore, in addition to the open air patio on the ground floor, it has been possible to limit the air conditioning to the bedrooms only.

This amazing location, so closed to the sea, is a dreaming place for living. This project tries to not miss this opportunity to offer to the guests a total and unique "seaside" experience.

In line with our practice, the materials are basic and the design is minimalist, focusing on the quality of each space with no sophistication.

CONTRIBUTORS

A-cero

A-cero joaquín torres & rafael llamazares architects is an architecture firm founded in 1996, vowed to the integral development of architectural, interior design and urban planning projects.

The studio has a team of more than 100 specialized professionals, led by architect Joaquín Torres Vérez, working in two main headquarters in Spain, located in Madrid and A Coruña, and a foreign projects office in Dubai.

The practice has evolved in parallel to its clients' demands, building a large portfolio that comprises residential estates, resorts, office buildings, mixed-use high-rises, corporate and interior design. We have the capacity to carry out an architecture project in all its stages, since its conception until the construction management.

Our working method is based on a detailed analysis of the client's needs and the project's program. The result is examined in all its dimensions in order to find every potential problem, all the possible solutions are studied and all the material possibilities for the new building analyzed during the design stage. The concept ideas are kept from the beginning to the end, as a conducting thread for the design process, in order to achieve the best possible results.

Passionate and motivated, A-cero designers develop innovative and visionary designs for our clients. Driven by our core values of individuality, respect, passion and integrity, our commitment to design excellence is integral to everything we do. At A-cero we want to experience the pride and excitement of creation and it is our commitment to be the very best that drives us forward.

Arch. Bernardo Hinojosa / Associates

Based in Monterrey, México, this architectural practice has a diversified practice, with over 2,500,000 m^2 designed in Master Planning, University Buildings, Private Houses, Industrial, Religious and Commercial Architecture. It is consider on of the top 5 most important architectural firms in Northern México.

ARQUIPLAN
BURO DE PLANIFICACIÓN Y ARQUITECTURA, S.C.
Arq. Bernardo Hinojosa Rodríguez, M.Arch., AIA Assoc.

More than 40 international, national and local prizes have been obtain for his distinct projects as well as publications of the web, architectural magazines and several books. His work has being exhibited in Netherlands, Belgium, Dallas, New York and Athens.

Bernardo Hinojosa´s architecture seeks "atemporality", which states all projects should look contemporary even with the passing of time, and it is characterize by its functional and rationalist bases.

We embrace any challenge to overcome it, with an excellent piece of architecture as a result.

Belzberg Architects

Belzberg Architects is about architectural innovation.

Design is a collaborative process, a dialogue, between client and architect.

Form is a merger of conceptual investigation with production methodology.

Practice is flexible, nimble, evolving, and unconventional.

Blaze Makoid Architecture

Blaze Makoid has been practicing architecture and design since graduating from Rhode Island School of Design in 1985. His company Blaze Makoid Architecture, located in Bridgehampton, NY, was established in 2001 and since its inception has created sophisticated, luxury residential architecture in the most sought after locations.

The firm's work has been recognized in The New York Times, Architect magazine, Hamptons Cottage & Gardens, Beach, Ocean Home, and the Robb Report for designs that acknowledge the lifestyle and day-to-day experience their clients' desire on beautiful, yet demanding sites.

Blaze and the firm have received numerous national and international design awards, including The Long Island AIA Commendation Achievement in Residential Design; The AIA Peconic Honor Award; The Boston Society of Architects' First Citation; and the Philadelphia AIA honor Award for Excellence.

Design studio Yuri Zimenko

Eponymous design studio, designs and design supervision of design projects: private houses, apartments, hotels, restaurants, cafes, offices, shops, as well as product design. In developing the project takes into account all the wishes of the customer.

Studio work has repeatedly won prizes at various competitions and many times were marked attention from the press.

GREGWRIGHT architects

GREGWRIGHT architects

GREGWRIGHT architects (GWA) was founded in 1995 by its sole member at the time, Greg Wright. The decision to break ties from a successful partnership with my previous partner and form a new practice was formed out of a need/desire to explore a new and separate vision for the making of buildings and to discover a different way in the delivery of both as a service and product that adhered to the principles and values held as important to Greg Wright. These principles still underpin the ethos of the practice and include:

• The business of architecture should be inspired by the delivery of contemporary buildings founded on the values of integrity, honesty, and a commitment to offer positively to the built environment

• The belief in and commitment to ones ideas is the single most valuable currency we can invest in

• Work is driven by a desire to make buildings that reveal & revel in excellence of thought and execution – this soon became the credo of the newly formed GWA.

The practise continues to develop projects around these core values. A holistic approach is adopted for all projects and this often includes the design of interiors and bespoke one-off items for their clients. This approach has often resulted in projects being critically acclaimed and featured in various publications both locally and internationally as well as TV programmes such as our local Top Billing.

From humble beginnings of doing primarily residential work, the practise grown both in confidence and size taking on bigger challenges and completed the recent master plan for the Centenary City of Abuja, Nigeria together with key landmark buildings designs. Our work continues to expand into Africa with submissions to the Ivory Coast, work in Namibia and current new commissions in Luanda Angola.

In 2001 Greg Scott joined GWA and very quickly became a pivotal part of the success of the practise. This was acknowledged in his appointment as a director and shareholder in GWA in 2003, and has been instrumental in the growth of GWA and the extensive portfolio of work completed to date.

John Maniscalco

John Maniscalco, AIA, is the founding principal of JMA. He brings 25 years of professional experience as a Project Designer for a wide range of projects including master-planning, commercial office buildings, academic facilities, civic centers, transportation complexes, and wineries, as well as multi and single-

family custom homes. He is a graduate of Cornell University and has worked as a Project Designer in the offices of Gensler, Chong Partners, ROMA Design Group, and Ellerbe Becket. Since starting JMA in 2000, he oversees all phases of design and construction on JMA projects from conception to completion. His work has received numerous design awards and honors, and has been featured in national and international publications.

Keith Baker Design

KB Design (Keith Baker Design Inc.) was established by Canadian designer Keith Baker in Victoria, B.C. in 1989 as a residential design practice specializing in the design of unique

custom homes and well integrated renovations and additions. KB Design is a member of the Canadian Home Builders Association. Keith's work has been recognized over the years with an impressive 22Gold awards and 47 Silver awards on the local, provincial and national levels for excellence in categories ranging from Project of the Year, Best Custom Home in Canada, Best Custom Home, Best Master Suite, Best Interior, Best Bathroom, Best Renovation, Best Kitchen and the coveted People's Choice Award. His work has been widely published in local, national and international books and periodicals and featured on hundreds of websites profiling Contemporary West Coast and Modern residential design.

The company is a three person team consisting of two designers and one building technologist and enjoys the close client relationship afforded by a small high quality residential design practice.

Keith accepts design commissions in his home of Victoria, B.C. as well as across Canada, the United States and internationally.

Keith and his team, using state of the art 3D design technology coupled with his thirty plus years of professional design experience, are able to create unique and varied custom home design solutions.

Keith believes strongly in the need for green and energy efficient home design as well as the concept of biophilic design - the idea of the use of natural building materials and a profound connection with the natural world creating beautiful healthful living environments.

Kolenik Eco Chic Design

Robert Kolenik (b.1981) is one of the representatives of the new generation of Dutch Designers who are renowned worldwide for their down to earth mentality, excellence and innovative approach to design. In 2005 Robert took over his father's business and subsequently Kolenik Eco Chic Design was founded in 2008.

With a dedicated team of experienced architects, the multidisciplinary studio is responsible for a wide range of projects. From bespoke designs for private villas and product designs through special fields of interest to the development of elegant and luxurious total concepts for the hospitality industry. More recently the studio earned a great reputation working on several hotels, restaurants, bar and club designs all with their signature international and timeless allure.

The distinct and recognisable Kolenik style appeals to a wide international audience. It is best described as minimalist and warm, carefully marrying functionality and aesthetics to create harmony and balance.

Kolenik hotel and villa designs exude an inviting quality of peace and tranquillity, while restaurants and other hospitality designs are more daring, aiming to fascinate and excite their guests.

The use of materials like luxurious natural stone and even living nature add interest to their spaces and are the hallmark of Robert's style.

Each and every Kolenik design is unique; from the made to measure furniture to the most minute, beautiful details and innovative solutions.

The name Eco Chic Design deliberately reflects the designer's passion for nature.

Together with his team he tirelessly searches for original, smart and intelligent but sustainable solutions to take their work to a higher level.

Robert Kolenik is also co-founder of Plastic Soup Foundation Junior, a charity that educates children at a very young age about the dangers of polluting our the seas and oceans with plastics and its consequent impact on marine life.

Mário Martins Atelier

The company, mário martins - atelier de arquitectura, lda, based in Lagos, Algarve, Portugal, has been working in the field of architecture and urban planning for more than 20 years.

The company consists in a diverse team of permanent staff, a group of technical experts, who work together in the different areas and specializations of projects.

The company has been extremely busy over the past decades, which has resulted in a considerable volume and diversity of projects built: single family houses, collective housing, residential condominiums, tourist developments (hotels, aparthotels, tourist apartments, etc), restaurants/bars, various public facilities (sports, social, educational, recreational, etc), urban renewal and planning.

The projects have been recognised with prizes, nominations and publications over the years in Portuguese and international publications (magazines, books and online).

This presentation is based on houses (new and recovered) done during last 15 years is this area of the Algarve, Portugal following the concept: Respect for the site, environment, local culture and the people.

Reinterpretation of these aspects to archive a sustainable and contemporary result.

McClean Design

Paul McClean trained as an architect in Ireland and founded McClean Design in 2000.

Over the last fifteen years, MCCLEAN DESIGN has grown into one of the leading contemporary residential design firms in the Los Angeles area committed to excellence in modern design. We are currently working on more than twenty large homes across much of Southern California with additional projects in San Francisco, Vancouver and New York.

Our projects reflect an interest in modern living and a desire to connect our clients to the beauty of the surrounding natural environment. We make extensive use of glazing systems to maximize views and provide a warm light filled contemporary space. We strive for simplicity and an openness to the surrounding landscape that erodes the division between indoor and outdoor spaces; homes with an emphasis on texture and natural materials.

We are committed to environmentally sustainable design practices and have extensive experience in both Orange and Los Angeles counties with a proven ability to navigate complicated approval processes such as the Laguna Beach and Beverly Hills Design Review Board as well as Coastal Commission. We keep an open mind on questions of style preferring to strike a balance between the best solution for the site, our clients' preferences, and what is potentially approvable for each particular site.

We work with both homeowners and developers. Our staff offers a full range of design skills ensuring that our projects are completed in a timely manner and to the highest standards.

We continue to strive for excellence in design and to push the boundaries of imagination in creating extraordinary spaces that we hope will provide enjoyment for many years to come.

MCK Architects

MCK is a young team of multi-award winning architects based in Sydney, Australia.

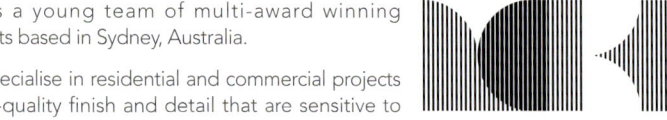

They specialise in residential and commercial projects of high-quality finish and detail that are sensitive to context and brief. Their distinctive aesthetic is known for its classic proportion and geometric form.

We enjoy using unexpected materials that challenge and sometimes even surprise. We also believe that good architecture and respect for the environment go hand in hand.

Metropole Architects

Metropole Architects was founded in 1997 by Nigel Tarboton. Tyrone Reardon joined the office in 2002, and became a partner in 2004. Our office is situated in Durban, Kwa-Zulu Natal, South Africa.

As a practice, Metropole Architects, are inspired by the energy of the city, as it unceasingly moves, radiates and evolves like a vast living organism. We aim to generate design that stakes out new territory, and explore ideas that are intuitive, inventive, exuberant and daring. Enthused by visionary architects like John Lautner and Santiago Calatrava, we aspire to create iconic and progressive architectural wonders that capture our collective imagination.

MM++ architects

My An Pham Thi, Architect, Graduated from University of Hanoi. After more than 10 years of practice in different international offices she founded Mimya co. (MM++ architects) in 2010. Michael Charruault, Architect, Graduated from the French architecture school Paris-Belleville. Based in Vietnam since 2007, co-founder.

Nico van der Meulen Architects

As an architectural practice that is well renowned throughout the African continent, NICO VAN DER MEULEN ARCHITECTS supplies creative solutions that are customized to suit each client's personal requirements. Through working closely with all its clients to ensure optimal satisfaction, the practice has accomplished astounding success in the design of upmarket residential homes. The company's innovative architectural vision is evident in its ability to continuously produce outstanding and artistic architectural designs that are personalized in accordance with the homeowners' lifestyle requirements.

OPENSPACE DESIGN Co., Ltd.

OPENSPACE DESIGN is a Thailand based architecture & interior design company founded in 2005. Their multidisciplinary design team is composed of architects, interior designers, graphic designers, R&D specialists. Professionally, they work together in the synchronized manner enabling them to serve their clients completely.

There are 4 main types of design services provided as follows: Architectural Design, Interior Design, Landscape Design and Graphic Design.

OPENSPACE DESIGN has accumulated design proficiency and experience through various types of projects such as office, commercial building, shopping mall & retail, hotel-resort-spa, residence (housing/condominium), educational building, hospital, master planning & landscape, etc. Their services cover projects both in Thailand and abroad including government's and private's sectors.

OPENSPACE DESIGN provides full package of design services from the client's requirement analysis, project's feasibility study, design strategy to achieve the uniqueness of the project-undoubtedly, several different design alternatives are meticulously compared before creating the final one, working with our client closely until the project's completion. With their service-mind and true determination, they always make sure that each project meets high efficiency, client's satisfaction and the users' aesthetical experience.

Pitsou Kedem Architects

Pitsou Kedem Architects was founded in 2002 and today employs nine architects (Pitsou Kedem ,Irene Goldberg, Nurit Ben Yosef, Raz Melamed, Noa Groman, Ran Broides, Hila Sela, Tamar Berger, Emanuel Amsalem).

pitsou kedem architect
פיצו קדם
אדריכל

The office was established by Pitsou Kedem, a graduate of the Architectural Association in London and mentor of final projects at the Technion Haifa's Faculty of Architecture. In the past two years, the office has received five awards in the Israeli "Design Award" competition, and has been chosen Architect Office of the Year in the "Private Construction" category by Israeli Construction and Housing magazine.

The office designs private as well as commercial projects such as B&B Italia's Tel Aviv flagship store, a boutique hotel on the city's prominent Rothschild Boulevard and an events hall.

Rolf Ockert Design

At Rolf Ockert Design we continuously aim to find individual and optimised solutions for any design task we can get our hands (and minds) on.

ROLF OCKERT DESIGN

Having lived and worked in Europe, Asia and Australia and having travelled the world extensively Rolf draws on a wide range of visual, practical and design experience.

For us it is still fascinating how different architectural solutions for the same task can be. The solutions then are a reflection of the designers experience, taste, preference, etc. We call it the mosaic of life, every little bit of input forming a vital part of the whole piece.

Rolf Ockert Design, commenced in 2004, has in a relatively short period of time created a rich portfolio of work, ranging from high end residential design to commercial and retail projects, product and furniture design, master planning and much more. Projects to date have been located throughout Australia as well as overseas, most recently in New Zealand, Japan and Switzerland. Many projects have been published in national and international publications.

SAOTA

SAOTA is a firm of architectural designers and technologists including in-house CGI and marketing teams, as well as a strong support staff. It is driven by the dynamic combination of Stefan Antoni, Philip Olmesdahl, Greg Truen and Phillippe Fouché who share a potent vision easily distinguished in their design. This, paired with both an innovative and dedicated approach to the execution of projects, has seen SAOTA become internationally sought-after, receiving numerous awards and commendations from some of the most respected institutions worldwide.

Capitalising on a unique understanding of an ever-evolving industry, SAOTA continues to build on past experiences and is well positioned to offer expert services to the corporate, institutional, commercial and residential marketplace.

With roots in South Africa, SAOTA now has an international footprint with projects on five continents.

Stuart Narofsky

Stuart Narofsky, AIA,LEED AP is the principal of Narofsky Architecture, a multi-discipline design firm founded in 1983 that also offers design build and interior design services. His partner Jennifer Rusch oversees ways2design, the interior division.

Stuart is former President of the American Institute of Architects-Long Island Chapter. For ten years he was an Associate Professor of Architecture at New York Institute of Technology, overseeing a design studio and teaching furniture design. More recently as a visiting Professor of Architecture at Pratt Institute, where he taught an upper class Design Studio, specializing in modular construction. Stuart has over the past three years he has been visiting a professor in workshops at the faculties of Architectures at Universities in Argentina (La Plata) and Bolivia (Santa Cruz, Cochabamba, Sucre and La Paz), on the subjects of Sustainable Architecture and practicing architecture in New York.

His projects have received many awards: Architectural Digests best Home Competition; Queens Chamber of Commerce Award for his competition winning scheme for a Ronald McDonald house; numerous architecture awards from the AIA, including AIA Long Island Chapter, where his Patel residence garnished multiple awards in residential design, and best project of the year; the Society of American Registered Architects; and AIA New York State.

Recently, a single family house on Long Island obtained the 2012 Long Island AIA Chapter Archi Award for a sustainable residence.

The Agency

The Agency is a full-service, luxury real estate brokerage representing clients worldwide in a broad spectrum of classes, including single-family residential, new development, resort and hospitality, residential leasing, luxury vacation rental and property management. The Agency was founded by Mauricio Umansky, who was recently recognized by The Wall Street Journal as the #1 top-producing real estate agent in Southern California and #7 in the U.S., and design and architectural specialists Billy Rose and Blair Chang, whose Rose + Chang team was named multiple times as one of the Top 100 U.S. real estate sales teams by The Wall Street Journal. Shunning the traditional brokerage model of cut-throat agents competing against each other, The Agency fosters a culture of partnership in which all clients and listings are represented in a cooperative environment by all its agents, thereby ensuring its clients and listings have the competitive edge. Leveraging the most emergent technologies and social media strategies, The Agency envisions itself as more than just a real estate brokerage; it is a lifestyle company committed to informing and connecting global communities. The Agency tailors global marketing solutions for buyers, sellers, developers and landlords

Urbane Projects

Urbane Projects was founded in 2003 by Managing Director, Steve Gliosca.

Urbane Projects has established itself as a premium boutique builder in WA, specialising in designing and building luxury homes across Perth with a focus on providing every client with personalised, tailored attention.

Urbane Projects' Managing Director, Steve Gliosca, is both the designer and builder – a rare luxury in today's construction industry which ensures the homes coherence and success from conception to implementation.

The goal at Urbane is to provide every client with an enjoyable, stress-free building experience and it speaks volumes about their quality of service that almost all of their business generates from word of mouth.

The distinguishing feature of building with Urbane Projects is "Our People". The team at Urbane Projects offers exceptional service, complete transparency and our in-house solutions provides each client with a combined skillset of a designer, interior architect, estimator and builder all under the one roof. Of course, Urbane recognise that without clients there is no product and they are privileged to have worked with a vast array of people that now formthe Urbane family of clients. It is their dedication and trust in Urbane Projects that have enabled the design and construction process to be pushed to the limits – to strive to set new benchmarks that serve as an inspiration to others.

Urbane Projects offers a complete turnkey package. From design conception to completion we assist every client with individual detailing of all key selections for both the exterior and interior of the home. Our homes have distinctive curb appeal whilst ensuring a floor plan that is unique to each client and their individual lifestyle.

Whipple Russell Architects

Marc Whipple, the founder of Whipple Russell Architects, is the son of an American Diplomat, Marc Whipple grew up across Europe, Asia and Africa, whose rich cultures helped to shape his eclectic approach. Following his education at Eton College and London's prestigious Architectural Association School of Architecture, he became the protégé of internationally renowned architect George Vernon Russell. Russell, creator of show-stoppers like the Trocadero on Sunset Boulevard, the Flamingo in Las Vegas, as well as Samuel Goldwyn's home in Beverly Hills and the expansive University of California at Riverside campus, further broadened Marc's vision.

Twenty-five years ago, when Marc opened his own firm, he honored his late mentor by including his name in that of the practice. Since that time, Marc Whipple has demonstrated a range of scale and innovation that extends from intimate west coast life-style specific homes in the Hollywood Hills to the Sienna Hotel Spa Casino in Reno to a master plan for an island-spanning resort in the Caribbean. His firm, whipple russell architects, is noted for applying authentic materials, natural light and green technology to the marriage of elegant form and efficient function.

Whipple Russell architects, formerly known as The Russell Group Architects, has been featured in periodicals that include Metropolitan Home, Dwell Maga zine, Robb Report, the Los Angeles Business Journal, Home Beautiful, In Style Home, The Los Angeles Times and The New York Times.

ARTPOWER

Acknowledgements

We would like to thank all the designers and companies who made significant contributions to the compilation of this book. Without them, this project would not have been possible. We would also like to thank many others whose names did not appear on the credits, but made specific input and support for the project from beginning to end.

Future Editions

If you would like to contribute to the next edition of Artpower, please email us your details to: artpower@artpower.com.cn